RUTH WODAK

THE POLITICS OF FEAR

WHAT RIGHT-WING POPULIST DISCOURSES MEAN

Los Angeles | London | New Delhi
Singapore | Washington DC

Los Angeles | London | New Delhi
Singapore | Washington DC

SAGE Publications Ltd
1 Oliver's Yard
55 City Road
London EC1Y 1SP

SAGE Publications Inc.
2455 Teller Road
Thousand Oaks, California 91320

SAGE Publications India Pvt Ltd
B 1/I 1 Mohan Cooperative Industrial Area
Mathura Road
New Delhi 110 044

SAGE Publications Asia-Pacific Pte Ltd
3 Church Street
#10-04 Samsung Hub
Singapore 049483

Editor: Mila Steele
Assistant editor: James Piper
Production editor: Imogen Roome
Copy-editor: Solveig Gardner Servian
Proofreader: Leigh C. Timmins
Indexer: Silvia Benvenuto
Marketing manager: Michael Ainsley
Cover design: Jen Crisp
Typeset by: C&M Digitals (P) Ltd, Chennai, India
Printed and bound by CPI Group (UK) Ltd,
Croydon, CR0 4YY

Library of Congress Control Number: 2015932198

British Library Cataloguing in Publication data

A catalogue record for this book is available from
the British Library

MIX
Paper from
responsible sources
FSC
www.fsc.org   FSC® C013604

ISBN 978-1-4462-4699-3
ISBN 978-1-4462-4700-6 (pbk)

At SAGE we take sustainability seriously. Most of our products are printed in the UK using FSC papers and boards.
When we print overseas we ensure sustainable papers are used as measured by the Egmont grading system.
We undertake an annual audit to monitor our sustainability.

This book is due for return on or before the last date shown below.

For Jakob

CONTENTS

LIST OF FIGURES, TABLES, IMAGES AND VIGNETTES

Figures

Tables

Images

Vignettes

PREFACE

Every day, when opening the newspapers in the morning, big headlines catch my eye, the most recent galvanizing provocation by a particular right-wing populist party or yet another success of such a party at recently held European, national or regional elections is discussed – the rise and, indeed, discursive prominence of right-wing populist parties currently seems to be without end. Thus, at some point, I had to take a difficult and deliberate decision: to stop collecting data and to finish this book. Other books will no doubt pick up the challenge and continue documenting the development of the European Union, the 28 EU member states and their political systems as well as follow the US primaries and the potential success of Tea Party candidates in various regional and national elections. In any case, it is undisputable that right-wing populist parties have moved away from the margins in many EU member states and beyond; that they have indeed become mainstream parties and movements. Many people react to this with surprise, asking themselves, how could this happen? And why is it happening now?

No simple explanations seem viable – this book therefore presents an attempt to trace, understand and explain the trajectories of such parties from the margins of the political landscape, transformations from fringe parties originally ridiculed and made light of, to the centre, manifesting a general move to the right in their figurative wake. Currently, we observe a normalization of nationalistic, xenophobic, racist and antisemitic rhetoric, which primarily works with 'fear': fear of change, of globalization, of loss of welfare, of climate change, of changing gender roles; in principle, almost anything can be constructed as a threat to 'Us', an imagined homogenous people inside a well-protected territory. Post-war taboos such as the expression of blunt racism and antisemitism in public have been breached in the course of these changes and, frequently, we are left with the impression that the political arena at present follows the dictum 'Anything goes!' and that few, if any, alternatives to such a stance exist, because mainstream parties have incorporated many of the previously rejected proposals into their policy preferences and, indeed, effective legislation.

In 1989, at the momentous occasion of the fall of the so-called Iron Curtain which had divided Europe into West and East, nobody expected that the immigration from the former Communist countries, Turkey and the Middle East would entail a rise in xenophobia and fear of losing jobs, and cause a division into 'Us' and 'Them', into the real 'Austrians, Brits, Swedes, Germans or Danes' and the 'Others', that is, foreigners. Old borders were dismantled and new borders were erected: via visas, language and citizenship tests, a veritable multitude of rules and regulations.

Of course, immigration from the East is not a new phenomenon; before 1989, however, these migrants were refugees fleeing a totalitarian system; or they were so-called 'guest-workers' who were welcomed and, indeed, often fetched in the 1960s and 1970s in order to help out with jobs which nobody else wanted to take on. Many such guest-workers stayed in Scandinavia, Germany or Austria and have since acquired a new citizenship and belonging. After 1989, however, people leaving Eastern European countries were perceived as 'economic' migrants who voluntarily left their homes, in most cases legitimately searching for better lives. These new fears merged with traditional racist and antisemitic beliefs and discrimination against minorities that had already lived for many decades (and, in many cases, centuries) inside Western EU member states, for example, against the guest-workers, against Roma, Jews and other ethnic and religious, autochthonous minorities. 'Modern strangers' (to borrow Georg Simmel's term) or 'post-modern strangers' (in the words of Zygmunt Bauman) were constructed as a ubiquitous threat to welfare, the economy and culture, even to 'civilization' as a whole.

The horrendous events of 9/11 were another tipping point in this development: Muslims were suddenly perceived as an acute danger to security in many Western countries. More restrictions for immigration were quickly legitimized via security measures presented as necessary and therefore rarely challenged. Turkey's potential accession to the EU triggered even more debates and evoked old collective memories of the victory of the Habsburgs against the Ottoman Empire in the 16th and 17th centuries, thus defending the 'Christian Occident' against 'Islam and the Orient'. And, finally, EU enlargement in 2004 led to a merging of the concepts of refugees, migrants and asylum seekers: an enemy image of *the* 'Other' started to dominate political struggles and debates. This image has taken many local forms and shapes; it is a floating signifier, indeed an empty signifier which anybody can articulate for their political interests. In the US, moreover, the election of Barack Obama to President triggered the rise of the Tea Party movements in opposition to the government's economic, security and health care policies – most probably also in reaction to a 'black man' sitting in the White House.

As will be elaborated throughout this book, however, there exists no one-size-fits-all explanation for the continuing rise and success of right-wing populist parties. Many factors contribute to this success, such as renationalizing nativist tendencies, border narratives and ideologies, economic fears, and the many dramatic pasts – revealing similarities and differences between countries. Regarding the latter, for instance, countries with fascist and national-socialist pasts differ significantly from countries without such pasts. The scapegoats constructed by rich countries differ from those constructed by poor countries that have been vehemently struck by the economic and Eurozone crises since 2008. It is a notable, though far from coincidental, fact that many frequently violent and polemical debates are conducted over the regulation of female bodies – gender roles have changed, and it seems as if the ultimate 'Other' is currently personified by and identified with the headscarf and burqa, with the ways Muslim women choose to dress (or are sometimes forced to dress).

Charismatic leaders and aggressive rhetoric are also important factors; indeed, for a long time, right-wing populist parties were primarily identified with and recognized by their rhetoric, argumentation schemes and aggressive debate mode. However, these factors per se do not suffice as salient characteristics; they do not suffice at all in defining the complex phenomenon of right-wing populism. It is the *contents*, that is, the ideologies and beliefs, the proposals and imaginaries conveyed by such rhetoric, that have to be observed, analysed and understood; only in conjunction do they provide insights into the many facets of right-wing populism on the rise. Meaning is constructed by form and content, to be understood and explained via many layers of contextual knowledge – historical, socio-political, intertextual and interdiscursive, as well as situative.

In 2010, at the occasion of one of my public lectures on right-wing populist rhetoric and ideologies – this time in the town hall in Örebro, Sweden – my son, Jakob, who was present, challenged me on the point of possible similarities and differences with the US Tea Party, which, as mentioned above, had been launched as a vocal opposition to

Barack Obama's Presidency in 2008. He urged me to write a book that would also compare European right-wing politics and policies with the American political movement, which is absorbed largely in the Republican Party. Hence this book is ultimately an attempt to understand and explain at least some of these recent developments and to provide manifold examples intended to trace the *micro-politics* of right-wing populism, performing the many discourses, genres, images and texts in various more formal and also informal contexts. Fifteen *vignettes* serve this end throughout the book, approximating in-depth analyses of what we might consider snapshots of the political situation taken in Austria, Finland, Germany, Hungary, Italy, Poland, Switzerland, the Netherlands, the Ukraine, the UK and the US. The analyses of right-wing populist micro-politics are embedded in much contextual knowledge, in some facts and figures from various national and EU elections, and in important theoretical discourse-analytic, sociological, historical and political science theories. As a framework, they guide the fine-grained linguistic, pragmatic, rhetorical and argumentation analysis. Nevertheless, this book also and primarily addresses readers outside of academia pure – this is why I have made a point of employing a more popular, comprehensible style of writing while still doing justice to the requirements of systematic linguistic analysis.

I start out in Chapter 1 by introducing readers to the complex phenomenon of right-wing populism, to the many contradictions posed by their programmatic statements, and to the – obviously successful – construction of fear throughout our societies. In Vignette 1, I present one of many examples of the 'politics of denial' and the blame-game: how the current leader of the Austrian Freedom Party (FPÖ) Heinz-Christian Strache (brand name HC Strache), speaking in an interview on prime-time Austrian television, continually denies having intentionally posted an antisemitic cartoon on his Facebook page. In Chapter 2, I provide some factual background (election results on the European and national levels from the 1980s to the present, in 2014) as well as a brief (and necessarily incomplete) review of important sociological and political science literature on right-wing populism. Two vignettes illustrate two important aspects of these ideologies: Euro-scepticism and the long and difficult search for European identities; and the rewriting of narratives of the past manifesting the need for national foundational myths, that is, historical revisionism. Chapter 3 elaborates important aspects of the discourse-historical approach (DHA) to critical discourse studies, and focuses on some salient linguistic phenomena and devices as well as specific discursive strategies, rhetorical tropes, argumentation schemes and the notion of *topos*: the *topoi of urgency, threat, the saviour* and *history* occur throughout right-wing populist rhetoric. Moreover, discursive strategies of justification and legitimation are frequently employed in the recurring 'politics of denial'. Vignette 4 is dedicated to the in-depth deconstruction of discourses about security, analysing a speech by the Dutch right-wing populist politician Geert Wilders. The illustrated strategies can, of course, be applied to many other instances of security debates. Vignette 5 focuses on one of the key concepts used throughout this book: 'calculated ambivalence', the strategy of addressing multiple and contradictory audiences via a single, cleverly layered message. Indeed, Jörg Haider, the former leader of the FPÖ, took this strategy to new heights. Vignette 6 identifies another important discursive strategy amply used in right-wing populist (and exclusionary) rhetoric: the strategy of victim/perpetrator reversal. This strategy is part and parcel of the justification discourse and the many attempts of shifting blame, creating scapegoats and blame avoidance. A summary of the most relevant contents as well as rhetorical and discursive strategies is provided at the end of this chapter, addressing readers who might have only a passing interest in linguistic details.

Chapter 4 is dedicated to the first of five topic-oriented chapters, tackling discourses about nationalism. Here, I argue that right-wing populism is characterized by renationalizing tendencies that go far beyond the commonly used 'family and house metaphors': *body and border politics* are emphasized in ethno-nationalist discourses drawing on traditional racist and indeed fascist ideologies. In this chapter, I further argue that we are currently experiencing a *normalization* of exclusionary rhetoric and illustrate this claim with two vignettes (8 and 9) from mainstream politics in the UK: the so-called 'bus incident', that is, 'Operation Vaken' during which London buses carried posters asking 'illegal migrants' to leave the country; and several political speeches by protagonists of the UK coalition government on restricting immigration. Furthermore, Vignette 7 exemplifies the above-mentioned body politics by analysing a poster series from Switzerland, Germany and Italy; Vignette 10 elaborates the new policies of gate-keeping via the emphasis on the 'mother-tongue', language and citizenship tests. Chapter 5 discusses the rise of antisemitism across Europe and traces significant differences in this respect between Western and Eastern European countries. I decided to restrict myself to analysing two instances of Holocaust denial, one each in Austria and in the UK, by way of two respective vignettes as case studies: Vignette 11 traces the 2010 election campaign for Austrian Presidency and the candidacy of the FPÖ MP Barbara Rosenkranz. Vignette 12 focuses on the BNP's leader Nick Griffin and his participation – for the first time in the history of the BBC – in the well-known Thursday evening discussion programme *Question Time*. Both protagonists employ variants of coded Holocaust denial which have to be deconstructed in systematic qualitative ways. This chapter illustrates very clearly that antisemitism and anti-Muslim sentiments can occur simultaneously; Islamophobia has thus not substituted traditional antisemitism. It also reveals that old and new antisemitic stereotypes occur in parallel or are even merged, via a strategy I label as the '*Iudeus ex Machina*' strategy, that is, whenever scapegoats are needed, the enemy image of 'the Jews' is readily seized and articulated in ever new variants.

Chapter 6 presents the many 'faces' of right-wing populist leaders and politicians, their performance across the social and more traditional media, be it on Facebook, in comic books or in backstage speeches. Here, I also draw on some fieldwork in Washington, DC, conducted in the spring of 2012 during the Republican primaries for the November 2012 US presidential election. The concept of 'authenticity', that is, what it means to be a 'real American', is discussed with the example of the polarized debate surrounding Barack Obama's presidency. Moreover, I introduce some aspects the US Tea Party and, more specifically, the underlying ideology of Sarah Palin's 'frontier feminism'. Vignette 13 presents a case study of one right-wing populist leader, HC Strache of the Austrian FPÖ, as an example of the media-savvy young and demagogic, successful and charismatic male leaders of right-wing populist parties.

Chapter 7 confronts a rarely discussed and controversial phenomenon: the gender ideologies and the discourses that seek to discipline and regulate women's bodies in right-wing populism. It is, as a matter of fact, somewhat surprising that the debates about the 'burqa and headscarf' as well as about 'abortion and contraception' have not been noted as salient for both European and US right-wing populist ideologies. Indeed, I claim that these debates function as litmus tests between conservative values and progressive values. Political struggle has shifted from focusing on social class to focusing on values that cut across the traditional left/right cleavage. New frames are adopted by politicians from all parties and by both women and men. Vignette 14 illustrates the fear that is strategically and intentionally triggered by the constructed danger to 'our' Western culture through Muslim dress conventions. Vignette 15 elaborates on the debate about abortion, usually carried by male politicians, throughout

US politics. The final Chapter 8 brings the many aspects discussed throughout this book together and poses the pertinent question about alternative politics: How can we all avoid falling into 'the trap' cleverly constructed day-in and day-out by right-wing populist ideologies and its rhetorical manifestations? While a ready-to-go recipe or check-list to this end is clearly beyond the scope of any single book, prospective critique implies not taking anything for granted and opening up alternatives. The glossary provides facts and figures of the most important right-wing populist parties across Europe and beyond, thus aspects of the necessary socio-political context for the various analyses throughout this book.

Many friends and colleagues have contributed immensely to this book over the past three years of intensive research and writing (although this topic has continuously occupied my research agenda and thoughts since 1989 and our first research project on media reporting about immigration from 1990, after the fall of the Iron Curtain, resulting in articles and books in the 1990s). Rainer Bauböck, Rudolf de Cillia, Helmut Gruber, Franz Januschek, Tony Judt, Katharina Köhler, András Kovács, Verena Krausneker, Theo van Leeuwen, Jay Lemke, Bernd Matouschek, Anton Pelinka, Alexander Pollak, Martin Reisigl, Maria Sedlak-Arduç and Teun van Dijk were all part of discussions and research about the Austrian Freedom Party FPÖ, its then leader Jörg Haider and his 'infamous' rhetoric in the 1990s and early 2000s. Without these important discussions and our teamwork in various projects, the interdisciplinary foundations for these new and unexplored research agenda would not have been established. Debates on many occasions at Civil Society events (with Ernst Berger, Walter Manoschek, Rubina Möhring, Doron Rabinovici, Heidi Schrodt, Peter Weinberger and many others) after 2000 and the instalment of the so-called 'black and blue' government in Austria (a coalition comprising the Austrian People's Party ÖVP and the FPÖ) also contributed to the understanding of the enormous and unforeseen impact of changes implemented by this government, acknowledging that this was the first time the *European cordon sanitaire* was breached: a right-wing populist party with frequently coded racist, nativist, revisionist and antisemitic utterances became part of a government in the EU. These activities lastly formed my ethnography; I was able to experience the effects of such policies first-hand.

From 2003 to 2005, I participated in a European Fifth Framework Project with the acronym XENOPHOB ('The European Dilemma; Institutional Patterns and Racial Discrimination', http://cordis.europa.eu/project/rcn/67097_en.html) as Principle Investigator of the Austrian team, together with Michał Krzyżanowski and Fleur Ulsamer. In this project we were able to conduct focus groups and thus record and analyse 'voices of migrants' in systematic detail, documenting many narratives about traumatic experiences. Via my work as Director of the Austrian National Focus Point, of the then European Monitoring Centre against Racism and Xenophobia (EUMC; under the leadership of Beate Winkler) from 2000 to 2002 (and later on as Vice-Director), I had the privilege of meeting many European experts and attending important workshops on developments after 9/11. Apart from Michał and Fleur, I am indebted to Brigitte Beauzamy, Tom Burns, Gerard Delanty, Helena Flam, Paul Jones, Jens Rydgren and Nicos Trimikliniotis, for inspiring discussions and their many exciting ideas.

When I moved to Lancaster in 2004, I continued with this work, for example in the Economic and Social Research Council (ESRC)-funded project RASIM (http://ucrel.lancs.ac.uk/projects/rasim/), together with Paul Baker, Costas Gabrielatos, Majid Khosravinik, Michał Krzyżanowski and Tony McEnery. This media study opened new horizons, both methodologically and theoretically. We were able to analyse substantial amounts of data via corpus linguistic tools and then analyse a smaller corpus using qualitative discourse analysis; we provided much evidence for the continuous production and reproduction of exclusionary rhetoric via print media. During my time at Lancaster and in the UK, I had the great pleasure of working and publishing extensively with John Richardson on related topics – a truly wonderful experience. Many conversations at Lancaster, with David Barton, Paul Chilton, Jonathan Culpeper, Anne-Marie Fortier, Neil Foxlee, Bob Jessop, Maureen McNeil, Greg Myers, Lynne Pearce, Andrew Sayer, Jacky Stacey, Ngai-Ling Sum, John Urry and Sylvia Walby proved extremely fruitful. The 'Dynamics of Memory' Research Group, including Mercedes Camino, Agata Fialkowski, Patrick Hagophian, Aristotle Kallis, David Seymour, David Sugarman and Naomi Tadmor, contributed many insights through the comparison of right-wing populist politics with the past experiences of totalitarianism in many other European countries and beyond. I was extremely lucky to receive much feedback at various stages of my research. In 2010, I was able to fund and organize an international and interdisciplinary symposium with Brigitte Mral and Stig-Arne Nohrstedt at the University of Örebro where I had been awarded the Kerstin Hesselgren Chair of the Swedish Parliament in 2008. The interesting discussions in a wonderful Swedish lake environment provided the opportunity to address the many contradictory aspects, both general and specific, of right-wing populism with prominent international experts. During my semester at Georgetown University, Washington, DC, in spring 2014, as Davis Chair for Interdisciplinary Studies, I was able to spend much time with close friends and colleagues, with Deborah Tannen, Paul Portner, Anna de Fina, Marilyn Merrit and Heidi Hamilton. While walking through the woods, Deborah and I discussed, amongst many other topics, the gender politics of the Tea Party as well as the linguistics of apologies and disclaimers.

Most importantly, however, I am extremely grateful to my former and current PhD students: it was and continues to be a great pleasure and challenge to work with them, to discuss not only their research but also mine; I owe many insights to their critical, inspiring and knowledgeable questions and comments: Ana Tominc supported me in my research on the Tea Party, transcribed the *Question Time* episode analysed in Chapter 5 and became an expert in drawing diagrams; Salomi Boukala helped in collecting the complex and diverse facts about the various European right-wing populist parties and discussed the ongoing crisis in Greece as well as the rise of the Golden Dawn Party with me; Sten Hansson provided much insight on blame avoidance and found many websites and documents about the UK and UKIP; Federico Sicurella told me about the peculiar role of nationalistic intellectuals in post-Yugoslavia, Johnny Unger about the impact of social media for political movements, Bernhard Forchtner and Karin Stögner about the intricacies of the Frankfurt School, Kristof Savski about 'Slovenian language-only' movements, Can Küçükali about recent political developments in Turkey and José Manuel Ferreiro Gomez about past and present in Chile. I am also very grateful to Shaimaa Zaher, Soudeh Ghaffari, Zoe Arezoo and Taira Amin who all taught me a lot about the complexities of Islam and the various Muslim communities. Tony Capstick traced the difficult journey for Pakistani immigrants to Lancashire in the UK, and thus documented the many obstacles facing migrants in our globalized world. Reaching the end of this list, I have come to realize that there would be much more to say! Let me conclude, therefore, with a summary 'Thank you' to the many students, colleagues and friends who have also played an important role in conceptualizing this book.

Finally, I am extremely grateful to Andrew Sayer, who commented on the draft manuscript of this book and provided very useful comments, and to the anonymous reviewers of the book proposal and manuscript who detected important gaps and inconsistencies. Of course, this book would not have been finished without the support of Markus Rheindorf. Markus read many drafts of the chapters, revised my English, and frequently detected inconsistencies, redundancies and contradictions. I am very grateful to him for his patience and his loyalty. I am also indebted to SAGE Publications and specifically to Mila Steele, who always managed to heave me out of black holes whenever I fell into them during my writing, as well as to Imogen Roome and Solveig Gardner Servian who were both responsible for the careful copy-editing of the book manuscript.

My son Jakob not only triggered the idea for this book, he also had to listen to my worries and fears, and commented on my final draft chapters. I have learnt so much from his profound intellectual critique, from his differentiated views about politics, and from his informed questions and comments. This summer, Jakob spent a month in Vienna and we shared the same office – Jakob working on his PhD thesis and I on this book. Sometimes, we interrupted each other, though meaningfully; Jakob was always ready to listen, to read and to discuss. My loving partner Georg frequently had to live without me during the writing of this book: literally, because we commuted between Lancaster and Vienna; and metaphorically, because I sometimes vanished into my study – into the self-imposed isolation of writing – when focused entirely on finishing the last chapters. Our many discussions at dinner, on the phone, in the holidays, in the range of everyday situations in recent years were dominated by aspects of this book. His contributions are invaluable, his patience endless, and his support was always forthcoming. I am so grateful to both of you, thank you!

Ruth Wodak

ACKNOWLEDGEMENTS

I am indebted to:

Salomi Boukala and Ashgate, for the reuse of some parts of Geert Wilder's speech and parts of our analysis of this speech (Wodak and Boukala, 2014)

Jakob Engel and Routledge/Taylor and Francis, for the reuse of parts of the analysis of the 'Rosenkranz Affair' (Engel and Wodak, 2013)

John E. Richardson and *Controversies*, for the reuse of Image 7.2 and parts of our analysis of this image (Richardson and Wodak, 2009a)

Martin Reisigl and Wiley-Blackwell, for the reuse of Image 6.10 and parts of our analysis of this image (Wodak and Reisigl, 2015; in press)

Journal of Language, Identity, and Education, for the reproduction of two images (Images 4.6 and 4.7) and parts of the analysis of these images (Wodak, 2013c)

Nicole Doerr, for the use of Image 4.4

All the respective parts of analyses mentioned above have been shortened and also partly changed, refocused and rewritten. All the co-authors mentioned above have given me their explicit written permission for such use in this book.

1 POPULISM AND POLITICS: TRANSGRESSING NORMS AND TABOOS

'For fundamentalist elites all over the world, fear is an effective antidote against the secularizing effects of communicative freedom.'

Matteo Stocchetti (2007, 229)

Analysing the Micro-Politics of Right-wing Populism

Whenever I lecture about right-wing populism and right-wing populist rhetoric, people in the audience pose many questions, such as:

Are not all politicians populists?

Don't other politicians sometimes construct scapegoats and use similar rhetorical tropes as do right-wing populist politicians?

Don't the so-called right-wing populist politicians all draw on the same plethora of linguistic, pragmatic or rhetorical devices as already used by Cicero and other rhetoricians from antique times?

Such challenges raise the pertinent question of the novelty of this topic. What kind of new knowledge or which kind of explanations could anybody actually add to what we have long known about this complex phenomenon? Let me start with some brief answers to these and similar questions.

Most importantly, right-wing populism does not only relate to the *form* of rhetoric but to its specific *contents*: such parties successfully construct fear and – related to the various real or imagined dangers – propose scapegoats that are blamed for threatening or actually damaging our societies, in Europe and beyond.

Moreover, tendencies of *renationalization* across the EU and beyond can be observed; tendencies of creating ever new borders (and even walls), of linking the nation state and citizenship (naturalization) with nativist (frequently gendered and fundamentalist religious) *body politics*, lie at the core of right-wing populist ideologies. We thus seem to be experiencing a revival of the '*Volk*' and the '*Volkskörper*'[1] in the separatist rhetoric of right-wing populist parties, for example, in the Ukraine, Russia, Greece as well as Hungary. At the same time, very real walls of stone, brick and cement are also being constructed to keep the 'Others' out, who are defined as different and deviant. *Body politics are therefore integrated with border politics.*

Of course, much research in the social sciences provides ample evidence for the current rise of right-wing populist movements and related political parties in most European Union (EU) member states and beyond.[2] On the one hand, we observe neo-Nazi movements in the form of extreme far-right parties and horrific hate crimes such as that committed by Anders Breivik in July 2011 in Norway, from which all right-wing populist parties immediately distanced themselves publicly;[3] on the other hand, a salient shift is occurring in the forms and styles of political rhetoric of 'soft' right-wing populist parties which could be labelled as 'the *Haiderization* of politics', a label relating to the former leader of the Austrian Freedom Party (Freiheitliche Partei Österreich or FPÖ), Jörg Haider. Haider's performance, style, rhetoric and ideologies have become the metonymic symbol of such parties' success across Europe. Indeed, the FPÖ has paved the way for the dissemination of a new, frequently *coded* xenophobic, racist and antisemitic, exclusionary and anti-elitist politics since 1989 and the fall of the so-called Iron Curtain.[4]

Right-wing populist parties across Europe and beyond draw on and combine different *political imaginaries*[5] and different traditions, evoke (and construct) different nationalist pasts in the form of *identity narratives*, and emphasize a range of different issues in everyday politics: some parties gain support via flaunting an ambivalent relationship with *fascist* and *Nazi* pasts (e.g. in Austria, Hungary, Italy, Romania and France); some parties, in contrast, focus primarily on a *perceived threat from Islam* (e.g. in the Netherlands, Denmark, Poland, Sweden and Switzerland); some parties restrict their propaganda to a *perceived danger to their national identities* from ethnic minorities and migrants (e.g. in Hungary, Greece, Italy and the UK); and some parties primarily endorse a *traditional Christian (fundamentalist) conservative-reactionary agenda* (e.g. in the US).[6] In their free-for-all rush for votes, most right-wing populist parties evidently pursue several such strategies at once, depending on the specific audience and context; thus, the above-mentioned distinctions are primarily of an analytic nature. In any case, I claim that:[7]

- all right-wing populist parties instrumentalize some kind of ethnic/religious/linguistic/political minority as a *scapegoat* for most if not all current woes and subsequently construe the respective group as dangerous and a threat '*to us*', to 'our' nation; this phenomenon manifests itself as a '*politics of fear*';

- all right-wing populist parties seem to endorse what can be recognized as the '*arrogance of ignorance*'; appeals to common-sense and anti-intellectualism mark a return to pre-modernist or pre-Enlightenment thinking.

In this book I am concerned with the *micro-politics* of right-wing populist parties – *how they actually produce and reproduce their ideologies and exclusionary agenda in everyday politics, in the media, in campaigning, in posters, slogans and speeches.* Ultimately, I am concerned with how *they succeed (or fail) in sustaining their electoral success.* The dynamics of everyday performances frequently transcend careful analytic categorizations; boundaries between categories are blurred and flexible, open to change and ever new socio-economic developments.

Below, I first elaborate on the many ways in which fear is continuously invoked and legitimized by right-wing populist parties; I then briefly trace the history of populist movements and present a working definition of right-wing populism that should help in understanding the impact of these political movements in the 21st century. Moreover, by way of example, I illustrate the typical *politics of denial* that characterizes much of right-wing populist rhetoric – the specific ways in which media scandals are provoked and then dominate the agenda, forcing all other important topics into the background. Indeed, instrumentalizing the media, both traditional and new, is part and parcel of the immediate success of such political movements. After discussing the example in Vignette 1, I identify some of the typical characteristics and rhetorical patterns of right-wing populist parties in a range of national contexts selected due to the distinctions made above, such as Austria, Denmark, France, Germany, Greece, Hungary, Italy, Sweden, Switzerland, the Netherlands, the UK and the US.

Right-wing Populism: Form and Content

Returning to the questions raised above, we see that they are not difficult to answer: For example, the sociologist and media expert Dick Pels (2012, 31ff.) emphasizes that it would be dangerous to regard modern populism as void of serious content or to reduce the new right-wing populism to a 'frivolity of form, pose and style' and thus to downplay its outreach, its messages and resonance. Indeed, it would be, Pels continues, 'erroneous to think there is no substance behind its political style. [...] It is precisely through its dynamic mix of substance and style that populist politics has gained an electoral lead position in current media democracy' (ibid., 32; see also Reisigl 2013, 159). Pels lists various important socio-political challenges that currently concern voters, especially during times of financial and environmental crises, and which are related to a multitude of fears, disaffection and pessimism: fear of losing one's job; fear of 'strangers' (i.e. migrants); fear of losing national autonomy; fear of losing old traditions and values; fear of climate change; disappointment and even disgust with mainstream politics and corruption; anger about the growing gap between rich and poor; disaffection due to the lack of transparency of political decision making and so forth (Rydgren 2007). Thus, when analysing right-wing (or, indeed, left-wing) populist movements and their rhetoric, it is essential to recognize that their propaganda – realized as it is in many genres across relevant social domains – always *combines and integrates form and content*, targets specific audiences and adapts to specific contexts. Only by doing so are we able to deconstruct, understand and explain their messages, the resonance of their messages and their electoral success.

Right-wing Populism: Creating Scapegoats

'Populism simplifies complex developments by looking for a culprit', states the political scientist Anton Pelinka (2013, 8). He argues that:

[a]s the enemy – the foreigner, the foreign culture – has already succeeded in breaking into the fortress of the nation state, someone must be responsible. The élites are the secondary 'defining others', responsible for the liberal democratic policies of accepting cultural diversity. The populist answer to the complexities of a more and more pluralistic society is not multiculturalism. [...] right-wing populism sees multiculturalism as a recipe to denationalize one's (own) nation, to deconstruct one's (own) people.

(ibid.)

3

Right-wing populist parties seem to offer simple and clear-cut answers to all the fears and challenges mentioned above, for example by constructing scapegoats and enemies – 'Others' which are to blame for our current woes – by frequently tapping into traditional collective stereotypes and images of the enemy. The latter depend, I further claim, on the respective historical traditions in specific national, regional and even local contexts: sometimes, the scapegoats are Jews, sometimes Muslims, sometimes Roma or other minorities, sometimes capitalists, socialists, career women, non-governmental organizations (NGOs), the EU, the United Nations, the US or Communists, the governing parties, the elites, the media and so forth. 'They' are foreigners, defined by 'race', religion or language. 'They' are elites not only within the respective country, but also on the European stage ('Brussels') and global level ('Financial Capital'). Important fissures and divides within a society, such as class, caste, religion, gender and so forth, are neglected in focusing on such 'Others' or are interpreted as the result of 'elitist conspiracies'. The discursive strategies of 'victim–perpetrator reversal', 'scapegoating' and the 'construction of conspiracy theories' therefore belong to the necessary 'toolkit' of right-wing populist rhetoric. In short, anybody can potentially be constructed as dangerous 'Other', should it become expedient for specific strategic and manipulative purposes. Pelinka recently observed a shift in the construction of the 'Other' and particularly emphasizes that

> contemporary populism does not so much mobilize against the (perceived) enemy above but more against the (perceived) enemy from abroad. Populism has become more and more ethno-nationalistic. Populist anti-élitism today is directed against those who seem to be responsible for Europeanization and globalization, and especially for mass migration, against élites who have opened the doors to foreign influence and to foreigners. [...] And, of course, the tendency to see individuals (politicians – the 'classe politica', or intellectuals – 'the chattering classes') as responsible for modern-izing trends is beyond any realistic and empirically sound analysis of the trend which tends to put an end to the nation state.

(2013, 9)

It is therefore important that we attempt to understand and explain *how* right-wing populist parties continuously *construct fear* in order to address the collective common-ground as well as their reasons and (rhetorical and communicative) means. This is necessary in order to understand *why and how* right-wing populist parties are achieving ever more success across Europe and beyond, especially in recent national and European elections. This is the main question that I attempt to answer throughout this book, by exploring and systematically analysing a range of different socio-political contexts, histories and empirical examples.

Creating Fear: Legitimizing a Politics of Exclusion

Obviously, the phenomena of right-wing extremism and right-wing populism are not new. And neither is their focus on fear. Indeed, David Altheide in his book *Creating Fear* (2002) very convincingly presents the ways in which scenarios of danger have been constructed ubiquitously in US media and politics for many years. He argues that

> fear has become a dominant public perspective. Fear begins with things we fear, but over time, with enough repetition and expanded use, it becomes a way of looking at life.

Therefore, it is not 'fear of crime', for instance, that is so interesting to me, but rather how fear has emerged as a framework for developing identities and for engaging in social life. Fear is one of the perspectives that citizens share today; while liberals and conservatives may differ in their object of fear, all sides express many fears and point to 'blameworthy' sources – often each other! The fear 'market' has also spawned an extensive cottage industry that promotes new fears and an expanding array of 'victims'.

(2002, 3)

Altheide goes on to emphasize that a large number of social scientists and experts are now marketing 'their self-help books, courses, research funds and expertise' which address anxieties related to the 'self' (2002, 3). Best (2001, 6) substantiates Altheide's arguments and claims that the media produce and reproduce fear and, simultaneously, sell solutions related to moral assumptions to a quite passive audience in the US. Of course, such threats and dangers easily refer to scenarios and horror stories created during the Cold War and continued after 9/11 (e.g. Stocchetti 2007; Stone 2002). In the US (and elsewhere), these debates are frequently instrumental in legitimizing proposals for either more gun control or less gun control – a conflict which has found its way into European debates as well; of course, the horrific 'Breivik incident' lends itself to such debates.

Right-wing populist parties successfully create fear and legitimize their policy proposals (usually related to restricting immigration and so forth; see Wodak and Boukala 2014, 2015) with an appeal to the necessities of security. As will be elaborated later, such arguments became eminent after the end of the Cold War in 1989 and were, of course, forcefully invigorated after 9/11. Each crisis contributes to such scenarios, as can be observed with respect to the financial crisis and the Euro-crisis (Angouri and Wodak 2014; Stråth and Wodak 2009). In such crisis situations, both politics and media tend to reduce complex historical processes to snap-shots which allow constructing and triggering Manichean dichotomies – friends and foes, perpetrators and victims, and so forth. As argued by Murray Edelman in his seminal book *The Symbolic Uses of Politics* (1967), crises are promoted to serve the interests of political leaders and other interest groups who will most certainly benefit from such definitions (e.g. Altheide 2002, 12). We are therefore confronted by a contingency of factors that serve to facilitate dichotomist perspectives, create scapegoats and play into the hands of right-wing populist parties: traditional and new threat scenarios, real and exaggerated crises as well as related horror and moral narratives, real and exaggerated security issues, media reporting that reproduces fear scenarios, and political parties which instrumentalize all these factors to legitimize exclusionary policies. It is evident that all of these factors are related to each other: that they are, in fact, interdependent. This contingency is best understood by recalling the relevant observations made by Berger and Luckmann:

Legitimation as a process is best described as a 'second-order' objectivation of meaning as it produces new meanings that serve to integrate the meanings already attached to disparate institutional processes. The function of legitimation is to make objectively available and subjectively plausible the 'first-order' objectivations that have been institutionalized.

(1966, 110–111)

Moreover, the authors emphasize that

[t]he problem of legitimation inevitably arises when the objectivations of the (now historic) institutional order are to be transmitted to a new generation [...] when the unity

of history and biography is broken. In order to restore it, and thus to make intelligible both aspects of it, there must be 'explanations' and justifications of the salient elements of the institutional tradition. Legitimation is this process of 'explaining' and justifying. Legitimation justifies the institutional order by giving a normative dignity to its practical imperatives. It is important to understand that legitimation has a cognitive as well as a normative element. In other words, legitimation is not just a matter of 'values'. It always implies 'knowledge' as well.

(1966, 110–111)

Right-wing Populism: Crisis and Rising Unemployment

Following the above definition of legitimation, Van Leeuwen and Wodak (1999) introduced a framework for analysing the language of legitimation with four major categories: authorization, moral evaluation, rationalization and mythopoesis. Authorization is legitimation by referring to authority, be that a person, tradition, custom or law. Moral evaluation means legitimation by reference to value systems. Rationalization is legitimation by reference to knowledge claims or arguments. Mythopoesis is legitimation achieved by narratives; these are often small stories or fragments of narrative structures about the past or future. These main types involve a number of sub-types and are also frequently connected. Thus, to understand the specific dynamics of legitimation in particular contexts, such as the financial crisis of 2008 for example, it is important to focus on the typical patterns and characteristics of these discursive strategies in context. Indeed, it is of interest to understand what kind of arguments are put forward and resonate with the public; for example, when legitimizing further austerity measures, governments tend to justify new cuts with necessity or responsibility – arbitrary cuts are then essentialized as necessary in order to protect the nation state and its people (Sayer 2015). When analysing right-wing populist rhetoric, we usually detect legitimization by moral evaluation and mythopoesis: the use of specific moral stances and exemplary reformulated historical narratives (myths) to legitimize 'Othering' and typically implement ever more restrictive immigration measures.

Accordingly, Dettke states that

> [n]ationalist and radical right parties have emerged everywhere in Europe. East and West, and once nationalist radical right wing parties become a stronger force also on the European level, it will be more difficult to preserve the legitimacy and authority of European institutions.

(2014, 10)

More specifically, Dettke (ibid.) argues that the collapse of the Soviet empire has allowed long-suppressed national aspirations and goals to find their outlet in radical ethno-nationalist parties and movements, whereas in Southern Europe youth unemployment has become a – or perhaps *the* – salient problem, with more than one quarter (or even half) of the younger generation facing unemployment. In the spring of 2014, youth unemployment in Greece stood at 62.5 per cent, in Spain at 56.4 per cent, in Portugal at 42.5 per cent, and in Italy at 40.5 per cent;[7] youth unemployment therefore might in fact unleash a new wave of xenophobia, chauvinism and radicalism. These phenomena frequently remind us of the collective experiences of the 20th century and the staggering economic crisis of the 1930s. However, the analogy does not account for the impact of neo-liberal policies since the 1970s and 1980s, the disastrous effect of privatization of many domains of our societies and the deregulation of the financial sector as well as the resulting austerity policies to combat the financial crisis since 2008. As Sayer convincingly argues in his comprehensive analysis of the impact of neo-liberal austerity policies as response to the financial crisis,

> [a]usterity policies fall most heavily on those at the bottom while the top 10%, and particularly the top 1%, are protected ... How ridiculous that the answer to our economic problems is seen as wasting more of our most important asset – people.

> (2015, 1)

The rise and success of right-wing populist parties can certainly also be explained as reaction to such policies, as uniting the modernization losers, the people 'who are left behind' (Mileti and Plomb 2007, 25). Oesch (2008) elaborates in great detail, while comparing five right-wing populist parties (the Austrian FPÖ, the Belgium VlB, the French FN, the Norwegian FrP and the Swiss SVP [see glossary for more information on these parties]), why many workers who traditionally voted for left-wing parties have recently tended to switch to right-wing populist parties. His results (while investigating preferences of male workers) illustrate well that fear-mongering has been successful in many instances, albeit in different ways: in the FPÖ and SVP, negative attitudes towards immigrants and fear of losing one's jobs dominate. Also, fear of negative influence on 'one's culture' is important. In Belgium, however, dissatisfaction with the government and the state of the Belgian democracy as well as cultural protectionism seem to be the primary motifs for voting for the VlB. The same holds true in Norway. In France, however, all three factors – dissatisfaction, fear of wage dumping, fear of the culture being undermined by immigration – prove salient (2007, 366–8). As the socio-cultural fears are also influencing other segments of society, old cleavages prove to be more and more obsolete and values are perceived as more important than social class and traditional class struggles (Marsdal 2013).

The Concept of Populism

Right-wing Populism: A First Definition

Right-wing populism can be defined as a political ideology that rejects existing political consensus and usually combines laissez-faire liberalism and anti-elitism. It is considered populism because of its appeal to the 'common man/woman' as opposed to the elites; this appeal to a quasi-homogenous *demos* is regarded as salient for such movements (see Betz and Immerfall 1998, 4–5). As Betz rightly argues,

> their [the 'elites'] inability to restore the sense of security and prosperity, which steady material and social advances in the post-war period had led their citizens to expect from their leaders, has become a major cause of voter alienation and cynicism. [...] It is within this context of growing public pessimism, anxiety, and disaffection that the rise and success of radical right-wing populism in Western Europe finds at least a partial explanation.

> (1994, 41)

Mudde and Kaltwasser elaborate this definition further and emphasize that populism (both left-wing and right-wing) 'considers society to be ultimately separated into two homogenous and antagonistic groups, "the pure people" and "the corrupt elite"' (2012, 8). Moreover, they claim that populism always perceives 'politics to be an expression of the *volonté générale* of the people' (ibid.). This makes antagonism and the Manichean division into good and bad, friends and foes, we and 'the other' salient characteristics of populism. Mudde and Kaltwasser conclude their conceptual analysis by arguing that three core concepts necessarily belong to any serious definition of populism: the people, the elite and the general will; and its two direct opposites – elitism and pluralism (ibid., 9).[8]

When tracing the history of the concept of 'populism', we quickly discover that the word 'populism' stems from the Latin word *populus*, which means 'people' in English (in the sense of 'folk', 'nation', as in 'The Roman People' (*populus Romanus*) or the German '*Volk*', not in the sense of 'multiple individual persons', e.g. Musolff 2010):[9] 'populism' espouses 'government by the people as a whole'. This stands in contrast to elitism, aristocracy or plutocracy, each of which define an ideology that implies government by a small, privileged, specifically selected group above the masses (i.e. selected by birth, wealth, election, education and so forth). Populism has been a prominent political phenomenon throughout history. The *Populares*, for example, were an unofficial faction in the Roman senate whose supporters were well known for their populist agenda. Some of these senators, such as Tiberius Gracchus, Gaius Marius, Julius Caesar and Caesar Augustus, were very prominent. They all eventually employed referenda to bypass the Roman Senate and appeal directly to the people (NB women, slaves and foreigners were not permitted to vote).

Populism in the 19th and 20th Centuries: Historical Developments and National Differences

Populism as a modern phenomenon with a more direct impact on politics emerges in different forms, beginning with the 19th century. Such movements – from the so-called 'Agrarian populism' in the North American West to 'Peronism' in Argentina – all aimed for a better, 'real' democracy (e.g. Canovan 1981; Pelinka 2013). Although populism in the US and Europe currently tends to be associated mostly (but not only) with right-wing parties, the central meaning of populism – that democracy should reflect the 'pure and undiluted' will of the people – implies that it can accommodate ideologies of both the traditional right and left. However, while leaders of populist movements in recent decades have claimed to be on either the left or the right of the political spectrum, there are also many populists who reject such dichotomist categorizations and claim to be neither 'left wing', 'centrist' nor 'right wing' (e.g. Betz 1994; Canovan 1981). In this way, one can in theory claim that populism supports popular sovereignty and majority rule; moreover, populists usually accept representation by someone of 'the people', but not of 'the elite' (Mudde and Kaltwasser 2012, 17). Of course, it is the populists who define – quite arbitrarily and depending on their interests – who should belong to which group.

Left-wing and right-wing populist parties differ in important aspects, namely in that the latter are inwards looking, thus primarily nationalist/chauvinist, referring to a nativist body politics, while left-wing populist parties are traditionally oriented towards internationalism or post-nationalism. Pelinka (2013, 5) defines the beginning of populism as a form of protest against the overwhelming power of specific privileged elites in the 19th century: economic elites like the 'trusts' in the US; social elites like the dominant aristocracies; political elites like elected representatives who were perceived not to care enough for the interests of 'the people'. As Pelinka convincingly argues (ibid.), the intellectual and analytical weakness of populist democracy always seems to be rooted in the inherent hegemonic assumption that such a *homogenous people* exist. Who is included in and who is excluded from the *demos* is thus not related to social and cultural developments but seen as a very simplistic dogma, a quasi-discrete definition that ignores social differentiation, distinctions and fragmentations (Laclau 2005). National as well as ethnic and racialized identities are discursively constructed to create an imaginary of nativist (essentialized) and quasi-natural borders between 'Us' and 'Them'. Differences (of any kind) within 'the people' are therefore denied. Populists create a *demos* which exists above and beyond the divides and diversities of social class and religion, gender and generation.

Populism was also exceedingly influential in South American nation states. For example, in Argentina in the 1940s, a local brand of fascist populism termed 'Peronism' emerged, named after its leader Juan Perón. Its roots lie in the intellectual fascist movement of the 1920s and 1930s that delegitimized democracy in Argentina (Blamires 2006, 26). More recently, South American leaders such as former President Hugo Chavez in Venezuela endorsed a more left-wing populism. Moreover, recent research on populist politics and policies in South America (e.g. Peru and Venezuela) provides ample evidence that we are dealing with an 'inclusive populism' in these contexts, whereas right-wing populism in Europe manifests itself as an exclusionary force. Accordingly, Roberts justifiably claims that

Chavez's self-proclaimed 'Bolivarian Revolution' was authentic, and it provided a textbook illustration of the ways in which populism's inclusionary dynamic can expand opportunities for democratic participation at the same time that its majoritarian logic restricts institutional spaces for effective democratic contestation.

(2012, 138)

There have also been several versions of populist parties in the US, some inspired by the Populist Party of the 1890s, the party of the early US populist movement in which millions of farmers and other working people successfully enacted their anti-trust agenda (Pelinka 2013, 3, 15). Other early populist political parties in the US included the Greenback Party, the Progressive Party of 1912 led by Theodore Roosevelt, the Progressive Party of 1924 led by Robert M. La Follette, Sr., and the Share Our Wealth movement of Huey Long in 1933–1935. Populism continues to be an important force in modern US politics, especially in the 1992 and 1996 third-party presidential campaigns of billionaire Ross Perot and in the so-called 'Tea-Party' since Barack Obama's first term in 2008 (Schweitzer 2012).

Ralph Nader's 1996, 2000, 2004 and 2008 presidential campaigns also endorsed a strong populist programme. Of course, any strict comparison between earlier populist movements and those of today is impossible because of significant changes in the so-called interests of the common people as well as socio-political changes and local and global developments. In one of the most recent examples of populist movements in 2012 and 2013, participants of the left-wing populist Occupy movement chose the widely popular slogan 'We are the 99 per cent'. The Occupy leadership used the elliptic and metonymic label 'the 1 per cent' to refer to the 1 per cent of Americans who are regarded as the wealthiest citizens; the 1 per cent that is commonly said and statistically proved to possess more than 50 per cent of the country's wealth (Sayer 2015). The Occupy movement emphasized that this 1 per cent was responsible for huge economic instability and inequality. Lowndes and Warren (2011) thus maintained that Occupy was the 'first major populist movement on the US left since the 1930s'.[10]

Finally, it is important to mention Silvio Berlusconi, leader of the People of Freedom Party and former Prime Minister of Italy for almost 10 years. When Berlusconi entered politics with his party Forza Italia in 1994, he established a new kind of populism which focused on the media's total control via ownership and censorship (Ruzza and Balbo 2013) – I label this form of populism *Berlusconisation*. Berlusconi and his allies have won three elections (1994, 2001 and 2008), the latter with his new right-wing party People of Freedom. In 2009 Beppe Grillo, a former comedian, blogger and activist, founded the so-called Five Star Movement. This party advocates direct democracy and free access to the Internet, and strongly condemns corruption. The movement's programme also contains elements of right-wing populism and American-style libertarianism. The party is considered populist, ecologist and Eurosceptic. Grillo is a highly successful performer and speaker, and comes across as authentic, close to the people and anti-elitist (Molé 2013). In the 2013 Italian election the Five Star Movement – to the surprise of all media and observers – gained 25.5 per cent of votes, winning 109 deputies and 54 senators (Fella and Ruzza 2013; Fusi 2014). Explanations range from deep disappointment with all parties of the establishment, anger about austerity measures, anti-Berlusconi vote, Euro-scepticism and protest to enthusiastic support for new creative forms of politics.

Populism and Fascism

Some researchers have argued that populist elements have always also appealed to and appeared in far-right authoritarian or fascist movements.[11] For example, conspiracy theories combined with scapegoating as employed by various populist movements can create 'a seedbed for fascism' (Rupert 1997, 96). Certainly, national socialist populism interacted with and facilitated fascism in interwar Germany and Austria (Posch et al. 2013).

Along the same vein, Schmitt maintains that the Führer-state represented the 'people's will' more efficiently and more truthfully than the liberal parliamentarianism of Weimar or Westminster (e.g. Pelinka 2013, 5). Thus, the national-socialist Führer or the fascist Duce continuously emphasized and thus legitimized (via mythopoesis) that they acted on behalf of *the* people, as saviours, sent as messenger by some mythical (frequently religious) *persona*. In practice, this meant that the people should applaud the actions of the leader and, in so doing, legitimize them (Schmitt 2007, 80–96). Legitimation qua authority also played a decisive role in these ideologies – in German, this specific discursive strategy is labelled the *Sendebotentrick* (see Maas 1985). Post-war, the terminology changed to *Robin Hood*, the commoner who saves the 'common man and woman on the street'. The *topos of saviour* occurs widely in right-wing populist rhetoric and refers to a simple argumentation scheme such as: 'If danger is to be expected because of X and if A has saved us in the past, then A will be able to save us again' (Wodak and Forchtner 2014).

Thus, ever since the end of World War II, revisionist ideologies have circulated and been adopted by neo-Nazi or right-wing extremist parties such as the FPÖ, the French Front National (FN), the Sweden-Democrats and the British National Party (BNP) (e.g. Beauzamy 2013a; Oje and Mral 2013; Richardson 2013a, 2013b; Wodak and Richardson 2013). While resemblances to older, well-known ideologies can be identified in many of the 'new' right-wing discourses (Mammone 2009), Betz (1996) rightly points to the fact that right-wing populism differs from those other trends as it does not convey a coherent narrative and ideology but rather proposes a mixed, often contradictory array of beliefs, stereotypes, attitudes and related programmes which aim to address and mobilize a range of equally contradictory segments of the electorate.

Below, in Vignette 1, I illustrate some typical discursive and rhetorical strategies employed by right-wing populist parties in their attempt to dominate the political agenda and media reporting, and thus to determine the hegemonic discourse, by briefly analys- ing a television interview with the current leader of the FPÖ, HC Strache. This vignette will reappear at various points throughout this book: in Chapters 2 and 3, some of the pertinent theoretical dimensions will be elaborated in more detail. In Chapters 5, 6 and 7, I will point to salient elements of visual rhetoric and argumentation (i.e. multimodality) which are prominent in the example discussed below. There, I will also analyse various television interviews and debates between right-wing populist politicians and television moderators. In the last chapter of this book, I discuss the implications of such hegemonic politics of denial as propagated by right-wing populist parties and their protagonists.

'Anything goes!': Setting the Agenda via Provocation and Scandalization

Right-wing Populism: Taking Advantage of the Media

Currently, we are witnessing the development of a 'media-democracy' across Europe and beyond, in which the individual, media-savvy performance of politics seems to become more important than the political process (Grande 2000; Wodak 2010; Stögner and Wodak 2014). Accordingly, politics is reduced to a few slogans thought comprehensible to the public at large. This development can be recognized also in the fact that contemporary politics does not only rely on the media as 'the most important source of information and vehicle of com- munication between the governors and the governed' (Strömbäck 2008, 230). The media have also contributed to the transformation of politics through more and continuous emphasis on 'frontstage performances' (Goffman 1959; Wodak 2011a). As argued by Forchtner et al. (2013), the manifold patterns of media communication and the clever and ubiquitous appro- priation of media agenda and frames employed in the recent success of populist-right parties cannot be dismissed or marginalized as a mere coincidence. Furthermore, the dispropor- tionate success of some of these parties, Ellinas (2009) goes on to suggest, can probably be explained by the excessive exposure that these parties receive in the media, despite their lack of what used to be regarded as required organizational and political structures (ibid.). As Bos et al. (2010, 3) illustrate, successful right-wing populist leaders have actually managed to achieve a delicate balance between, on the one hand, appearing unusual and populist, or anti-establishment, and on the other, authoritative and legitimate; thus they counter the elites but do not oppose the liberal democratic system per se. Frequently, this is achieved by scan- dalization (Wodak 2013a, 2013b) or by what Albertazzi labels 'dramatization', that is, 'the need to generate tension in order to build up support for the party […] by denouncing the tragedies that would befall the community if it were to be deprived of its defences' (2007, 335). Scandalization also implies manifold references to the allegedly charismatic leaders of such parties, who construct themselves as knowledgeable, saviours, problem solvers and crisis managers, which may lead voters to have more confidence in the effectiveness of the politics of the populist right-wing (see Chapter 6).

Of course, politics, media and business have always, to some degree, been interdependent.[12] The aforementioned changes have recently led to a further blurring of the boundaries between entertainment and information as well as between private and public domains, between marketing, advertising and campaigning, between politicians and celebrities and so forth (Higgins 2008; Street 2010); a blurring of boundaries, in other words, that used to be seen as vital and essential to the structure of modern, democratic societies. Wodak (2011a, 157) has described this process as the *fictionalization of politics*, that is, 'the blurring of boundaries in politics between the real and the fictional, the informative and the entertaining' that creates a reality for the viewer which appears ordered and manageable – and thus presents a deceptively simple illusion in contrast to the very real complexity and pluralism of present-day societies. Moreover, Hay (2007) contends that public discontent with contemporary politics (on which the rise of populist parties partly rests) has led not to a decrease but to an increase in what is expected of politicians; most parties have responded to these increased expectations by reducing an increasingly complex world to media-savvy personalities and their simplistic slogans. Criticism directed at mainstream programmes and content is routinely responded to by admitting that 'things have not been communicated well' or even 'not sold well' in the diction of the parties themselves and by asserting that the only thing that needs to be improved is communication (by implication via the media) (Hansson 2015). Although Karvonen (2010) stresses major differences in the amounts and modes of personalization and performativity across EU member states, the case of the FPÖ is a telling example of this tendency.

Current analyses also stress the transformation of discourses and performances of political action and their representation in contemporary Europe in terms of the *celebrity culture* in the political field.[13] For example, beginning in the early 1990s, the Austrian politician Jörg Haider changed the character of the political game in significant ways (Krzyżanowski and Wodak 2009). The former Italian Prime Minister Silvio Berlusconi (Mancini 2011; Semino and Koller 2009) exemplified this new type of political leader in Italy. The way the tension between extraordinariness and being 'one of us' (i.e. being 'authentic') was cleverly managed by Haider on frontstage and further developed by his successor, HC Strache (as he is branded), in many different publics and genres, from television interviews to snippets caught on video while dancing in a disco, from pamphlets and manifestos to posters and comic booklets, all of which are accessible on HC Strache's homepage[14] and disseminated via Facebook[15] (see Chapter 6).

Media democracies and the hybridity of political and everyday practices imply an increase in quasi-informality and 'democratisation', arguably also in 'politics as usual' (Wodak 2011a). Indeed, following Alexander (2006), the *symbolic dimension* of 'doing politics' must be understood as central to *all* efforts of a politician's performance, in the media, at election rallies, in parliament, at press conferences and so forth (Forchtner et al. 2013). While Alexander is certainly not the first scholar to emphasize the symbolic dimension of politics, his approach reaches further than both Edelman (1967) and Goffman (1959) in their focus on the symbolic dimensions of frontstage performance.[16] Alexander not only stresses the need to create a collective representation which is attractive to, and resonates with, the audience in election campaigns (and beyond), he also emphasizes that these performances must hook into the background culture, symbols, narratives and myths of the respective society in order to be successful. In other words, if such symbolic practices are supposed to resonate, they have to draw on and mobilize a common cultural structure, via appeals to common knowledge of epistemic communities, to the *endoxa* by using presuppositions, insinuations and other pragmatic devices as well as specific argumentation schemes. The details of the linguistic, rhetorical and argumentative analysis of right-wing populist text and talk will be examined in Chapter 3. Vignette 1 serves as an introduction to the analysis of the micro-politics of right-wing populist politics of denial, as typically performed in media debates and interviews.

VIGNETTE 1
THE POLITICS OF DENIAL: 'THERE IS NO STAR OF DAVID'

On 18 August 2012, the leader of the FPÖ, HC Strache, posted a caricature on Facebook (Image 1.1) which recontextualized an American caricature from 1962 (Image 1.2) into a caricature which obviously alluded to antisemitic caricatures from the Nazi era that were published daily in the 1930s in the infamous German newspaper *Der Stürmer*. After the – predictable – scandal had erupted over explicit antisemitic features of the caricature, most newspapers in Austria and Germany published editorials and news reports about this incident; Strache was also interviewed on television on 20 August 2012;[17] he first denied having altered the original caricature; he then denied that the stars visible on the cufflinks of the banker were Stars of David; and finally he categorically denied any resemblances to antisemitic caricatures.

Image 1.1 Caricature posted by HC Strache on Facebook, 18 August 2012

Image 1.2 American caricature, 1962

The explicit differences between Images 1.1 and 1.2 are easy to detect: the nose of the sweating and greedily eating banker had been changed to a crooked, so-called 'Jewish nose' and the cufflinks had been decorated with the Star of David. These two changes both insinuate,

(Continued)

(Continued)

and resonate with, images of the Nazi past, with the stereotypical image of 'the ugly Jewish banker' who exploits the poor (metonymically embodied by the image of a poor worker from the 1960s) and patronises the government that tries to ingratiate itself with the powerful and rich Jew by serving him an opulent meal and pouring wine. Image 1.3 shows this in detail.

Image 1.3 Details of the 'greedy banker'

By making these changes and posting the altered caricature with an extended comment (see Image 1.1), Strache utilized the theme of the financial crisis in at least three ways: first, to accuse the government of wrong policies and of submitting to the EU; second, to create a scapegoat that can be blamed for current woes by triggering traditional anti-semitic stereotypes of world conspiracy and powerful Jewish bankers and capitalists; and third, to provoke a scandal and thus attract media attention and set the news agenda. The caricature is accompanied by a text panel on the right that explains the caricature in some detail and accuses the government of selling out to EU policies and foreign punters. This insinuates some other well-known anti-Jewish stereotypes: the world conspiracy and the Jewish capitalist. I will return to this text and its role in the scandal below. The 'Facebook incident', as I like to refer to the lengthy scandal surrounding the posting of the antisemitic caricature, will be employed to demonstrate several aims through-out this book: it introduces readers to the typical rhetorical strategies of *provocation*, *calculated ambivalence* and *denial*; it emphasizes the power of digital media in their use of traditional genres and the rapid spiral of scandalization; moreover, this example illustrates the importance of an in-depth and context-sensitive, multi-layered analysis when trying to understand and explain the dynamics of right-wing populist propaganda and manipulation.

The dialogue below is taken from the beginning of a television interview from 22 August 2012 (i.e. four days after the caricature was posted) on ORF II (ZIB 2; Austrian Broadcasting Company, daily news programme at 10 p.m.), and illustrates perfectly the politics of denial propagated by HC Strache (AW is Armin Wolf, anchor-man on the main Austrian news programme ZIB II; HCS is Strache).[18]

Text 1.1

[1] AW Now, last week you managed once again to make it into international

[2] AW headlines, and you did it by using this caricature, which you posted
HCS Hmhm

[3] AW on your Facebook page. The Zeit,
HCS Hmhm

[4] AW a respected German weekly newspaper, refers to this as 'antisemitic

[5] AW provocation', the Spiegel refers to is as 'a picture, just as in times of NS-

[6] AW propaganda', and even the BBC reported on it. Are you

[7] AW proud of that?
HCS No. This is absolute nonsense! I got

[8] AW You did
HCS this, um, caricature, um, shared by a user

After asking HC Strache whether he is now 'proud' of being discussed in so many serious newspapers and radio stations across Europe (*Die Zeit*, *Der Spiegel*, the BBC), Strache utters his first denial (lines 7–9), an act-denial:[19] 'No, this is absolute nonsense, I got this caricature shared by a user.' Anchor-man Armin Wolf immediately falsifies this claim and shows that Strache actually posted this caricature himself by pointing to a print-out of the relevant Facebook page (line 9). Strache then concedes that he first said something wrong and starts – by way of justification – to explain the caricature as illustrating the unfair and unjust redistribution of money taken away from the Austrian people. Here, Wolf interrupts in line 16 and qualifies the bankers as Jews ('who are Jews in your caricature'). At this point, the second round of denials starts and Strache says (lines 16–19):

Text 1.2

[16] HCS No, no, they are not,
AW What then?

[17] HCS Mister Wolf. And, um, with all due respect, I have

(Continued)

(Continued)

[18]	**HCS**	many Israeli, but also Jewish friends, who

[19]	**HCS**	have, um, seen this caricature, and not one of them can recognise antisemitism

Via a well-known disclaimer ('I have many Israeli, Jewish friends'), Strache denies that the caricature should or even could be read as antisemitic, a typical intention-denial: the fallacious argument (*post hoc, ergo propter hoc* fallacy) is obvious: if his many Jewish friends do not classify the caricature as antisemitic, it cannot be antisemitic. Such disclaimers are widely used to prove that an utterance *cannot* be categorized as racist, sexist or antisemitic because 'Turkish, Arabic, female or Jewish friends' share the speaker's or writers' opinions. Moreover, the justification implies that if one has Jewish friends, then one is incapable of saying something antisemitic (see Wodak et al. 1990 for the analysis of similar fallacious argumentative moves).

After this unsuccessful denial, Wolf points to the Stars of David on the cufflinks and asks who might have put them there if not Strache himself. In his third attempt to deny wrongdoing and antisemitic stereotypes, Strache refuses to recognize the Star of David on the cufflinks (lines 23, 24) and starts a counter-attack with an *ad-hominem argument*: he claims that Wolf obviously cannot see well, his glasses are probably not strong enough; even if one would magnify the cufflinks, Strache further claims, no Star of David would be visible. Wolf then shows a Star of David he has brought with him to the studio and asks Strache if he can spot any similarity (line 32); Strache denies again and states that the picture on the cufflinks is blurred and that there is no star but actually something like a diamond. After this fifth (act) denial, he refers to his 'Jewish friends' again who, Strache claims, believe that somebody is intentionally conspiring against him. In this way, Strache accuses the media and the public of conspiring against him by quoting his 'Jewish friends' – another typical justification strategy: claiming victimhood via victim–perpetrator reversal. Wolf continues his line of questioning and asks Strache why he apparently finds it impossible to simply apologize for posting such a caricature and why he would rather use a strategy of victim–perpetrator reversal instead of an apology. Strache answers by repeating his denials: there is no Star of David; the caricature is not antisemitic (this staccato-like question–answer sequence continues for several minutes).

Text 1.3

[20]	**AW**	Mister Strache …
	HCS	in this. If you see something else in this,

[21]	**HCS**	um, then, um, you have to ask yourself the question, why do you want to see

[22]	**AW**	Because you have three Stars of David here. Because you put three
	HCS	something else in this, because there is no antisemitism

[23]	**AW**	Stars of David here, or someone put them there …
	HCS	That is incorrect, Mister Wolf.

[24]	**AW**	No? You do not see three Stars of David here.
	HCS	Well … No, maybe you should have the

[25]	**AW**	Yes
	HCS	strength of your glasses checked, if you magnify this picture,

[26]	**AW**	Yes Really? Okay. We did
	HCS	you can see no Stars of David. Yeah.

[27]	**AW**	magnify the picture, Mister Strache. We did
	HCS	I can show you, too, yes.

[28]	**AW**	magnify the picture and you cannot see any Stars of David here?
	HCS	Exactly. Yes. Yes. No,

[29]	**AW**	Mister Strache, you don't see any Stars of David?
	HCS	there are no Stars of David to be seen, because …

[30]	**AW**	Mister Strache, I also brought you
	HCS	No! There are no Stars of David to be seen here.

[31]	**AW**	a Star of David for comparison. And
	HCS	Yes…. and this picture … That is one! Yeah? No, that is

[32]	**AW**	there are not three Stars of David here?
	HCS	one. No, that's a star with continuous

[33]	**AW**	Good.
	HCS	lines, there is no way you can see that with that blurry picture.

In line 74, Wolf shifts to the meta-level and frames the entire discussion as a provocation strategy intentionally triggered by Strache to attract media attention. This interpretation is, not surprisingly, again denied by Strache (a goal-denial). The interview continues with other questions about Strache's programme for the autumn 2012.

(Continued)

(Continued)

Text 1.4

[70]	**HCS**	regarding that nose, I have already seen worse caricatures of my own

[71]	**HCS**	there we, I can only think of Mister Sinowatz or as a

[72]	**HCS**	neighbour, as a political neighbour, um, Mister Khol, or possibly

[73]	**HCS**	Mister Konrad as a comparison, but certainly not what you

[74]	**AW**	Well. Mister Strache, is it possible that you are
	HCS	are trying to create here.

[75]	**AW**	in reality quite pleased with the situation? Well,
	HCS	No, I am not pleased at all!

[76]	**AW**	well, you have once again created a lapse to provoke, the
	HCS	Quite the contrary. Yes, yes.

[77]	**AW**	outrage is enormous, um, not only in Austria, but also internationally,

[78]	**AW**	and you can once again present yourself as the poor and the persecuted, now

[79]	**AW**	you are the victim, suddenly, and can enjoy the headlines.
	HCS	Yes, yes.

After the interview, many commentators accused Armin Wolf of having been too 'strict' on Strache; some newspapers like the widely read tabloid *Neue Kronenzeitung* wrote that the line of questioning had been unfair and not acceptable for this kind of interview genre; others equated the interview style with a tribunal or an interrogation.[20] These media comments show that Strache had obviously been quite successful in constructing himself as victim on the one hand and as a saviour of the Austrian people on the other hand, by telling the Austrians the 'truth' about the economic crisis, by discovering the causes of the crisis (allegedly, the 'Jewish banker') and by thus providing a scapegoat that everybody could blame for the crisis. However, simultaneously, the state prosecutor started to investigate whether the Facebook incident could be persecuted as hate incitement. In April 2013, the court decided that Strache's posting could not be regarded as a case of hate incitement – I will come back to this verdict in the final chapter of the book as the outcome of this investigation cannot be regarded as unique or exceptional. In fact, it is quite typical for the ways in which courts of law deal with right-wing populist discriminatory and exclusionary rhetoric. In short, the lack of legal consequences seems to confirm that 'anything goes'.

By systematically employing genres such as caricatures and comic books to convey xenophobic and antisemitic messages, right-wing populist parties cleverly play with the fictionalization of politics and frequently argue that no discriminatory message was intended as such genres play with humour and are inherently ironic or even sarcastic (Wodak and Forchtner 2014). The blurring of boundaries between fiction and reality, caricature and image, or between comic book plot and historical narrative is one of many ways of staging the strategy of *calculated ambivalence*, thus simultaneously addressing multiple audiences with – frequently contradictory – messages (Wodak 2013b; Engel and Wodak 2013; Wodak and Reisigl 2002). Facebook potentially adds to this strategy at least in one way: denying having posted the incriminatory content oneself and using the (seeming) anonymity of the Internet.

The Right-wing Populist Perpetuum Mobile

Of course, as already mentioned above, the rise of right-wing populist movements in recent years would not have been possible without massive media support, inadvertent as it may have been in many cases. This does not imply that all newspapers share the same positions, although naturally some tabloids do. For example, the former leader of the Austrian Freedom Party (FPÖ), Jörg Haider, frequently appeared on the cover of weekly magazines such as *News* or *Profil*, thereby ensuring higher sales for these publications but at the same time adding to his visibility in the public sphere. The Austrian tabloid *Neue Kronenzeitung*, similar to the *Sun* or the *Daily Mail* but with a larger outreach in relation to the country's population (approx. three million Sunday readers in a country of eight million), campaigned for Haider both explicitly and implicitly: headlines, editorials, images and letters to the editor were all streamlined to provide support.

Right-wing populist politicians, as illustrated by Vignette 1, intentionally provoke scandals by violating publicly accepted norms (Köhler and Wodak 2011; Wodak 2013a, 2013b). In this way, the media are forced into a 'no-win' situation: if they do not report a scandalous racist remark or insinuation, such as Strache's caricature, they might be perceived as endorsing it. If they do write about it, they explicitly reproduce the prejudicial utterance, thereby further disseminating it. If they critically interview the politician, they give him/her more face time and an opportunity for perpetrator–victim reversal. This triggers a predictable dynamic which allows right-wing populist parties to set the agenda and distract the media (and the public) from other important news.

This dynamic consists of several stages which I refer to as '*The right-wing populist perpetuum mobile*': this implies that such parties and politicians have developed discursive and rhetorical strategies which combine incompatible phenomena, make false claims sound innocent, allow denying the obvious, say the 'unsayable', and transcend the limits of the permissible. Usually, they get away without being sanctioned and, even if they have to apologize, they do so in a calculated and ambivalent way (see Chapter 3). Rarely do they have to resign and, even if they do, some of them seem to 'bounce back' quite quickly.

The specific dynamic is easily deconstructed:

- First, *scandal* (e.g. the posting of the antisemitic caricature) is *intentionally provoked* by the FPÖ.

- Once evidence for the inherently racist meaning is produced by the opposition, the offensive meaning of the image is immediately *denied* (intention and goal denials);

- then the scandal is *redefined* and *equated* with entirely different phenomena (by redefining and reformulating the meaning of concepts or by employing analogies and metaphors, or by constructing contrasts or arguing via *topoi of history*). In Vignette 1, the FPÖ employed the discursive strategy of *calculated ambivalence* and succeeded in conveying a *double-message* – readers could either share the opinion that any similarity with an antisemitic caricature was utterly coincidental, or they could share the antisemitic meanings insinuated by the crooked nose and the particular cufflinks.

- This strategy allows, as a further step, the respective politician to claim *victimhood* as he or she is accused of racism or antisemitism by the opposition and some media.

- The event is then *dramatized and exaggerated*, that is, the FPÖ/Strache claims to have been wrongly accused of having posted a racist or antisemitic slogan.

- Furthermore, the politician could emphasize the right of freedom of speech for himself as a *justificatory strategy*: 'Why can one not utter critique?', or 'One must be permitted to criticize Turks, Roma, Muslims, Jews …!' or '*We* dare say what everybody thinks' and so forth. Such utterances immediately *shift the frame and trigger another debate* – unrelated to the original scandal – about freedom of speech and political correctness, and thus serve as a distraction and allow evasion of the primary scandalous issue.

- Moreover, the accusation is instrumentalized for the construction of a *conspiracy*: somebody must be 'pulling the strings' against the original culprit of the scandal, and *scapegoats* (foreigners, liberal intellectuals, the Jewish Community, the opposition, etc.) are quickly discovered.

- Once the thus accused finally have a chance to present substantial counter-evidence, a *new scandal* is launched.

- A '*quasi-apology*' might follow in case 'misunderstandings' should have occurred, an apology based on a condition that is presented as unlikely, even surreal: by apologizing for other people's misunderstanding (rather than for one's own ambiguity), the apology is rendered a farce; and the entire process begins afresh with a new scandalous utterance, again an instance of calculated ambivalence.

This pattern illustrates how right-wing populist parties cleverly manage to set the agenda and frame media debates; other political parties and politicians as well as the media are, in turn, forced to react and respond continuously to ever new provocations. Few opportunities remain to present other frames, values and counterarguments, or any other relevant agenda. As a consequence, mainstream politics moves more and more to the right and the public becomes disillusioned, de-politicized and 'tired' of ever new scandals; hence, right-wing populist rhetoric necessarily becomes ever more explicit and extreme and continuously attracts further attention.

Constructing a 'Politics of Fear'

After having presented a typical example of the 'politics of denial', it is worth summarizing the various characteristics of right-wing populist parties introduced in this chapter. I propose nine features, which are, I claim, common to most if not all right-wing populist parties (see also Wodak 2013a; Reisigl 2013) and which will be discussed in the following chapters in greater detail.[21]

- Right-wing populism is based on a generalized claim to represent '*THE people*' in the sense of a homogenised ideal based on nativist ideologies, thus on *traditional body politics*. The construction of these groups is contingent on many historical, national and socio-political factors. This dogma is accompanied by a *revisionist view of history*. The *rhetoric of exclusion* has become part and parcel of a much more general discourse about strangers within and outside the 'body', that is, the nation state. Such minorities include the Roma and the Jews on the one hand and migrants on the other, following the overall motto: '*We*' (i.e. the Occident or Christian Europe) have to defend '*Ourselves*' against '*Them*' (i.e. the 'Orient': Roma, Jews, Muslims). Right-wing populist movements are based on a specific understanding of the '*demos*/people', thus denying complexity within society. These parties continuously construct themselves as the 'saviours of the Occident' who defend the man/woman on the street against both 'those up there' and 'the Barbarians' who might take away 'Austrian (British, Dutch, Belgian, Italian) jobs from Austrian (British, Dutch, Belgian, Italian) workers' and who 'do not want to integrate and adapt to our culture'. Similar slogans employing parallel scenarios abound.

- Right-wing populism[22] employs a *political style* that can relate to various ideologies, not just to one. We encounter left-wing and right-wing populist parties; the difference relates to the *political imaginaries* they put forward as well as to the parties' structures and recruitment patterns.

- Right-wing populism cuts across the traditional left/right divide and constructs *new social divides*, frequently related to many, sometimes legitimate and justified, fears about globalization and the subsequent rise of nationalism and chauvinism, the failure of current mainstream parties to address acute social problems, like the financial crisis and so forth.

- Right-wing populist parties' success depends on *performance strategies* in modern *media democracies*. This implies extensive use of the media (press and television, new media such as comics, homepages, websites, Facebook, Twitter and so forth). Moreover, right-wing populist politicians are usually well trained as media personalities, and have frequently transformed a 'thug-like' appearance into that of a 'slick' mainstream politician: they appear youthful, handsome, fit and well dressed. In short, they assume the habitus of serious but young, involved and approachable statesmen and stateswomen. This image transformation is not always successful. Mainstream parties in particular often find it difficult to adopt similar strategies (as they do with the use of new media).

- The *personalization* and *commodification* of current politics and politicians lead to a focus on 'charismatic' leaders; right-wing populist parties usually have a hierarchical structure with (male) leaders who exploit modern trends of the political profession to perfection.[23] Recently, female leaders have also come to the fore (in France, Denmark, Norway and the US).

- Leading populist politicians employ *frontstage performance* techniques that are linked to popular *celebrity culture* (well-known from tabloids and sensationalist media reporting): They oscillate between self-presentations as a *Robin Hood*-like figure (i.e. saviour of 'the man and woman in the street', 'defender of the common people') and self-presentations as 'rich, famous and/or attractive' (i.e. an 'idol' to aspire to), frequently leading to a 'softer' image, adapted to mainstream values, but only on frontstage. Hence, such politicians carefully prepare their *appearance* and *performances* for different audiences; their rhetoric and programmatic proposals are heavily *context-dependent*. This implies a specific selection of meeting places (beer tents, pubs, stages, market places, discos, and the so-called 'tea-parties' in the US), the clothes they wear (from suits to casual leather jackets, T-shirts or folklore dress), their selection of spin-doctors and accompanying 'performers' on stage, the music, posters and logos on display and so forth.

- Right-wing populism usually correlates with *anti-intellectualism* and, as a result, with what I term *arrogance of ignorance*. Appeals to common-sense and traditional (conservative) values linked to aggressive exclusionary rhetoric are, for example, particularly apparent in some parts of the US *Tea Party* movement, performed and instrumentalized almost 'perfectly' by politicians such as Sarah Palin or Michelle Bachmann.

- Linked to anti-Muslim rhetoric and campaigns, right-wing populist parties currently endorse pseudo-emancipatory *gender policies* which, on second view, are extremely contradictory; in this vein, the US Republicans claim, for example, to support a so-called 'right-wing feminism' ('frontier-feminism'), which links feminist values to traditional family values and campaigns against pro-choice movements. Thus, on the one hand, traditional family values are emphasized (which position women primarily as mothers, caring for children and their families); on the other hand, although 'freedom for women' is propagated, this refers solely to Muslim women, who are depicted as wearing headscarves or burqas not by choice but by oppression. Gender becomes instrumentalized and linked to rhetoric of exclusion, for example, the exclusion of Turkish migrants. The so-called 'freedom' of women is contrasted with fundamentalist Islam, which presupposes that every woman wearing a headscarf is at the same time suppressed and potentially dangerous in terms of terrorism. The theme of security is thus easily linked to the so-called 'freedom of women' by what is perceived as their common 'root of evil'.

- There is a distinct difference between populist styles and rhetoric in *opposition* and in *government*. Few right-wing populist parties maintain their strength or survive if elected into government because they lack the necessary experience, programmes, strategies and skills. In the Netherlands, for example, the extreme right lost immediately once they formed part of the second chamber in the Dutch government (2002–2006) after the assassination of Pim Fortuyn on 6 May 2002.

Endnotes

1 These terms were primarily used in the 19th and 20th centuries to describe the 'people' from a racist and biological/biologistic perspective, i.e. nativist. Ultimately, these terms were salient in national-socialist ideology and propaganda and directed primarily against so-called 'parasites' who were allegedly threatening the 'host-body', i.e. Jews, Slavs, homosexuals and Roma (see Musolff, 2010, for an extensive discussion and discourse-historical analysis of these terms and related metaphors of body-politic).

2 See Feldman and Jackson (2013), Gingrich and Banks (2006), Harrison and Bruter (2011), Mudde and Kaltwasser (2012), Sir Peter Ustinov Institut et al. (2013), Wilson and Hainsworth (2012), Wodak et al. (2013).

3   For example www.news.at/a/anschlaege-norwegen-fpoe-hetzt-302711, accessed 3 May 2013.

4   See e.g. Krzyżanowski and Wodak (2009), Matouschek et al. (1995), Pelinka and Wodak (2002), Reisigl (2013), Wodak and Pelinka (2002) for more details. It is important to emphasize at this point that right-wing populist parties have appeared and gained much support in the former Eastern Bloc countries such as Bulgaria, Hungary, Poland and Romania (Dettke 2014). Unlike their counterparts in 'the West', they find it less difficult to promote explicit xenophobic, antisemitic and antiziganist messages (see Chapters 2, 4 and 8). They also draw on traditional antisemitic beliefs shared widely across the population, but these differ in their quality and explicitness from antisemitic resentments in the UK or France, e.g. where opinions about hegemonic Israeli politics are always integrated into debates about Jews (thus sometimes also insinuating world-conspiracy themes) (see Kovács 2013; Mădroane 2013).

5   Political imaginaries are defined as being in a 'landscape of power as a space of political action signified in visual and iconographic practices and objects as well as in the literary-textual field that depicts the political scene, its structure, and its stakes' (Bob Jessop, personal communication, 10 February 2010).

6   See the Glossary for important facts related to all right-wing populist parties.

7   See www.statista.com/statistics/266228/youth-unemployment-rate-in-eu-countries/

8   Recent studies define and frequently analyse populism in terms of metaphors such as a 'virus', 'syndrome' or 'modern problem' (Taggart 2000; Taguieff 1984) or characterize populism as 'anti-democratic', 'anti-parliamentary' or as a 'dangerous excess' (Mény and Surel 2002). These accounts do not, however, directly contribute to a differentiated analysis of this complex phenomenon.

9   See also Latin *popularis*, referring to the 'people' (Latin *populus*; in French *populaire*, 18th century, which led to the German *populär* – which differs in meaning from 'populist') (Kluge 1999, 641).

10 See www.dissentmagazine.org/online.php?id=551.

11 See De Cleen (2012), Fieschi (2004), Wodak and Richardson (2013) as well as Richardson and Wodak (2009a, 2009b).

12 See Bourdieu (1999, 2005), Chouliaraki and Morsing (2010).

13 See Corner and Pels (2003), Forchtner et al. (2013), Street (2004), Wodak (2010, 2011a) as well as Wodak and Forchtner (2014) for more details on the fictionalization of politics.

14 See www.hcstrache.at/, accessed 2 May 2013.

15 See Horaczek and Reiterer (2009), Köhler and Wodak (2011), Reisigl (2013), Scharsach (2012), Wodak (2013a, 2013b), Wodak and Köhler (2010) and Wodak and Reisigl (2014) for recent detailed studies and research on the FPÖ and HC Strache.

16 See Wodak (2011a, 14ff, 32ff, 190ff) for a summary and integrated model of frontstage and backstage political communication where I draw primarily on identity theories, Bourdieu's theory of habitus and capitals, Goffman's metaphor of theatre and performance, and Lave and Wenger's approach to communities of practice.

17 See http://derstandard.at/1345164507078/Streit-um-antisemitisches-Bild-auf-Strache-Seite, accessed 12 March 2015.

18 The transcription here follows rudimentary transcription rules developed for conversations. Such a transcription allows following the dynamic of the conversation and presents all voices as they interact, overlap and interrupt each other. This is a simplified presentation of the full transcript, which follows the HIAT rules for transcriptions.

19 See Chapter 3 for an extensive discussion of denials, justification strategies and disclaimers (van Dijk 1992).

20 See http://derstandard.at/1345165340089/Strache-Interview-im-Weichspuelmodus. The *Kleine Zeitung* commented on how Strache had succeeded in presenting himself as victim: www.kleinezeitung.at/nachrichten/politik/2936602/opferumkehr-des-h-c-strache.story; other politicians were angry about Strache's attacks on his former mentor Jörg Haider and so forth: www.heute.at/news/politik/art23660,763710. In any case, the interview (and the provocation via the Facebook incident) proved to be agenda-setting (all links accessed 5 May 2013).

21 Reisigl (2013, 145–6) lists five relevant dimensions that coincide with some of the nine aspects listed above – but he does not yet consider the important and constitutive role of '(gendered) body politics' in enough detail (see Chapters 4 and 7 in this volume). He proposes two dimensions as overriding all other aspects: the use of synecdoche and the use of the topos of 'people', i.e. the *argumentum ad populum*. De Cleen (2013) emphasizes four dimensions, where populism marks one of the four, the others being nationalism, authoritarianism and conservatism. There are, of course, other taxonomies as well. I will come to a more detailed discussion of a range of theoretical approaches in Chapter 2.

22 I prefer the term 'right-wing populism' to both 'radical' and 'extreme right-wing populism', as these superlatives are a question of relative scale and perception.

23 Silvio Berlusconi is an obvious case in point, due to his ownership of almost all the relevant Italian media.

2

THEORIES AND DEFINITIONS: THE POLITICS OF IDENTITY

'In twenty-six definitions of right-wing extremism that can be derived from the literature no less than fifty-eight different features are mentioned at least once.'

Cas Mudde (2000, 11)

Typologies and Definitions

While investigating right-wing populist politics and rhetoric, it quickly becomes obvious that a vast number of different theories, definitions and typologies exist that attempt describing, categorizing and making sense of the recent success of such parties and movements. Before embarking on my empirical studies, it is, of course, important to consider relevant theories developed in the political sciences and sociology inasmuch as they attempt to explain the complex phenomenon of 'the rise of right-wing populism' from different perspectives, thus benefitting the detailed analysis of right-wing populist micro-politics in text and talk.

In the following I therefore focus primarily on such approaches that contribute to explaining and understanding the diverse and manifold ways of constructing fear in everyday politics as well as to showing *why* such scenarios, strategies and tactics are successful.

To begin with I provide a brief and condensed overview of the most relevant theoretical approaches to right-wing populism; I then discuss some recent statistics on the electoral success of right-wing populist parties in the European Parliament and Western Europe; this is important in order to 'get the facts right'. Thereafter, I focus on identity politics related to EU-scepticism and the politics of the past, both of which are constitutive elements of right-wing populism, in two vignettes. As no one-size-fits-all explanation exists, it strikes me as essential to investigate specific national and even local contexts in order to be able to make sense and understand the electoral gain of such parties, while taking into account the nine dimensions presented in Chapter 1.

Despite the great differences within the scholarly debate on right-wing populism (Skenderovic 2009a, 14–16), *three recurring and central concepts* can be recognized as generally used to characterize this phenomenon: first, the notion of 'the people' is a crucial feature.[1] This notion is conceptualized as a 'heartland' (or 'homeland') positioning 'the people' as a central community (Taggart 2000). It construes a (racially) 'pure' community with an unequivocally central position, in many ways referring to the anachronistic conceptual metaphor of 'nation as a body' as apparent, of course, in National Socialism (Musolff 2010).[2] Second, most scholars argue, this heartland is predominantly *opposed to* or *antagonistic towards* 'others', among them 'elites' (ethnic or religious), 'minorities' or 'immigrants'.[3] The concept of 'the heartland' (or 'homeland', 'fatherland') implies inward-looking and the exclusion of the demonized 'Other'. Third, populism can also be characterized as a syndrome which incorporates a distancing dynamic (Reisigl 2013, 159). This dynamic constructs and sustains an antagonistic relationship between 'the people', 'the elite(s)' and 'the (dangerous) others'; populism thus employs a discourse of *distancing* (from the 'Others'/'Them') and of *proximity* (to 'the people'/'Us') (Reisigl 2013, 141–2; Reisigl and Wodak 2001). In this way, populism is defined as a *relational* concept between 'the people' and 'others'. Sometimes the 'others' are the elites; sometimes it is a distinctive 'Other', that is, the foreigners, the Muslims, the Jews or the Roma. In all cases, however, the salient feature is that each of these elements gains substance through the antagonistic relationship with another element (De Lange 2008).

Demand-side and Supply-side Models

Beauzamy (2013a) convincingly distinguishes between '*demand-side models*' and '*supply-side models*' when categorizing the many different explanatory approaches in this field in respect to the French right-wing populist Front National's success. Her categorization, however, could certainly be applied to other similar parties as well. I summarize some characteristics of these two models in turn.

Demand-side models, which explain the far-right vote with *socio-economic factors*, relate to the so-called 'modernization losers thesis' (Beauzamy 2013a, 179). This term was originally coined by Betz (1994) and connects the impact of unemployment and progressive marginalization of the working class in post-industrial, neo-liberal states to the increasing rejection of older political parties (Betz 1993). And, as already noted in Chapter 1, socio-economic factors, such as unemployment, obviously have a significant impact on the vote for the right-wing populist parties. Other authors, such as Minkenberg and Perrineau (2007, 32–42), maintain that radical-right voters see themselves as 'modernization losers' in *subjective* rather than objective terms, and share a strong level of anti-immigrant feeling; this result confirms Veugelers' emphasis on the importance of *racial prejudice* in predicting far-right voting (2005, 424). Such theorizing strongly supports the more socio-psychological approach, originally put forward by Adorno et al. (1967) about the impact of the 'authoritarian personality', which, as Kitschelt and McGann (1995) maintain, forms a salient part of the policy preferences of radical-right voters when integrated with right-wing economic liberalism (Beauzamy 2013a, 180; see Chapters 5 and 7). Beyond psychological factors, the appeal of *authoritarian politics* and a dislike of foreigners therefore appear to be ideologically connected for many voters of right-wing populist parties.

Supply-side explanatory models of the electoral rise of right-wing populist parties emphasize the *strategic means* used by its party leaders to shape and appeal to the respective electorate. Accordingly, as Beauzamy (2013a, 181) suggests, parties have to retain support from core like-minded communities: cultural approaches emphasize the key role of *extreme-right subcultures* that intermediate between right-wing populist parties and their constituency. For example, such links have been repeatedly observed in the French and Austrian cases, stretching from skinheads and 'identity rock' fans to small élitist and even occultist groups (Horaczek and Reiterer 2009). Minkenberg (2002) argues that radical-right social movements do not represent a radicalized and more dangerous form of extreme-right politics than established political parties, but they do prepare the ground for them when they rely less on violent modes of action. Moreover, many scholars (e.g. Forchtner et al. 2013; Ignazi 1992) have emphasized the *agenda-setting role* of right-wing populist parties concerning issues such as immigration, national identity or opposition to a corrupt system. This impact on the mainstream political agenda reveals the *normalization* of such parties' standpoints (especially with regard to immigration) and should therefore be understood as a crucial element in obtaining more electoral success (see Chapter 8). In sum, Beauzamy (2013a) rightly argues that it is necessary to go beyond quite simple socio-economic and socio-cultural explanations for the success of right-wing populist parties. Many factors of an objective and subjective kind – from the demand- and supply-side – apart from the specific socio-political context, have to be integrated in order to make sense of the increasing appeal of right-wing populism.

In 'The sociology of the radical right' – a more supply-side oriented approach – Rydgren (2007, 242) emphasizes that the new radical right-wing parties particularly share an emphasis on 'ethno-nationalism rooted in myths about the distant past'. They focus on strengthening the nation by emphasizing a homogenous ethnicity and by returning to traditional values. Similarly to Pelinka (2013), Rydgren also observes a shift from 'enemies within' to 'enemies outside' of national boundaries, that is, internationalism, paired with anti-establishment populism. Important themes are law and order as well as family values (a programme which coincides with some leitmotifs of the US Tea Party; see Chapters 6, 7). Moreover, Rydgren points to a relevant contradiction in the self-definition of such parties: although they strive to remain inside of the semantic space of democracies by accepting procedural democracy, they actually endorse ethnocracy as their ideal imaginary, which in many ways contradicts the pluralistic values of all liberal democracies (ibid., 241). Rydgren defines 'right' in this case as endorsing economic liberalism and specific conservative positions on sociocultural politics such as a focus on national identity, law and order, restrictive immigration policies, anti-abortion and so forth. Such positions were traditionally framed as *Kulturkampf* and can also be found in the US Tea Party's agenda. In sum, however, Rydgren argues that anti-immigration issues should be perceived as the core message of the radical right:

> For the radical right, immigrants are a threat to ethno-national identity; second, they are a major cause of criminality and other kinds of social insecurity; third, they are a cause of unemployment; and fourth, they are abusers of the generosity of the welfare states of Western democracies, which results in fewer state subsidies, etc., for natives.

> (ibid., 242)

Skenderovic (2009a, 17) summarizes the core-agenda even more succinctly; in his view, the 'radical right minimum' consists of all kinds of 'manifestations of exclusionary ideology'.

Authoritarianism or Re-politicizing Democracy?

Butterwegge (1996, 64ff.) discerns between at least seven different approaches that attempt to explain the phenomenon of populism,[4] some of which I have already briefly summarized in Chapter 1, namely viewing right-wing and left-wing populism as 1) reactions to our globalized risk-societies and as 2) reactions to crisis, competition and immigration, thus to globalized and national economic developments. These demand-side oriented approaches mainly define right-wing populist parties and movements as the refuge or gathering pool of modernization-losers, that is, of those who have lost out due to new socio-economic and cultural trends in neo-liberal societies (e.g. Heitmeyer 1996). Along this vein, Harrison and Bruter (2011, 35) demarcate two main dimensions in which right-wing populist parties are defined: *authoritarianism* and the so-called *negative identity* dimension. These two main axes can be further differentiated into four groups of right-wing populist parties: xenophobic repressive (e.g. the BNP), repressive (e.g. the FN), reactionary (e.g. UKIP) and xenophobic reactionary (e.g. the FPÖ) (see ibid., 107).

The social conception of the authoritarian dimension implies 'a utopian ideology [which] entails devotion to a posited ideal civilisation. This civilisation may take the form of a city, town, locality, or, in the most extreme case, the entire world' (ibid, 37). This utopian ideology, they argue, is strongly opposed to or might even reject the status quo. The cultural political identity defines belonging to this utopian society; the negative identity, therefore, excludes those that are perceived as different (ibid., 39). In differentiating the two main dimensions, Harrison and Bruter (2011) state that the reactionary component implies (the) proposal(s) to return to a traditional way of life, with established morals and (usually Christian) values; the repressive element emphasizes 'law and order' ideologies, thus a strong state and an authoritative leader. The negative identity dimension suggests contrasting 'our community' with dangerous 'others'. And, finally, the populist discourse maintains that the power should be placed in the will of the (arbitrarily defined) 'people'. While this – more demand-side oriented – typology is most useful, it neglects the historical dimension, that is, which European right-wing populist parties draw on fascist/national-socialist traditions and which do not (see Pelinka 2013, 12ff.).[5]

Butterwegge (1996, 79ff.) also emphasizes that right-wing populist and extremist movements have gained followers when cloaked as anti-establishment movements, directed against the elites, the teachers, the media, the mainstream politicians, the intellectuals, the capitalist society and so forth, thus emphasizing the supply-side in this case. In such protest movements, right-wing populist leaders and parties are constructed as saviours, saving 'the people' from threat and danger (mostly from 'outside'), and as saving the welfare state for 'Us'. This leads to the final two explanatory attempts put forward by Butterwegge (ibid.): viewing right-wing populism and right-wing extremism as stemming from fascism and, secondly, as related to vehement chauvinism and sexism (Stögner 2014). It seems quite apparent that different electoral groups are addressed and attracted, frequently simultaneously via discursive strategies of calculated ambivalence (see also Klein 1996): blue-collar voters; young people; unemployed; prejudiced (racist, antisemitic, antiziganist) voters across the professional spectrum. This is why Mouffe stresses that one solution to the danger of the growing right-wing populist mobilization might be 'to revive the opposition between left and right, in order to offer the voters real alternatives' (2005, 67).

There are further important explanations for the rise of right-wing populism. For example, Laclau (2005) maintains that populist movements per se are not to be viewed only in a negative way. As he puts it, 'Populism is, quite simply, a way of constructing the political' (2005, 6). Populism, in Laclau's understanding, would remind democracy of itself, that is, of a (direct) presence of 'the people'. Consequently, it is argued that populism plays a crucial role in democracy by re-politicizing democracy (Schinkel 2010, 68). The people 'is never a primary datum but a construct' (Laclau 2005, 48); the reality of representative democracy necessarily creates frustration among those segments of society that do not feel represented by a rather élitist establishment. The frustration and anger of members of the '*demos*', directed against the official and legal representatives, are the sources, Laclau argues, of contemporary populist movements and populist parties.

In fact, according to such political populism, democracy does not merely exist for its own sake. 'Bureaucrats in Washington', 'technocrats in Brussels', 'liberal elites' or 'the broken/corrupt system' are metonymic nominations and metaphors criticizing a dominant and inward-looking *self-referentiality* (i.e. a democracy for its own sake). Political populism challenges such rigidness and inwardness of the political system – a challenge that is most attractive to many (young) voters who are disillusioned by mainstream politics and the apparent lack of new programmes and reforms, as well as by exorbitant corruption. That is why political populism postulates that it wants to change or reform 'the system', promises to provide 'new politics' or highlights that 'our nation' or 'our country' must come first. Such parties position themselves outside the political status quo by condemning 'particracy' or 'lobbycracy' in the name of 'the people' (Lucardie 2000; Pelinka 2013, 7–8).

Although political populism might at first seem quite refreshing for traditional demo-cratic systems, much political antagonistic content is neglected in such assessments (see Pels 2012): empirical evidence from Austria and the Netherlands, for example, illustrates that right-wing populist parties, should they succeed in their struggle to be integrated into government coalitions, are usually doomed to fail and lose most of their electorate as they have neither the resources nor the experience to govern successfully (Forchtner et al. 2013). Their polarizing rhetoric and Manichean ideology are not suited to the policies, strategies and tactics that are necessary when in government, where finding compromises through careful negotiation is an important skill and priority.

The Rise of Right-wing Populism

Since the 1990s, right-wing populist parties have become established in various democracies across the globe, including Canada, Norway, France, Israel, Russia, Romania and Chile, and have entered into coalition governments in Switzerland, Austria, the Netherlands, Denmark, New Zealand and Italy (Norris 2004, 2). These parties were successful in the polls by challenging the legitimacy of the democratic process and so-called 'multicultural' or diverse societies. Even though 'ultra-nationalist populism' has been discussed in the Social Sciences as a reaction of this 'third wave' of right-wing extremist parties, the situation has changed further since 2000: until recently, there was no agreement on how populism was to be evaluated in the long-run in differ-ent European countries. Some countries, such as France (due to Le Pen's Front National), have witnessed rather stable long-term support for ultra-nationalist and ethnocentric populism. Other countries, such as the UK or Sweden, were not considered to be prone to right-wing populism. To the contrary, this was believed to be a marginal phenomenon that would pass rather quickly; we now know that such predictions proved to be mistaken and that the Sweden Democrats, for example, succeeded in passing the 4 per cent threshold for entering the Swedish Parliament in the national election of 2010 and now occupy 20 seats, having won 5.7 per cent of the votes.

Although right-wing movements in the US have been studied separately, normally labelled as 'radical right', some writers consider them to be the same or a similar phenom-enon (Beirich 2013; Kaplan and Weinberg 1998, 1–2; Pelinka 2013, 14). At this point, it is important to emphasize that right-wing populism is usually (but not always) quite distinct from the historically (also fascist) Right (Betz 1994, 24; Kaplan and Weinberg 1998, 10–13; Wodak and Richardson 2013; Woodley 2013). Different scholars use different terminology, sometimes referring to right-wing populism as 'radical right' (Rydgren 2007; Skenderovic 2009a, 2009b) or right-wing extremism (Kaplan and Weinberg 1998, 10–11). While referring to such terminological confusion, Norris states that

standard reference works use alternate typologies and diverse labels categoris-
ing parties as 'far' or 'extreme' right, 'new right', 'anti-immigrant', 'neo-Nazi' or
'neofascist', 'antiestablishment', 'national populist', 'protest', 'ethnic', 'authoritarian', 'antigovernment', 'antiparty', 'ultranationalist', or 'neoliberal', 'libertarian' and
so on'.

(2005, 44)

Hence, scholars should define both their terms and their contents precisely to avoid predictable misunderstandings. I believe that the terms 'extreme right' or even 'fascist right' should
be reserved for parties that explicitly and openly endorse fascist and Nazi ideologies and
physically violent traditions. Having said that, it must be acknowledged that boundaries
between right-wing populism and the extreme/fascist right are sometimes blurred and that
some extreme right parties have also succeeded in winning seats at democratic parliamentary elections while simultaneously maintaining and supporting violent paramilitary troops
(such as the Hungarian Jobbik and the Greek Golden Dawn; e.g. Angouri and Wodak 2014;
Dettke 2014; Kovács 2013) and masking their violent agenda: in these cases, backstage and
frontstage rhetoric differ significantly. Indeed, as Richardson (2013a, 106ff.) illustrates, party
leaders such as Nick Griffin (BNP) are on record when advising their core followers to mit-
igate their beliefs in public, that is, 'to forget about racial differences, genetics, Zionism,
historical revisionism, and so on – all ordinary people want to know is what we can do for
them that the other parties can't or won't' (*Patriot* 4, 1999,[6] cited ibid., 107).

Election Results since the 1990s

The results of the European Parliament (EP) elections of 25 May 2014 and socio-political
developments thereafter across EU member states and beyond mirror the continuous
trend of rising right-wing populism. The turnout in 2014 was 43 per cent, slightly more
than in 2009; 129 MEPs can be classified as belonging to a total of 15 right-wing
populist parties from 14 countries. In Denmark, France and the UK, the right-wing populist parties took first place (with 25 per cent in France, 26.8 per cent in the UK and 26.6
per cent in Denmark), whereas in the Netherlands, Sweden and Italy, they lost several
seats. The FPÖ received 19.7 per cent of the votes, Jobbik 14.7 per cent and the Greek
Golden Dawn 9.4 per cent. Altogether, there is an enormous increase of right-wing populist seats in comparison to 2009 (from 38 to 129 seats).[7]

When observing the emergence of new ultra-nationalist and xenophobic parties that are
built on so-called 'new' and 'old' identity concepts, it is obvious that right-wing populism
is not a passing phenomenon. Although such parties were frequently a marginalized phenomenon in the beginning (e.g. Sweden and the UK), they have now become nationwide
and transnational, European phenomena. Therefore it seems useful to draw on the definition
of the phenomenon offered by the so-called *modernization theory* (see above): According
to this definition, the 'radical right' (including right-wing populism) is based on ultra-nationalist (homogenous) ideas that are directed (in tendency, not necessarily directly) against
liberal democracy. Of course, European elections are frequently heavily influenced by protest votes against the current respective national government – this was most apparent in
the UK, Sweden and France. In Italy, the new social-democratic government doubled its
votes, and Berlusconi's party lost. Table 2.1 offers an overview of the distribution of seats
according to parties in the European Parliament: overall, the mainstream conservative and
liberal parties lost 71 seats, the mainstream left-wing gained seven seats, and the huge range

Table 2.1 Overview of European parties, losses and gains after European Parliament elections 2014 (adapted from Arsenal for Democracy 2014; http://arsenalfordemocracy.com/2014/06/01/eu-elections-the-rising-populists-and-why-europe-is-worried/2014-european-election-results-table/#.U-8IT7I__mR) (accessed 16 August 2014)

Pan-European Party Affiliation	# of MEPs Elected (+/− Change from 2009)
European People's Party (centre-right)	214 (−51)
Party of European Socialists (centre-left, social-democrats)	191 (+7)
Alliance of Liberals and Democrats (liberal/centrist)	64 (−20)
Greens – European Free Alliance (environmentalism and regionalism)	52 (−3)
European Conservatives and Reformists (eurosceptic right-wing)	46 (−8)
European United Left/Nordic Green Left (radical left, socialists, communists)	45 (+10)
Non-aligned Members (mainly nationalists, far right)	41 (+8)
European Freedom and Democracy (sovereigntist, eurosceptic and anti-EU right-wing)	38 (+6)
Others (new elected MEPs without affiliation including populists, far-right, radical left and stunt candidates)	60

of differing populist right- and left-wing parties are widely regarded as the winners by the media across Europe and beyond.

Right-wing populist parties, thriving on EU criticism and on ultra-nationalist and ethnocentric concepts, improved their results in comparison to the elections in 2004 and 2009. Most likely, the issues that led to the rise of right-wing populist parties, such as UKIP in the UK, will remain relevant or spread even further as economic austerity plans and the Eurozone crisis cause and reinforce a widening gap between rich and poor as well as stark polarization of societies such as Greece, Spain, Italy and Portugal. Furthermore, growing Islamophobia in the West and hostilities against Roma and Jews (predominantly) in the East (Hungary, Slovakia, Czech Republic, Bulgaria and Romania) serve as additional mobilizing factors amongst quite different population segments – both educated and less educated people, employed and unemployed, young and old, rural and urban groups of voters tend to follow the slogans and programmes of these parties (Kovács 2013).

Traditional explanations seem unable to grasp this very complex and fluid phenomenon; the most successful right-wing populist parties currently observable in Europe – the Swiss People's Party (Schweizer Volkspartei, with approximately 27 per cent of the votes in 2011) and the Austrian Freedom Party (Freiheitliche Partei Österreichs or FPÖ with 20.51 per cent of the votes in 2013) – actually thrive and flourish in the wealthiest European countries with the lowest unemployment and least financial losses caused by the financial crisis since 2008. The same holds true for the third prospering European country, namely Denmark (where the Dansk Folksparti won 12.3 per cent at the last national election in 2011). Accordingly, alternative and more complex explanations have to be sought which would allow integrating *inter alia* context-specific factors, socio-political traditions and histories, party-political histories, cultural hegemonic tendencies, the media landscape and economic developments, thus integrating demand- and supply-side models. One factor, however, remains constant and resilient: *fear of strangers related to vehement nativist nationalism built on the populist myth of a quasi-homogenous nation state which has to be preserved and protected against (usually fictive) external or internal dangers.* Denying the rapid change from relatively homogenous nation states to diverse, multicultural and multi-ethnic societies lies at the core of such beliefs (see above).

Along this vein, Zygmunt Bauman concludes in his 2009 lecture entitled 'Europe of Strangers'[8] that

> in the language of vote-seeking politicians, the widespread and complex sentiments of *Unsicherheit* are translated as much simpler concerns with law and order (that is with bodily safety and the safety of private homes and possessions), while the problem of law and order is in its turn blended with the problematic presence of ethnic, racial or religious minorities – and, more generally, of alien styles of life.
>
> (2009, 11)

In this lecture, Bauman argues that due to globalization and the vast complexity of modern societies, politicians search for simple answers to unsolvable problems. It is easy, he claims, to find culprits and scapegoats who can be blamed for the causes of our current woes: everybody who is 'different' and who does not 'belong' to 'Us', that is, strangers, both within and outside. As the causes for present troubles, Bauman implies, are not immediately visible and frequently distant, and as politics always remains a more 'local affair', explanations and remedies are sought in areas closer to the home-ground of daily experience. Threats to collective identity (stemming from individual insecurity), Bauman continues, are easily countered:

> local state powers may still be used to close the borders to the migrants, to tighten the asylum laws, to round up and deport the unwelcome aliens. The governments cannot honestly promise its citizens secure existence and certain future; but they may for the time being unload at least part of the accumulated anxiety (and even profit from it electorally) by demonstrating their energy and determination in the war against foreign job-seekers and other alien gate-crashers, the intruders into once clean and quiet, orderly and familiar, native backyards.
>
> (2009, 10–11)

The search for local scapegoats has lent itself, for centuries, to achieving quick electoral success (see Chapter 1). Of course, not all 'others' are discriminated against: our societies, we are told again and again by our governments, need qualified experts who may also be 'foreigners'; however, poor and unqualified migrants are not welcome. Moreover, the threat frequently does not only relate to fear of unemployment and losing one's job: if foreigners also 'look or behave differently', racist, antisemitic and nativist stereotypes are easily evoked; these draw on collective stereotypes and traditional prejudice narratives and stories and are then instrumentalized for political ends. Thus, we have to conclude, collective memories, ingrained and internalized fears of 'strangers' and 'others', new and old insecurities triggered by new socio-political developments, and many other factors converge to support the rise of right-wing populist movements at different points in time.

Electoral Success – Overview

Let us now consider more recent developments of some important West-European right-wing populist parties (developments in Eastern Europe differ significantly; I will come back to the differences between Western and post-Communist Eastern Europe below and in Chapter 8). For example, the statistics of electoral success of right-wing populist parties in the UK, Austria, France, and Italy (in national[9] and European Parliament elections[10]) (Tables 2.2–2.7) illustrate that substantial differences exist between countries and parties as well as electorates, which have to be accounted for in great detail (e.g. Harrison and Bruter 2011; for more facts and figures, please refer to the glossary).

Table 2.2   Results of the British National Party (BNP) in European Parliament elections 1994–2014

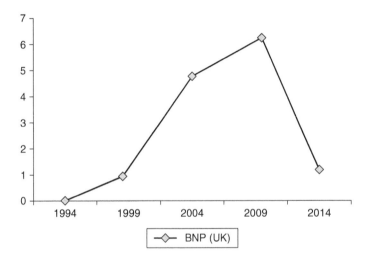

Table 2.3   Results of the Austrian Freedom Party (FPÖ) in European Parliament elections 1996–2014

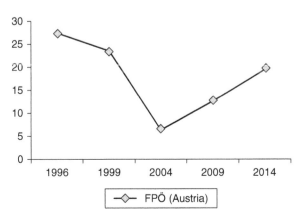

Table 2.4 Results of the Front National (FN) in European Parliament elections 1984–2014

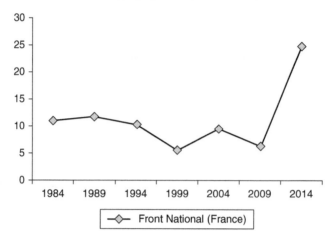

Interestingly, the BNP has lost many votes in recent elections (UKIP has, however, steadily increased, especially on the European level, see Table 2.6), whereas the Austrian Freedom Party has (almost) continuously gained votes (see Tables 2.3 and 2.7). The Front National oscillates between 6 and 10 per cent nationally (Table 2.7) but has reached first place on the European level (Table 2.4), and the Lega Nord continued to win more seats in each election until 2009 (Tables 2.5, 2.7). These differences can only be explained by considering both internal national (and even regional) socio-political developments in combination with the apparent dissatisfaction with EU policies as well as with intensified migration and the effects of the global financial crisis.[11]

Table 2.5 Election results of Italian right-wing populist parties 1992–2013, national elections

	1992	1994	1996	2001	2006	2008	2013
Lega Nord (Italy)	8, 65	8, 4	10, 07	3, 94	4, 58	8, 3	4, 1
Alleanza Nazionale (Italy)		13, 5	15, 66	12, 01	12, 34		
Five Star Movement (Italy)							25, 5
Forza Italia		21	20, 4	29, 4	23, 7		
People of Freedom (Lega Nord, Forza Italia, Alleanza nazionale)						37, 4*	29, 1

*Alleanza Nationale and Forza Italia merged in to one party, People of Freedom

More recently, in Britain the UK Independence Party (UKIP) has overtaken the BNP nationally and on the European level (see Table 2.6) and is causing considerable panic in the political mainstream: protest against EU legislation and proposals for more restrictions against migrants are leading the governing coalition to align with some anti-immigration slogans of UKIP.[12]

If one listens carefully to the speeches and interviews of leading UKIP politicians and MPs, one can easily discern that simple messages lie at the heart of the UKIP strategy: less or no EU membership would imply more freedom; and less or even no immigration would imply less unemployment and more Britishness. Because of some local and regional successes, mainstream politicians are following the path of UKIP and are swerving more and more to the right. Such strategies on the part of the mainstream have already been proven to lead to failure (in Austria and elsewhere): people tend to vote for the party or MPs they believe most authentically stand for specific opinions and policies, not for those who appear to copy policies out of fear of losing votes. Table 2.7 provides an overview of the national election results of the parties briefly discussed above; of course, national (and regional) elections after 2013 in the UK and France display significant new developments: both UKIP and FN have gained much more votes.

Table 2.6 Election results of United Kingdom Independence Party (UKIP) in European Parliament elections 1994–2014

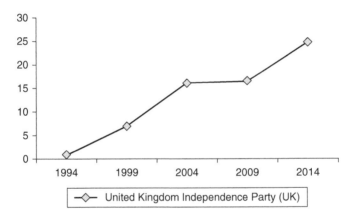

Identity Politics – Exclusionary Politics

In defining the concept of populism and characterizing the core elements of right-wing populism, the focus on exclusion of 'strangers' (both within and outside the nation's borders) is obviously and unanimously perceived as salient by most scholars in the field (e.g. Bauman 1995). Exclusionary politics imply 'border politics', emphasizing both the criteria of belonging and territorial boundaries. I will elaborate extensively on the interdependence of body and border politics (and, related to this, aspects of citizenship legislation) in Chapter 4, and on dimensions of racist and antisemitic discrimination in Chapter 5. Here, however, it is important to point to two other constitutive aspects of right-wing identity politics: first, the impact of '*banal nationalism' related to revisionist politics of the past*; and second, to *EU scepticism* which fuels the success of right-wing populist parties, as illustrated in the election results at national and EU elections above. As these two elements are constitutive of right-wing populist identity politics, they will be dealt with in some detail at this stage.

Table 2.7 Selected European right-wing parties 1986–2013, national elections

	1986	1988	1990	1992	1993	1994	1995	1996	1997	1999	2001	2002	2005	2006	2007	2008	2010	2012	2013
United Kingdom Independence Party (UK)*				0,01					0,34		1,48		2,2				3,10		
British National Party (UK)				0,1					0,1		0,2		0,7				1,9		
FPÖ (Austria)**	9,7		16,63			22,9	22			26,9		10,01		11,04		17,54			20,6
Front National (France)***	9,8	9,8			12,69				14,9			11,12			4,3			13,66	
Lega Nord (Italy)				8,65		8,4		10,07			3,94			4,58		8,3			4,1
Alleanza Nazionale (Italy)****						13,5		15,66			12,01			12,34					
Five Star Movement (Italy)																			25,5
Forza Italia (Italy)						21		20,4			29,4			23,7					
People of Freedom (Alleanza Nazionale, Forza Italia)																37,39****			29,1

* At the election on 7 May 2015, UKIP reached 13,5%.

** 5 April 2005, the FPÖ split in to two parties (FPÖ, with party leader HC Strache; and BZÖ [Bündnis Zukunft Österreichs], with jörg Haider as party leader). The BZÖ won 4,11% 2006, 10,7% 2008 and dropped out of the Austrian parliament 2013, with 3,53%.

*** At the presidential election 2002 in France, the FN (with J.M. Le Pen as party leader) reached 16,9%.

**** In 2009 Alleanza Nazionale merged with Forza Italia into 'The People of Freedom' (party leader Silvio Berlusconi); the 2008 result is already a joint result.   28 June 2013, Berlusconi announced the revival of Forza Italia, after having lost 15,8% at the 2013 election.

VIGNETTE 2
EXPERIENCES OF TOTALITARIANISM –
DEALING WITH THE PAST(S)

Identity politics form a core of right-wing populist politics: founding myths become revitalized to legitimize the myth of a 'pure people' who belong to a clearly defined nation state. Most right-wing populist parties thus re-imagine and rewrite their national histories to legitimize their present agenda and future visions. They draw on the past to relive allegedly successful victories and/or previously grand empires. Indeed, many studies illustrate in detail that right-wing populist parties show a particular interest in debates over history and the ways in which politics and the public is and should be dealing with the past (Engel and Wodak 2013; Herr et al. 2008; Krzyżanowski and Wodak 2009; Wodak et al. 2009). At different moments in the 1990s and 2000s, they intervened in debates over the role that the respective European countries had played during the periods of fascism and communism as well as in the activities of remembrance of specific historical events related to these periods (Mudde 2007). For example, the then-leader of the FPÖ, Jörg Haider, infamously commemorated 'decent' (*anständige*) victims of World War II while explicitly referring to former Austrian members of Nazi Waffen-SS units. Accordingly, history is rewritten to highlight foundation myths of a 'pure people' in homogenous nation states (Wodak and Forchtner 2014).

The Hungarian Jobbik, for example, yearns for the past of the Hungarian Empire; the Ukrainian Svoboda and related 'groupuscules' of Neo-Nazis for the lost power they briefly held during the Nazi era and the 'Third Reich' (see below). Symbols of the past re-emerge, such as flags, logos, uniforms, hymns, slogans and so forth,[13] and reinforce the revisionist ideologies of such right-wing populist and radical extremist parties. Flags and their related traditions 'can be simultaneously present and absent, in actions [such as flag waving] which preserve collective memory without the conscious activity of individuals remembering' (Billig 1995, 42). The emphasis of nationalist groups on intertextual references to national emblems, logos and flags as semiotic resources is a way of relating to the remembered (or imagined) present or past national, frequently imagined grand or grandiose cultures, communities and practices. Simultaneously, such symbols function as marketable brands which guarantee recognizability and – via indexicality – condense metonymically the agenda and programme of the respective party.

In Hungary, the official emblem of Jobbik members looks like the Árpád stripes which date back to the 13th century and were reused in the 1930s and 1940s by the fascist and virulently antisemitic Party of the Arrow Cross (see Dettke 2014, 5; McGlashan 2013).

The Jobbik poster slogan clearly presents the Árpád stripes and reads 'radical change' (in this image the slogan has been covered with oppositional slogans 'Rotten Nazis', 'the Gypsies should work', 'The Arrow Cross should hang' and a Hitler moustache has been painted on the poster to indicate the proximity to Nazi ideology and insignia, and functions as subversive resistance). As McGlashan suggests,

> [t]here is evidence here, through the lack of inclusion of the alternating horizontal red and white Árpád stripes, to suggest that Jobbik's logo is a form of calculated ambivalence. Earlier adopters of the Arpád stripes such as the nationalist Margyar

(Continued)

(Continued)

Gárda and the Arrow Cross drew from the same coat of arms that Jobbik have in their symbolic behaviour, however, the Arpád stripes have strong connotations in modern Hungary with nationalist groups; as part of *'the Garda'* as a brand.

(2013, 306)

Image 2.1 Jobbik poster for Hungarian election 2010

On 30 April 2014, the blog *RT Novosti* displayed some images from a commemorative march in Lvov on that very day, in honour of the Ukrainian Waffen-SS division[14] (Image 2.2). As Rudling (2013) elaborates in great detail, this cult of the Waffen-SS Galizien, a Ukrainian collaborationist formation established by Heinrich Himmler in 1943, is combined with celebrations of an alleged anti-Nazi resistance struggle, in a most contradictory way:

> The enjoyment of in the many nationalist rituals and processions in post-Soviet Lviv is partly commercial. Ultra-nationalist ideologues have found both effective and lucrative ways to work with entrepreneurs to popularize and disseminate their narrative to the youth. The OUN-UPA[15] theme restaurant *Kryivka,* [lurking hole] in Lviv is but one example of this. Its guests have a choice of dishes like 'Cold boiled pork "*Hände Hoch*,"' 'Kosher *Haidamaky*-style *salo* (pork lard),' and 'Combat serenade' *salo. Kryivka's* dining room walls are decorated with larger-than-life portraits of Bandera, the toilet with Russian and Jewish anecdotes. The same Lviv entrepreneur also runs the Jewish theme restaurant *Pid Zolotoiu Rozoiu,* (Beneath the Golden Rose), where the menu lists no prices for the dishes, but where one instead is required to haggle, 'in the Jewish fashion,' with the waiters.

(ibid., 233)

In this way, a new narrative of the past is formulated which addresses different parts of the electorate, former collaborators and their sympathizers, as well as anti-fascists, all at the same time, and thus employs the strategy of calculated ambivalence in embracing both fascist symbols as well as nationalist Ukrainian ones.

Image 2.2   March in Lvov in honour of the Waffen-SS 28 April 2011

Specific countries do not allow display of symbols that insinuate or copy National Socialist insignia (e.g. Austria, Germany, France and the Netherlands), other countries believe that such symbols belong to and should be protected under their respective 'freedom of speech' legislation (e.g. Poland, Hungary, Sweden, Denmark, Finland and the Baltic States). Historical experiences and memories always also affect the present (Heer et al. 2008). Different historical experiences have shaped the images of democracy and perceptions of fundamental values. The differences between perception and expectation, however, are particularly striking between old and new EU member states: Western Europe's dominant historical experience is National Socialism or Fascism (with the exception of the previously divided Germany: the former GDR has also experienced Communism). Central and Eastern European countries have experienced National Socialism, Fascism and Communism. The legacy of a totalitarian past and the associated difficulties of understanding and accepting heterogeneity, as well as difficulties in coping with societal change, have paved the way for current trends of right-wing populism as a means of preservation of some stable and conservative past and related values (see Chapter 8). Particularly, as already mentioned amongst the nine dimensions characterizing right-wing populism, nationalist and xenophobic populism creates or rewrites its own concepts of history, charging them with nationalist ideas of homogeneity, and is able to fuel political conflicts between states and groups by using arguments (*topoi*) which appeal to past collective experiences or common-sense narratives. Of course, *topoi* are never per se right or fallacious – it always depends on the respective context. This is why appealing to and learning from the past could sometimes be a most useful, reasonable and sound argument; in other instances, such as the above, the *topos of history* is used in a misleading and simplistic, fallacious way. The related argumentation scheme, which claims that learning from the past is important for the present and that – such is implied – the past should be preserved, can be depicted as shown in Figure 2.1.

Through various research networks, projects and policy resolutions, the European Commission has attempted and continues to attempt to cope with the fascist, colonial and Nazi past of EU member states in the 19th and 20th centuries. For example, as a result of an

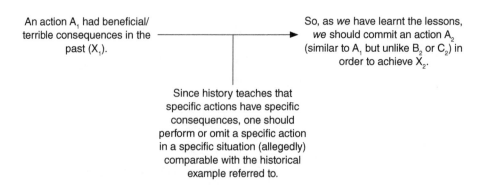

An action A_1 had beneficial/ terrible consequences in the past (X_1).

So, as *we* have learnt the lessons, *we* should commit an action A_2 (similar to A_1 but unlike B_2 or C_2) in order to achieve X_2.

Since history teaches that specific actions have specific consequences, one should perform or omit a specific action in a specific situation (allegedly) comparable with the historical example referred to.

Figure 2.1 *Topos* of history

initiative by the Czech EU Council Presidency, the European Parliament adopted a resolution on 'European Conscience and Totalitarianism' on 2 April 2009. The resolution attempts to place historiography and memory of Europe's totalitarian past in an up-to-date European context and thereby seeks to respond to different memory cultures and needs for commemoration (such as the memory of the Holocaust, remembrance of the victims of National Socialism, memory of totalitarian suppression by communist states and remembrance of their victims). In opposition to the violation of fundamental Human Rights by totalitarian regimes, the EU Resolution confirms the Fundamental Rights of European democracies, in particular Human Rights.

This resolution also displays the range of difficulties encountered when judging history. In rejection of any totalitarian claims on the existence of a so-called 'absolute truth', it is emphasized that 'no political body or political party has a monopoly on interpreting history, and such bodies and parties cannot claim to be objective'.[16] Here, conflicting memories provide an enormous challenge. For example, the understanding of the competition between victim groups of Nazi and communist power, and conflicts between differing historical cultural memories concerning these phases of totalitarian power, have to be confronted (Wodak and Auer-Boreo 2009). Who, one must also ask, is in possession of such an objective 'truth'? And, furthermore, does an objective truth or narrative about history exist apart from established facts? Revisionist narratives of the past are part and parcel of right-wing populist rhetoric and propaganda. Since the memory of the past shapes the conception of current collective identity, right-wing populist parties usually see their engagement in politics of the past as an integral part of their overall identity politics. In particular, some revisionist intellectuals and historians have been consistently involved in efforts to present their distinct versions of collective memory in academic and public discussions.

VIGNETTE 3
EU-SCEPTICISM AND EUROPEAN IDENTITIES

The issues raised by today's right-wing populists and argued in debates on historical cultural memories are frequently related to the search of, and debates about, a new European identity (or *identities*) and of 'belonging' (Krzyżanowski 2010; Wodak and Boukala

2014, 2015; Wodak et al. 2009). For example, political parties and movements such as the Austrian FPÖ, the French FN, the British BNP and UKIP, and the Hungarian Jobbik are developing – or have developed – a broader 'integrative' identity concept, related to nativist body politics. In such cases, the actors succeed in not only attracting votes exclusively on social determination issues, but also by offering inclusive foundation myths, and positive identity and identification concepts as well as, most importantly, both traditional and new scapegoats.

Thus, understanding the rise of populism in Europe makes it necessary to analyse the formation of new and old cultural spaces as well as cultural identities (de Cleen 2012, 2013). However, the existence of a cultural space favourable for populist endeavours may not immediately transform into electoral success. For example, in Poland such a cultural space was already being created from the 1990s onwards, but it was only in 2001 that a separate group became visible and a related movement established (Krzyżanowski 2013b). Two political parties succeeded in developing an agenda which allowed adapting to those political milieus: The League of Polish Families draws on the traditions of the 1930s, while the second Polish far-right party, Samoobrona, refers to vague ideological orientations spread among farmers, including populism and a strong nationalism with violent elements.

Many studies on European identity seem to agree on one aspect: that a 'democracy deficit' is apparent, and thus the communication between EU institutions and decision-makers on the one hand, and EU citizens on the other, does not function well (Triandafyllidou et al. 2009; Wodak 2011a). Various measures, policy papers, discussion forums and so forth have been created to counter the emerging and growing democracy deficit (Wodak and Wright 2006, 2007); moreover, due to the so-called *Eurozone crisis* and the various measures to counteract this, national politicians and parliaments have warned time and again that democracy could be at risk more than ever before, frequently invoking admonitory parallels to the 1930s.

At the time of publication, EU-acceptance/satisfaction is at a one-time low of 32 per cent. The economic policies and developments have, of course, supported the growth of EU-sceptic movements: parties like the Greek Golden Dawn blame the EU, the German or French governments, the bankers or the migrants, in most simplistic ways, for the crisis;[17] they demand more security against 'outsiders' and also a return to forms of traditional nativist nationalism/chauvinism.

The financial crisis (since 2008) has led to the rise of EU-sceptic political ideologies that are not only expressed by ultra-national, far-right parties, such as Jobbik and Golden Dawn or by right-wing populist parties such as Marine Le Pen's Front National, but also by the adoption of various austerity measures and immigration restrictions against 'outsiders' that are imposed by mainstream national governmental coalitions. One of the main arguments suggested by Smith (1995) to explain why the implementation of a hegemonic European identity has failed to date is the fact that this concept was based on an elite-centred vision (ibid., 126–8). In other words, European identity was invented through the actions and programmes of business, administrative and intellectual elites whose needs transcended national borders (ibid.). Checkel and Katzenstein (2009) similarly claim that European identity is an elite project. However, identity constructions imply specific cultural and emotional dynamics which transcend political projects. For this reason, according to Cinpoes (2008), the political elites of the EU have employed various myths and values across European nations in order to cultivate a sense of belonging among Europeans but – as we know and experience daily – in vain; this remains a somewhat futile project if strategies of participation and legitimization do not reach out to European

(Continued)

(Continued)

citizens in more accessible ways. The creation of a European flag, a European anthem and even a European day are some examples of measures meant to increase the sense of unity among the members of the EU (ibid., 4–7), and these have, in part, succeeded in establishing a kind of 'banal nationalism', that is, in embedding the EU and a related nationalistic feeling into everyday life practices, always in contrast to the US, Japan, China, India and so forth (Billig 1995, 6; Wodak and Boukala 2014, 176).

The discursive forms of inclusion and exclusion have significant importance for the cultivation of European identity(ies), since they define 'the Europeans' and create an 'imagined community' of 'Us' which excludes the 'Others', that is, 'those that are not worthy of becoming Europeans' (Wodak 2007b, 651). By employing discursive strategies for the construction of in-groups and out-groups and making the distinction between 'Us' and 'Them', the 'non-Europeans', the EU redefines its relations with the 'Other' in context-dependent ways. Whenever it is necessary to legitimize new immigration policies or citizenship policies, new criteria are launched that allow some people to come and belong to 'Us', and keep others out.

In order to understand voters and citizens who feel attracted by right-wing populism, it is thus important to put all the above-mentioned issues into context. European societies are challenged by rapid social change. However, politics and society should be aware that right-wing populist parties have found an entry-point for raising identity issues and delivering identity concepts. They benefit from overall feelings of insecurity and use them to launch protest against the current social order. Minkenberg (2002) argues that while (right-wing) populist parties across Europe draw upon revisionist concepts of the past, Eastern European populist parties even more strongly relate to past concepts of authoritarian rule and minority questions (Kovács 2013; Mădroane 2013). On the other hand, their counterparts in the West are predominantly occupied with questions of immigration and their migrant populations. These parties seek hegemony for their revisionist interpretation of the past and the present by presenting integrated identity concepts that undermine the very existence of the EU and trigger and foment Euro-Scepticism. One of the newly arising or newly promoted identity concepts within the populist context seems to merge with 'gender issues' and gendered body politics. In the political struggle across Western Europe, the rhetoric of 'defence of liberal values' is often used as a strategy against Islam and the 'headscarf' is appropriated as a symbol of that struggle (Fortier 2012; Köhler and Wodak 2011). Here, cultural heritage and issues of religion are linked with the reformulation of Christian values or the framing of anti-Muslim values in the perception of gender equality. Moreover, the liberal values of 'freedom for women' also appeal to some groups in a progressive and left-wing electorate. In this way, gender issues may well serve as an overarching framework integrating voters from both the left and the right (Chapter 7).

Summary: The Normalization of Identity Politics?

The results of the elections to the European Parliament in May 2014 have caused great concern in the various national governments of EU member states as well as in the European organizations: although expected by opinion makers and predicted by opinion polls, it was nevertheless surprising that the FN won first place in France (with just under 24.9

per cent) and UKIP first place in the UK (with 27.5 per cent).[18] The electoral success of these two Eurosceptic, nationalistic/chauvinistic and xenophobic parties dominated media reactions across Europe and beyond, leading many politicians and journalists to proclaim the foreseeable end of the EU. In the midst of such outcries, other results were neglected and contradictory tendencies overlooked.

For example, the FPÖ won fewer votes in Austria than expected and took third place (with around 20 per cent); in Italy Matteo Renzi's Democratic Party (belonging to the Party of European Socialists) almost doubled its seats, whereas the extreme right lost more than 50 per cent of theirs. In Sweden, the Socialists won the election and the governing conservative party lost more than 5 per cent; in Greece, the opposition populist left-wing party Syriza gained over 22 per cent on its vote share from 2009. In Hungary, however, the Jobbik received just under 14.7 per cent.

As elaborated above, we are dealing with contradictory tendencies across Europe that are not easily explained by North/South or East/West cleavages. Indeed, the many theoretical approaches and diverse taxonomies presented in this chapter cannot fully explain these complex developments; moreover, each approach seems to foreground one single aspect and neglect many others. Obviously, the economic crisis did not influence the elections to similar effects all across Europe: Austria and Denmark belong to the richest countries of the world and have some of the most successful right-wing populist parties. In other EU member states, however, the global financial crisis since 2008 certainly supported the emergence or re-emergence of parties similar to Neo-Nazi and fascist organizations (such as Golden Dawn in Greece and Jobbik in Hungary) who both also employ physical violence against migrants, Jews and Roma. The overall election was ultimately won by the conservative European People's Party, albeit with massive losses, and the Party of European Socialists took second place.

Consequently and understandably, speculations about the reasons for such developments are manifold: they range from a purported broad disillusionment and anger with politics per se and blaming governing parties for the global financial crisis, to discontentment with austerity politics and the growing gap between rich and poor. For most parties, the fear of migrants and asylum seekers has become a hegemonic agenda as well as a forceful argument for the necessity to protect the 'Christian Occident' as a constitutive part of European identity. In other cases, particularly in Eastern European countries, old traditional antisemitic, racist and antiziganist prejudices were explicitly functionalized in order to construct scapegoats wherever and whenever needed. And, certainly, media-savvy charismatic leaders such as Marine Le Pen, Nigel Farage or HC Strache and their rhetoric are recognized as at least a partial cause of such success. And, finally, nationalistic oppositional interests were frequently played against governing parties and their politics – hence transforming the European elections into (at least partly) national elections. In short, there is no one explanation and no clear uni-directional development to be identified in such complex and contradictory results.

As I have argued throughout this chapter, extreme right-wing populist parties are united in their endorsement of a chauvinist, nativist view of 'the people', as well as by creating specific chauvinistic identity myths which idealise and rewrite history, and an anti-elistist, revisionist and anti-intellectual stance combined with strong Euro-scepticism. According to the latter, one can also observe a tendency to favour plebiscitarian methods and to downplay representative democracy, while proclaiming the search for 'true democracy' and denouncing 'formalistic democracy'. Democracy should be reduced, such parties argue, to the majority rule of 'the people'. By triggering such debates, populism might, Laclau (2005) claims, possibly play a crucial role by re-politicizing democracy, at least as long these parties are not in any national government. Clearly, there is no one-size-fits-all explanation for this complex phenomenon, and the following chapters will attempt to explore its most important dimensions in order to allow understanding and explanation of these new global and glocal developments in Europe and beyond.

Endnotes

1 See Canovan (1999), Laclau (2005), Mouffe (2000), Mudde (2004), Reisigl (2013), Taggart (2000), and Taguieff (1984).

2 Conceptual metaphors are not understood as a linguistic expression or a rhetorical formula, but as a tool for the conceptualization of meaning based on the association between two cognitive domains. Conceptual metaphor theory functions by establishing connections or mappings (Lakoff and Turner 1989, 4) between aspects belonging to both cognitive domains. The source domain provides a conceptual schema that gives rise to a number of subcategories which, in turn, correspond to many other subcategories that belong to the conceptual schema of the target domain. The target and source concepts are part of cognitive and cultural models (Lakoff 1987) known as 'knowledge structures representing the collective wisdom and experience of the community, acquired and stored in the individual minds of the members of a community' (Dirven et al. 2007, 1217) (see also Pinero-Pinero and Moore, in press, for an elaborated discussion of a range of definitions and theories of conceptual metaphors).

3 See Kitschelt (1997), Laclau (2005) and Mudde (2004).

4 Butterwegge, however, mainly focuses on developments in Germany, before and after unification. Moreover, his main concerns are post-fascist and post-totalitarian political phenomena, especially right-wing extremism. Of course, it is not easy, as he also suggests, distinguishing between the range of expressions and forms of extremism, which is why combinations of various dimensions seem to hold more explanatory potential.

5 In the Glossary, all right-wing populist and extremist parties are briefly summarized according to a few salient criteria (their political programmes, their main agenda, their history, leading protagonists, and their electorate).

6 *The Patriot* is a magazine edited by Tony Lecomber in support of the BNP; see www.whatnextjournal.org.uk/Pages/Politics/Copsey.html for more details.

7 http://arsenalfordemocracy.com/2014/06/01/eu-elections-the-rising-populists-and-why-europe-is-worried/#.U-8BULI__mQ, accessed 16 August 2014.

8 For the entire text, see Zygmunt Bauman, 'Europe of Strangers,' in *docs.google.com*, 2009, available at http://docs.google.com/viewer?url=http://www.transcomm.ox.ac.uk/working%20papers/bauman.pdf, accessed 23 July 2011.

9 The starting dates are chosen as they immediately precede 1989 and the fall of the Iron Curtain – a tipping point for the rise of the right-wing populist parties in Austria and France.

10 Different starting dates in the diagrams below point to the different dates the respective right-wing populist parties first stood for elections to the European Parliament.

11 For more details on national developments in the last two decades, since the fall of the Iron Curtain in 1989, and current statistical differences, see Wodak et al. (2013). Moreover,

Harrison and Bruter (2011) and Mudde and Kaltwasser (2012) provide ample statistical evidence for these specific developments. For brief overviews of national developments, see also the Glossary.

12 Sources: www.ukpolitical.info/ResultsFull01.htm; www.bbc.co.uk/news/uk-politics-22396689, accessed 12 March 2015.

13 See Billig (1995), Wodak et al. (2009) and McGlashan (2013).

14 http://rt.com/news/155364-ukraine-nazi-division-march/, accessed 12 March 2015.

15 As Rudling (2013, 229) explains, 'in Western Ukraine, the Organization of Ukrainian Nationalists (OUN) was founded in 1929 through the merger of several far right groups, such as the Ukrainian Military Organization, consisting largely of war veterans, student fraternities and groups like the Union of Ukrainian Fascists [...] OUN relied on terrorism, violence, and assassinations, not at least against other Ukrainians, to achieve its goal of establishing a totalitarian and ethnically homogenous Ukrainian nation-state. In 1938, the movement split into two wings, the followers of Andrii Melnyk and Stepan Bandera, known as Melnykites, OUN(m), and Banderites, OUN(b). Both wings enthusiastically committed to the new fascist Europe. Stets'ko supported "the destruction of the Jews and the expedience of bringing German methods of exterminating Jewry to Ukraine, barring their assimilation and the like," his chief propagandist Stepan Lenkavs'kyi advocated the physical destruction of Ukrainian Jewry. During the first days of the war, there were up to 140 pogroms in Western Ukraine, claiming the lives of 13,000–35,000 people. In 1943–1944, OUN(b) and its armed wing, the Ukrainian Insurgent Army (UPA) carried out large scale ethnic cleansing, resulting in the deaths of over 90,000 Poles and thousands of Jews.'

16 See www.europarl.europa.eu/sides/getDoc.do?pubRef=-//EP//TEXT+TA+P6-TA-2009-0213+0+DOC+XML+V0//EN, accessed 14 July 2014.

17 See www.opendemocracy.net/opensecurity/kristina-bor%C3%A9us-tobias-h%C3%BCbinette/hate-speech-and-violent-right-wing-extremism-in-scandi; www.opendemocracy.net/opensecurity/ruth-wodak/security-discourses-and-radical-right.; www.opendemocracy.net/opensecurity/salomi-boukala/grammars-of-enmity-golden-dawn-of-contemporary-greek-democracy, accessed 23 May 2014.

18 Here, I elaborate some dimensions of my commentary published by the LSE EUROPP blog after the elections for the European Parliament, 25 May 2014: http://blogs.lse.ac.uk/europpblog/2014/07/23/it-would-be-dangerous-to-regard-modern-european-populism-as-devoid-of-serious-content-or-as-a-triumph-of-style-over-substance/, accessed 12 March 2015.

3   PROTECTING BORDERS AND THE PEOPLE: THE POLITICS OF EXCLUSION

'Political speech and writing are largely the defence of the indefensible. Things like the continuance of British rule in India, the Russian purges and deportations, the dropping of the atom bombs on Japan, can indeed be defended, but only by arguments which are too brutal for most people to face, and which do not square with the professed aims of the political parties. Thus political language has to consist largely of euphemism, question-begging and sheer cloudy vagueness. [...] All issues are political issues, and [...] when the general atmosphere is bad, language must suffer.'

George Orwell (1946, 43)

Discourses, Genres, and Right-wing Populist Agenda

Orwell primarily focused on euphemisms, that is, sophisticated ways of talking about terrible events and distressing actions in mitigated, 'soft' language. Quite masterfully, he was able to deconstruct the 'double-think' we are all confronted with daily, in the media, in newspapers, or when listening to politicians promising reforms and a better future – or cloaking difficult decisions in neologisms and managerial jargon. In his dystopia of 1984, Orwell intuitively pointed to many discursive strategies and lexical innovations which have become part and parcel of populist rhetoric across all political parties since 1945. Indeed, inspired by the language used in national-socialist as well as in Communist totalitarian states, he unmasked the second reality frequently imposed by politicians to cover up uncomfortable facts.

After experiencing the horrific consequences of totalitarianism in the 20th century, most politicians nowadays turn to a more subtle, coded version of previously blunt exclusionary text and talk. It is this coded language that I am concerned with when analysing right-wing populist micro-politics and related rhetoric; the insinuations to common-sense of those 'in the know', the euphemisms that serve to mask crises and discriminatory policies, the arguments and legitimation strategies employed to justify the unjustifiable or speak the unspeakable. Most importantly, the *calculated ambivalence* that serves to address multiple and contradictory audiences simultaneously, and the *provocative statements* which colonize the agenda of our daily news programmes, have to be considered in systematic detail. In this way, the strategy of calculated ambivalence relates well to the Orwellian notion of '*double think*', that is, creating assumed associations between contradictory meanings.[1] All these linguistic strategies in text and talk keep right-wing populism alive and kicking. These are the most important discursive strategies, rhetorical tropes and pragmatic devices as well as argumentation schemes employed to express and realize both form and content of right-wing populist ideologies, which I focus on in this chapter.

'Double-think', Left-wing and Right-wing Populism

Populism can be viewed as a political style in the sense of a complex 'syndrome' (used here not in any pathological sense) which mixes heterogeneous and theoretically incoherent elements in a strategic way – of course, these elements need not all emerge simultaneously. In addition to this quite formal, stylistic and technical definition, 'populism' can also be concretely categorized with respect to the content of opinions and beliefs expressed. At this point, it is important to emphasize – again – that 'right-wing populism' has to be distinguished from 'left-wing populism' with respect to the attitude of populist politicians towards National Socialism, fascism, racism, antisemitism and xenophobia as well as to their understanding of *inter alia* social and cultural policies, migration policy, gender issues, environmentalism and security policy (Pelinka 2013). Right-wing populism endorses a nativist notion of belonging, linked to a chauvinist and racialized concept of 'the people' and 'the nation'. This has to be kept in mind as both types of populism (left-wing and right-wing) otherwise share some features of style, form and mediated performance. In short, right-wing populism presents itself as serving the interests of an imagined homogenous people *inside* a nation state, whereas left-wing populism or other parties also employing populist strategies have an international stance, look *outwards* and emphasize diversity or even cosmopolitanism (albeit in different ways).

With respect to the political role of populist politicians, we distinguish between an 'oppositional habitus', which is the classical stance of populism, and a 'governmental habitus' (Grande 2000; see Chapter 6). While observing the 'career-trajectory' of various right-wing populist parties across Europe, it becomes obvious that the oppositional habitus (opposing everything and especially 'those up there' while serving 'the man and woman on the street') suits the objectives of such parties better than having to find compromises when in government.

If we consider the social domain of politics and related fields of action, then populist rhetoric has to be regarded a matter of 'external political communication'. The rhetoric of oppositional populism manifests itself in (1) the field of political advertising; (2) the field of political control; and (3) the field of formation of public attitudes, opinions and will. Generally, the field of political control is the traditional and typical place of oppositional populism, which develops as a form of protest against hegemonic governmental policy. In contrast, the rhetoric of governmental populism is usually articulated in the field of formation of public attitudes, opinions and will. Moreover, governmental populism has gained some importance in the field of the political executive and administration, for example in the case of 'issueless politics', in which political action is simulated primarily by symbolic rituals (Figure 3.1; adapted from Reisigl 2007, 1128ff.; Wodak 2011a, 41).

Different fields of action are defined by different functions of discursive practices (Girnth 1996). For example, in the arena of *political action*, we distinguish eight different political functions as eight different fields (see Figure 3.1). A 'discourse' about a specific topic such as immigration can emerge within one field of action and proceed through another; for

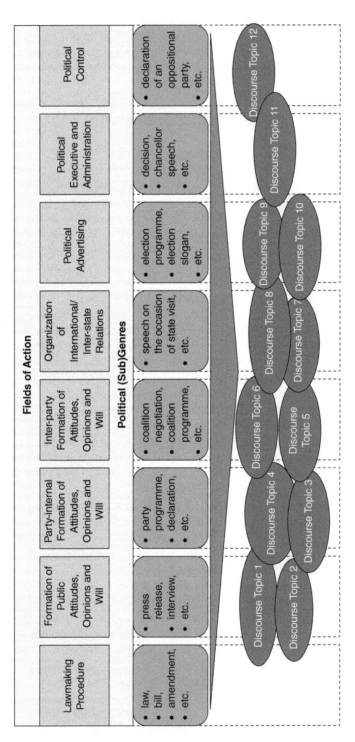

Figure 3.1 The 'Political Field': Functions, genres, discourses and discursive practices

example, debates about immigration could be launched in a party-internal meeting to form the opinions of party members and then be recontextualized as a political leaflet in an election campaign (with the function of political advertising). Discourses often 'spread', or are intentionally spread, to different fields and relate to or overlap with other discourses. In this way, the discourse about immigration could draw on discourses about security and citizenship, and also be disseminated to other fields, like education or foreign affairs.

Figure 3.2 illustrates the various discourses and the specific ideological positionings of right-wing populist parties, the many topics which are talked about and framed in

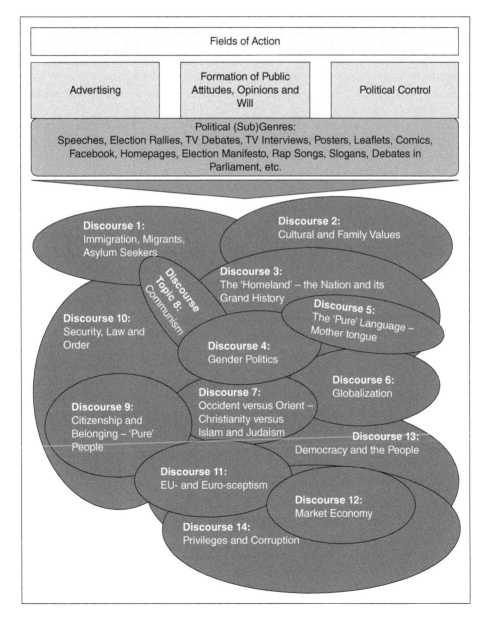

Figure 3.2   Discourses about right-wing populist agenda

specific ways, and the range of genres employed when advertising, influencing public opinion and will as well as intervening into political control. The agenda relate to the theoretical approaches discussed in Chapters 1 and 2, and to the various examples analysed throughout this book.

Discursive Strategies and Exclusionary Argumentation

The study of discriminatory practices necessarily implies qualitative in-depth analysis, as traditional methods of measurement encounter enormous obstacles when trying to account for racist, antisemitic or xenophobic attitudes. Indeed, much research has provided ample evidence that better educated people understate their prejudiced beliefs (Kovács 2010); moreover, the ideological value of tolerance is widespread in contemporary capitalist societies, so that the explicit promulgation of exclusionary politics conflicts with the generally accepted values of liberalism. Hence, discriminatory utterances tend to be 'coded' in official rhetoric so as to avoid sanctions; *pragmatic devices* such as *insinuations*, *implicatures*, *inferences* or *presuppositions* are frequently comprehensible only to insiders. Indeed, the very terms 'discrimination', 'exclusion' or 'prejudice' carry a range of negative connotations. Thus, few would admit in public or when interviewed to agreeing with the exclusion of or prejudice or discrimination against minority groups. This is why opinion polls and interviews are inherently doomed to fail as investigations into racist belief systems. Usually, people deny these beliefs and try to present themselves in a positive light as they are aware that such opinions are taboo or might even be associated with extremist right-wing political affiliations. This implies studying how discursive practices can accomplish exclusion in its many facets without the explicitly acknowledged intention of actors; exclusion has become 'normality' and thus acceptable, and has been integrated into all dimensions of our societies. According to Reisigl and Wodak, racism/discrimination/exclusion manifests itself discursively: 'racist opinions and beliefs are produced and reproduced by means of discourse [...]; through discourse, discriminatory exclusionary practices are prepared, promulgated and legitimized' (2001, 41).

In the following section, I first briefly present key concepts of the discourse-historical approach (DHA) (i.e. the concepts of 'con/text, discourse, and discursive strategies') relevant to the understanding and deconstruction of right-wing populist rhetoric, as well as some implications for the analysis of the various data sets and genres presented throughout this book.[2] Second, I use several examples to illustrate some of the most important characteristics of right-wing populist rhetoric.

The Discourse-historical Approach

The *discourse-historical approach* (DHA) allows relating the macro- and meso-level of contextualization to the micro-level analyses of texts. Such analyses consist primarily of *two levels*: the so-called 'entry-level analysis' focusing on the thematic dimension of texts, and the 'in-depth analysis' which scrutinizes coherence and cohesion of texts in detail. The general aim of the *entry-level* thematic analysis is to map out the contents of analysed texts and then to assign them to particular discourses. The key analytical categories of thematic analyses are *discourse topics*, which 'conceptually, summarize the text, and specify its most important information' (van Dijk 1991, 113). The *in-depth analysis*, however, is informed by the research questions. The in-depth analysis consists of the analysis of the genre (e.g. television interview, policy paper, election poster, political speech or homepage), the macrostructure of the respective text, discursive strategies and of argumentation schemes, as well as of other means of linguistic realization (Krzyżanowski 2010; Reisigl and Wodak 2009; Wodak et al. 2009).

First and most importantly, the DHA focuses on *texts* – be they audio, spoken, visual and/or written – as they relate to structured knowledge (*discourses*), are realized in specific *genres*, and must be viewed in terms of their *situatedness*. That is, many texts – including posters, speeches, comics, television debates, postings and other web 2.0 genres – owing to their inherent ambiguities as *texts*, cannot be fully understood without considering different layers of *context*. Here, I follow a *four-level model* of context that includes the historical development of the respective political party (the *socio-political/historical context*), discussions which dominated a specific debate/event (*the current context*), a specific text (*text-internal co-text*) as well as other related events, utterances, discources, and texts which have influenced the specific discursive practice in manifold ways (*intertextual and interdiscursive relations*; Reisigl and Wodak 2001, 40ff.). The terminological pair interdiscursivity/intertextuality denotes the linkage between discourses and texts across time and space – established via explicit or implicit references. If text elements are taken out of their original context (de-contextualization) and inserted into another (re-contextualization), a similar process occurs, forcing the element in question to (partly) acquire new meaning(s) (Wodak 2011a).

Second, the DHA defines *discourse* as a set of 'context-dependent semiotic practices' as well as 'socially constituted and socially constitutive', 'related to a macro-topic' and 'pluri-perspective', that is, linked to argumentation (Reisigl and Wodak 2009, 89). Taking such a perspective, the 'Facebook incident' (Vignette 1) can be understood as drawing on existing opinions and collective memories about Austrian history, on manifold prejudicial identity constructions, stereotypes as well as current discourses on immigration and the financial crisis in Europe, and furthermore *mobilizing* and *radicalizing* these discourses. Third, positive self- and negative other-presentation is realized via *discursive strategies* (Reisigl and Wodak 2001, 45–90). Here, I primarily focus on nomination (how events/objects/persons are referred to) and predication (what characteristics are attributed to them). A paradigmatic case might be the 'naming' of a protagonist or an institution metonymically (*pars pro toto*), for example Merkel for Germany, or as synecdoche (*totum pro pars*), for example the EU for all individual EU organizations. The strategy of perspectivization realizes the author's involvement, for example, via deïxis, quotation marks, metaphors and so forth.

Argumentation Schemes, *Topoi* and Fallacies

The DHA draws on the concept of *topos* apart from employing and elaborating Toulmin's model (2003) when appropriate (see also Chapter 2).[3] Kienpointner (2011, 265) defines *topoi* as 'search formulas which tell you how and where to look for arguments. At the same time, *topoi* are warrants which guarantee the transition from argument to conclusion' (2011, 265).[4]

Rubinelli (2009, 13) suggests that *topoi* are strategies of argumentation (see Figure 3.3) for gaining the upper hand and producing successful speeches. *Topoi* can be made explicit as conditional or causal paraphrases such as 'if x, then y' or 'y, because x' (Reisigl and

Figure 3.3   A simplified model of argumentation

Wodak 2001, 69–80). Focusing on such conclusion rules, Kienpointer (1996) distinguishes between various content-abstract, that is, formal argumentation, schemes (while drawing on Aristotle's taxonomy) which occur frequently in argumentation, such as the *topos of defini-tion*, the *topos of the species and the genus*, the *topos of comparison* (*topos of similarity* versus *topos of difference*), the *topos of the part and the whole*, the *topos of authority*, the *topos of example* and the *topos of analogy*. For example, the *topos of authority* can be deconstructed as follows:

Conclusion rule:	If authority X says that A is true, A is true.
A:	X says that A is true.
C:	Thus, A is true.

On the other hand, Wengeler (2003a, 2003b) emphasizes a content- and context-specific definition of *topoi* as this allows deconstructing presupposed and frequently fallacious prejudices embedded in everyday common-sense conversations about specific topics. The notion of common-sense (or everyday) argumentation is salient in our case as many studies focus on understanding more or less explicit preferences of specific electoral groups or political parties. For Aristotle, *topoi* are linked to the subject of *dialectic*, called *endoxon* [accepted opinion]. He uses the concept of *endoxon* in order to describe an opinion that can be accepted by the majority of people, because it represents *tradi-tional knowledge* but not necessarily *true knowledge* (Boukala 2013, 18). Accordingly, van Eemeren (2010, 111) also claims that *endoxa* are defined as commonly held beliefs or generally accepted commitments which are linked to normal beliefs and are accept-able for the audience.

Tables 3.1 and 3.2 present the two different types of *topoi* (formal and content-related), based on Wengeler (2003a, 2003b) and Kienpointner (1996).[5] When considering these two cat-egories of *topoi*, it becomes apparent that a logical continuity exists, extending from *rhetorical topoi* to the definitions proposed in Kienpointner's approach and the DHA (Wodak 2014a). At this point it is important to emphasize that *topoi* are not necessarily fallacious. Many examples below manifest flawed logic, but in particular contexts, arguments using a specific *topos* could be right: *topoi* are therefore, neutrally speaking, a useful shortcut appealing to existing knowl-edge. Therefore the *use* of *topoi* in specific ways and contexts (which are often very complex), what they ignore or sidestep, *can* be fallacious and manipulative.[6]

In summary, the DHA focuses on ways in which power-dependent semiotic means are used to construct positive self- and negative other-presentations ('Us' and 'Them', the good people and the scapegoats, the pro and contra of the crisis or any other topic/event). This also captures the ability to select specific events in the flow of a narrative as well as increased opportunities to convey messages through opening up space for '*calculated ambivalence*'

Table 3.1 Selected list of formal *topoi*

Topos	Principle and/or Example
Topos of opposites	If the contrary of a predicate belongs to the contrary of a subject, then this predicate belongs to this subject.
	'If the war causes us all this damage, then we should make peace.'
Topos of definition	*'If someone believes that evil is related to the gods, then he believes in the existence of the gods.'*
Topos of syllogism that starts with something specific and concludes with something general	*'If some human beings do not trust their horses to people who do not protect the horses of other human beings, then they cannot trust their salvation to people who do not succeed in saving other human beings.'*
Topos of the consequential	If an act has both good and bad consequences, then on the basis of the good/bad consequences this act can be exhorted/blamed.
	'If one is educated, then he can be wise. If one is educated, the others envy him.'
Topos of cause	If the cause exists then so does the effect. If the cause does not exist, then there is no effect.

Table 3.2 Selected list of content-related *topoi* in right-wing populist rhetoric

Topos	Warrant
Topos of people	If the people favour/refuse a specific action, the action should be performed/not performed.
Topos of advantage or usefulness	If an action under a specific relevant point of view will be useful, then one should perform it.
Topos of uselessness or disadvantage	If one can anticipate that the predicted consequences of a decision will not occur, then the decision has to be rejected.
Topos of threat or *topos of danger*	If there are specific dangers or threats, one should do something against them.
Topos of burden or weighing down	If a person, an institution or a country is burdened by specific problems, one should act in order to diminish those burdens.
Topos of finance	If a specific situation or action costs too much money or causes a loss of revenue, one should perform actions that diminish those costs or help to avoid/mitigate the loss.
Topos of reality	Because reality is as it is, a specific action/decision should be performed/made.
Topos of numbers	If the numbers prove/don't prove a specific standpoint, a specific action should be performed/not be carried out.
Topos of saviour	If danger is to be expected because of X and if A has saved us in the past, then A will be able to save us again.
Topos of history	Since history teaches that specific actions have specific consequences, one should perform or omit a specific action in a specific situation (allegedly) comparable with the historical example referred to.

(Engel and Wodak 2009, 2013). The latter is defined as the phenomenon that one utterance carries at least two more or less contradictory meanings, oriented towards at least two different audiences (see the 'Facebook incident', Vignette 1). This not only increases the scope of the audience too (e.g. the Austrian people and international audiences), but also enables the speaker/writer to deny any responsibility: after all, 'it wasn't meant that way'. Finally, the power of discourse creates regimes of quasi 'normality', that is, what is deemed 'normal', for example, with regard to the political messages circulating during the financial crisis and the heated debates related to it.

Appealing to Security – Justifying Exclusion

EU-scepticism and 9/11

The ethno-nationalist form of populism mentioned in the previous chapters frequently employs strategies of appealing to, or presupposing, national sameness, unity and cohesion. These strategies are usually based on the *fallacy of sameness* and on the *fallacy of argumentum ad baculum*. The *fallacy of sameness* imagines the 'own' nation as a culturally homogeneous community. The *fallacy* or *argumentum ad baculum* refers to (alleged) dangers that threaten this so-called national homogeneity. On the other hand, ethno-national populism relies on the strategy of presupposing or stressing difference. This strategy resorts to the *fallacy of difference*, which emphasizes the clear distinction and distinctiveness from other nations or ethnic minorities in order to draw a rigid dividing line (see Wodak et al. 2009). In this way, all persons considered members of allegedly different nations or minorities are automatically excluded. Additionally, nationalistic populism makes use of the *strategy of singularisation*, that is, of constructing oneself as unique and superior. This strategy necessarily integrates the explicit or implicit *fallacy of comparison*: the superiority of one's own nation to all other nations and ethnic minorities is thus overemphasized and exaggerated. Moreover, as elaborated in Vignette 3, right-wing populist movements also tend to have an ambivalent approach to 'Europe' and support EU-scepticism. When it fits their political agenda, even right-wing populist politicians such as the former leader of the FPÖ, Jörg Haider, who usually indulged in anti-EU views (i.e. the *Feindbild* of 'Europe'), strategically invoke 'Europe' and a 'European identity'. This was the case, for example, when he tried to exclude groups of people not considered 'European', that is, Turks, Muslims or other people from the 'developing countries' (Wodak et al. 2009, 221–2), alluding to the Christian or even Judeo-Christian traditions in Europe – a theme frequently repeated by Geert Wilders of the Dutch Freedom Party or by Jarosław Kaczynski of the PiS, the Polish Right and Law Party (see Krzyżanowski 2013b; Wodak and Boukala 2014, 2015).

Exclusionary measures and exclusionary rhetoric are also legitimized via security measures (Matouschek et al. 1995; van Leeuwen and Wodak 1999): the terrorist attacks in the US on 11 September 2001 had – and still have – global consequences and continue to have an enormous impact on Europe and all European nation states, most specifically by linking immigration restrictions to security measures instead of Human Rights conventions or other social and economic considerations and policies. The FPÖ and the Jobbik or the Vlaams Blok and UKIP thus attempt to functionalize 9/11 as a persuasive vehicle to create or strengthen a European identity, against the danger of 'invading masses' or so-called 'uncivilized barbarians' (see below).

For example, about two and a half weeks after 9/11, Jörg Haider proposed that the EU should only accept asylum seekers from Europe and that asylum seekers from other continents would have to wait for a decision in an (allegedly) safe third country outside Europe (e.g. in Asia). This request undoubtedly violated Human Rights laws and the Geneva Refugee Convention. In this way, Haider stated – cynically – that it would be useful to reach agreements with third (non-European) countries where asylum seekers could be 'dumped' (the German '*deponiert*' used by Haider evokes the metaphor of 'a waste disposal site') (Wodak et al. 2009, 223).[7] Haider's demand was obviously based on Islamophobic prejudice, while appealing to and legitimizing his demands via the necessity of more security policies. He presupposed, it appears, that mainly potential terrorists were emigrating from unspecified non-European countries to Europe, to live and hide here as 'sleepers', who would then carry out suicide attacks in the near future. Haider's proposal clearly illustrates how European right-wing populist parties sometimes advocate a rigid patriotic chauvinism no longer only limited to national identities, but extended to an unspecified European identity whenever politically opportune.

VIGNETTE 4
GEERT WILDERS[8] AND THE 'JUDEO-CHRISTIAN HERITAGE' IN EUROPE

In debates or media reporting about immigration and religious difference, speakers/writers frequently employ arguments about 'culture', depicting it as an essentially bounded entity whose integrity is threatened by the presence of residents supposedly belonging to a different 'culture' and thus not willing to learn and adopt 'our' conventions and norms, that is, to assimilate; in these argumentative sequences, deictic elements acquire salience and culture is regarded as a static entity which somebody either knows about or does not, has or does not have. Culture is thus essentialized in such debates.

Let us look at a typical example: in 2011, the Italian government decided to issue Schengen visas to Tunisian refugees so that they could cross the borders into other European countries – a measure supported by the former EU Commissioner for Home Affairs, Cecilia Malmström.[9] The former Italian Minister for Interior Affairs, Roberto Maroni, officially requested support and solidarity from neighbouring EU member states. The latter, however, did not want to comply: in a press conference on 26 April 2011, the former French President, Nicholas Sarkozy, and the former Italian Prime Minister, Silvio Berlusconi, emphasized that Schengen borders should be closed again, even though this would contravene EU policy. Many national media seemed (and still seem) to support this new campaign for a 'Fortress Europe'.

In this context, Geert Wilders, the leader of the Dutch Freedom Party, delivered a speech in Rome on 25 March 2011 and claimed that:[10]

Text 3.1

'[...] the failure to defend our own culture has turned immigration into the most dangerous threat that can be used against the West. Multiculturalism has made us so tolerant that we tolerate the intolerant [...] if Europe falls, it will fall because, like ancient Rome, it no longer believes in the superiority of its own civilization. It will

(Continued)

(Continued)

> fall because it foolishly believes that all cultures are equal and that, consequently, there is no reason why we should fight for our own culture in order to preserve it.'

Wilders defines immigration as the 'most dangerous threat against the West' (*topos of definition*) and links immigration to multiculturalism, thus employing a *topos of threat* and a metaphorical scenario of a presupposed danger from multiculturalism. Here, I draw on Musolff's concept of metaphorical scenario:

> '[W]e can characterise a scenario as a set of assumptions made by competent members of a discourse community about "typical" aspects of a source situation, e.g. its participants and their roles, the dramatic storylines and outcomes, and conventional evaluations of whether they count as successful or unsuccessful, permissible or illegitimate, etc. These source-based assumptions are mapped onto the respective target concepts.'

> (2006, 28)

Moreover, Wilders compares modern Europe to ancient Rome and maintains the necessity to fight for the defence of European culture. This argument is further developed by the *topos of threat*, which relies on the conditional: 'If immigration creates a specific threat against Europe and European culture, then the Europeans should fight against it.' Finally, he highlights the causes of multiculturalism for Europe via the fallacy that accepts as a cause something that is not a cause (*post hoc, ergo propter hoc* fallacy) and which can be linked here to the conditional: 'If Europe accepts multiculturalism and denies the superiority of European culture, then Europe will fall.' He then emphasizes the end of the Roman Empire by drawing a very tenuous analogy to current immigration flows from North Africa (Tunisia), Turkey and the Middle East (*topos of comparison*):

Text 3.2

> 'Rome did not fall overnight. Rome fell gradually. The Romans scarcely noticed what was happening. They did not perceive the immigration of the Barbarians as a threat until it was too late [...]. People came to find a better life, which their own culture could not provide. But then, on December 31st in the year 406, the Rhine froze and tens of thousands of Germanic Barbarians crossed the river, flooded the Empire and went on a rampage, destroying every city they passed. In 410, Rome was sacked.'

Wilders presents the fall of the Roman Empire as an unavoidable consequence of the mass migration of 'barbarians' into Roman provinces, and thus intentionally 'rewrites history'. In fact, as many historians have indicated, it is highly unlikely that keeping barbarians from crossing the frontiers would have prevented the invasion of 406–407 and the subsequent defeat of Rome (see Pohl and Wodak 2012). Labelling non-Western civilians as 'barbarians' leads to a distinction between Westerners and non-Westerners/ barbarians and thus to the discursive construction of in-groups and out-groups. Wilders further maintains that 'together with Jerusalem and Athens, Rome is the cradle of our Western civilization – the most advanced and superior civilization the world has ever known'. And he adds:

Text 3.3

> 'As Westerners, we share the same *Judeo-Christian culture*. I am from the Netherlands and you are from Italy. *Our national cultures are branches of the same tree.* We do not belong to multiple cultures, but to different branches of one single culture. This is why, when we come to Rome, we all come home in a sense. We belong here, as we also belong in Athens and in Jerusalem. Ordinary people are well aware that they are witnessing a population replacement phenomenon. Ordinary people feel attached to the civilization which their ancestors created. They do not want it to be replaced by a multicultural society where the values of the immigrants are considered as good as their own. It is not xenophobia or Islamophobia to consider our Western culture as superior to other cultures – it is plain common sense.' (Emphasis added)

In this extract, he refers to the historical unification and cultural similarity of Europe and moves beyond the rhetoric of European populist parties[11] that deny the coexistence of Judeo and Christian traditions within European territory. Quite to the contrary: he employs a conceptual metaphor – a tree with various branches but the same roots symbolizing the cradle of civilization. Moreover, he redefines the limits of European civilization via another conceptual metaphor ('the nation as a home'; Norocel 2013) in order to substantiate the continuity and unification of European culture; he strongly emphasizes the alleged superiority of this specific civilization (see Chapter 4) and – via a *topos of threat* – repeats that a multicultural society necessarily implies a threat to ordinary (European) people.

This argument is further elaborated by the *topos of (common) European culture*, which is based on the conditional: 'If we share the same Judeo-Christian culture, then we are citizens of Europe.' Wilders excludes people from Islamic countries from Europe in an indirect way, in so far as he does not refer to them directly but gives weight to the borders of European civilization and distinguishes between 'Us', the Europeans (of Judeo-Christian roots), and 'Them', the non-Europeans, defined by 'religion and culture' (and not by territory), thus in a typical ethno-nationalist way. This argument is further substantiated by the *topos of definition*, which refers to 'Europeans' and can be reconstructed as 'If a group of people is named as Europeans, then they feel attached to the (European) civilization that their ancestors created', and thus indirectly refers to people with different cultural backgrounds who are necessarily, Wilders maintains, excluded from this group. Thus, the aforementioned *topoi* establish and legitimize the opposition between 'Us', the 'Europeans', and the 'Others'. Finally, Wilders concludes:

Text 3.4

> 'Now that Tunisia is liberated, young Tunisians should help to rebuild their country instead of leaving for Lampedusa.[12] Europe cannot afford another influx of thousands of refugees.'

At this point he employs a 'flood metaphor', that is, the 'influx of thousands of refugees', and supports his argument via the *topos of threat*; such metaphors are frequently employed in the context of migration (Reisigl and Wodak 2001, 54–61). In this way, he intensifies the idea of the dangerous 'Other'. The discursive construction of the in-group

(Continued)

(Continued)

of 'Europeans' and the out-group of 'Others/Muslims' that dominates Wilders' rhetoric could also be viewed as related to the constructive macro-strategies identified by Wodak et al. (2009, 33–42) in the context of the discursive construction of national identities. One could argue that Wilders equates a transnational Europe with a nation state, in the manner of exclusive nationalism; he highlights the common culture of different European nations and attempts to unify them by emphasizing a common threat. Wilders thus cultivates a quasi-national, elite identity based on a cultural hybrid and the *discursive construction of fear*.

The Denial of Racism: Disclaimers, Denial and Justification Strategies

Clearly linked to positive self-presentation and the construction of positive group and collective identities is what Teun van Dijk (1992) calls 'the denial of racism'. Van Dijk (1992, 92) provides a useful typology of denial as part of a general defence/justification strategy when accused or blamed of having uttered a racist remark or of being racist. These types are:

- Act-denial ('I did not do/say that at all')

- Control-denial ('I did not do/say that on purpose', 'It was an accident')

- Intention-denial ('I did not mean that', 'You got me wrong')

- Goal-denial ('I did not do/say that, in order to …')

- Mitigations, downtoning, minimizing or using euphemisms when describing one's negative actions

Moreover, van Dijk (ibid.) assumes that there are also cognitive and social strategies which could be regarded as 'stronger forms of denial': blaming the victim and victim–perpetrator reversal (see Vignette 6 below). Van Dijk's approach can be integrated with an innovative theoretical framework provided by Hansson (2015) which serves analysing and explaining 'blame avoidance' in political (government) communication; strategies of denial and justification obviously form an important part of the so-called 'blame game'. When returning to Vignette 1 in Chapter 5, I will illustrate that HC Strache primarily employs act- and intention-denials; however, when analysing apologies (see below), intention-denials, goal-denials, control-denials and relativizing/downplaying serve as justification strategies, whereas act-denials do not occur.

Van Dijk (ibid.) also mentions the use of *disclaimers*: recall the well-known examples of justification discourses, such as 'I have nothing against …, but', 'My best friends are …, but', 'We are tolerant, but …', 'We would like to help, but the boat is full' and so on. All these utterances, labelled as *disclaimers*, manifest the *denial of racism or exclusion* and emphasize *positive self-presentation*. Usually, such speakers seek to justify the practice of exclusion without employing related overt rhetoric. Overt denials of prejudice basically involve two presuppositions. First, they presuppose the existence of 'real' prejudice. In this regard, the existence of extreme, outwardly fascist groups enables defenders of mainstream racism, exclusion or discrimination to present their own rhetoric as being unprejudiced – by comparison, thus also constructing an implicit *straw man* fallacy. Second, speakers, in denying prejudice, will claim that their criticisms of minority group members are 'factual', 'objective' and 'reasonable', rather than based upon irrational feelings, and will accordingly employ a range of discursive strategies of legitimization. Speakers can, of course, use similar denials of prejudice and arguments of reasonableness when invoking different forms of discrimination, such as sexism, racism, antisemitism or religious discrimination. Additionally, each type of exclusionary practice will integrate particular themes, stereotypes and *topoi*, all contributing to the *syncretic nature of mainstream discriminatory discourse*.

For example, when analysing postings following an article by Helen Smith in the *Guardian* (2013) about the financial crisis in Greece and the rise of the Greek extremist right-wing party Golden Dawn, Angouri and Wodak (2014) were able to identify numerous utterances, such as:

Text 3.5

'I don't condone *violence* but clearly the governments of Europe aren't listening to their people any longer and *real* alternatives are popping up.'

In such utterances, the writer clearly first positions him/herself as rejecting violence, but then legitimizes the use of violence when no other alternatives seem available to make one's voice heard. To provide another example, we can return to the Facebook incident presented in Chapter 1, during which antisemitic attitudes were denied by Strache in pointing to his 'many Israeli friends' (a typical intention-denial):

Text 3.6

[16]	**HCS** No/ No, they are not,
	AW What then?

[17]	**HCS** Mister Wolf. And, um, with all due respect, I have

[18]	**HCS** many Israeli, but also Jewish friends, who

[19]	**HCS** have, um, seen this caricature, and not one of them can recognise antisemitism

The argument reads as follows: if somebody has Israeli (i.e. Jewish) friends, it must follow that one cannot endorse any antisemitic or anti-Jewish beliefs, a *post hoc, ergo propter hoc* fallacy. Moreover, not only does having Jewish friends put HC Strache above reproach, but they also approve the caricature and, therefore, nobody else should criticize it. Two propositions are causally linked here, although they obviously are not in any way indicative of a causal relationship; we are thus dealing with a fallacy presented in the form of a typical disclaimer.

Justifications usually attempt to turn blame into credit, for example, when claiming to be saving the country/nation/fatherland from terrorists, or migrants, or from any other danger, although these measures may also have involved some restrictions of Human Rights. The related argumentation may be based, as Hansson (2015, 308) elaborates succinctly, on emphasizing one's own qualities (*argumentum ad verecundiam*), evoking the audience's emotions (*argumentum ad populum*), and the use of fallacies or the incorrect application of argumentation schemes (e.g. false analogies; *post hoc, ergo propter hoc* fallacy, straw man fallacy and so forth). Moreover, politicians trying to avoid blame may employ a 'rescue narrative' frame in order to cast themselves as saviours (see *topos of saviour*, Chapter 2; Hansson, ibid.). Justifications may include various types of denial, apart from control-denial: the blame taker usually does claim responsibility for the actions or events (see discussion of apologies below). As Hansson maintains, justifications employ 'the full range of legitimations, based on authority ('We proceeded according to the law adopted by the Parliament'), moral evaluation ('Our actions are based on Britain's values'), rationalization ('This helps to get our economy back on its feet') and mythopoesis (e.g. telling a cautionary story about what could have happened if a particular decision had not been made)' (2015, 308–9) (see also Chapter 1).

Justification can also involve *problem-denial*, combined with a *counter-attack*, accompanied with negative Other-presentation, that is, attacking the (sometimes only alleged) accusation and accuser (Wodak 2006). In this case, the argumentation is frequently based on victim–perpetrator reversal (*trajectio in alium*), on discrediting the opponent (*argumentum ad hominem*), on threatening the opponent (*argumentum ad baculum*) or on an alternative claim, applied to shift blame (e.g. *post hoc, ergo propter hoc* fallacy) (see Vignette 1; Hansson 2015, 309). Moreover, relativizing and trivializing strategies are applied, frequently by using (fallacious) comparisons or equating strategies: 'Roma/Jews/Turks are also criminal'. Sometimes, the *Bad Apple frame* is used by referring to an alleged villain within the opposition or in a stigmatized minority group; or a conspiracy is constructed as caused by a strategically 'useful' scapegoat. The *Bad Apple frame* is based on the proverb 'One bad apple spoils the barrel', triggering a simple solution: Get rid of a bad apple and the barrel will be saved (Hansson 2015, 301; Lakoff 2008, 163–7). This frame can, of course, also be used for scapegoating and for shifting blame as well as for victim–perpetrator reversal. Indeed, I suggest that this frame could be reconceptualized in body politics, for the *nation as body* metaphors, the metaphors of immigration perceived as contagious *disease/illness* and minorities (Jews or Roma) as *parasites* threatening the nation (see Chapter 4).

VIGNETTE 5
JÖRG HAIDER AND THE POLITICS OF THE PAST – CALCULATED AMBIVALENCE

A further example will illustrate the theoretical and methodological considerations of the current chapter, linking to a salient dimension mentioned in Chapter 2 – the rewriting of history and creating national myths from a revisionist point of view, specifically in countries with a fascist or national-socialist past, on the one hand, to justification and denial strategies, on the other. In this way, guilt for alleged or real war crimes is downplayed, atrocities are euphemized and perpetrators are purged from memory. As a case in point, Jörg Haider's implicit conception of history became apparent in an interview in the weekly *Profil*, 21 August 1995:

Text 3.7

Haider: 'I have said that the soldiers of the Wehrmacht have made democracy in its existing form in Europe possible. If they had resisted, if they hadn't been in the East, if they had not conducted military campaigns, we would have ...'

Profil: 'What does that mean "resisted" ... after all, it was a war of conquest of the German Wehrmacht.'

Haider: 'Well, then we have to ask what really happened.'

What did 'really' happen? By emphasizing the adverb 'really', Haider might also be indicating that something different had actually happened, something that is 'being kept from us'. Implied in this reading is a conspiracy theory, that is, that somebody (who?) is hiding something that *really* happened. Via the *strategy of calculated ambivalence* Haider leaves the answer open for the audience. Moreover, the use of the adverb 'really' in this context also opposes the statement of the *Profil* journalist and implies for some readers that Haider's first answer ('the Wehrmacht have made democracy') would actually be the 'real and right answer'. The macro-strategy informing this short sequence could be described as a move to a meta-level and to a different conversational frame: Haider does not follow the required question–answer scheme that is part of the interview genre. He poses his own question as an answer. This question, however, has to be understood as a rhetorical question. Moreover, Haider's response could also be perceived as a way of using an answer to one question to invite another question on something he also would like to communicate. In this way, he uses defence as attack. The answer is – this is obviously implied – already available to the readers or could be easily extracted out of the co-text. And this leads us back to the intentional and strategic use of presuppositions and implicatures mentioned above.

Haider continues and adds more defensive and justification strategies: distortion, redefinition and reformulation, the offsetting of old myths and the creation of new ones. The result is that a hegemonic narrative is formulated and presented as the authentic one, the one that many war veterans would probably agree with. It is well known that this 'Haider version' of history is frequently welcomed by some of the so-called 'future generations' (as Haider used to label himself and other people who were born after 1945 and thus *per definitionem* incapable of endorsing a Nazi ideology, a fallacy which obviously establishes a false causality). This historical narrative allows maintaining the so-called Austrian 'victim myth' (Wodak et al. 1990), which has shaped the understanding and conception of the Nazi past for many Austrians for decades after 1945. This narrative also includes the practice of equating National Socialism with Stalinism, or the Wehrmacht's war of annihilation with any 'normal war' and so forth (Heer et al. 2008). Along this vein, Haider, when asked whom he perceived as the biggest war criminals of the 20th century (thus 'unrespectable' people by extension of his wording), equated Hitler with Stalin and Churchill. His answer blatantly disregards the differences between the ideologies, systems of government, their respective consequences and results as well as the difference between aggressors and victims or defendants. The victims, too, are equated by him:

Text 3.8

Profil: 'Do you consider the Nazi dictatorship a dictatorship like any other?'

Haider: 'I believe that one should not make gradual distinctions when talking about totalitarian systems. One should reject them altogether [...]. There was an era

(Continued)

(Continued)

> of military conflicts in which our fathers were involved. At the same time, there were operations occurring within the framework of the Nazi regime that cannot be accepted. But no family members of mine were involved in the latter.'
>
> *Profil*: 'Do I understand you correctly? "Operations"? What exactly do you call "operations"?'
>
> *Haider*: 'Oh well, activities and measures against parts of the population that were blatant human rights violations.'
>
> *Profil*: 'Do you have any problems calling it genocide or mass murder?'
>
> *Haider*: 'If you like, then it was mass murder.'

In this sequence, we can distinguish several discursive strategies, argumentation schemes and conversational moves. Again, there is a plethora of vague answers which allow for different readings and interpretations and address multiple audiences via the strategy of calculated ambivalence. On the one hand, Haider allows for identification with the war generation and the 'fathers'; on the other hand, he rejects (indeed, in this situation he has to reject) some of the 'operations' of the Nazi time, an obvious vague and abstract euphemism for the Holocaust and genocide – an example of the kind of euphemism pointed to by Orwell in the introductory quote to this chapter. Haider also quickly adds, by shifting frames and employing a very concrete, casual non-standard register, that his own family had no part in these 'operations'. This move indicates that he obviously knows precisely what he is talking about: the Holocaust. The use of such euphemisms is part and parcel of the strategy of calculated ambivalence. His third move, 'If you like, then it was mass murder', suggests that he is conceding a point to the journalist, but only superficially and not because he might believe so himself. It is made recognizable as a gesture to please the journalist by hedging and a concession ('If you like'). Thus, he indicates to his preferred audience of core party followers and believers that this is not really his opinion but an attempt to be politically correct in the public sphere.

Ambivalent Apologies

After making offensive statements, politicians are expected to apologize publicly. As Robin Lakoff elaborates in much detail, '[a]pologies have a tendency to be ambiguous' (2001, 204). The ambiguity implies that, sometimes, apologies are not regarded as sincere; or they do not acknowledge misbehaviour in the necessary explicit way; or they do not accept responsibility adequately but sound like a meaningless ritual (Tannen 1994). Sometimes, apologies relate solely to the style but not the content of language-based transgressions (i.e. the words used are admitted to have been inappropriate, but no mention is made of the content); sometimes, apologies only relate to one of many components that comprise the transgression (and the speakers seem to hope that nobody will notice that they have not apologized for the entire scandalous incident; Kampf 2009, 2265–6). Apologies can also aim at blurring the offence by using a euphemistic or vague term to refer to the offensive remark (i.e. by talking about 'mistakes' or 'things' or 'being sorry about that' in characterizing an offensive utterance); or speakers might only apologize for the consequences of a transgression but not for the transgression itself (e.g. by mentioning the possible damage or harm for recipients but not the insult). This kind of selectivity is characteristic of apologies in political contexts.

Moreover, avoiding responsibility might also be realized as non-performative: Thus, as Kampf (ibid., 2262) explains, such apologies consist of expressing the will or duty to apologize, a promise to apologize, or reference to a past apology – instead of using an active verb in the present tense and thereby actually performing the apology ('I hereby apologize'). In this way, evasive language is used to avoid blame and in order to survive a 'talk scandal' (Ekström and Johansson 2008). Here, the concept of the '*credibility test*' becomes relevant: such a 'test' emerges when an actor (or organization such as a political party) is called on to make an apology which is acceptable to many different parties, with different expectations and differing interpretations of the incident. As Kampf (ibid., 2259) argues, such credibility tests might lead to punitive atmospheres and to attempts of humiliating the wrong-doer. The latter is then forced to apologize while keeping face and, simultaneously, convincing the other audiences of his or her sincerity. Moreover, the media tend to document the offensive statement as well as the apology; this recontextualization, in sequence, creates a specific story, reported by many other media outlets, on social media and so forth, and thus gains notable momentum. Politicians try to pass the 'credibility test' by placating important public actors and audiences who might have different perceptions with respect to the responsibility or guilt of the actor. It is precisely in such complex contexts that apologies tend to become ambiguous; politicians tend to employ the *strategy of calculated ambivalence* to satisfy the various actors involved.

Right-wing populist politicians, such as Jörg Haider (see Texts 3.7 and 3.8), who have frequently (and also intentionally) transgressed norms, have become 'infamous' by performing evasive or selective apologies, by minimizing responsibility or by performing apologies that address multiple audiences with contradictory messages. For example, on 13 June 1991, in a debate in the regional parliament of Carinthia, a Socialist politician attacked Haider's plan of reducing unemployment payments for people seen as 'freeloaders', calling it forced work placement reminiscent of Nazi policies. Haider replied by making an unacceptable comparison between Nazi politics and the post-war democratic Austrian government: 'No, they didn't have that in the Third Reich because in the Third Reich they had a proper employment policy which not even your government in Vienna can manage to bring about.'[13] Haider first reacted – not surprisingly – with denial, and then claimed that the legislators had probably understood his comment wrongly, as a criticism of the present Austrian government, but in the days that followed the Austrian Social-Democratic Party (SPÖ) joined with the Austrian People's Party (ÖVP) in a vote of no confidence against him[14] (Köhler and Wodak 2011).

Clearly, in his apology, introduced by 'Actually, I have to apologize' (*Eigentlich muss ich mich entschuldigen*), Haider did not apologize for the content. Moreover, by employing the adverb 'actually', he indicated that he was apparently 'forced' to apologize, but that he 'actually' stood by his opinion. Many other similar examples could be cited. In this way, Haider clearly satisfied his core followers; the general public was only partially satisfied, but no more apologies could be demanded. Frequently, fallacious and completely unacceptable comparisons between the Nazi dictatorship and present-day Austria have occurred, uttered not only by Haider but also by other members of the FPÖ. By employing the strategy of evasive/selective and ambiguous apologies, such politicians were able, in essence, to escape unscathed after their scandalous utterances – although the insincere apologies, in fact, were never able to account for the horrific comparisons.

On 24 March 2014, Andreas Mölzer, MEP and former FPÖ candidate for the election of the European Parliament, also had to apologize: for calling the EU a '*Negerkonglomerat*' (conglomerate of 'Negroes') and for comparing the EU with the Third Reich, as the quality broadsheet *Süddeutsche Zeitung* had reported:

Text 3.9

'The [European] Union is a dictatorship, by comparison the "Third Reich was probably informal and liberal", the newspaper quoted. Furthermore, it had been stated that the EU must ask itself whether it was a "Conglomerate of Niggers", dominated by a "gang of lobbyists".'[15]

Mölzer had first denied these utterances; however, the newspaper had been able to record them and could therefore provide ample and substantial evidence. Mölzer eventually had to apologize; the Austrian newspaper *Der Standard* reported on 24 March 2014:[16]

Text 3.10

'In a press release he stressed that he "could not remember" this statement and called it a "semantic slip". "The choice of words was mistaken and also not intended that way", said Mölzer.'[17]

Obviously, Mölzer attempted to minimize the wrongdoing by claiming that he was emotionally involved (intention-denial); that he could not remember and that the utterance had been a mistake. He had never intended to use those words – a typical example of an apology focused on the words instead of the content. The scandal grew to enormous proportions and dominated the media for several weeks. Meanwhile it followed the predictable dynamic of the *right-wing perpetuum mobile* (see Chapter 1): Mölzer claimed to be a victim of a campaign directed against him personally and against the FPÖ in general.[18] Eventually, Mölzer had to resign and leave the FPÖ when it transpired that he had published – using the pseudonym '*Dr Seltsam*' (i.e. Dr Strangelove) – explicitly racist attacks against a famous and very successful black Austrian soccer player in the FPÖ newspaper *Zur Zeit*, of which he was and remains chief-editor.[19]

VIGNETTE 6
ANTISEMITISM IN HUNGARY: VICTIM–PERPETRATOR REVERSAL

In a recent study about racism and antisemitism as manifested in the propaganda of the Hungarian Jobbik since 2000, Kovács and Szilágyi (2013, 221–3) provide strong evidence that the strategy of 'victim–victimizer reversal' has become a reccurring element of explicit antisemitic discourse in present-day Hungary, different in some aspects from the virulent antisemitism of the 1940s (see Chapter 5). This – traditional and quite ubiquitous – strategy literally 'turns the tables': the victims are transformed into the powerful perpetrators, and the perpetrators into victims. A variation of this posits that the victims are themselves to blame for their terrible and dangerous fate, actually inviting it, acting irresponsibly or deserving some form of 'punishment'.

Nowadays, the authors (ibid.) argue, antisemitism primarily fulfils a function of constructing positive group-identities opposed to the danger and threat allegedly manifested by Jews. Such a discourse implies that by removing/expulsing/exterminating Jews, the danger could/would be removed. Furthermore, the authors illustrate that the *topoi of danger* and *threat* are necessarily integrated with the strategy of victim–victimizer reversal. Let us look at two examples (see ibid., 221 for an extensive analysis):

Text 3.11

'Decisions made by your kind [of people] are always dictated by whatever happens to "pay off" at a particular point in time, whatever is profitable for you, that is, whatever results in money or power. Common values are replaced by antifascist slogans and anti-Hungarian sentiment, and other ways of bringing "our kind" [of people] under control.' (Alfahír 2008a)

'Your kind (intend us to be) obedient subjects, servants and domestics, in an impoverished and maimed Hungary that has been turned into a third-world colony.' (*A Népszava megint Morvai Krisztinát gyalázza – Krisztina nyílt válaszlevele Várkonyi Tibornak* December 5, 2008)

The discourse leaves little doubt as to the identity of the 'Other'. Formulated in economic terms and thus referring to the traditional stereotype of the 'rich and greedy Jew', Krisztina Morvai, a MEP and representative of Jobbik in the European Parliament, accuses 'the Jews' ('your kind of people') of trying to dominate Hungary and the Hungarian people; moreover, apart from seeking domination, Jews are, she argues, per se disloyal (anti-Hungarian), thus evoking the stereotype of the 'disloyal Jew' (an old religious antisemitic stereotype insinuating Judas' betrayal of Jesus Christ) and would also strive to turn Hungary into a poor country, thus taking everything away from Hungarians and turning the latter into servants, implying that Jews actually possess the power to do so (stereotype of the 'mighty, powerful Jew'). Text 3.11 combines positive self- and negative other-presentation with the defamation of Jews (*argumentum ad hominem*) and the attribution of various traditional negative stereotypes to Jews. Furthermore, the text suggests that Jews are dangerous and powerful and would therefore intentionally damage Hungary and the Hungarians.

Text 3.12

'If, after the fifty years of your communism, there had remained in us even a speck of the ancient Hungarian prowess, then after the so-called "change of regime" your kind would not have unpacked your legendary suitcases, which were supposedly on standby. No. You would have left promptly with your suitcases! You would have voluntarily moved out of your stolen [...] villas, and [...] you would not have been able to put your grubby hands on the Hungarian people's property, our factories, our industrial plants, our hospitals ... We shall take back our homeland from those who have taken it hostage!' (Alfahír 2008b)

Text 3.12 accuses Jews of having been part of, and collaborated with, Communist Hungary by attributing it as 'your communism', hence rewriting history (*topos of history*). By claiming sarcastically that Jews would have left voluntarily (or stayed voluntarily) with their 'legendary suitcases' – alluding in an extraordinarily euphemistic and cynical way to the forced deportation of Jews to Nazi extermination camps, where they were allowed to carry only one suitcase with their belongings – the author relativizes or even denies the Holocaust in

(Continued)

(Continued)

order to evade responsibility for the bad economic situation currently faced by Hungary. Moreover, Jews are accused of having stolen the Hungarians' property, thus of never having owned any legitimate property in Hungary; here the fallacy of *shifting the blame* is used. This fallacious accusation implies that Jews are not Hungarians; they are construed as an out-group, as strangers 'at hand' (Kovács 2010), not part of the Hungarian *Volk*. In this way, tables are turned and victims transformed into perpetrators despite the well-established fact that Jewish property was stolen ('aryanized') by the Nazis and their Hungarian collaborators, not vice-versa. In short, Jews are blamed for all of Hungary's problems and economic disasters, a typical fallacious argument (straw man fallacy, combined with the fallacies of *shifting blame* and *hasty generalization*; Kienpointner 2009). Kovács and Szilágy suggest that these rhetorical elements are 'means, in the current antisemitic discourse, for constructing a narcissistic national self-image and self-identity' (ibid., 222). In other words, antisemitism functions as a code for a 'real' Hungarian political identity, part of a nativist body politics.

Summary: The Micro-politics of Fear

Summarizing the salient characteristics of right-wing populist rhetoric, it is important to distinguish two levels: on the one hand, specific contents; on the other, specific discursive strategies that realize these contents (but could, of course, be employed as resources with other contents in other contexts by other political parties and positionings as well).

I follow Michael Billig (2006) in positing that four factors typically have to be considered when analysing discriminatory and exclusionary rhetoric in post-war Europe:

1. Exclusionary practices occur in situations of differential power.

2. The powerful actors need not possess a conscious goal or intention; indeed, they may deny that any discrimination/exclusion has occurred.

3. The powerful actors consider their own actions 'reasonable' and 'natural'.

4. The actions that lead to exclusion are usually conducted through 'coded' language; overt exclusionary language is rarely to be observed.

Below, I list the specific phenomena related to right-wing populist rhetoric, starting with the contents I have introduced throughout the first three chapters of this book and related to the nine dimensions listed in Chapter 1:

- First, right-wing populist parties focus on a homogenous *demos*, a *populum* (community, *Volk*) which is defined arbitrarily and along nativist (blood-related) criteria, thus endorsing a nativist body politic.

- Second, and related to the former, right-wing populist parties stress a *heartland* (or homeland, *Heimat*) which has to be protected against dangerous outsiders. In this way, *threat scenarios* are constructed – the homeland or 'We' are threatened by 'Them' (strangers inside the society or from outside; migrants, Turks, Jews, Roma, bankers, Muslims etc.).

- *Protecting the fatherland* (or heartland, homeland) implies belief in a common narrative of the past, where '*We*' were either heroes or victims of evil (of a conspiracy, evil enemies, enemies of the fatherland etc.). In this way, *revisionist histories* are constructed, blending all past woes into success stories of the *Volk* or stories of treachery and betrayal by others.

- 'They' are different and are conspiring against 'Us'. *Conspiracies* are part and parcel of the discursive construction of fear and of right-wing populist rhetoric. Such conspiracies draw on traditional antisemitic and anti-elitist tropes – conspiracies are, it is believed, organized by bankers, the media, oppositional parties, traitors to the fatherland and so forth.

- Furthermore, apart from nationalism and nativism as well as the populist agenda, right-wing populist parties endorse *traditional, conservative values and morals* (family values, traditional gender roles) and want to maintain the status quo.

- They also support *common sense simplistic explanations and solutions* (anti-intellectualism), and need a *saviour, a charismatic leader* who oscillates between the roles of Robin Hood (protecting the social welfare state, helping the 'man and woman on the street') and 'strict father' (see Lakoff 2008). Such charismatic leaders necessarily require a hierarchically organized party and *authoritarian structures* in order to install law and order and to protect the *Christian Occident* against the *Muslim Orient*.

As mentioned above, not all right-wing populist parties endorse all these contents; nevertheless, these contents can be largely generalized and typify right-wing populist beliefs and ideologies. It is worth mentioning at this point that the Tea Party movement in the US shares many of the above-listed characteristics; most importantly, anti-intellectualism and an abundance of (frequently anti-elitist and sometimes antisemitic) conspiracy theories are to be found across all Tea Party rhetoric of recent years. I will discuss some differences and similarities between European right-wing populist parties and the Tea Party movement with respect to gendered body politics in Chapter 7.

Turning to the discursive strategies employed to realize the above-listed contents in right-wing populist rhetoric, I would like to emphasize:

- The continuous campaigning mode that implies Manichean divisions. Right-wing populist rhetoric divides the world into good and bad, into '*Us*' and '*Them*', insiders and outsiders, by constructing simplistic dichotomies and by positive self- and negative other-presentation.

- Following the aggressive campaign mode implies the use of *ad hominem arguments* as well as other fallacies, such as the straw man fallacy or the *hasty generalization fallacy*. Politicians tend to *deny and justify* even obvious 'mistakes' and quickly find somebody else to blame; under much pressure, *ambiguous*, *evasive* and *insincere apologies* may occur.

- Related to such a dichotomist worldview are *victim–perpetrator reversal* and the construction of scapegoats by *shifting of blame* (another fallacy).

- Moreover, the *topos of history* and the *topos of saviour* serve to realize revisionist historical narratives and the myth of the saviour who protects *Us* against *Them*.

- Constructing conspiracies necessitates *unreal scenarios* where some perpetrators (lobbies, parties, bankers and the 'Other') are allegedly pulling the strings; these are frequently dramatized and exaggerated. Lies and rumours are spread which denounce, trivialize and demonize the 'Others', following the slogan of 'Anything goes'!

- Finally, and importantly, the *strategy of calculated ambivalence* and the *strategy of provocation* lend themselves to aggressive campaigning and the addressing of manifold audiences as well as to setting the agenda in the media. In this way, the *perpetuum mobile* of right-wing populist rhetoric is set in motion, time and again.

Endnotes

1 Orwell (1949, 32) defines 'double-think' as 'To know and not to know, to be conscious of complete truthfulness while telling carefully constructed lies, to hold simultaneously two opinions which cancelled out, knowing them to be contradictory and believing in both of them, to use logic against logic, to repudiate morality while laying claim to it, to believe that democracy was impossible and that the Party was the guardian of democracy, to forget, whatever it was necessary to forget, then to draw it back into memory again at the moment when it was needed, and then promptly to forget it again, and above all, to apply the same process to the process itself – that was the ultimate subtlety; consciously to induce unconsciousness, and then, once again, to become unconscious of the act of hypnosis you had just performed. Even to understand the word "doublethink" involved the use of doublethink.'

2 The DHA is elaborated extensively in Reisigl and Wodak (2009) and Wodak (2011a, 2013a, 2013b, 2014a, 2014c). I refer readers to these publications for more information on linguistic details.

3 Which kind of persuasive and rhetorical means can be used depends on topic, genre and audience orientation as well as intention; these factors thus also determine which argumentation schemes seem most adequate and appropriate. In the concrete analysis, therefore, it will sometimes be Toulmin's model (2003), sometimes Walton's practical reasoning, and sometimes van Eemeren's Pragma-dialectics that make sense (see Walton 1996).

4 Charteris-Black, however, proposes to conceptually distinguish between warrants and content-related *topoi* (2013, 145), as does Boukala (2013), but for different reasons. Charteris-Black states that formal *topoi* could also be seen as warrants, but not in terms of Wengeler's content-related *topoi* (2003a, 2003b). To avoid confusion, he suggests labelling only the latter as *topoi* and to distinguish them from warrants. Boukala (2013) elaborates on both the Aristotelian and Cicero's concept of *topos* (84 BC) and illustrates their different meanings (warrants; common places) and the conflation in their meanings, which may be a further reason for much controversy and confusion.

5 Reisigl (2014, 78–9) presents an elaborated list of topoi which are – he claims – specific to right-wing populist rhetoric; I also believe that the *topos* of people (*argumentum ad populum*) is most relevant; however, I would add the *topos* of the saviour and the *topos* of history to this list as both are certainly salient throughout my data.

6 I am very grateful to Andrew Sayer for pointing out to me that this differentiation should be made explicit in order to avoid confusion and misunderstandings.

7 See http://derstandard.at/725783/FPOe-fuer-Verschärfung-des-Asylrechts, accessed 28 September 2001.

8 Geert Wilders is a Dutch right-wing politician and the founder and leader of the Party of Freedom (PVV). In 2010, after its electoral success (it won third place) the PVV agreed to

participate in a governmental coalition. However, the PVV withdrew its support in April 2012 (see Wodak and Boukala 2014, 180ff., for an extensive analysis of this speech). See Glossary for more information.

9 See also Wodak and Boukala (2014) for an extensive analysis of the background to this speech.

10 www.americanthinker.com/blog/2011/03/geert_wilders_in_rome_defendin.html.

11 Golden Dawn and Laos in Greece, National Front in France, FPÖ in Austria etc.

12 Lampedusa is the port of entry in Sicily for refugees and immigrants coming from North Africa.

13 See www.nationalsozialismus.at/Themen/Umgang/zitiert.htm

14 See https://www.google.at/webhp?sourceid=chrome-instant&ion=1&espv=2&ie=UTF-8#q=k%c3%a4rntner%20landtags%20protokolle%2013%20juni%201991

15 See https://soundcloud.com/sz-magazin/moelzer. After these utterances, even the President of Austria, Heinz Fischer requested Mölzer's resignation: www.gmx.at/themen/nachrichten/oesterreich/40b6r3s-heinz-fischer-legt-andreas-moelzer-ruecktritt-eu-wahl-nahe, both links accessed 21 July 2014.

16 See http://derstandard.at/1395362877057/Moelzer-soll-EU-mit-dem-Dritten-Reich-verglichen-haben, accessed 15 April 2015.

17 http://derstandard.at/1395363004736/Deutsch-Moelzer-soll-Kandidatur-zurueckziehen; see also www.kleinezeitung.at/nachrichten/politik/3584399/moelzer-entschuldigte-sich-fuer-sager. story, both links accessed 16 March 2015.

18 www.gmx.at/themen/nachrichten/oesterreich/46b6ie2-eklat-david-alaba-andreas-moelzer-wehrt-rassismusvorwuerfe, accessed 12 March 2015.

19 www.gmx.at/themen/nachrichten/oesterreich/00b6d6o-andreas-moelzer-david-alaba-rassistisch-beleidigt, accessed 12 March 2015.

4 LANGUAGE AND IDENTITY: THE POLITICS OF NATIONALISM

'[People who are] unable to speak English as those living here or not really wanting or even willing to integrate [...] have created a kind of discomfort and disjointedness in some neighbourhoods.'

David Cameron (Speech on Immigration, 14 April 2011)[1]

(Re)inventing Nationalism

Nationalism, once declared an obsolete force, especially after World War II and the establishment of the EU, has obviously returned with renewed vigour. Nationalism nowadays must be perceived as a global phenomenon – we encounter passionate nationalist movements everywhere, in Africa, South-America, the Middle East, Southern Europe, and in the successor states of the former Soviet Union. Frequently, new nationalisms emerge, tied to religious beliefs such as Islamic nationalism. Indeed, it seems to be the case that, in spite of an ever more unified and globalized world, more borders and walls emerge, defining nation states and protecting them from dangers both alleged and real.

Of course, it is important to emphasize that the idea of the nation also encompasses inclusiveness and solidarity; simultaneously, belonging to a nation is frequently defined through ethnic and even racist categories (rather than, e.g., legal citizenship), thus excluding 'Others' who do not possess these characteristics and are marginalized as outsiders, as strangers. In this way, our identities are inherently tied to subjective feelings of belonging, as well as to imposed nationalistic, religious and ethnic categories.

Identity, in this complex struggle over belonging, is never static and defined once and for all; identity and identities are dynamic, fluid and fragmented; they can always be renegotiated, according to socio-political and situative contexts as well as to more global social change and ideologically informed categories. This is why the German sociologist Theodor W. Adorno famously claimed, '[i]dentity is the prototype of ideology' (1966, 151).

Taking Adorno's words on board, the manifold ways in which national identity and nationalism are functionalized nowadays by right-wing populist parties with the aim of, on the one hand, constructing the 'real' Hungarians, Austrians, Dutch, Finns or British and, on the other, of excluding all the 'Others' who are considered as not belonging to the respective group, have to be investigated. Delanty and Kumar rightly emphasize that 'nationalism is present in almost every aspect of political community and social arrangements. It pervades the global and local dimensions and can even take cosmopolitan forms' (2006, 3). The 'real' people are defined not by having obtained citizenship to a specific country (*ius soli*), but by having been born to parents who already belonged to the respective country, that is, by nativist principles or *ius sanguinis* (Mudde 2007). If push comes to shove, this can even be extended to a vaguely defined *cultural or even linguistic 'belonging'*. Such opinions are held not only by the far-right; they are endorsed more and more strongly by mainstream parties who, out of fear of losing votes, accommodate such right-wing populist views. Because of continuous fear-mongering related to debates about security and the protection of 'our social welfare' (social welfare chauvinism), the ground has shifted.

Accordingly, in many countries across Europe and beyond, linguistic competence in the language of the majority serves as a 'gate-keeping device': the 'real' Hungarians, Austrians, Dutch, Finns or British are also defined via their language use. A large number of European states have made specific linguistic skills, defined according to Common European Framework of Reference for Languages (CEFR) levels, a requirement for permanent residence, citizenship or even the acquisition of an entry visa (Extramiana et al. 2014). Although European legislation presents language requirements and language testing as a means of 'integration', language requirements seem to represent an obvious formal legislative obstacle to migration and determine who should or should not belong to the EU (de Cillia and Dorostkar 2013).

Of course, the results of recent national and European elections demonstrate that such ideological shifts are not always successful or may even be counter-productive (on the strategic level): those voters who really want to keep the 'Other' out still vote for the far-right parties, whereas such opportunistic shifts of the mainstream frequently alienate traditional voters; they either abstain or vote for more liberal, anti-racist parties. Thus, mainstream parties lose in any case – they have, in effect, helped construct a no-win situation for themselves.

Five assumptions serve as foundations for this chapter:

1. Identities are always (re)created in specific contexts. They are 'co-constructed' in interactive relationships. They are usually fragmented, dynamic and changeable, but not mutually exclusive – everyone has multiple identities.

2. Identity construction always implies inclusionary and exclusionary processes, that is, definitions of 'Us' and 'Them'. Linguistic competence of the national language ('the mother tongue') has acquired the status of a gatekeeper in defining 'Us' and posing obstacles for migrants.

3. Identities that are individual and collective, national and transnational are also (re)produced and manifested symbolically, in many genres, while drawing on a range of linguistic/pragmatic/rhetorical/narrative and argumentative resources.

4. Right-wing populist nationalism inherently endorses an essentialized concept of nationalism expressed in ever more restrictive (nativist) body politics (*Kulturnation*).

5. Mainstream political parties accommodate more and more to essentialized national body politics in order to keep their electorate from voting for the far-right parties and their values.

Language Policies: Defining the 'Real' Hungarian

Let me start out with a telling example: in Hungary, new laws about preserving 'the' Hungarian language were passed in 2014. Legislation identifies the 'real' Hungarian language as something that should be preserved in a prescriptive, normative way; new institutions have been established to control language behaviour and to protect Hungarian against 'deterioration'. The recent decree implemented on 1 April 2014 states:

Text 4.1

Government Decree 55/2014 (III.4) on the founding of the Hungarian Language Strategy Institute [Nyelvstratégiai Intézet [lit. 'Language-strategical Institute']]

With the rights as defined in § 15:3 of the Constitution ('Basic Law'), within the task area defined in § 15:1 of the Constitution, the Government decrees the following:

1. The legal position of the Hungarian Language Strategy Institute

§ 1 To guarantee the *development of the Hungarian linguistic legacy, the deeper knowledge of the language and in connection with it the culture, to cultivate and maintain it* and to cater for the tasks defined in § 4: 1, the Government will found the Hungarian Language Strategy Institute (henceforth: The Institute).

§ 2 (1) The Institute is a state organ.

(2) The Institute will be directed by the Prime Minister.

(3) The Prime Minister will direct the Institute by way of the State Secretary in charge of the Prime Minister's office.

(4) The Institute will reside in Budapest.

[…]

2. The tasks of the Institute

§ 4 (1) The tasks of the Institute are

1. to direct and professionally monitor the preparation of a medium-term Hungarian language strategy, 2. to conduct research into the internal structure, characteristics and functioning of the Hungarian language, into its connections to our culture as a whole, and to apply the results from this research in public education, as well as to encourage the development of language data bases, 3. to coordinate the conscious development of diverse professional language forms (terminologies), to conduct contrastive research into Hungarian terminology beyond the borders and in the motherland, to compile contrastive terminological dictionaries, 4. in the area of information technology: to participate in the formulation of principles of supporting Hungarian-language databases and in their coordination 5. to give expert opinions in questions of language policy for public administration and public media, 6. to investigate new scientific approaches, to employ doctoral students of linguistics in a system of project scholarship applications and commissions. [...] 8. *to maintain the richness of language, with special respect to the Hungarian dialects and registers or sociolects, 9. to protect linguistic minorities, especially the endangered Hungarian language communities, to investigate the situation of trans-border language varieties, 10. to cultivate language-strategic foreign relations, especially with linguistically related language minorities, 11. to develop guidelines to the Government for fighting the devalorisation of the Hungarian language* [....], 14. to undertake further tasks to counter the devalorisation of the Hungarian language.

§ 5 This decree will enter into force on April 1, 2014.

(Viktor Orbán, Prime Minister; emphasis added)

In this decree, we encounter the Hungarian government's fear of 'devalorization' and the loss of 'richness' of the Hungarian language, of the 'mother tongue', as well as the conception of special means to protect the centrally defined and protected norms by a specifically created, strategic 'Language Institute'. The institute should, it is proposed in the document, be vested with substantial powers and responsibilities: to monitor school books, all institutions of education, as well as the language rights of Hungarian-speaking minorities inside and outside of Hungarian borders. This new legislation was met with much criticism and resistance, for example by the Hungarian Academy of Sciences (HAS), which sent the following statement on 31 March 2014 to linguists and linguistic departments across the globe[2] (emphasis added):

Text 4.2

Department I of the HAS wishes to point out in connection with the establishing of the 'Hungarian Language Strategy Institute' that any decision, strategic or political, which is related to language, or any scientific or cultural or artistic activity, *must be based on scientific investigation.* Scientific investigation can be conducted in research institutions monitored by *international quality control criteria.* (This general truth is, furthermore, worded in Article X (2) of Hungary's Fundamental Law.)

Department I of the HAS thinks it essential that decisions on language policy be made with careful preparation. *The Department notes with deep concern that, on establishing the 'Hungarian Language Strategy Institute', the establisher –* did not consult the Hungarian Academy of Sciences, which is the depository of the scholarly cultivation of the Hungarian language, being 'the nation's counsellor', or generally with the scientific and research institutions at large; – did not declare the necessity of maintaining contact with, and utilizing the scientific results of, other centres of research; nor did it mention cooperation with scientific institution in minority Hungarian areas in the neighbouring countries, but practically isolates the new Institute from these; – *failed to ensure quality control according to internationally recognized standards in the newly established Institute.*

Department I of the HAS wishes to emphasize that the research institutes of the HAS as well as the relevant departments and research groups of universities have *achieved outstanding results in the different areas of Hungarian scholarship, and that they will be able to do so in the future, and are ready to contribute to a sound scientific preparation of decisions related to the Hungarian language.* This wide-ranging and open activity is able, at all times, to provide the scientific foundation of political decisions to be made in various areas of cultural life.

(http://www.aitla.it/wp-content/uploads/2014/10/language-strategy-institute_hungary.pdf)

The statement explicitly rejects the new official language policy imposed by the government and insists on scientific criteria and international review procedures according to a long-established tradition in the Hungarian academic institutions. The HAS thereby distances itself from the new government project and implies that the new institute does not conform to the internationally recognized criteria of language policy research. This statement thus delegitimizes the new legislation (and, by consequence, any activities of the newly established Institute) and presents the HAS as the legitimate authority on issues of language and language policy. The statement restricts itself to more formal aspects of the new legislation, that is, the non-transparent and authoritarian decision making, while excluding the academic community. It also avoids entering into any debate concerning the alleged 'devalorization of the Hungarian language', a fear frequently expressed by conservative politicians and linguists in relationship to the concept of 'mother tongue' which, it is assumed, requires protection (see Rheindorf and Wodak 2014; see also below). The concept of 'mother tongue' relates well to the previously mentioned 'body and border politics' of right-wing populist nationalism.[3]

Body and Border Politics

'Border politics' are part of national identity politics and are now increasingly defined by the national language ('the mother tongue'), by ethnicity and culture, transcending the political borders of the nation state. Such language policies imply a return to national language policies which essentialize the nation state, projecting a homogenous culture, language and territory; correspondingly, old slogans and symbols of Hungary's fascist period in the 1930s are revived (see also Chapter 2). Instead of cosmopolitanism, post-nationalism, a European citizenship and the common European language policies which promote multilingualism (Krzyżanowski and Wodak 2011), we seem to be witnessing a (re)inventing of traditional, parochial, closed nation states. Such tendencies have also been observed by Skenderovic who, while analysing the Swiss right-wing populist party's (SVP) policies and history, concludes that 'the radical right's conception of nationhood and national identity offers patterns of interpretation premised on the idea that sociocultural, political or historical groups are based on natural distinctions' (2009a, 18–19). Griffin (1999, 316) accordingly concludes that the radical right 'takes on highly culture-specific forms, largely because it draws on nationalist myth whose contents are by definition unique to each cultural tradition' (ibid.). Obviously, the concept of 'mother tongue' relates to nativist 'body politics' of viewing and conceptualizing the nation as a body with the mother tongue symbolizing the national language (Musolff 2010). Indeed, Musolff argues that

the *body-state* metaphor and its *illness* and *parasite* scenarios have been 'declared dead', 'moribund' or at least deserving to be extinct in several schools of conceptual history. Its anti-Semitic associations have made it suspect on account of the memory of its use by the Nazis. Its semantic coherence has been seen as weakened in the modern era due to the demise of the humoral source of knowledge system and its replacement by new mechanically orientated scientific paradigms. [...] In its use by the Nazis, the metaphor helped to advance a genocidal ideology in its most brutal form, which is still remembered. [...] But the 'German case' is not unique.

(ibid., 137–8)

Moreover, Musolff continues that '[i]n US American English, *body politic* has its own characteristic connotations that invoke an inclusive view of society (as in President Obama's appeal to overcome 'racial and religious tensions within the body politic')' (ibid., 139). A close look at election posters by the Hungarian Jobbik in 2010 reveals that body politics combined with the discourse about parasites is experiencing a revival (see Image 4.1).

Image 4.1 Jobbik poster for Hungarian election 2010

This poster represents a mosquito embedded in a stop sign. The colours of the Hungarian flag (red, white and green) evoke nationalism and imply that Hungary, represented by the right-wing populist Jobbik, should not be bothered or damaged by such pests, which come in swarms and may cause pain or even severe illness by transmitting contagious disease. Hungary, in short, should get rid of mosquitoes. However, an abstract noun is employed: 'parasitism', which implies that this is a notable phenomenon, not just trivial everyday mosquitoes. This is a serious condition that has befallen Hungary and one that Jobbik will stop. If this is a condition, then one necessarily poses the questions: Who causes or has caused this condition? Who are the parasites, that is, mosquitoes? In the context of the 2010 Jobbik campaign, the answers are not difficult to find: Roma and Jews living in Hungary (see Vignettes 2 and 7). Accordingly, the report by the Human Rights First group states that

[t]hese two parties [i.e. Golden Dawn and Jobbik] are arguably among the most extreme in the E.P. in their rhetoric, which is designed to fan hatred and legitimize its expression, and in the violence they have fomented. Their stance goes far beyond the Euroscepticism that was seen the primary driver of the victory of many other European far-right parties in the E.P. elections. In fact they are so antisemitic and extreme that even Marine Le Pen, whose Front National won the French election with a record 24.86 percent of the vote, and Geert Wilders of the Netherlands declined to form a coalition with them in the European Parliament—thereby forfeiting the extra money, speaking time and influence they could have received by forming a parliamentary group.

(2014, 30)

The report further maintains that 'Jobbik used the crisis to pursue its anti-Roma agenda while Golden Dawn seized on it as an excuse to drive out migrants who were "taking Greek jobs" out of the country' (ibid., 43). Jobbik have revitalized hatred against Roma, homosexuals and Jews, 'all of whom were targeted by the Nazis, and added new targets of hatred – including Israel, Muslims, and Western-leaning socialists. And it began to organize grass-roots activists willing to act on those hatreds' (ibid., 45). Of course, when accused of hate incitement in the case of Image 4.1, the text producers would deny any discriminatory intentions (intention-denial and goal-denial). In this way, the strategy of calculated ambivalence is employed – people can infer the intended meaning. The abstract noun serves as a further linguistic trace for the metaphorical reading: getting rid of minorities not considered pure Hungarians and thus not accepted as Hungarian citizens in a Hungarian state.

This poster (amongst many other examples from the FPÖ, Golden Dawn and FN) illustrates that renationalizing tendencies can be observed across several EU member states and that therefore a nativist body politics seems to be 'celebrating' a revival. By extending the model of Norocel (2013, 94), I claim that not only does the 'family' as source domain imply the 'nation' as target domain in right-wing nativist discourse, but that the original source domain actually consists of the human (male) 'body' (the *Volk*), which spreads to a 'family' (multiple bodies incorporated by the *Volk*) and then encapsulates the 'nation'[4] (see Figure 4.1).

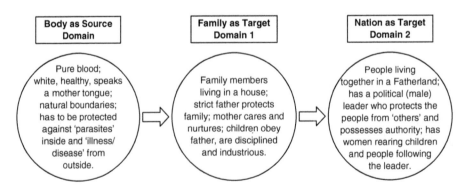

Figure 4.1 Body politics and the 'nation'

Thus, in contrast to discursive and social constructivist approaches to nationalism (Anderson 1983; Wodak et al. 2009), 'nation' as defined by right-wing populist parties is a limited and sovereign community that exists and persists through time and is tied to a specific territory (space), inherently and essentially constructed through an in/out (member/non-member) opposition and its out-groups. Access to national identity/membership is defined via heritage and ancestry, thus via 'blood' (de Cleen 2012, 97).[5] Such a notion of nation and nationalism is, of course, closely tied to concepts underlying racism; however, it is important to emphasize here that neither is racism necessarily nationalist, nor nationalism necessarily racist. For example, the connection to a territorial space must be perceived as a structural component of nationalism but not of racism. While racism as ideology and practice depends on the definition of groups and their fallaciously generalized alleged negative characteristics, due to biological categories, nationalism need not. Nevertheless, the conceptual boundaries are certainly blurred (de Cleen 2012; Reisigl and Wodak 2001).

Nationalism and Belonging

In this chapter, I draw on previous research on the discursive construction of national and transnational identities.[6] Following the seminal research by Benedict Anderson (1983, 15ff.), I assume that nations are defined as mental constructs, 'imagined communities', which political subjects perceive as discrete political entities. The discursive construction of the nation is accompanied by deep-seated feelings of belonging (Fortier 2012), which in itself is perceived as a 'consciously desired value' (Freeden 1998, 754). These feelings of belonging might also explain, according to Anderson, why people sometimes state that they might even be willing 'to die for a nation'. This meaning of nation is closely related to other heavily emotionally laden concepts like 'fatherland' or '*Heimat*'. The nation is conceived as a container, as a family to which one obviously belongs by birth (Norocel 2013).

As Wodak et al. (2009) have argued, such a concept of nation and national identity implies a complex of similar conceptions and perceptual schemata (or frames), of similar emotional dispositions and attitudes, and of similar behavioural conventions, collectively shared by bearers of this 'national identity' and internalized through socialization (education, politics, the media, sports or everyday practices). In our case, the common *conceptions* shared by British, Hungarians, Finns or Austrians include ideas of a *homo/femina nationalis*; of a common homogenous culture extending into the past, present and future; of a distinctive national territory; and of notions of and attitudes towards other national communities and their culture, history and so on.

The shared *emotional dispositions* relate to the attitudes towards both 'Us' and 'Them'; emotions that members of a given in-group have towards other members of that in-group, as well as those towards members of an out-group. Thus, this attitude implies solidarity with one's own group as well as animosity towards or, at least, clear-cut distinctions from 'Others' by excluding them from this constructed collective. Finally, it must be emphasized that discursive constructs of nations and national identities primarily essentialize national uniqueness and intranational uniformity but largely ignore intranational differences, especially when dividing the world into two distinct groups: 'Us' and 'Them'. In imagining national singularity and homogeneity, members of a national community simultaneously exaggerate distinctions between themselves and other nations, specifically when the other nationality is believed to exhibit traits quite similar to those of one's own national community (Sigmund Freud labelled this phenomenon the 'narcissism of small differences'; 1930, 243). Homogeneity is, as mentioned above, usually constructed discursively in a hegemonic identity narrative, encompassing a collective past, a collective present and future, a common culture, a common territory and a *homo/femina nationalis*. Such imaginaries clearly correspond to the concept of *Kulturnation* and, in its extreme version, to body politics, that is to the '*nation/state as body*' conceptual metaphor.

In exploring discourses of nationalism as created and employed by right-wing populist parties, a 'social-constructivist approach' provides a useful framework. Unlike essentialist approaches to nationalism such as the above-mentioned primordialist one, constructivism maintains that nations are the result of elite-driven processes aimed at meeting the needs of modern industrial societies. Indeed, the emergence of a national consciousness in the form of an imagined community was made possible only by the convergence of capitalism and printing technology, and is commonly viewed as the basis for the establishment of modern states (Anderson 1983). The existence of a national community – homogeneous in terms of language and cultural references – is obviously instrumental to the functioning of the core assets of the modern state, that is, industrial production, bureaucracy and citizenship. Hence, nation-building comprises continuously imposing an impersonal and codified high culture on a people – mostly by means of the mass educational system and the mass media – in order for a state to gain and maintain consensus and thus to function properly (Gellner 1983). Among the various dimensions that the constructivist approach to nationalism has highlighted, two deserve particular attention. First, the acknowledgement that nationalism is an eminently *discursive phenomenon*, which finds its most significant expression in the idea of studying the nation through its narrative address (Billig 1995). Second, the emphasis put on the central role played by the so-called national *intelligentsia* (frequently writers, journalists and also academics), whose role consists of promoting the construction of the national community and of sustaining and legitimizing its existence by virtue of its authority (Boukala 2013; Sicurella 2015; Wodak et al. 1994).[7]

In exclusionary rhetoric, language (and other symbolic systems) is used to determine and define similarities and differences; to draw clear *boundaries* between 'Us' and 'Them' (see Chapters 1 and 3). The distinction between 'Us' and 'Them' is explicit not only in the discourses of various right-wing parties, but also in EU Commission papers proposed since 9/11, on security issues, and national policy papers on citizenship measures[8] that present an 'existential threat' (Williams 2003, 514–15), call for counter-measures and lead to the stigmatization and exclusion of the 'Other' in various ways. These differences are subsequently evaluated and thereby an ideological moment is often implicitly (and sometimes also explicitly) introduced through various kinds of categorization. Constructions of identities, therefore, always presuppose that there are similarities/equivalences and differences (*idem* and *ipse*; Ricoeur 1992). Indeed, the study of mainstream voices (Krzyżanowski and Oberhuber 2007) illustrates how European elites, like the Members of the European Parliament (Wodak 2011a), define Europeanness and how they continuously produce 'in-groups' and 'out-groups' through *discursive strategies of positive-Self and negative-Other representation*. Furthermore, hegemonic discursive forms of inclusion and exclusion define 'the Europeans' and create an 'imagined community' that does not comprise the 'Others', 'those that are not worthy of becoming Europeans' (Wodak 2007b, 651) and are usually represented as 'enemies'. Here, I also draw on Lamont's work on racial and ethnic boundaries (Lamont 2000; Lamont and Molnar 2002). Lamont suggests that groups can create and cross boundaries simultaneously and that people construct 'boundary ideologies' distinguishing between 'Us' and 'Them' in their everyday discourse while drawing on 'the cultural resources to which they have access to and the structural conditions in which they are placed' (Lamont and Molnar 2002, 167ff.). The analysis of Image 4.1 provides an illustration of such racist exclusionary boundary ideology.

While illustrating current border politics, I will first trace the trajectory of an 'infamous' Swiss poster representing exclusionary immigration policies, adopted and used by several right-wing populist parties across EU member states, always recontextualized into the specific local context (of Germany, Italy, Catalonia and so forth). Second, by analysing opinions expressed by national politicians, I illustrate typical definitions of 'Us' and 'Them' based on exclusionary rhetoric. To put it even more succinctly: alleged or real threats to European and national security (to 'Us') are functionalized more and more as legitimation for drawing new borders between 'Us' and 'Them', the 'real Europeans' (Austrians, Finns and so forth) and 'Others', and for deciding on ever more restrictive measures to keep 'Others' out (Cutts and Goodwin 2013). Of course, the borders between 'Us' and 'Them' or the 'Others' are not set in stone; boundaries can be shifted, allegiances change and are changed, depending on political and other interests. Third, and more specifically, I trace the trajectory of how the traditional and value-laden concepts of 'mother tongue' and 'fatherland' have been foregrounded in recent national citizenship policies to accommodate requests and proposals from nationalistic far-right parties; I attempt to answer the question of what kind of symbolic values are (again) attributed to these concepts by drawing on the analysis of some recent citizenship policies across EU member states. In conclusion, I argue that current debates on citizenship have led to a (re)emergence of the concept of 'mother tongue' – as a centre-stage value in many nation states and a salient category defining the *homo* and *femina nationalis*.

Protecting the Borders, Family/Body and Nation

VIGNETTE 7
SWISS BORDER POLITICS: THE RECONTEXTUALIZATION OF EXCLUSIONARY VISUAL RHETORIC

In its Swiss national electoral campaign of 2007, the SVP launched a poster showing three white sheep standing on the Swiss flag, one of them kicking a single black sheep away (Image 4.2).[9]

Image 4.2   Black sheep poster, Swiss SVP 2007

(Continued)

(Continued)

This poster was greeted with much criticism because of its explicit racist image.[10] Here, the SVP insinuates the Swiss nation and its national identity by depicting the Swiss flag, and employs the widely known Christian religious white and black sheep symbolism. Although Switzerland is currently amongst the wealthiest nations on earth, the SVP enjoys much public support, specifically due to its anti-immigration stance.[11]

Quickly, this SVP poster was disseminated through mass media and various party homepages as well as right-wing blogs, accessed by thousands of sympathizers. By integrating the DHA (see Chapter 3) with visual analysis, it is possible to trace images historically and ideologically back to the image producers and also to deconstruct their recontextualized meanings due to different local and national contexts (see Richardson and Wodak 2009a). The SVP poster was soon re-used and radicalized by German right-wing groups (Image 4.3). Interviewed by the *New York Times* correspondent in September 2007, an SVP party member argued that the 'black sheep' was not to be understood as a racist symbol but instead 'just gives a simple message' – a typical rhetorical move of reformulating the predication and simultaneously mitigating and changing its content; this is a pattern which was already described in Chapter 1 in analysing the 'Facebook incident' (Vignette 1) and the many reformulations and denials of HC Strache when confronted with the antisemitic meaning of the caricature of the Jewish banker posted on his Facebook page.

Such reformulations are, of course, also indirect denials. Further along in the interview, the SVP candidate maintained that '[t]he black sheep is not any black sheep that doesn't fit into the family. It's the foreign criminal who doesn't belong here, the one that doesn't obey Swiss law. We don't want him'.[12] Thus, it is obvious who the 'black sheep' is supposed to represent: the generic criminal foreigner, dehumanized, and implying a fallacy of hasty generalization, namely that all foreigners are, first, easily discernible – they look different, and second, that they are all criminals.

Image 4.3   Black sheep poster, German NPD 2008

After the launch of this poster, other populist and extreme right-wing parties followed suit, for example in Germany, Italy and Spain, thus adopting the Swiss ethno-nationalist politics (Images 4.3 and 4.4).

Image 4.3 retains most of the visual elements of the original SVP poster, while recontextualizing its meaning from a national to a transnational right-wing and extreme right-wing public. The white sheep – now only one – symbolizing 'the nationals', the brand of the German NPD, remains on the Swiss flag symbolized by the colours of the Swiss flag (and not the German one), and kicks the black sheep out. Moreover, they promise to 'clean up the province (Hessen)'. It remains vague as to what or whom they will get rid of: foreigners, obviously, but also 'chaos' or 'dirt' in some other sense? The Nazi jargon usually employed the notion of *säubern* [cleansing] for cleaning in such contexts (directed against Jews, primarily), not *aufräumen* [to clear up] (see Richardson and Wodak 2009a). We can only speculate whether this slogan allowed for associations with Nazi slogans and ideology, and whether this was intended or not. In Northern Italy, the Lega Nord recontextualized the poster as shown in Image 4.4.

Image 4.4   Black sheep poster, Italian Lega Nord 2008

Here, one can observe notable changes of colour and symbolism: the Swiss flag with its red cross has been replaced by the symbolizm of the wheel and the colour green, representing the separatist ideology of the North Italian *Lega Nord*. This recontextualized image might have 'helped the Lega Nord to successfully increase its electoral support by connecting with both local and Italian memories of fascism and a modern, Europeanist discourse' (Doerr 2013, 7). In general terms, the symbolic expulsion of the black sheep remains the same. However, the linguistic message of the Swiss poster has also been changed: now, 'Security at home' is campaigned for, clearly insinuating the family metaphor, as 'lessons from the North'. Following the controversial success of the initial black sheep poster (Image 4.2), the SVP continued to use representations of 'criminal and dangerous foreigners' who threaten the Swiss nation/family/body and who, accordingly, should be not allowed to enter the country or be deported in case these foreigners do not accommodate to Swiss legislation (see Chapter 7).

VIGNETTE 8
BRITISH MAINSTREAM DISCOURSES –
'THEY DON'T BELONG TO US'

Here I analyse aspects of official British politics concerning migrants and immigration during the financial crisis of 2008 and its aftermath, thus illustrating the attempts to accommodate populist right-wing rhetoric demanding to 'Keep them out!'. The British

(Continued)

(Continued)

Prime Minister David Cameron's address to the British Conservative Party on 14 April 2011 was dedicated to the so-called 'immigration problem':

Text 4.3

'That's not to say migration from Europe has been insignificant. Since 2004, when many large eastern European countries joined the EU, more than one million people from those countries have come to live and work in the UK – a huge number. We said back then that transitional controls should have been put in place to restrict the numbers coming over. And now we're in government, if and when new countries join the European Union, transitional controls will be put in place. But this remains the fact: when it comes to immigration to our country, it's the numbers from outside the EU that really matter. In the year up to June 2010, net migration from nationals of countries outside the EU to the UK totalled 198,000. This is the figure we can more easily control and should control.'[13]

Cameron's speech, not surprisingly, makes reference to the migration of a vague number of European citizens, and especially citizens of Eastern European countries. He underlines the 'huge number [one million people] who came to live and work in the UK' and the importance of transnational controls, thus of border politics. Hence, he emphasizes issues of security and represents Eastern Europeans (who, of course, are also EU citizens) as a huge problem within Europe. This argument is developed on the basis of the *topos of internal threat*, which is based on the conditional: 'If immigration from Europe is a threat against the UK, then the British government should control it.'

Later on, Cameron explains that 'it's the numbers from outside the EU that really matter' and only then restores the opposition between Europeans and non-Europeans supported by the *topos of threat*. In Cameron's speech, three different social actors are constructed and represented: the British government, migrants within Europe and non-European migrants. The role of the government is elaborated by the *topos of responsibility*, which is based on the conditional: 'If the British government is responsible for its people (i.e. the family), then it should control immigration.' Moreover, Cameron highlights the numbers of immigrants and at this point triggers an intensification of fear that is related to the *topos of threat*.

Cameron's warnings resonated well with the British public: therefore, during the continuing financial crisis in 2012, when reports from the European Commission[14] illustrated that the financial and social crisis had destabilized the Greek social structure and created a new generation of middle-class, well-educated Greek migrants (who are, of course, EU citizens), the British conservative newspaper the *Telegraph* interviewed the Home Secretary Theresa May (Winnett and Kirkup 2012); she referred to the arrival of Greek migrants in the UK, thus obviously and intentionally neglecting the fact that Greece is still a member of the EU and will likely remain so, and that Greeks are thus EU-citizens as well as Europeans. Therefore, the EU's principle of free mobility for citizens of EU member states (freedom of movement) is valid.[15]

Indeed, Greek citizens are suddenly transformed into post-modern strangers, as acutely defined by Bauman (1995, 2–3). Zygmunt Bauman distinguishes between two strategies of modern and post-modern societies to cope with strangers. The first consists of 'devouring them', that is, swallowing them and making them indistinguishable from oneself, in other words, assimilating them. The second strategy implies exclusion or 'vomiting the strangers', making them invisible, by locking them into ghettos or removing them from one's territory. These metaphors are related to body politics, that is, imagining a human being when eating and digesting food. It seems to be the case that current immigration policies continue to oscillate between these two extremes. Specifically, the editor of the newspaper mentioned that '[t]he Government is drawing up plans for emergency immigration controls to curb an influx of Greeks and other European Union residents if the euro collapses, the Home Secretary discloses today' (Winnett and Kirkup 2012). The phrase 'emergency immigration controls' implies that the Greek migrants will be very dangerous and that, therefore, control systems are necessary and urgent. Three *topoi* are employed in this argumentation: the *topos of threat* and the *topos of urgency*, combined with the *topos of responsibility* (here, of the government to protect British citizens).

The editor then quoted May's arguments:

Text 4.4

'But *Mrs May* said the Government was "looking at the trends" on immigration from struggling European economies. She said there was no evidence of increased migration at present, adding that it was "difficult to say how it is going to develop in coming weeks". Asked whether emergency immigration controls are under consideration, Mrs May said: "It is right that we do some contingency planning on this (and) that is work that is ongoing." Mrs May suggested that the "abuse" of freedom of movement within the EU more generally was under consideration.'

Here, the newspaper focuses on the immediate threat of immigration within the EU, and especially from Greece, because of the financial crisis; moreover, the expression "*abuse*" of freedom of movement' insinuates illegality. By stating that '[t]he Government is drawing up plans for emergency immigration controls to curb an influx of Greeks and other EU residents', she points to an undefined and unpredictable, vague number of potential immigrants and underlines the necessity for 'emergency immigration controls'. The British Home Secretary confirms these concerns when she mentions that it is difficult to say how migration is going to develop in the coming weeks. Hence, this rhetoric is based on the *topos of internal threat* and constructs a distinction between the UK and the 'struggling European economies', clearly implying that the UK is not a struggling economy (see Wodak and Boukala 2015). She also adds that 'emergency immigration controls and the freedom of movement within the EU are under consideration' and emphasizes the necessity of a 'Fortress Europe', while at the same time presenting the British government as the guarantor of national security via the *topos of responsibility*. While the political situation in Greece remained unstable and the country proceeded to a second election (17 June 2012), the British Prime Minister, fearing Greece's possible exit from the Eurozone, declared in a statement to the cross party House of Commons liaison committee on 3 July 2012:[16]

Text 4.5

'Britain is prepared to take measures to avoid a major influx of Greek citizens. I would be prepared to do whatever it takes to keep our country safe, to keep our banking system strong, to keep our economy robust. At the end of the day, as prime minister, that is your first and foremost duty.'[17]

(Continued)

(Continued)

In this statement, the Greeks are clearly and explicitly represented as dangerous migrants who threaten the stability of the UK, the collocation 'major influx of Greek citizens' is repeated. This claim is further elaborated by the *topos of internal threat*. Moreover, Cameron emphasizes the danger presented by the *Greek Other* and underlines his role as Prime Minister via the *topos of responsibility*. Cameron anthropomorphises the country and the banking system, and constructs a Manichean dichotomy in the opposition between a British 'Us' and the Greek migrants' economy, presenting himself as the saviour of the nation who will 'do whatever it takes' to protect Britain. This text illustrates well how European allies are suddenly transformed into 'Others', that is, strangers, in moments of crisis, also by mainstream parties and not only by right-wing populist politicians (Triandafyllidou et al. 2009; Wodak and Boukala 2015). Needless to state that since 2012 and the success of the UK Independence Party (UKIP) in the 2014 European Parliament elections, Cameron's appeals to change the EU's principle of freedom of movement and related legislation on benefits resonate more and more among the British public (Ford and Goodwin 2014).[18]

VIGNETTE 9
NORMALIZATION OF EXCLUSION: ASKING 'ILLEGAL MIGRANTS TO LEAVE'

As a pilot project, on 22 July 2013, vans were driven through the streets of especially multicultural parts of London, carrying large posters calling on illegal migrants to turn themselves in to the police voluntarily in order to be returned home (outside the country) without cost (see Image 4.5). Failure to do so, the posters said, would lead to arrest or detention. At the same time, policemen were arbitrarily conducting identity checks on people of colour and demanded to see their residence permits; in many cases, as might be expected, these were British citizens or citizens of EU member states. It is evident that such measures are, in fact, very useful means of fear-mongering; and it comes as no surprise when, at the same time, they are seen as a rather clumsy and blunt attempt to curry favour with the xenophobic UKIP (or its voters). Even Nigel Farage, party leader of UKIP, saw this project as a clumsy move on the Conservative government's part and thus exposed it as such.

But who are the thus invoked 'illegal migrants'? In a recent study on the representation of refugees, asylum seekers and migrants (abbreviated as RASIM) in British newspapers over 10 years (1996–2006), we were able to provide evidence that the concepts of migrants, refugees and asylum seekers are merged into one large category of 'Others', that is, strangers, in media reporting including both tabloids and quality newspapers (although less so in the latter) (Baker et al. 2008). KhosraviNik concludes in his summary of findings that in general,

> [t]he tabloids [...] construct a very sharp 'Us' vs. 'Them' categorisation. This process, in effect, constructs a 'panic' state of affairs among its readership, legitimising and urging them to take on a more active role within this (constructed) 'stand-off' while at the same time, it attributes only negative evaluation to all people who are perceived as 'the other' overwhelmingly. [...] There are also noticeable discrepancies between the conservative broadsheets and tabloids in terms of the modes and degree of incorporation of different elements of perspectivisation. [...] Overall, the conservative broadsheet creates a more 'sophisticated' and probably less obviously xenophobic impression of

Image 4.5   Vans in London carrying posters of 'Operation Vaken' 2013

RASIM while the tabloid is at ease in reproducing the existing general-ambiguous prejudices and positions itself as a consumer and proliferator of the negativity. The *Guardian* and the *Observer* generally try to incorporate a wider variety of topics relevant to RASIM, while the conservative press systematically ignores almost any topics which do not fit into the macro-structure of negativisation of RASIM. The emerging pattern is that the newspapers give more space and direct quotations to an in-group member, while citations to out-group members are given only when they are (or can be represented as being) inarticulate, extremist, illogical or threatening.

(2010, 22–3)

In other words, almost all newspapers carry some degree of negativity when reporting on refugees, asylum seekers and migrants. However, tabloids do so without hedging and euphemisms, while more centre-left newspapers also refer to humanitarian crises and report individual stories of suffering. In contrast, conservative newspapers (both tabloids and broadsheets) commonly dehumanize all strangers and focus on young, non-white dangerous males by default.

These findings resonate with earlier studies on the representation of refugees and migrants such as post-1989 in Austria (Matouschek et al. 1995), where similar flooding metaphors as well as *topoi of criminality, danger and burden* were identified. Such diverse findings allow us to conclude that much discourse about migrants and immigration seems to bear (several) almost universal features, throughout Europe and beyond, which can be explained well by social theories about 'Othering' and the discursive construction of 'the stranger' and 'fear of the stranger' mentioned above. Border and identity/body politics converge to keep specific strangers out and let others in. Moreover, poor and destitute insiders are suddenly defined as strangers and also excluded (such as the Greek citizens mentioned above).

Therefore, neighbours can easily and abruptly transform into strangers, as evidenced by many historical examples such as the implementation of the Nuremberg Laws (1933),

(Continued)

(Continued)

which turned German-Jewish neighbours into unwanted 'Others', that is, Jews. Georg Simmel in his seminal book (1950) defines 'the Jew' as the prototypical stranger of modernity, as having an intrinsically different identity which could not be changed and who remained a non-member forever (see Vignette 1; Chapter 5).

Let us briefly recapitulate Operation Vaken, as the bus policy mentioned above (Image 4.5) was officially named: a premonition can probably be gleaned from listening carefully to David Cameron's speech on immigration on 25 March 2013, in which the PM explicitly talks about 'removing illegal migrants faster'.[19] The association to the house/container frame and body politics is easily established when he mentions that 'we should be showing them the door'. Only specific migrants should be welcomed, he promises, referring to the 'hardworking, wealth creators'. The *topoi of danger, burden, criminality* and *urgency* are evoked lexically and in the underlying argumentation scheme that is easy to detect. Moreover, polarization and a *reductio ad absurdum* are also evident – as if a 'red carpet' *were* extended for immigrants. The differential treatment to so-called 'wealth creators', meaning those migrants with incomes above a certain amount, fits the hegemonic neo-liberal ideology and its willingness to instrumentalize class differences whenever suitable. While political neo-liberalism may generally be anti-immigration (and creates scapegoats), other more theoretical discourse of neo-liberalism is pro-immigration (and, obviously, some of the very rich are immigrants-as-tax-exiles themselves) (Sayer 2015). Cameron therefore states:

Text 4.6

'[A]nd, once we've found them, we're going to make it easier to remove them: faster deportation; stopping the payment of legal aid for the vast majority of immigration appeals; and we're even going to look at how we can change the law so that wherever possible people are deported first and they can appeal second from their home country. Put simply, when it comes to illegal migrants, we should actually be rolling up that red carpet, and showing them the door. So, that's how we're changing immigration in this country. Getting net migration down radically. Making sure that the people who come here, wherever they come from, are coming for the right reasons. Breaking out of the old government silos and making immigration a centrepiece of our economic policy, so that we train our young people to fill more of the jobs being created in our economy with genuine incentives to work, and so we attract the hardworking, wealth creators who can help us to win in the global race.'

(Speech on 'immigration and welfare reform',
held March 25, 2013, at University Campus Suffolk, Ipswich.
Transcript of the speech as delivered)

On 22 July 2013, the operation was launched without consulting the six London councils where the buses circled. The following day, London-Brent's council member Muhammed Butt stated that he was 'horrified over government plans to drive vans through his borough with adverts calling on illegal immigrants to leave' (BBC News 2013c). Indeed, he argued that it was not the migrants' fault if their applications had not been processed yet and they were waiting for their work permits. On 29 July 2013, Downing Street issued a statement that justified this pilot project, stating that the scheme was working well. On 22 October 2013, the *Guardian* reported that Home Secretary Teresa May 'admitted that the Home Office's controversial "go home" vans had been "too much of a blunt instrument", as she confirmed they would not be extended nationwide'. She admitted that 'politicians should be willing to step up to the plate and say when they think something actually hasn't been as good an idea, and I think they were too blunt an instrument' (*Guardian* 2013). This assessment coincides with the opinion of the Liberal Democrats, the junior partner in the then Coalition: indeed, Minister Vince Cable had immediately called the pilot project 'offensive and stupid' in an interview on the Andrew Marr Show: 'It is designed, apparently, to sort of create a sense of fear [in the] British population that we have a vast problem with illegal immigration. [...] We have a problem but it's not a vast one. It's got to be dealt with in a measured way dealing with the underlying causes' (BBC News 2013d).

The Evaluation Report issued on 'Operation Vaken' in October 2013, however, stated that 60 voluntary departures had taken place and 65 further cases were being progressed to departure (Home Office 2013, 2). In a more detailed survey, the report concludes that only 11 cases (18 per cent) had chosen voluntary departure after seeing the van with its advertisement. Moreover, the evaluation report argues that such a project costs much less than an explicitly enforced removal. The enforced removal of an individual, the report states, costs up to £15,000, whereas Operation Vaken cost £9,740. Further numbers are brought into play to substantiate this argument (*topos of means*): 'As every person living illegally in the UK is estimated to cost ca. £4,250 to public services, the return of 60 people may therefore have saved an additional estimated £225,000' (ibid., 4). Numerous tables and diagrams throughout the report are meant to lend even more statistical validity to the pilot project, based on the rather small sample of 172 (a number which diverges from the official numbers mentioned above). On its very last page (28), the report mentions a further 'success', namely that the Operation Vaken team 'were contacted by 28 individuals offering to provide intelligence on illegal immigration' (ibid., 28). In other words, the operation instigated the denunciation of likely innocent people, frequently British citizens. The 'Operation Vaken affair' has a surprising coda, after it had already been stopped in 2013: on 8 February 2014, Immigration Minister Mark Harper resigned. The *Guardian* reports with some irony that[20]

Text 4.7

'[t]he immigration minister, Mark Harper, has resigned for employing an illegal immigrant as a cleaner, Downing Street said on Saturday. Number 10 said there was "no suggestion that Mr Harper knowingly employed an illegal immigrant" but the prime minister, David Cameron, had "accepted his resignation with regret". Last year Harper launched a government advertising campaign that targeted racially mixed areas with mobile billboards warning illegal immigrants to "go home or face arrest"'.

(*Guardian* 2014)

The fact that such projects and measures are being considered and implemented is not surprising. The more success attributed to the UK Independence Party (UKIP) and the more council elections and by-elections that are lost by the government and won by UKIP and other opposition parties, the more the government seems to feel pressure to outflank UKIP's policies and slogans on Euro-scepticism and immigration. Playing 'the immigration card' attracts voters. If one studies UKIP's policies, it becomes apparent that their language use does not differ much from the governmental policies and Cameron's speeches mentioned above. Indeed, the statement of principles on which detailed policies are to be based on UKIP's website mention, for example, under Point 6 and 8:

Text 4.8

6. 'Measures would be taken to identify illegal immigrants and remove them to their country of origin. Exceptions may be made in limited circumstances, but there would be no general amnesty for illegal migrants.'

8. 'UKIP would withdraw from the European Convention of Human Rights and the European Convention on Refugees. This would enable us to deport foreign criminal and terrorist suspects where desirable. UKIP would allow genuine asylum applications in accordance with our international obligations.'

(UKIP 2013b)

UKIP is regarded as a niche party on the British political party spectrum (Lynch et al. 2012, 735). Such niche parties thrive and depend on a single or, at most, two distinctive issues – in the case of UKIP, this issue is anti-immigration, necessarily coupled with Euro-scepticism inasmuch as many of their policies would be in conflict with the Convention of Human Rights and the Freedom of Movement legislation. Accommodating to the policies of UKIP and their populist agenda has become part and parcel of the Conservative–Liberal UK government's strategies, specifically of the Conservative Party. It remains to be seen if these strategies will be successful in retaining and/or attracting votes (see Chapter 2).

'Mother Tongue' and Citizenship

Bauböck and Goodman-Wallace (2012) argue that naturalization is the most debated and most densely regulated form of access to citizenship. 'Naturalization' is defined as 'any acquisition after birth of a citizenship not previously held by the person concerned that requires an application to public authorities and a decision by these' (ibid., 1).

Via naturalization regulations, the 28 member states of the EU determine who *belongs* or *does not belong* to the EU, and therefore who remains 'outside' and who is allowed to venture 'inside' Europe (i.e. the EU). But it is not only mobility and travel that are determined in this way, as belonging also implies access to work, education, housing and, importantly, citizenship rights such as participation in elections (Delanty et al. 2011; Wodak 2012, 2013c). Therefore the status of what is to be perceived as a 'real/authentic citizen' – though we might well ask by whom – is explicitly defined (ibid.): citizens are allowed to travel and move freely inside the EU, they are eligible for work, and most importantly they do not have to pass any citizenship or language tests to receive or enact these rights.

Naturalization conditions vary enormously, however: Belgium, for instance, only requires three years of residence as a precondition for ordinary naturalization, whereas Austria requires 10. Moreover, 15 countries still require renunciation of any previously held citizenship (although each of these allows for specific exceptions). Bauböck and Goodman-Wallace (2012) also provide evidence for ever more restrictive regulations: in 1998, only six states had citizenship and/or language tests; by 2010, the number had grown to 18, by 2013 to 23 (see Table 4.1; note that this table is already outdated and the situation is constantly changing).

Table 4.1 Citizenship and language requirements in selected EU countries (A = language test before entering; B = language test required for working permit; C = language test required for citizenship) (adapted from Extramiana et al. 2014)

	Language Requirement 2009	Language Requirement 2013
Austria	B, C	A, B, C
Belgium – French Community		C
Cyprus		B
Czech Republic	B, C	B, C
Denmark	A, B, C	B, C
Estonia	B, C	B, C
Finland	A, B	A, B, C
France	A, B, C	A, B, C
Germany	A, B, C	A, B, C
Greece	B, C	B, C
Italy	B, C	B
Lithuania	B, C	B, C
Luxembourg	A, B, C	A, B, C
Netherlands	A, B, C	A, B, C
Poland	C (repatriation)	C
Slovenia	B, C	C
Spain		B, C
Sweden		
United Kingdom	A, B, C	A, B, C
	A = 8	A = 7
	B = 16	B = 18
	C = 17	C = 19

Sixteen states offer naturalization to close relatives of citizens or to persons who are perceived as and acknowledged to be ethnically or linguistically related to the majority population (Bauböck and Joppke 2010; Michalowski 2011). Of course, such definitions allow for a plethora of interpretations – after all, who defines what is regarded as similar or different and on what authority? What criteria are used for comparison? How integrative or assimilationist are these new policies in the specific socio-political context? How do new regulations accommodate to, or contradict, national laws and ideological traditions (Wodak and Fairclough 2010)? And, finally, what kind of knowledge is tested – more to the point, what is conceived by whom as condensing or indicating salient knowledge of a language or of the hegemonic political and cultural knowledge of a specific country? It is important to add at this point that these requirements contradict important strategies of the EU's multilingual policies, which explicitly recommend acceptance of difference and diversity with respect to language and culture (see Ersbøll et al. 2010).

The discourse about citizenship and its related language for specific purposes constitutes new categories, new groups, new 'real' citizens and 'Other' people who are regarded as having 'deficits' of some kind. They thus construct and essentialize new realities, which will remind every sociolinguist of the rather anachronistic debates in the 1970s about 'deficit or difference', that is, polemics between theories proposed by Basil Bernstein and William Labov, respectively (see the overview in Michalowski 2011, 750–52; Wodak et al. 2010).

Goodman-Wallace refers to differences in citizenship regimes and identifies *four categories of citizenship strategy*: prohibitive, conditional, insular and enabling (2010, 755). She successfully categorizes differences among countries with citizenship tests and other integration requirements, depending on what she terms the countries' *open or closed citizenship regimes*. Countries with 'traditionally exclusive citizenship' have 'arduous or even prohibitive conditions for outsiders gaining access to membership' so as to 'preserve a concept of citizenship identity largely unaffected by post-war mass immigration' (ibid., 765). Countries with a more open citizenship regime make the concept of citizenship more coherent and meaningful through civic criteria, whereas citizenship tests in countries with closed citizenship regimes express a rather 'ethnic understanding' of the nation (ibid., 766). These concepts are certainly useful when analysing recent debates about inclusion and exclusion, about 'real citizens' or those with 'deficits', and allows/may allow a recontextualization of the concept of '*dis-citizenship*' traditionally employed in disability studies (Arneil 2009; Prince 2009; Wodak 2013c).

'Dis-citizenship' might grasp new, ideologically influenced membership categorizations concerning migrants' status as naturalized citizens of EU member states. Devlin and Pothier define *dis-citizenship* as 'citizenship minus' (2006, 2), as a form of citizenship that denies certain rights to people with disabilities, but – as I propose here – the concept can also be extended to describe the way in which migrants are not viewed as 'real' or 'authentic' citizens with full rights in a specific country. It might therefore also refer to ethnic and religious groups who are traditionally discriminated against in specific national contexts (e.g. Jews and Roma in Hungary; see Chapters 2 and 3).

Such policies give rise to polarized conflicts in many EU member states between far-right populist parties (such as the Austrian Freedom Party, the Greek Golden Dawn, the French Front National and the Hungarian Jobbik), some mainstream conservative parties (such as the Tories in the UK or the Austrian People's Party) and more progressive parties such as the Greens or the Social Democrats across the EU (Wodak et al. 2013). The latter parties endorse a more open concept of citizenship and more liberal immigration policies than the conservative and radical right-wing parties, but they do so in context-specific ways; their policies are not homogeneous because specific groups within them hold differing opinions as, for example, the trade unions in the case of the Social Democrats traditionally oppose liberal immigration regulations (see the former British Labour Party Prime Minister Gordon Brown's slogan *British Jobs for British Workers*; Richardson and Wodak 2009b).

VIGNETTE 10
'MOTHER TONGUE' AND THE 'GERMAN-ONLY POLICY'

During the campaign leading up the regional election in Vienna 2010, the Austrian People's Party (ÖVP) launched the slogan '*reden wir über bildung. am besten auf deutsch.*' ('let's talk about education. best in german.') (see Image 4.6), thus emphasizing a

'German-only policy' while ironically ignoring standard capitalization rules of German spelling. The next example illustrates how the People's Party had thus accommodated the policies of the Freedom Party (see Image 4.7): *'Deutsch statt nix versteh'n'* ('German instead of not understand', the ungrammatical construction being a deliberate slur) refers to the so-called *Gastarbeiterdeutsch* (guest-workers' German) of the 1960s, when migrants from then Yugoslavia were stereotypically represented as speaking a very restricted German, for example, always employing infinitive verbal forms.

The Austrian flag typically symbolizes the FPÖ's attempt at constructing the German language metonymically as part of being 'a true Austrian'. Image 4.8, reproduced from a comic book which may be downloaded from HC Strache's website as part of the above-mentioned campaign (obviously appealing to the young electorate), depicts the contrast between the Social Democratic Party (SPÖ) and the FPÖ. The former is metonymically represented by the current and former leaders of the SPÖ, Werner Faymann and Alfred Gusenbauer, both sweating and dressed in red, who allegedly bribe generic foreigners (here depicted without individual faces and in grey) to vote for the SPÖ and, in return, promise them citizenship. In stark contrast, the latter is metonymically represented by HC Strache transformed into 'HC-Man' (thereby insinuating superhero-like qualities) as saviour, flying in to save 'the Austrians' from foreigners who might not even know the German language. Thus, only people who speak German should be given access, but not citizenship.

Here, the role of the mother tongue is emphasized even more strongly. The comic book condenses the common-sense argumentation – only if you know German will you be allowed to enter the country legally (in contrast to the views of the SPÖ). The use of posters and comic books also illustrates the broad range of materials employed in the FPÖ's campaign and the many resources and genres addressed to many different audiences (see also Chapter 6).

Image 4.6   ÖVP poster, Vienna election campaign 2010

(Continued)

(Continued)

Image 4.7   FPÖ poster, Vienna Election Campaign 2010

Image 4.8   FPÖ comic book, Vienna election campaign 2010

The idea of using citizenship tests and other integration requirements as mechanisms for assimilation is countered by some political theorists who argue that integration requirements are an instance of political liberalism (see Michalowski 2011, 573–4). Joppke (2010), for example, has described integration requirements as a form of *repressive liberalism*. He uses the term 'repressive' because the tests are obligatory and can restrict access to citizenship and 'liberalism' because the goals pursued are those of liberalism and largely comparable with other obligatory but 'capacity-enhancing' measures proposed by some European welfare states. However, the everyday practices as described above illustrate that Joppke's approach fails to capture political realities as such regulations clearly serve a discriminating function. This function has been well described by Orgad for German citizenship tests which

> mirror not only what German culture is, but also what the Germans want it to be […]. Although the Länder tests have been replaced by a federal test, they indicate an ideological concept of Kulturnation. By adopting these policies, Germany embraces a strict rule of forced cultural assimilation.
>
> (2010, 69–70)

Many European countries are thus promoting a *(re)nationalization* in respect to language and culture – in spite of being part of the multilingual and multicultural transnational entity that is the EU. The concept of 'mother tongue' as salient prerequisite of belonging has become part and parcel of new citizenship laws, regulations and requirements, advocated or even championed not only by the far-right, but by mainstream political parties in government. Interestingly, as will be illustrated below, the concept of 'mother tongue' has, however, vanished from EU documents since approximately 2004. It seems to be the case that, on the EU level, the concept of *Staatsnation* (civic nation) is foregrounded, whereas on the national level the concept of *Kulturnation* has been (re)invented and (re)discovered (as ethnic, cultural nation; see also Musolff 2010). The 'mother tongue' as salient attribute for *the homo* and *femina nationalis* goes back to the 19th and first half of the 20th centuries.[21]

Historically, it is important to note that the conceptual history of 'mother tongue' presents relevant findings which support my argument: in the year 1119, we first encounter the notion of '*Materna lingua*' (*lingua nativa*; *lingua vernacula* versus 'Latin'), used in French to label the vernacular everyday language as opposed to the language of the elites (*Langaige maternel (françois)*; Lebsanft 2000, 9). In the 16th century, the German notion of '*Muttersprache*' as 'Language of the Germans' can be found in the meaning of vernacular, but it is only in 1782 that nation and mother tongue are inherently related (Adelung 1782). In the 19th and 20th centuries, due to rapid nationalization ideologies, the concept of 'mother tongue' becomes racialized and a nativist attribute of a/the 'pure' German (see Chamberlain's quote below). This culminates under Nazi domination, which uses the concept of '*Muttersprache*' as part of its ideology (Ahlzweig 1990, 35ff.):

> And as the German soul is inextricably bound to the German language, thus is the higher development of humanity bound to a powerful Germany, asserting the holy heritage of its language far across the Earth. (H. S. Chamberlain *Briefe 1882–1924* Munich, quoted in Townson 1992, 118)

In a strikingly similar fashion, we today find the *topos of the true Finn/Austrian/British* (i.e. if you speak the mother tongue and are born from parents who also speak this mother tongue and are Finnish/Austrian/British, then you are one of us); and the *topos of a mythical and essentialized nationhood*, such as Britishness, Finnishness or Hungarianness embedded in most populist right-wing programmes but, as illustrated above, also in conservative parties' propaganda. In other words, all Hungarians by birth and ancestry belong to our people's 'home' because they are real Hungarians (in the sense of belonging to the Hungarian *Volk*); by extension, the *topos* implies that if people behave like X and are born as X and speak X, then they embody true X/Hungarianness/Britishness/and so on. The explicitness with which such *topoi* are presented by right-wing parties is noteworthy:

> Finnishness is Finland's gift to the world and the key to success for our society.

> Basic Finnish immigration policy should be based on the fact that the Finns should always be able to decide for themselves the conditions under which a foreigner can come to our country and reside in our country.

> (Programme of the True Finns, the third largest party in the Finnish Parliament; Worth 2011 and https://www.perussuomalaiset.fi/kielisivu/in-english/; Finnish Language Policy; https://www.perussuomalaiset.fi/wp-content/uploads/2013/12/ps_language_policy.pdf; accessed 23 April 2015)

Jobbik considers its most important task to be the reunification of a Hungarian nation unjustly torn apart during the course of the 20th century. We will guarantee every Hungarian the right to Hungarian citizenship, and thus, to have their voices heard in matters concerning the national interest.

(Programme of Jobbik, Hungary's third largest party; 'closer relationships with those nations related to us by culture and descent' www.jobbik.com/foreign_affairs_policy; accessed 30 April 2014)

Many other examples could be presented and analysed here. It is obvious that we are dealing with nativist ideologies of ethnic nationhood, related to birth, blood and a mystical notion of a homogenous *demos* and history. Thus, acquiring citizenship is made into an enormous obstacle: only those who belong to 'Us' (i.e. are true Austrians, Finns, Hungarians and so forth) will be accepted. To qualify for inclusion, they must speak the mother tongue, have the right ancestry and should return to their 'fatherland'. Others might be welcome, but the decisions as well as the conditions for residence vary (see above).[22]

Endnotes

1 www.guardian.co.uk/politics/2011/apr/14/david-cameron-immigration-speech-full-text, accessed 9 June 2013.

2 This statement was issued by the Department I of Languages and Literatures of the Hungarian Academy of Sciences (HAS) concerning the 'Hungarian Language Strategy Institute' established with Government Decree No 55/2014 (III. 4.). See http://listserv.linguistlist.org/pipermail/ura-list/2014-April/001451.html and www.aitla.it/wp-content/uploads/2014/10/language-strategy-institute_hungary.pdf for more details.

3 Governmental intervention into language policy in order to 'preserve' the 'pure mother tongue', be it German, Hungarian or any other language, is part and parcel of many totalitarian regimes (e.g. Ahlzweig 1990; Blackledge 2006; Fortier 2010; Schmidt 2002; Townson 1992; Wodak and Kirsch 1995).

4 Here, I will not dwell on other approaches to the conceptual metaphor of the NATION AS BODY/FAMILY as proposed by Musolff (2010) and Hart (2010). The latter also elaborates this metaphor by integrating the concept of *blending*, i.e. blending of two conceptual metaphors – metaphor of the HOUSE and metaphor of IMMIGRATION as threatening the house. In this chapter, I focus specifically on body and border politics – this diagram thus serves heuristic functions. In Chapters 5 and 7, I also draw on body politics when discussing antisemitism, Islamophobia and sexism, i.e. gendered body politics in populist right-wing rhetoric.

5 Other scholars also use the terms 'ethno-nationalism' and 'ultra-nationalism' in this context (Rydgren 2005).

6 See Billig (1995), Boukala (2013), de Cleen (2012), Krzyżanowski (2010), Wodak (2011a) and Wodak et al. (2009).

7 The insight that discursive practices encapsulate power structures is grounded in longstanding philosophical traditions encompassing, amongst others, Foucault, Gramsci, Habermas, Laclau and Mouffe – to mention only the most prominent authors. Its conceptual premise draws on Gramsci's idea that 'culture' is the site of real political struggles and not merely their distorting mirror, as postulated by classical Marxism.

Gramsci claims that social dominance implies the capacity of the ruling class to establish its moral and intellectual leadership – i.e. its hegemony – over society, and that intellectuals (and other elites) play a salient role in this undertaking (Boukala 2013; Gramsci 1975).

8 For example, the Commission of the European Communities (CEC) and the Council of the EU focus on security measures in relation to immigration issues, determination of the external borders of the EU and in response to the 2004 terrorist attack in Madrid. See: www.statewatch.org/news/2001/nov/illimm672.pdf, accessed 12 March 2015; Council of the EU (2003); and European Commission (2004).

9 In Chapter 7, I analyse another SVP poster, launched during the referendum about banning the building of minarets in Switzerland. See the Glossary for more information about the SVP. Richardson and Colombo (2014) have also analysed the Swiss posters in detail, however without including the transnational comparative dimension.

10 See, e.g. *FAZ*, 19 October 2007; *NY Times*, 8 September 2007; *The Times*, 10 October 2007.

11 At an invited lecture at Boston University, Boston MA, on 24 February 2014, when I used this example in my lecture, I had the pleasure of talking with Nicole Doerr (of Harvard University). She told me that she was also analysing this same Swiss poster and its trajectory, albeit in a different context, completely independently of my work (Doerr 2013). We spent much time discussing this kind of visual propaganda and exchanged publications. I am very grateful to Nicole for allowing me to use the Italian version of the poster in this chapter, which I had not noticed to date; I had only found the Swiss, German and Catalan examples.

12 *NY Times*, 8 October 2007.

13 Speech available at www.theguardian.com/politics/2011/apr/14/david-cameron-immigration-speech-full-text, accessed 23 August 2014.

14 Quarterly Review on EU Employment and the Social Situation, June 2012.

15 At this point it is important to mention that Britain is not a member of the Eurozone and that, historically, British governments have not always supported the idea of European integration; indeed the Thatcher government was known for being very opposed to more integration and emphasized a fedral union with primarily economic goals. Thus, the financial crisis in Europe and especially in Greece increased the Conservative government's interest in European politics for purported reasons of national security (see also Weiss 2002; Wodak and Weiss 2004; and Wodak and Boukala 2015 for more information on this case).

16 See www.publications.parliament.uk/pa/cm201213/cmselect/cmliaisn/484/120703.htm for details.

17 See www.c-span.org/video/?306895-1/impact-european-debt-crisis-british-economy, accessed 23 August 2014.

18 See BBC report from 28 November 2014 where the British Prime Minister presents his plans to curb migration from EU member states; www.bbc.com/news/uk-politics-30224493, accessed 16 December 2014.

19 See www.gov.uk/government/speeches/david-camerons-immigration-speech, accessed 29 April 2014.

20 See www.theguardian.com/uk-news/2014/feb/08/immigration-minister-resigns-illegal-immigrant-mark-harper, accessed 29 April 2014.

21 It is important to emphasize that the status of the required language might differ: English and French (and to a lesser degree German) are hegemonic in the EU, although

EU multilingualism strategies propose that all national languages of EU member states are equal (Krzyżanowski and Wodak 2011). Nevertheless, English and French (and Spanish) are used globally much more than e.g. Hungarian, Dutch, Greek or Finnish. Obstacles to immigration thus differ in respect to immigrants from former British or French colonies, who necessarily know and speak English or French (or some variety of these languages).

22　The new brochure on the Austrian citizenship test (*Staatsbürgerschaftsbroschüre*) contains the amendments to the new Austrian citizenship law and tries to make the questions posed in the citizenship test and other formalities and obstacles more comprehensible and accessible to applicants with first languages other than German (see also Wodak 2013c).

5 ANTISEMITISM: THE POLITICS OF DENIAL

'To deny the issue of antisemitism in Europe on the grounds that Europe has learned the lesson from the Holocaust, or to deny the issue of antisemitism on the left on the grounds that the left is inherently anti-racist, or to deny the issue of antisemitism within radical Islam on the grounds that Muslims are oppressed within Europe and have a history of tolerance, is in every case a kind of closure, a refusal to engage critically with the legacies of European, left and Muslim antisemitism.'

Robert Fine (2009, 477)

Jews as Eternal Scapegoats[1]

It is terrible and telling that a book on right-wing populism in the 21st century still has to include this topic. Many readers might be inclined to believe that antisemitism has vanished from the political arena and has become a 'dead prejudice'. Or that anti-Muslim beliefs and Islamophobia have more or less completely replaced antisemitism and that antisemitic beliefs have thus been marginalized. However, when following political debates in the East and West, it is obvious that we are still confronted with massive prejudices directed against Jews as a homogenous group, in many forms and realizations. Antisemitism still occurs in various contexts, for example, in the public sphere and anonymously in online postings. Both antisemitism and Islamophobia can also appear together, as recent public debates about banning Halal and circumcision in Austria, Germany and France illustrate.[2]

There is always a specific history and context to be considered and accounted for when investigating prejudiced beliefs and ideologies. They sometimes appear simultaneously, and sometimes one specific type of prejudice is foregrounded. Any prejudice is, and this has to be emphasized, always irrational, always cloaked in a fallacious generalization of specific (frequently biological) attributes projected onto a group that is imagined as homogenous – be it an ethnic, religious or sexual minority.

Closely related to the expression of antisemitic beliefs in public are denials and disclaimers. This phenomenon can be easily explained: due to the Shoah and the horrific war crimes committed in World War II, a taboo surrounds explicit antisemitic rhetoric in public. Thus, when uttering negative prejudices about Jews as a group, speakers choose a coded rhetoric, frequently introduced by stating that 'their best friends are Jewish' or 'that they have nothing against Jews' and so forth.

After some theoretical observations about the (re)occurrence of antisemitism in Europe and beyond, I present a definition of antisemitic beliefs and rhetoric as well as related strategies of denial. Examples of recent developments in political discourse, as discussed in previous chapters, show that the issue is pertinent to this book: the Hungarian Jobbik, the Greek Golden Dawn, the French Front National (particularly under Jean-Marie Le Pen), the Austrian FPÖ, the British BNP and the Polish PiS, amongst many other right-wing populist parties, manifest explicit and coded antisemitic beliefs in context-dependent ways, mostly related to fascist and national-socialist or religious historical traditions of the respective parties and countries. Furthermore, I argue that antisemitic rhetoric has persevered, even after World War II and the Shoah, albeit frequently but not necessarily in coded forms due to both legal regulations prohibiting hate incitement and the denial of the Holocaust in several EU member states. I will also discuss a notable tension between regulations prohibiting hate incitement and Holocaust denial, and laws allowing 'freedom of speech' in many countries, such as Sweden, Denmark, the UK and the US.[3] Finally, in two vignettes, I focus on just one form of antisemitic prejudice – the most extreme – that is, Holocaust denial, which has become characteristic of some right-wing populist and extreme right-wing parties.[4]

Returning to the Facebook Incident

In Chapter 1, I presented the debate over an antisemitic caricature posted on Facebook by the leader of the Austrian Freedom Party (FPÖ), HC Strache, as an example of the *politics of denial* (Vignette 1). In the extracts of the subsequent television interview between the anchor-man of the Austrian public broadcasting service ORF and Strache, several disclaimers and discursive strategies of denial could be observed. First, Strache insisted that because he had 'some Israeli friends' nobody could possibly accuse him of being antisemitic – a typical disclaimer in discriminatory discourse (a goal-denial). Second, he claimed that not he but somebody else had distorted the previous American caricature, thus fallaciously shifting the blame, a good example of control-denial. Third, he denied recognizing the Star of David on the cufflinks of the banker, portrayed as a Jew via stereotypical antisemitic characteristics such as the hooked nose, although the Star of David was recognizable to everybody else, thus performing an act-denial. Denying the obvious and evading all rules of cooperativeness are part and parcel of right-wing populist rhetoric as elaborated in Chapter 3. At this point, HC Strache argued with the *topos of definition*: 'If I, HC Strache, define this as X, then this is X (and not Y)'. Fourth, he claimed that a conspiracy of political opponents was behind the accusations against him and 'hunting' him down, thus constructing himself as the victim of a dangerous conspiracy, which is another typical justificatory strategy of right-wing populist rhetoric and an inherent part of the right-wing populist *perpetuum mobile* as described in Chapter 1. The politics of denial seem to have worked well in this particular case: HC Strache was subsequently declared innocent of having explicitly contributed to hate incitement by the then Minister of Justice, Beatrix Karl. She claimed that the employed stereotypes were not antisemitic as they did not target *all* Jews – a noteworthy and peculiar *topos of definition* in itself (see also Chapter 8).

As apparent from various examples in the preceding chapters (Vignettes 1, 2 and 7), antisemitic stereotypes as well as latent and explicit antisemitic utterances occur continuously and systematically in many right-wing populist parties: in the FPÖ, Jobbik, the Organization of Ukrainian Nationalists (OUN) and Golden Dawn. As will be illustrated below, they also occur in the BNP. Indeed, as the Human Rights First Report (2014, 30) states, antisemitism has remained a constitutive element of neo-Nazi and right-wing populist ideologies and rhetoric across Europe, frequently alongside anti-Muslim, homophobic and antiziganist beliefs and stereotypes (Wodak and Richardson 2013).[5] This could confirm, as Stögner (2014) argues, the view put forth by Adorno et al. (1967) that we are dealing with an 'authoritarian syndrome': racism, antisemitism, xenophobia, homophobia and sexism reinforce each other and converge into one exclusionary nativist belief system.

Alarmism or Denial? The Phenomenon of Secondary Antisemitism

The reoccurring antisemitic activities across Europe contradict scholars who claim that Islamophobia has replaced antisemitism in Europe in the 21st century and that antisemitism consequently has to be considered an ideology of the past. The sociologist Robert Fine (2009) provides an extensive summary of the debate between so-called 'alarmists' and so-called 'deniers'. Alarmists, he maintains, view antisemitism as an immutable element of European history; the deniers, however, challenge the salience of any current antisemitic manifestations. Both sides primarily disagree in their assessment of the Israeli–Palestinian conflict and how critique directed towards the Israeli government should be perceived (ibid., 465ff.; Bunzl 2007): alarmists usually perceive critique of Israeli activities against Palestinians as antisemitic, whereas the deniers argue that any critique against Israeli policies is justified. This strict opposition seems to leave no space for any differentiated views and opinions about this complex conflict and its history or, for that matter, about any specific related context-dependent utterance – the debate is polarized into two extremes. Of course, criticism of Israel and Israeli actions can be uttered in an antisemitic way, but it need not be. At the same time, however, it is equally fallacious to assume that Israel or the Israelis would all endorse the same opinion, that is, to presuppose that Israel is a homogenous nation and not divided into many political parties or other political movements and groups endorsing many different views.

Such Manichean divisions are never fruitful for rational discussion – many exaggerations and fallacious arguments occur in such polarized debates. Both sides provide new versions of past events, their narratives of 'what really happened', and frequently employ the *post hoc propter hoc* fallacy, claiming causality for very complex interdependent phenomena.

Soon after the end of World War II, Adorno (1963) coined the term 'secondary antisemitism' (see also Kovács 2010) in order to address public opinions present in post-war Germany, which claimed that the Jews were exploiting Germany's guilt over the Holocaust. In many antisemitic instances, analysed in this book, we are dealing with secondary antisemitism (e.g. Vignette 6). Usually, justifications and denials when being accused of antisemitic beliefs or utterances abound in political debates and in the media, as illustrated in Vignette 1, typically as elements of blame avoidance (Hansson 2015; Wodak et al. 1990). Victim–perpetrator reversals frequently occur as well, as is visible in Vignette 6, specifically when Jews are (again) instrumentalized as scapegoats for common woes. In a nutshell, as the historian Tony Judt states, 'what is truly awful about the destruction of the Jews is not that it mattered so much, but that it mattered so little' (2008, 14). In other words, no or few lessons were learnt from the past. This is why, as Fine (2009, 476) argues, it is necessary to trace and deconstruct new forms of expressing and representing antisemitic (and all other racist and xenophobic) beliefs. As the open, explicit expression of antisemitic prejudice has been tabooed in many Western European countries since the Holocaust (but not in the former

Eastern Bloc countries; see Chapter 8), indirect, subtle and coded prejudicial discourses about Jews have emerged. These have to be carefully analysed in order to uncover whether this is 'old wine in new bottles'.

Consequently, antisemitism in post-war (Western) Europe, specifically in countries with a fascist and national-socialist past, must therefore be viewed primarily in relation to the various ways employed in dealing with alleged or real guilt, with alleged or actual accusations about the Nazi and fascist pasts. Discursive manifestations may be found not only in the large, traditional reservoir of antisemitic prejudice and in a general discourse of collective experiences and attitudes, but in several new *topoi* as well. The forms of expression chosen vary significantly: they may be manifest or latent, explicit or very indirect. But each and every one appears to be embedded in a *discourse of justification* (see also Wodak 2011c; Wodak et al. 1990).

Defining Antisemitic Rhetoric: The *'Iudeus ex machina'* Strategy

Syncretic Antisemitism

It is important to emphasize that 'antisemitic language behaviour' may imply explicitly held and/or articulated hostility towards Jews, but it necessarily implies the presence of prejudicial assumptions about 'the Jews' as a group. For example, the slogan 'Kill Jews' painted on the Sigmund Freud monument in Vienna in 1988 clearly does contain an explicit, albeit anonymous, imperative call for the most hostile of actions against Jews. On the other hand, a Jewish joke, which can have various meanings depending on the setting, the participants and the function of the utterance, also forms part of what we term 'antisemitic language behaviour', but only in circumstances where the joke expresses anti-Jewish prejudices (Wodak et al. 1990). Thus, analysing the context of an utterance is indispensable in determining whether an utterance expresses antisemitic prejudice or not. Which antisemitic contents are expressed depends, among other things, on the setting (public, private or media), the formality of the situation, the participants, the topic and the presence or absence of Jews. Antisemitic language behaviour, moreover, covers a wide range of speech acts, ranging from explicit remarks or appeals for action to mere allusions. Antisemitic language behaviour includes all levels of language, from text or discourse to the individual word or even sounds, for example, the Yiddish intonation of certain words or phrases, when used in derogatory ways.

Ideally, the systematic in-depth linguistic analysis of hate speech and antisemitic utterances of Holocaust denial should, according to the DHA (see Chapter 3), draw on:

- historical analysis of antisemitism and its verbal expressions (i.e. 'coded language');
- socio-cognitive analysis of collective memories and frames guiding the acquisition of specific knowledge so as to be able to understand 'coded language';
- socio-political analysis of ongoing debates and political parties taking part in them – these two dimensions form the broad context;
- genre theory, considering, for example, the functions of television interviews and television discussions (persuasive strategies, positive self-presentation/negative other-presentation, populist rhetoric etc.);

- the setting, speakers and so on of specific utterances, that is, the narrow context;

- the co-text of each utterance;

- and, finally, verbal expressions have to be analysed in terms of linguistics, that is, pragmatic and/or grammatical theories (presuppositions, insinuations, implications etc. as characteristics of specific 'coded antisemitism').[6]

As Jews are perceived as the universal and ultimate evil in such antisemitic rhetoric, contradicting moments can be combined within one argument, in the sense of what I suggest labelling as the '*Iudeus ex machina*' strategy – it allows all antisemitic stereotypes to work together whenever needed and can be functionalized for political ends, even when individual arguments are in contradiction of each other (Wodak 1989). There is, of course, a whole range of stereotypes that combine nationalism and antisemitism, their core meaning being that Jews are not trustworthy in terms of their commitment to any nation state despite being citizens. Other roots of antisemitism lie in Christian religion, where Jews are considered to be the murderers of Christ (Wodak et al. 1990). Nowadays, the various roots of antisemitism (drawing on nationalist, religious and racist ideologies) are usually merged into what I call '*syncretic antisemitism*'. This implies that any traditional stereotype can be evoked when useful for political debates, thus employing the *Iudeus ex machina* strategy.

Some Antisemitic Stereotypes

The accusation of Jews being untrustworthy clearly stands in the tradition of an ancient antisemitic trope: 'Ahasver, the eternally wandering Jew.' This myth, reaching back into the 13th century, has been a core element of Christian Jew hatred since the 17th century and was placed at the centre of national-socialist antisemitic propaganda (see Körte and Stockhammer 1995). In the 19th century, when European nation states were established, the lack of a homeland is reinterpreted as rootlessness; forced exclusion from European societies is turned into an essential and essentialized Jewish characteristic. The effect of this prejudice is to suspect Jews of not being fully reliable with regard to their loyalty to the nation state, thereby subtly drawing on the Christian myth that Jesus Christ allegedly damned Ahasver to eternal wanderings because of his disloyalty. Denied the capability of building an 'authentic' nation in the modern sense, Jews were regularly regarded as aliens, and sometimes as 'parasites', within nations (Musolff 2010). Thus, Jews were vulnerable to being viewed as cosmopolitan 'anti-nationalists'. The figure of the anti-national Jew was therefore also used as a projection surface for the unacknowledged uncertainties, fragilities and antagonisms of the modern nation state – which resonates with the right-wing populist imaginary of a homogenous nation state as elaborated in Chapters 1, 2 and 4.

Furthermore, in antisemitic prejudice, Jews are usually viewed as overstated intellectuals, as people who would live in their books rather than the 'real world', thus having no real home country and not being part of a nation. The critical element in the spirit ascribed to the Jews is connected to social mobility and thus has a strong connotation with the age of emancipation. Anti-intellectualism goes hand in hand with the particular *fin de siècle* ideology of authenticity. This ideology, drawing on social and political movements like the youth movement and inspired by philosophy of life in the *fin de siècle*, is connected to a conservative, even reactionary, critique of economy, anti-urbanism and nationalism. Modest and straightforward behaviour and thinking, practicality, wholeness and unity are some major features of this ideology, which by definition excludes Jews (Stögner 2014, Stögner and Wodak 2014).

Closely related to the two stereotypes of the 'anti-national' and the 'intellectual Jew' is the antisemitic image of the 'Jewish Bolshevik', which has its origins in the Russian civil war. Jews were, for example, accused of (being responsible for) the murder of the Tsarist family by the opponents of the revolution. These accusations were the onset of horrible pogroms with more than 100,000 Jewish victims (Pipes 1997). After World War I, this stereotype spread to the West, including Germany, the UK and the US, and became an important component of ideologies concerning an alleged 'Jewish world conspiracy'. The stereotype of the 'Jewish Bolshevik' was also important in national-socialist ideology (Musolff 2010), where it was paradoxically combined with anti-liberalism and ostensibly anti-capitalist rhetoric. While this might seem contradictory at first glance, it turns out to be another manifestation of antisemitism as an ideological syndrome, as a world-view, characterized by a combination of contradictory elements, that is, *syncretic antisemitism*. Thus, in this form of antisemitism, Jews are viewed as evil (finance) capitalists *and* as representing bolshevism – and these motives do not so much compete against each other as combine (Stögner and Wodak 2014, 2015). This trope was massively employed – as illustrated in Chapter 1 – during the financial crisis of 2008: Jews are thus portrayed as guilty of all common woes.

Strategies of Blaming and Denying

Teun van Dijk describes the strategies of denying racism in great detail (1992, 89ff.; e.g. Chapter 3). He claims that

[o]ne of the crucial properties of contemporary racism is its denial, typically illustrated in such well-known disclaimers as 'I have nothing against blacks, but ...' [....] The guiding idea behind this research is that ethnic and racial prejudices are prominently acquired and shared within the white dominant group through everyday conversation and institutional text and talk. Such discourse serves to express, convey, legitimate or indeed conceal or deny such negative ethnic attitudes.

(ibid., 87–8)

Van Dijk's insights remain relevant to this day, as already discussed in Chapter 3. They are also relevant for antisemitic rhetoric where more motives converge when denying anti-Jewish beliefs. Indeed, T.W. Adorno in his seminal 1959 lecture '*Was bedeutet Aufarbeitung der Vergangenheit?*' maintained that in German (and also Austrian) discourse about the Nazi past and the Shoah, roles were reversed (Wodak 1990). Thus, Jews were causally linked to the Shoah; victims were turned in to quasi-perpetrators, that is, the Jews themselves were blamed for their suffering. Subsequently, a 'justification-discourse' evolved which projected guilt onto aggression via what Anna Freud termed 'identification with the aggressor' (Freud 1992). Wodak et al. (1990) analysed the infamous 'Waldheim Affair' in Austria, which triggered a nationalist-antisemitic rhetoric 'defending Austria and Austrians against a world conspiracy accusing them of war crimes' – as was claimed – without grounds. The analysis revealed a range of discursive strategies of 'blaming and denying/justifying' when antisemitism and the Shoah were mentioned in public (Wodak 2006). Denials abounded, usually introduced by disclaimers such as 'I have many Jewish friends, but ...'. Singular incidents and unique bad experiences (real or fictional) with a Jewish person were fallaciously generalized onto the entire group, whereas good experiences were usually framed as an exception. Similar strategies and dynamics could be observed in many other cases where war crimes committed during World War II were debated in the public sphere (Heer et al. 2008; Wodak and de Cillia 2007; Wodak et al. 1994). Frequently, these justificatory strategies led to 'secondary anti-semitism' as already mentioned above. In short, a no-win situation was created where Jews were either constructed as guilty of the Shoah in the first place or as subsequently exploiting history for their interests, whenever the terrible past was mentioned.

In Chapter 3, I presented many discursive strategies as well as cognitive frames and argumentation schemes related to the dynamic of blaming, denying, justifying and legiti-mizing, which I do not want to repeat here in full. Below, I summarize the most important strategies and patterns that occur in the antisemitic justification discourse summarized above (e.g. Angouri and Wodak 2014; Wodak 2006):

1. The first three strategies *negate the very context of the occurrence of antisem-itism*, at least at the explicit level (i.e. act-denial): (i) this occurs everywhere (equation); all countries, all wars are the same (fallacious generalization; *tu quoque*); or (ii) claiming ignorance combined with a refusal to take a stance; or (iii) individuals claiming victimhood for themselves or for the entire country, thus shifting the blame to others.

2. The second major strategy raises the discussion to a more general level. Using the *strategy of scientific rationalization*, some people launch into extensive analyses of pre-war Germany, discussions about the past, debates about Israel and so forth. Many utterances make use of arguments embedded in a *topos of history*, drawing on collective memories and fallaciously equating the context of World War II and war crimes with current contexts. Such narratives, for example, might serve as justifica-tion for the re-emergence of the Golden Dawn as a necessary consequence of Greek history and a predictable, thus justifiable, response to crisis management (Angouri and Wodak 2014).

3. The third macro-strategy consists of *positive self-presentation*: the speaker narrates stories which portray him/her as having performed 'good and praiseworthy deeds', of helping those in need whenever possible. Speakers maintain to have acted respon-sibly so that they are morally without blame. This strategy can be further developed as: (i) trying to understand what happened; or (ii) trying to justify and/or deny the existence of 'problems' triggered by the rise of the right-wing and so forth.

4. The fourth macro-strategy serves to *relativize the facts*: people using this strategy will (i) start to enumerate similar problems and occurrences in other nations (bal-ancing, equating); or (ii) adopt further strategies seeking to provide *a (pseudo-) rational causal explanation* for the specific incident (e.g. fallaciously blaming the victims); or (iii) employ the '*Not we, but them*' strategy, which attributes the specific utterance to somebody else, another typical fallacy of shifting blame; or (iv) simply deny the fact that the Shoah happened at all (act-denial) and attribute such 'narra-tives or reports' to some kind of international (frequently Jewish) conspiracy. This final strategy constitutes Holocaust denial.

Holocaust Denial

Hate Incitement and Freedom of Speech

Article 4 of the *International Convention on the Elimination of all Forms of Racial Discrimination* (ICERD 1969) condemns all propaganda and organizations that attempt to justify or legitimize discrimination or are based on the idea of racial supremacy. The ICERD obliges parties 'with due regard to the principles embodied in the Universal Declaration of Human Rights' to adopt 'immediate and positive measures' to eradicate these forms of incitement and discrimination. Moreover, it obliges parties to '*criminalise hate speech, hate crimes and the financing of racist activities*', and to prohibit and criminalize membership of organizations that 'promote and incite' racial discrimination.

In line with various constitutional rights which guarantee 'free speech', a number of countries and parties have expressed reservations about this article, arguing that such a regulation would infringe on freedoms of speech, association or assembly. Accordingly, the ICERD has frequently and repeatedly criticized parties for failing to abide by it and views the provisions as necessary to prevent organized racial violence or 'discrimination on grounds of racial or ethnic origin' (European Commission, COM 2014/2, 2).[7]

From a linguistic and pragmatic-rhetorical point of view, it is apparent that no linguistic indicators are explicitly presented in the various international and national conventions and laws which cover detecting and substantiating allegations of hate speech occurrences. Indeed, this is impossible: first, because languages offer strikingly different resources to effectuate racist, antisemitic and xenophobic prejudices, which are furthermore context-dependent and frequently uttered indirectly; and, second, because explicit manifestations of racist and antisemitic attitudes are taboo in many countries post-World War II and the Holocaust, after the staggering number and scope of war crimes and mass murders committed as well as the high levels of institutional racism and discrimination implemented. But hate speech continues to exist, both globally and locally, and is still functionalized for political ends.[8] Hate speech can but does not necessarily have to lead to violent and physical acts as, inter alia, the socio-psychologist Gordon Allport evidenced in his seminal book *The Nature of Prejudice* (1979). Therefore it seems both timely and relevant to focus on the range of linguistic, pragmatic and rhetorical devices and argumentation schemes employed in different cultural and sociopolitical contexts which convey such agonistic and exclusionary meanings.[9]

Defining Holocaust Denial

In Austria, Holocaust denial is defined as the (fallacious) claim that the mainstream historical accounts of the Holocaust are either highly exaggerated or wrong, whereas historians, experts and witnesses almost universally regard Holocaust denial as untrue and the expression of antisemitic hate speech (Shermer and Grobman 2000, 3). Usually, Holocaust deniers emphasize that they do not deny per se that Jews, Roma, disabled people, homosexuals and political opponents were persecuted under the Nazi regime; they also usually do not deny that Jews were deprived of civil rights or that Jewish ghettos or concentration camps existed. And they normally admit that Jews died for a great number of reasons. But they *do* deny that there were mass murders; and they provide many fallacious arguments concerning the number of victims and the specific means of death, particularly related to the gas chambers and crematoria. Holocaust denials are frequently disguised as legitimate challenges to hegemonic historical theories and established facts; moreover, typically, such utterances appeal to freedom of opinion and freedom of speech, as realized in seemingly naive rhetorical questions such as 'Why cannot one (re)investigate the ...?' and demands like 'It must be possible/admissible to investigate ...'.

At this point, it is important to briefly discuss the dimensions of freedom of speech: freedom of speech is covered in Article 19 of the *Universal Declaration of Human Rights*, adopted in 1948: 'Everyone has the right to freedom of opinion and expression; this right includes freedom to hold opinions without interference and to seek, receive and impart information and ideas through any media and regardless of frontiers' (United Nations 1948). The right to freedom of speech, however, is also subject to limitations, as with libel, slander, obscenity, sedition (including e.g. inciting ethnic hatred), copyright violation, revelation of information that is classified or otherwise. For example, freedom of speech may be legally curtailed where it is found to cause religious or racial offence, such as by the Racial and Religious Hatred Act 2006 in the UK.[10]

In many countries, Holocaust denial is regarded as a criminal offence, for example in Austria, France, Germany, Israel, Belgium, Poland, Lithuania and Switzerland, and punishable by fines and/or jail sentences (see Engel and Wodak 2013). Because of such pending sanctions, denials of the Holocaust – an extreme case of hate speech – are usually uttered indirectly in order to allow the speaker to deny allegations of having committed a criminal offence.[11] This is why a critical discourse-analytic perspective is expedient, as it facilitates deconstructing 'the unsayable' when it occurs in official settings, in the media or on the frontstage in politics.

Below, I provide two recent examples of 'saying the unsayable' as vignettes: the first occurred during the election campaign for the Austrian presidency in spring 2010 and concerns specific utterances made by the presidential candidate of the Austrian Freedom Party (FPÖ), Barbara Rosenkranz. The second occurred during a discussion on the prominent BBC1 television programme *Question Time*, in the UK, in October 2009, when the leader of the British National Party (BNP), Nick Griffin, was invited as a discussant on the panel, the first time a member of the BNP had officially been invited to participate. Both parties, FPÖ and BNP, are well-known for their traditional racist and antisemitic beliefs, which continue to appear in various contexts in more or less implicit or explicit ways. In Austria, Holocaust denial is criminalized, a law which is justified by the national-socialist past of many Austrian perpetrators during World War II; in the UK such criminalization does not exist in the same way, as freedom of speech is regarded very highly and institutionalized differently.

The two incidents are quite similar as both protagonists, Rosenkranz and Griffin, breached taboos by insinuating Holocaust denial during television appearances. However, their status differs significantly: in the Austrian case, we are dealing with an official candidate for federal president of the Republic. In the British case, the scandal was already initiated by inviting Nick Griffin to a prominent BBC television show, which – as alleged by many politicians and journalists alike – constitutes a transgression and violation of a *cordon sanitaire*, that is, a 'red line' never to allow members of the BNP space on such programmes. Analysing the unfolding interactions and interdependencies between politics and media is thus, in both cases, at the centre of the following vignettes, though in different historical, media, legal and political contexts.

The Austrian Case[12]

The *Verbotsgesetz*

Central to this case is the complex history of Austrian de-nazification, and particularly the '*Verbotsgesetz*', a body of post-war legislation in Austria known simply as '*the prohibition law*', which effectively prohibits the glorification, mystification or denial of national-socialist crimes. De-nazification measures were passed in the immediate aftermath of World War II, on 8 May 1945, and were reformulated in 1947. The laws forbid, among other things, any National Socialism-related activity. De-nazification measures also required the registration of all NSDAP, SS and SA members, the payment of fines and participation in reconstruction works projects. Moreover, former Nazis were barred from public sector employment as well as from high-level private sector positions. However, in 1957, follow-ing an amnesty, many of the more punitive measures were lifted. As already mentioned above, in many other European countries there have been significant controversies around the *Verbotsgesetz*, most notably in its relationship to freedom of speech.[13] The European Court of Human Rights has, however, consistently rejected any claims against the law, argu-ing that it 'can be justified as necessary in a democratic society in the interest of national security and territorial integrity as well as for the prevention of crime'.[14]

The most relevant part of the *Verbotsgesetz*, §3, has been repeatedly amended since 1945 – most recently in 1992 – and presently states that 'even outside of these orga-nizations, no one may be active for the NSDAP or its aims in any form'. While §3a to §3f focus primarily on the re-establishment of organizations that disseminate National Socialist propaganda, or the dissemination of such materials in print or similar means, §3g states that:

Anyone who becomes active in the National Socialist sense in ways other than those specified in §§3a-3f – unless the offence carries a harsher sentence under other legislation – is punishable with imprisonment of one to ten years, and in case the offender is of exceptional danger of up to 20 years.

§3h of the *Verbotsgesetz*, which is most relevant in this case study, includes the following passage:

Prosecution according to §3g also applies to anyone who seeks to deny, flagrantly downplay [*gröblich verharmlost*], glorify or justify the National Socialist genocide or other National Socialist crimes against humanity in print material, a broadcast or other medium, or in any other form accessible to many people.

§3h, specifically, punishes public denial of the Holocaust, or other extreme revisionist views pertaining to national-socialist crimes.[15] The emphasis on the word 'flagrant' (*gröblich*) has in the past frequently allowed for the dismissal of Holocaust denial lawsuits, particularly against prominent individuals, since while the downplaying or mitigation of Nazi crimes could be established, these were found to be not flagrant (Wodak 2007a).

In recent years, there has been an increase in the number of trials for violations of the *Verbotsgesetz*, with 153 in 2010 (as opposed to 104 in 2009 and 17 in 2008).[16] Despite this, the number of convictions has remained relatively constant over the past years, implying that a growing number of lawsuits have been dismissed or resulted in acquittal.[17]

VIGNETTE 11
THE 'ROSENKRANZ AFFAIR'

On 28 February 2010, the leader of the Austrian Freedom Party (FPÖ), HC Strache, announced publicly that the FPÖ would nominate Barbara Rosenkranz as its presidential candidate[18] – even before the party's federal executive board had actually approved her. The rationale behind nominating a national-conservative candidate was, according to Strache, to place the so-called 'unresolved question of immigration' on the agenda ('ungelöste Zuwanderungsfrage').[19]

Barbara Rosenkranz was elected to the local Parliament of Lower Austria in 1993; she also became deputy chair of the FPÖ in the state of Lower Austria in 1996, and chaired her party group since 2000. The mother of 10 studied history and philosophy, was secretary general of the federal party from 1998 to 1999, and in 2003 was elected chair of the federal party. Between 2002 and 2008, she was a member of the Austrian Parliament. In 2007, Rosenkranz was awarded the *Decoration of Honour for Services to the Republic of Austria* (*Ehrenzeichen für Verdienste um die Republik Österreich*).[20]

Her husband, Horst Rosenkranz, is a publisher of far-right books and pamphlets and a former member of the now banned right-wing extremist National Democratic Party (NDP). She herself is the author of a book that criticizes feminism and efforts promoting gender mainstreaming (e.g. Chapter 7).[21] She opposes civil partnerships for homosexual couples because, she argues, the legal definition of marriage also includes the assumed intention to produce and raise children.[22]

Rosenkranz finally became widely known in the course of her candidacy for the Austrian presidential election in 2010. She also received significant support from the far right.[23] Most importantly, however, on 1 March 2010, Hans Dichand, owner and editor-in-chief of *Neue Kronen Zeitung* (NKZ), used his pseudonym CATO (NKZ, page 3) to announce his pro-Rosenkranz campaign in his newspaper, while stressing primarily her 'motherhood'. He thus implied that being a good mother to her children would also make her a 'good mother' to the 'Austrian family'; more generally, the praising of motherhood certainly relates to conservative and Christian family values:

Text 5.1

'A brave mother [...] A new federal president is up for election. A mother of ten children, who has already demonstrated what she is capable of in her political career, is in the running for a very high position. Let us vote for her; she will be a good president for Austria.'

On 2 March 2010, Rosenkranz was officially presented as candidate for the federal presidency by the FPÖ. In the evening news of the same day, in a radio interview (Ö1 *Morgenjournal*) on 3 March 2010, and in an interview in *Neue Kronen Zeitung* on 4 March 2010 (Text 5.2), she challenged the *Verbotsgesetz* (as she had already

(Continued)

(Continued)

done in 2006 when commenting on the so-called Gudenus affair; see Engel and Wodak 2013). Similar to Gudenus, she claimed that challenging the existence of gas chambers should fall under 'freedom of speech'.[24]

Text 5.2

Kronen Zeitung:	You have, however, repeatedly demanded that the *Verbotsgesetz* should be repealed?
Rosenkranz:	This is a question of freedom of speech: If one is in favour of this, one has to allow opinions to be voiced that one finds wrong, absurd or repulsive.
Kronen Zeitung:	Should Holocaust denial be permitted?
Rosenkranz:	I have repeatedly taken a stand on this issue. Laws against defamation and libel exist, and these of course keep freedom of speech within the bounds of civilized cooperation.

In this way, Rosenkranz draws on the *topos of freedom of speech* ('if freedom of speech exists, then wrong opinions can also be voiced/every opinion can be voiced'). When asked specifically about Holocaust denial, she redefines this offence implicitly (she does not mention Holocaust denial explicitly, but refers to it vaguely and euphemistically as 'this issue') as libel or defamation. Thus, she avoids further discussion about the Holocaust and Nazi crimes. When asked in an interview with Ö1 *Mittagsjournal* on 3 March 2010 whether she actually believed in the existence of gas chambers in the concentration camps during World War II, she replied that she had the knowledge of an Austrian 'who attended Austrian schools between 1964 and 1976 – this is the extent of my knowledge of history and I do not intend to change this'.

As stated in a dossier collected by the Green Party on Barbara Rosenkranz (2010, 15), this utterance seems to be part of a coded language amongst radical right-wing party members indicating a revisionist perspective of contemporary history, and most specifically a positive view of National Socialism: 'Blaming the schoolbooks' is obviously regarded as a suitable defence strategy. First, Rosenkranz assumes (rightly) that nobody would check the schoolbooks which she might have used many decades ago; second, it is also common knowledge that many Austrian schoolbooks in the 1960s and 1970s did not elaborate on World War II and Nazi crimes. This period was frequently summarized very briefly; war crimes were reported, but only if they had happened far away (Loitfellner 2003, 2008). She emphasizes the unchallenged and unchallengeable 'authority of schoolbooks' (*topos of authority*) as legitimation device ('if something is stated in a schoolbook, then it must be right'). All these meanings are coded in this statement, which thus clearly establishes its calculated ambivalence. Of course, on the surface of it, her statement does not breach any norms of political correctness. One might wonder, however, why she declares explicitly that she would never change her views or be open to new insights (particularly during her studies of history and philosophy at the University of Vienna during the late 1970s and early 1980s). This clause serves, as stated in the aforementioned dossier, as a salient indicator of revisionist ideology.

Following this remark, Vienna's Archbishop Cardinal Christoph Schönborn labelled Rosenkranz ineligible in his view for the presidency on 4 March 2010, a most unusual move for a representative of the Church in a secular state: 'When someone is running for high office in this country and simultaneously leaves room for ambiguity over the question of the *Verbotsgesetz* or the Shoah, then they are unelectable for me.'[25] This remark indicates that Rosenkranz's repeated statements had been well understood, in spite of the use of calculated ambivalence. On the same day, the then leader of the Austrian People's Party (ÖVP) and former Foreign Minister, Michael Spindelegger (a self-professed devout Catholic), supported the Cardinal's move: 'For me someone who has this kind of relationship to questions that affect our past is unelectable.' Through her strategy of provocation, Rosenkranz's nomination monopolized the agenda; thus, the media and most public debates revolved around her utterances.

However, on 6 March 2010, Hans Dichand, again under his pseudonym CATO, demanded a serious and honest *declaration of distance* from National Socialist beliefs and ideology:

Text 5.3

'As an independent newspaper, the *Kronen Zeitung* has always attempted to give outsiders a fair chance and to not exclude them. This is also the case in the ongoing presidential campaign, where we have provided Barbara Rosenkranz with the opportunity to present her ideas and views. Among these, there were also some that led to doubts. Therefore it is currently necessary that Barbara Rosenkranz distance herself under oath from all National Socialist ideas. Anything else would disqualify her as a presidential candidate.'

The same day, under obvious pressure, in an interview with the centre-right quality newspaper *Die Presse*, Rosenkranz was asked the question: 'Do you believe there is such a thing as an Austrian nation?' This question is linked to a similar question once posed to Jörg Haider, many years ago, to which he responded that Austria was an 'ideological miscarriage' ('*ideologische Missgeburt*'); of course, Haider triggered an enormous scandal with such a negative predication (Wodak et al. 2009). Rosenkranz responded by stating: 'Of course the Austrian nation-state exists.'[26] Again, we are confronted with a factually and politically correct statement; however, she avoids answering the question of whether she actually 'believes' in the Austrian nation. This move is another example of calculated ambivalence.

Finally, on 8 March 2010 at a public press conference, Rosenkranz felt compelled to sign a declaration distancing herself from National Socialism, as demanded by CATO, which, however, had no legal significance whatsoever (Engel and Wodak 2013, 88).[27] Thus, paradoxically, the eligibility of Rosenkranz' candidacy was re-established in the eyes of the most widely read Austrian tabloid, which exerted and manifested more power than any court, law or politician. On 9 March 2010, this declaration was reprinted in the NKZ, including a personal letter from Rosenkranz to Dichand (Image 5.1). In this letter she states, inter alia, that 'I condemn the crimes of National Socialism out of conviction and distance myself vehemently from the ideology of National Socialism'.[28]

On 18 March 2010, Rosenkranz, for the first time, explicitly acknowledged the existence of gas chambers: 'Of course gas chambers existed. Of course, awful crimes took place. No reasonable person questions this.'[29] This is a clear statement and seems not to contain any indicators of calculated ambivalence. However, her statement does not mention any perpetrators (actually no human beings are mentioned, whether as perpetrators or victims; the crimes simply 'took place' just as the gas chambers simply 'existed'), nor does it mention any specific territory or historical period. Hence, this

(Continued)

(Continued)

Image 5.1 Barbara Rosenkranz distances herself from National Socialism, *Neue Kronenzeitung*, 9 March 2010

statement could have been employed for any period of time and for any similar event in the entire world. In this way, abstraction and vagueness reinforce calculated ambivalence. On 25 April 2010, Rosenkranz received 15.62 per cent of the vote (voter turnout: 49.2 per cent). FPÖ party leader HC Strache had initially envisaged 35 per cent.[30]

The British Case

The BBC Programme *Question Time*

The second example concerns an episode of *Question Time*, a weekly British television format that stages a topical debate including representatives from at least three different political parties as well as other public figures. The audience can direct questions to the invited speakers, who are not told in advance which questions to expect. The programme is currently broadcast on BBC 1 every Thursday from 10.30 p.m. to 11.30 p.m. and has been presented by the prominent and very well-known moderator David Dimbleby since the mid-1990s.

Question Time was first broadcast in 1979 and has become very popular over the years.[31] The panellists, frequently prominent ministers, intellectuals, authors or journalists, are obliged to answer selected audience members' questions. This concept is adapted to suit the show, which consists of the panel, the host and the audience. David Dimbleby exerts much power in inviting turns, closing turns, inviting members of the audience to speak or disregarding them. He also determines the sequence of answers by inviting the panellists to respond directly to a specific question; he is the key figure of this show and keeps the discussions going, intervenes if politicians do not answer questions properly or digs deeper. Dimbleby sits in the middle of the panel at a table that faces the audience. The issues discussed are usually major political events currently taking place or other prominent news of the week. The programme is recorded in front of a live audience, approximately two hours before it is broadcast. The BBC therefore guarantees a convenient recording slot for the panel as well as for the audience, and claims that this is the only reason for not broadcasting this programme live. The specific episode analysed in this paper was broadcast on 22 October 2009, and triggered a great scandal and public uproar. Nick Griffin, leader of the BNP, was caught in the crossfire between the audience, the panel and the host, Dimbleby, for his statements about World War II, the Holocaust, British identity and homosexuality (amongst other topics).[32]

VIGNETTE 12
NICK GRIFFIN AND *QUESTION TIME*

Nick Griffin, born in 1959, has been the leader of the BNP since 1999 and was a member of the European Parliament for North West England until the European Parliament election in May 2014. At this election, the BNP lost both seats. Griffin then stepped down as leader of the BNP on 19 July 2014 and became the president of the organisation. On 1 October 2014 Griffin was expelled by the BNP and quickly founded the British Unity Party which to date has about 2000 members primarily on Facebook (see www.facebook.com/BritishUnity; accessed 12 June 2015). Nick Griffin was invited onto *Question Time* for the first time on 22 October 2009, causing widespread and polarized controversy amongst politicians, media and the public.[33] Before the show, Nick Griffin told *The Times*: 'I thank the political class and their allies for being so stupid ... [this invitation] gives us a whole new level of public recognition.' In this interview, he also labelled his fellow panellist and the former Minister of Justice, Jack Straw, contemptuously a 'very effective advocate' (ibid.).

Apart from Nick Griffin, the panel also consisted of: Jack Straw, former Labour Justice Secretary and previously Home and Foreign Secretary; Sayeeda Warsi, then Conservative Shadow Minister for Community Cohesion; Chris Huhne, then spokesman for the Liberal Democratic Party on home affairs; and Bonnie Greer, an African-American playwright and deputy chair of the British Museum.

The programme began with this question from the audience: 'Is it fair that the BNP has hijacked Churchill?' After approximately 10 minutes of discussion about World War II, the Holocaust and other issues concerning racism and antisemitism, Dimbleby took some comments from the audience, all of which were directed against Nick Griffin, before turning to the next main question, again addressed to Griffin: 'Why is Islam a wicked and vicious faith?' The question that followed also concerned the BNP: 'Can the recent success of the BNP be explained by the misguided immigration policy of our government?' A couple of short questions including attacks on Nick Griffin followed. Later on, the British immigration policy system was discussed and Jack Straw was forced to justify the Labour Party's policies during the New Labour government until 2010. The next prominent question concerned issues about attitudes towards homosexuality: 'Should the *Daily Mail* have published the Jan Moir article on Steven Gately?' This question triggered a discussion on homosexuality, with offensive arguments from Nick Griffin who was heavily criticized by the audience. The last question was: 'Might this programme be viewed as an early Christmas present for the BNP?' It becomes obvious that the whole programme was oriented towards issues related to the BNP and Nick Griffin. Although moderator Dimbleby tried to change the topic several times, questions from the audience again and again were directed at Nick Griffin.

(Continued)

(Continued)

Holocaust Denial and Blame Avoidance
Text 5.4

30 *Peter Loge*: Given that the Second World War was fuelled by the need to disarm oppressive and racist

31 regimes is it fair that the BNP has hijacked Churchill as its own?

32 *DD*: Is it fair that the BNP has hijacked Churchill. Jack Straw.

33 *JS*: Certainly not fair, and one of the extraordinary things about the Second World War and the First

34 World War was not only that we fought Nazism in the Second World War and defeated it, a party and

35 an ideology based on *race*, just like another party represented here today, based on race,

36 fundamental to its constitution, and it's that difference, by the way, the fact that BNP defines itself

37 on race, which distinguishes if from every other party that I can think of and what is common about

38 every other political party that I can think of regardless of the difference is that they have each have a

39 moral compass and they show respect and recognizable, moral compass for them based on

40 longstanding cultural and philosophical and religious values of western society. Nazism didn't and

41 neither I'm afraid does the constitution of the BNP. The other thing I just say is this. We only won

42 the war with the help of Black and Asian people from around the world.

43

44   [*Applause and woo*]

45

46 *JS*: My constituency is twinned with a little town in northern France called Péronne, it was

47 *massacred* in the First World War, the battle of the Somme, hundreds of people from East Lancashire,

48 young lads from East Lancashire were killed and if you go to the Péronne military cemetery, just

49 outside Péronne, you'll find 577 young men buried there. 257 of those come from East Lancashire,

50 they' we got names like Ainsworth and Barnes. The others, more than half, have Indian and Pakistani

51 sounding names like Mohammed Khan, from the 18th King's own Lancers, or Sheik Mohammed.

52 These people died together to fight for *us* [*DD*: OK] and that's why having a multiracial society and

53 ensuring that race based politics has no place in our society is *fundamental* to the decent British

54 values which are held by most people in this country.

55   [*Applause*]

56 [...]

61 *DD*: Nick Griffin, you said if Churchill were alive today his own place would be in the British

62 National Party. Why d'you say that? Why did you hijack his reputation?

63 *NG*: I said that Churchill belonged to the British National Party because no other party would have

64 him for what he said in the early days of mass immigration into this country or the fact that quote,

65 quote, 'they're only coming for our benefits system' and for the fact that in his younger and in his

66 earlier days he was extremely critical of the dangers of fundamentalist Islam in the way that would

67 now be described as Islamophobic. I believe that the whole the effort in the Second World War and

68 the First, a lot of effort was designed to preserve British sovereignty, British freedom which Jack

69 Straw's government is now giving away lock, stock and barrel to the EU and to prevent this country

70 being invaded by foreigners. Finally, my father was in the RAF during the Second World War while Mr

71 Straw's father was in prison for refusing to fight Adolf Hitler.

72   that's it, that's it [*from the public, small applause and boooo*]

73 [...]

76 *DD*: What, sorry, what what's that got to do, what's that got to do with it?

77 *NG*: Mr Straw was attacking me and I've been relentlessly attacked and demonised during the last

78 few days but the fact is that during the Second World War my father was in the RAF.

79   I can't believe this [*from the public*]

80 I am not a Nazi, I've never have been.

81 *DD*: The man there [*points towards audience*]

82 A man in the audience: Emmm, yeah, just to say to Nick Griffin on the whole issue of Europe and how

83 you seem to be against Europe while 80% of our trade is with Europe.

After a first unambiguous answer to Peter Loge's question that it is certainly unfair to 'hijack Churchill', Jack Straw immediately focuses on the BNP's racist policies which exclude diversity. Jack Straw positions himself very clearly on the other side of the political spectrum, thus distancing himself (and all other political parties) from the racist ideology of the BNP. Simultaneously, he presents a positive image of multicultural and diverse Britain and the many British soldiers from different ethnic origin who all together fought against the Nazis and won. He refers to his own constituency and its many soldiers who died in fighting the Nazis. This introduction thus draws a clear

(Continued)

(Continued)

distinction between 'Us', the anti-racist British public and politics, and 'Them', the racist BNP – all this intended as introduction and positive self-presentation before even venturing to respond more in-depth to the first question posed by the audience. Nick Griffin is asked to respond, both to the first question and to Jack Straw's evidence that Britain is a diverse, multiracial society and that many Pakistanis and Indians fought on Britain's side in World War II.

Of course, this extract could be analysed in much more detail and on many levels (see, for example, Bull and Simon-Vandenbergen 2014). Here, however, I focus primarily on the 'politics of denial' as manifested within it. Thus, Nick Griffin's overall argumentation in this passage can be deconstructed according to Toulmin's scheme of argumentation in the following way: the alleged fact that 'Churchill belonged to the British National Party' (l. 63) provides the claim. 'Because no other party would have him [Churchill] for what he said in the early days of mass immigration into this country' (ll. 63–4) as well as 'and for the fact that in his younger and in his earlier days he [Churchill] was extremely critical of the dangers of fundamentalist Islam' (ll. 65–6) are used as data (evidence). 'In the way that would now be described as Islamophobic' (ll. 66–7) serves as *warrant*. This utterance also implies that in Churchill's time, such opinions would not have been described as Islamophobic and that possibly, if one refers to the well-known critique frequently voiced by the far-right against any form of 'political correctness' that Churchill's alleged opinion would still be valid. The warrant is supported by the well-known *topos of burden*: 'they're only coming for our benefits system' (l. 65), using the conditional: If foreigners come, they are only here to claim benefits (money which belongs to us), and thus they should be kept out of the country. This warrant leads, in Nick Griffin's argument, to the *conclusion* that Churchill was right and were he alive today, would belong to the BNP through association with distinguished political leaders (*topos of authority* in the sense that if Churchill said something then it must be right), Griffin implies that it is the BNP which is standing up for traditional British values, not the other mainstream political parties.

The merging of past and present in this context is fallacious. Griffin continues with another claim: 'I believe that the whole effort in the Second World War and the First a lot of effort was designed to preserve British sovereignty, British freedom' (ll. 67–8). This claim is fallacious because Griffin does not mention other possible motives, such as fighting Nazism in Europe and beyond, for example. The latter could be interpreted as *argumentum ad ignorantiam*, that is, an argument that is regarded as true as long as it has not been refuted. Griffin continues this line of argumentation with a *topos of history* in order to attack the Labour Party and its pro-European position: 'which Jack Straw's government is now giving away lock, stock and barrel to the EU' (l. 69). Of course, in this case, two instances are linked with each other in a fallacious way: current immigration policies in the European Union have nothing in common with World War II and the fight for British freedom. Moreover, the European Union cannot be compared to the 'Third Reich'.

At this point, Griffin's argumentation shifts and he attacks Jack Straw directly: 'Finally, my father was in the RAF during the Second World War while Mr Straw's father was in prison for refusing to fight Adolf Hitler' (ll. 70–1) – this *argumentum ad hominem* is used by Griffin to personally discredit his opponent Straw by attacking his father, a conscientious objector. Thereby Griffin obviously seeks to undermine Straw's credibility, and thus invalidate his criticisms of the BNP. Here, Dimbleby intervenes and challenges Nick Griffin. He asks Griffin: 'What, sorry, what what's that got to do , what's that got to do with it?' (l. 76).

Griffin answers: 'Mr Straw was attacking me and I've been relentlessly attacked and demonized during the last few days but the fact is that during the Second World War my father was in the RAF' (ll. 77–8). Again, two instances are linked with each other which are unrelated, apart from the fact that Nick Griffin is his father's son, thus *post hoc* fallacy.

As is evident from the transcript, Griffin did not reply to the question. He uses an *argumentum ad misericordiam*, that is, an appeal to pity or related emotions to gain the acceptance of other people or of one's antagonist. He constructs himself as a victim so that everybody should sympathize with him. It is a discursive strategy of *positive self-presentation* including the previous argument (ll. 77–8) and *negative other-presentation*. Griffin's revelations, however, provoke harsh criticism from the audience. A man in the audience speaks up, defending Jack Straw and attacking Nick Griffin emotionally, uttering disgust and dismay, and predicating him in very negative ways: 'See, I think it's an absolute disgrace that you can't even sort of take on board what Jack Straw has said' (l. 91), and continues: 'yes you are, poison politics and poison the minds of people in this country. The vast majority of this audience, the vast majority of this audience, fine, would find what you stand for to be ... completely disgusting' (ll. 101–3). Griffin, instead of referring to and dealing with the accuser's points, changes the topic and uses another *argumentum ad misericordiam*: 'if you look at some of the things I'm quoted as having said in the *Daily Mail* and so, I'd be a monster. Those things are outrageous lies ...' Griffin offers no proof for his claim; Dimbleby digs deeper and asks for the specific quote. However, Griffin tries to avoid answering, but Dimbleby insists on an answer:

Calculated ambivalence and Holocaust denial
Text 5.5

110   *NG*: No doubt, I appreciate that but if you look at some of the things I'm quoted as having said in the

111   *Daily Mail* and so, I'd be a monster. Those things are outrageous *lies*.

112   *DD*: Which is the untrue quote? The Holocaust Denial possibly

113   [*general laugh, people speaking*]

114   [...]

116   *NG*: The. hh [*smile*]. the *vast* majority of them, far too many to go into, but

117   [*general laugh*]

118   *DD*:   But denying, denying of Holocaust,

119   did you deny the Holocaust? Yes you did

120   *NG*:   I, I do not have a conviction for Holocaust Denial

121   *DD*: But you did deny it.   Why are you smiling? It's not particularly amusing you see.

122   [*NG Smile*]

123   *NG*: I was, I was very much critical for the way Holocaust was and is in fact abused to prevent serious

124   discussion of immigration.

(Continued)

(Continued)

Instead of answering the question of whether he denied the Holocaust, Griffin replies with a strategy of calculated ambivalence (and act and intention denial): 'I do not have a conviction for Holocaust denial' (l. 120), which serves two aims: first, stating – after a second question by Dimbleby (l. 121) – that he was 'very critical of the Holocaust' (l. 123); however, the statement that he was never convicted does, of course, not preclude having denied the Holocaust. This claim provokes his opponents even more; Dimbleby angrily points to Griffin's inappropriate behaviour, that is, smiling when talking about a very serious issue concerning millions of people losing their lives (l. 121). Dimbleby does not let Griffin get away with his technique of blame avoidance and cites some quotes to prove that Griffin's claims of being incorrectly cited are simply fabricated, and reprimands him yet again later in the debate: 'D'you know what I'm saying? I can't find misquotations and apparently nor can you' (ll. 135–6). In Text 5.5, however, Griffin changes the frame and turns the tables. He claims that the way the Holocaust is discussed 'actually prevents a serious discussion of immigration'. In this utterance Griffin constructs a fallacious comparison between the Holocaust as historical event and the current phenomenon of immigration. Is immigration to be seen on an equal level with the Holocaust? Or is the taboo on denying the Holocaust perceived as analogous with being forbidden to speak critically about immigration? This is a straw man fallacy as nobody has ever been forbidden to criticize immigration and immigration policies. The link and comparison are thus fallacious in at least two respects: in comparing the Holocaust with immigration and thus de-historicizing and relativizing the Holocaust; and in providing an exaggerated claim by equating the taboo on denial of the Holocaust with an alleged rule regulating freedom of speech, that is criticizing immigration.

Moreover, Griffin was convicted in 1998 of 'publishing or distributing racially inflammatory written material', which is an offence under the 1986 Public Order Act. The material quoted in the verdict was Holocaust denial published in his magazine *The Rune*. This implies that his claim 'I do not have a conviction for Holocaust denial' is in fact a fallacious equivocation (see also Bull and Simon-Vandenbergen 2014, 4).[34]

Griffin and the KKK
Text 5.6

238   A male voice: Absolutely. *[and applause]*

239   *NG*: I was ... I was sharing a platform with David Duke, who was a head of KKK

240   who was once a leader of the Klu Klux Klan and almost a totally non, incidentally, no no no ...

241   *DD*:   oooo, wow

242   *[noise in the public, boooo]*

Griffin keeps on trying to ignore and deny facts about himself, for example, that he was caught in a video standing next to the head of the Ku Klux Klan (act-denial), and when he realizes that he cannot deny the truth any more he plainly states that David

Duke was 'a head of KKK who was once a leader of the Ku Klux Klan, and always a totally non-violent one' (ll. 239–40), thus relativizing and euphemizing Duke's agenda. At this point, the audience boos and the other panel members utter their disgust at this further attempt at denial. The debate is dominated by much turn-taking from the panellists. Dimbleby continues to take comments and questions in order to avoid an escalation of the discussion. Probably the most controversial moment is reached when Griffin suggests that he has changed his mind about the Holocaust and yet can give no reason for this, thus implying that the reason for his change of mind were potentially negative sanctions when travelling to France because of existing French laws against Holocaust denial:

Changing his opinion
Text 5.7

297   Audience: So ...

298   *DD*:   You've got white shirt, alright ... Go on.

299   Audience: So Winston Churchill put everything on the line so that my ancestors wouldn't get you

300   know slaughtered in the concentration camp. But here sits a man who says that that's a myth just like

301   a flat world was a myth [*NG shakes his head no*]. How could you say that, how could you?

302   *NG* [*to DD*]: Can I answer these three points, very briefly?

303   *DD*: Yes.

304   *NG*: First the first one, I cannot explain why I used to say those things, I can't tell you ...

305   [*booooooooooooo*]

306   any more than I can tell you why I've changed my mind, I can't tell you the extent to which I've

307   changed my mind, because European law prevents

      [...]

310   *JS*: This is rubbish, this is rubbish ...   there is no law *here* that stops you from explaining yourself

311   [*NG*: The European law prevents from]

312   *CH* [*has been talking simultaneously with JS until now*]: And we refused to a European

313   arrest warrant from precisely this from a ho [*?*], from a country that does require a Holocaust Denial

314   to be an offence and we refused that

315   *JS*:   as a justice minister, I promise you, if you want to explain why you

316   [*audience wooo and applauds*]

317   *BG* [*during applause*]: Nick, tell them, tell them, you gadit.

(Continued)

(Continued)

318 *JS* and *CH* [*interchangeably, during applause*]:   go on, come on …

319 *DD* [*to NG*]: You have, you have the freedom now to explain it.

320 [*laughter in audience, NG smiles too*]

321 *NG*: But unfortunately, the French courts and German courts would not recognize me that [*talks*]

322 *BG* and *another male voice*:   ooo ooo oooooo, woow …

323 […]

324 *BG* [*a call amongst other noises*]: This isn't justified

325 [*laughter, incl. NG*]

326 *Male voice*: [*talks loudly over DD*]

327 *DD*: I have, I have, I have – wait wait I have a question here. Have you actually changed your mind or do

328 you only say you've changed your mind because a law says it is illegal to be a Holocaust denier?

329 *NG*: I, I, I *have* changed my mind, yes, a lot's of it about the figures, and one of the [*someone says*

330 *'Figures'?*] – yes, yes – one of the key things that made me change my mind is British radio intercepts

331 of German transmissions about the *brutal* mass murders of innocent Jews on the eastern border

332 during anti-partisan warfare which changes the figures very much [*more talk*]

333 *JS*:   What about Holocaust? Does that not require an […]? What about Auschwitz?

334 *NG*:   Can I go back to my other point?

335 *JS*: Can people not see with their own eyes what happened at Auschwitz? It didn't need

336 subsequent radio intercepts to find out that people were gassed.

337 [*applause and a voice saying 'absolutely' and more talk*]

This extract illustrates a plethora of strategies of both calculated ambivalence and blame avoidance very explicitly. Although both Dimbleby and Justice Minister Jack Straw clarify that nothing could happen to Nick Griffin if he explains what he means in respect to the Holocaust when in the UK, where no legal measures against Holocaust denial exist, he does not answer and attempts drawing a line; obviously, he is afraid of litigation. Finally, he admits to having changed his mind (after an ironic question by Dimbleby, ll. 327–8), and again avoids talking about concentration camps and the gassing of Jews. Instead, he shifts to another topic and talks about the eastern border and the 'anti-partisan' warfare during World War II, thus employing a well-known Nazi term used to refer to civilians and resistance fighters (l. 332; Heer et al. 2008). Jack Straw intervenes, returns to the topic of concentration camps and the Holocaust, and states very emotionally that one does not need any new figures or facts when referring to Auschwitz (l. 333), implying that the extermination of Jews is a well-established historical fact. Throughout Text 5.5, Nick Griffin employs strategies of blame avoidance via calculated ambivalence, shifting blame, switching topics, not answering questions and the fallacy of *ignoratio elenchi* (ignoring counter-proof or counter arguments) (Reisigl and Wodak 2001, 73; Hansson 2015). As stated above, Griffin does not deny everything; he continuously uses fallacious analogies and comparisons (disingenuously invoking the *topos of history*) and emphasizes his freedom to speak. Implied throughout is that he does not want to state the Holocaust denial explicitly as otherwise he would not be able to travel to France anymore, where laws against Holocaust denial exist; thus his motivation to avoid Holocaust denial is purely practical. His self-confident smile could indicate to his core voters that he is well aware of the various strategies employed here, specifically that of calculated ambivalence. Hence he is assuring his core voters that he has not changed his stance, while superficially acknowledging that the Holocaust actually happened, albeit in a euphemistic and relativizing way.

Returning to the categorizations of denial as provided in Chapter 3 and the four macro-strategies of dealing with blame and accusations listed above, substantial differences can be detected between Griffin's and Rosenkranz's respective *blame-avoidance* and *discourses of justification* – these are also due to the different settings, of course, that is, being in a heated and polarized discussion, or being interviewed as a serious candidate standing for election to Austrian president. While Rosenkranz primarily employs the denial strategy of scientific rationalization, Nick Griffin resorts to total denial, intention denial, shifting of blame, asserting ignorance, and counter-attack via *argumentum ad hominem.* Both cases, however, exemplify the range of possibilities used when denying the Holocaust in 'coded' ways, which, however, remain comprehensible for the targeted audience of core followers and party members via the strategy of calculated ambivalence. Employing careful and detailed analysis, it is however possible to deconstruct the micro-politics of denial in systematic detail.

Conclusion: The Strategy of Provocation

While listing general characteristics of the radical right (including right-wing populist parties), Skenderovic argues that

> after the Second World War, overt statements of modern antisemitism, making use of blunt categorisations, have largely vanished from the public sphere and have become confined to marginal extreme right groups. [....] However, what some have termed 'post-Holocaust' or 'post-fascist' antisemitism has remained a potent force of anti-Jewish hostility in contemporary societies and is most commonly found among political and intellectual actors associated with the radical right.
>
> (2009a, 22a)

Skenderovic maintains that this form of antisemitism implies that a coherent antisemitic ideology has vanished. However, the manifold occurrences and examples across all right-wing populist parties combined with the forms of denial analysed in this chapter and throughout the book provide evidence that antisemitic rhetoric continues to be part and parcel of right-wing populism in almost all of its variants, more or less explicitly and more or less coded. Along this vein, Valérie Igounet (1998) states in *Le Monde Diplomatique*, while exposing Jean Marie Le Pen and his party Front National's manifold denials of the Holocaust, that 'Holocaust denial is a convenient polemical substitute for antisemitism' (Igounet). This insight is certainly evidenced by the two incidents analysed here.

In both vignettes, implicit and explicit denials of the Holocaust were made on public television, in Austria and in the UK, by well-known politicians and members of far-right parties. In both cases, the main protagonists succeeded in using various strategies of provocation and calculated ambivalence, denying their denial, but simultaneously signalling to their core constituencies what they really believed in. In both cases, strategies of provocation served to obtain wide media attention and to set the agenda for several weeks, at least in the media.

Rosenkranz's relatively brazen xenophobia was acceptable to the public, also to mainstream media and politicians. She had, as mentioned above, even received an important decoration from the Austrian state. However, her coy attempts to question historically established facts about the history of the *Third Reich* went too far for her supporters in the tabloid media and she was required to distance herself publicly – via a legally irrelevant oath – from National Socialist ideology in order to be accepted again in the mainstream of right-of-centre Austrian politics. However, this was only relevant as she was a candidate for the presidency; otherwise, she presumably would have not attracted the level of attention she did. In this way, one could speculate that the scandal she provoked had the intended or unintended benefit of allowing her to set the agenda in the ongoing election campaign in which, predictably, she had little chance of winning against an incumbent popular president running for a second term.

The specific *Question Time* programme analysed in this chapter was watched by more than eight million viewers. It was the first time a member of the BNP appeared on the programme; it was also the first time that representatives of other major parties had shared a platform with a member of the BNP. In the past, there had been an agreed policy of 'No Platform' in order to clearly mark the *cordon sanitaire*, that is, the established border to and the abnormality of extreme-right parties. This was breached for the first time ever with the 2009 broadcast.[35] Protesters gathered outside the BBC Television Centre and regional BBC offices. The BBC was closed down so that people invited to other shows were not able to enter. Six people were arrested, and some protesters and police officers were wounded.[36] After the broadcast, Griffin presented himself as the 'victim of a "lynch mob"' during his appearance. Moreover, in an interview given to the *Telegraph* on 23 October 2009,[37] Griffin demanded a repeat of the programme, as he felt unfairly treated by the panel and argued that the show had not been a typical *Question Time* event but rather a 'lynch mob against him'. A typical conspiracy theory was set in motion, many postings on various online forums agreed, and thus Griffin employed yet another victim–perpetrator reversal.[38]

Endnotes

1   In this chapter, I also draw on research on Holocaust denial in Austria, partly conducted together with Jakob Engel (Engel and Wodak 2009, 2013), as well as on a paper on hate speech and hate incitement (Wodak 2015). Moreover, I draw on recent research about

antisemitism as functionalized in British tabloids, investigated in much detail in respect to the tabloidization of media ('media-democracy') with Karin Stögner in *Osnabrücker Beiträge zur Sprachwissenschaft* (Stögner and Wodak 2014), as well as on instances of 'blaming and denying' related to the violent incidents instigated by the Greek party Golden Dawn, as apparent in postings to newspaper articles (Angouri and Wodak 2014). Ana Tominc transcribed the BBC *Question Time* episode; Sten Hansson supported me by collecting the media reactions to this specific episode.

2 See e.g. http://stream.aljazeera.com/story/201402252346–0023505, for a summary of this debate in Denmark, 25 February 2014, accessed 17 July 2014.

3 See e.g. Billig (1978), Engel and Wodak (2009, 2013), Kovács (2010, 2013), Pelinka and Wodak (2002), Richardson and Wodak (2009a, 2009b), Skenderovic (2009a, 2009b), Stögner and Wodak (2014, forthcoming), Wodak (1989, 2011c, 2015), Wodak and Richardson (2013) and Wodak et al. (1990).

4 In this chapter, I neglect debates about Israeli politics and related critique of Israeli governmental politics in respect to Palestinians as well as the sometimes occurring functionalization of such critique for antisemitic purposes (see Billig 1978, 339ff; Stögner 2014). Specifically, Billig (1978) analyses in much detail the attempt of members of the British National Party (BNP) to distinguish between anti-Zionism and antisemitism. The bonding of right-wing populist politicians with extreme right-wing Israeli politicians is certainly worth mentioning here (Betz 2013) and could be regarded as an attempt at strategic calculated ambivalence.

5 See also the centre-left French quality newspaper *Libération* on 23 July 2014, which dedicated an entire issue to '*Les Nouveaux Antisémites*' (The New Antisemites) after several synagogues in Paris and its neighbouring villages had been attacked. There, the authors Dominique Albertini and Willy Le Devin list several reasons for this 'new antisemitism' (2–3): radical Palestinians, pan-African supremacists, the extreme Right in the Front National, and some – as they are labelled in the article – 'pseudo-intellectuals' (e.g. Beauzamy 2013b). Deborah Lipstadt agrees with this assessment (20 August 2014; see www.nytimes.com/2014/08/21/opinion/deborah-e-lipstadt-on-the-rising-anti-semitism-in-europe.html?_r=1, accessed 24 August 2014), as does the centre-right French quality newspaper *Le Figaro* in the conclusion '*On sous-estime la haine dont les juifs de la France font l'objet*' [One underestimates the hate directed against Jews in France] (27 July 2014, 19).

6 Due to space restrictions, I will of necessity have to neglect some of these dimensions in my analysis below (for more details, see Engel and Wodak 2013; Wodak 2007a, 2011c, 2015).

7 See the overview of different signatories and salient cases as well as recommendations in http://en.wikipedia.org/wiki/Convention_on_the_Elimination_of_All_Forms_of_Racial_Discrimination (accessed 2 January 2014); Regulation 2000/43/EG of the European Commission, 29 June 2000; http://ec.europa.eu/justice/discrimination/files/com_2014_2_en.pdf, accessed 28 February 2014.

8 See e.g. the recent polarized debate triggered by the *Daily Mail* in the UK, directed against the former leader of the opposition Labour Party Ed Miliband (and his father, Ralph Miliband) (Stögner and Wodak, forthcoming); or the hate crimes and hate speech enacted almost daily by the Neo-Nazi party Golden Dawn in Greece (Angouri and Wodak 2014).

9 Kienpointner (2009, 63–4) argues that 'in highly exceptional cases, for example, if Austrian or German citizens deny the Holocaust, restrictions of freedom of speech can be rationally justified'. He states that the existence of gas chambers has been proved 'beyond reasonable doubt'; thus re-examining such issues would be a waste of intellectual energy and would, furthermore, be self-destructive and damage the public image of democracies (ibid., 66).

10 http://en.wikipedia.org/wiki/Racial_and_Religious_Hatred_Act_2006, accessed 5 January 2014. This law is mostly concerned with expressions of religious hatred.

11 See recent incidents of Holocaust denial: in Hungary, 27 May 2013, when an MP of the Jobbik Party claimed that the Auschwitz Death Camp museum 'may not reflect real facts' (www.eurojewcong.org/hungary/9492-jobbik-mp-in-holocaust-denial.html, accessed 16 February 2014); or the enormous scandal in Poland, following publication of the extreme right-wing Polish historian Dariusz Ratajczak's book, *Dangerous Themes*, in which he claims, inter alia, that the gas Zyklon B was only used for disinfection in the concentration camps, and other lies. He was suspended from teaching in 1999 (see www. revisionists.com/revisionists/ratajczak.html; accessed 21 April 2014). Ratajczak was supported by some members of the far-right League of the Polish Families Party. Many utterances by Jean-Marie Le Pen, starting in 1978, were classified as Holocaust denial and widely accepted within the Front National (http://mondediplo.com/1998/05/08igou; accessed 16 February 2014). Marine Le Pen, however, has recently strategically distanced herself, with respect to antisemitic and racist hate speech, from her father's usage in order to open the party to a bigger electorate. Thus, one can conclude that even today antisemitism and Holocaust denial are part and parcel of extreme and populist right-wing rhetoric across Europe (see also Mudde 2005 for more details and examples).

12 More details about this and other similar cases which took place in post-war Austria can be found in Engel and Wodak (2009, 2013), Kienpointner (2009), Wodak and Reisigl (2002) and Wodak et al. (1990).

13 See e.g. Lipstadt (1993) or Kahn (2005) for an overview of comparative legislation and controversies pertaining to Holocaust denial. Particularly, Lipstadt's *Denying the Holocaust* is notable not only for its thorough treatment of the subject, but also for the suit filed by David Irving against Deborah Lipstadt and her publisher, Penguin Books, in which he alleged that Lipstadt had libelled him in her book. Irving lost the case and the trial judge's 333-pages-long opinion in favour of the defendant detailed Irving's systematic distortion of the historical record of World War II.

14 www.menschenrechte.ac.at/orgi/98_5/Nachtmann.pdf, accessed 15 March 2012.

15 Benz (1995, 125) defines revisionism in the narrow sense as 'the denial of the proven historical fact that in the course of the Second World War millions of European Jews were murdered in gas chambers'.

16 Considerable international attention was attracted by the conviction of the (now released) British Holocaust denier David Irving to three years in prison in Austria on 21 February 2006 (the verdict was confirmed on 4 September 2006). Controversies around Irving's conviction led to a number of editorials in leading Austrian conservative newspapers objecting to the law for its limitations on the freedom of speech and its allegedly ineffective preventative effect.

17 Only a small percentage of trials actually end with conviction (5.2 per cent in 2013).

18 See www.krone.at/Oesterreich/Strache_schickt_Rosenkranz_ins_Rennen_um_Hofburg-Seite_an_Seite-Story-187536, accessed 12 March 2015.

19 See http://derstandard.at/1267131932485/Rosenkranz-wird-fuer-FPOe-kandidieren, accessed 12 March 2015.

20 Incidentally, on 13 November 2003, the European Court of Human Rights in Strasbourg decided that the journalist Hans-Henning Scharsach (*News*) was found to not be in contravention of libel laws for calling Rosenkranz a '*Kellernazi*' (the colloquial term, literally 'cellar Nazi', describes a person who supports National Socialist/anti-democratic ideas through clandestine activities).

21 *MenschInnen. Gender Mainstreaming – Auf dem Weg zum geschlechtslosen Menschen* (2008).

22 Rosenkranz argues that such partnerships contravene the contract between generations to ensure that the state has sufficient revenue to provide social services. She also opposes the right of homosexual couples to adopt children.

23 See: http://derstandard.at/1267132251749/Kandidatur-Rechtsextreme-NVP-unterstuetzt-Rosenkranz; http://derstandard.at/1268700952546/Rosenkranz-ist-eine-nationale-Sozialistin; cf. also www.kleinezeitung.at/nachrichten/politik/bundespraesident/2307151/zwei-gesichter-kandidatin.story, accessed 11 November 2012.

24 See www.vol.at/news/politik/artikel/bundespraesident---rosenkranz-steht-weiterhin-zu-umstrittenen-aussagen/cn/news-20100303–12292321; www.krone.at/Oesterreich/FPOe-Kandidatin_Rosenkranz_gegen_NS-Verbotsgesetz-Meinungsfreiheit-Story-188096, accessed 12 March 2015.

25 See www.worldjewishcongress.org/es/news/9109/far_right_politician_s_presidential_candidacy_sparks_outrage_in_austria, accessed 23 March 2014.

26 See http://diepresse.com/home/politik/hofburgwahl/544630/Rosenkranz_Kein-Zweifel-an-Gaskammern?_vl_backlink=/home/politik/hofburgwahl/544587/index.do&direct=544587, accessed 12 November 2011.

27 http://derstandard.at/1268402692605/Kommentar-der-anderen-Die-Nullnummer-des-Onkel-Hans, accessed 12 November 2011.

28 http://newsv1.orf.at/100308–48803/index.html, accessed 12 November 2011, for the precise wording of the letter.

29 See http://diepresse.com/home/politik/hofburgwahl/547110/Rosenkranz_Selbstverstaendlich-gab-es-Gaskammern, accessed 12 November 2011.

30 See http://diepresse.com/home/politik/hofburgwahl/543588/Rosenkranz_Ueber-Identitaet-des-Landes-diskutieren?direct=543061&_vl_backlink=/home/politik/index.do&selChannel=101, accessed 12 November 2011.

31 The literal meaning of 'Question Time' is: 'a period of time set aside each day for members to question government ministers' (http://dictionary.reverso.net/english-definition/question%20time, accessed 10 January 2014.

32 See e.g. 'BNP on *Question Time*: Nick Griffin uses BBC appearance to attack Muslims and gays', *Telegraph*, 22 October 2009, published immediately after the show was broadcast (www.telegraph.co.uk/news/politics/6410764/BNP-on-Question-Time-Nick-Griffin, accessed 24 October 2013); 'Keeping Nick Griffin off air is a job for parliament, not the BBC', was the tenor of Mark Thompson, BBC's director, when justifying the invitation (*Guardian*, 21 October 2009; www.theguardian.com/commentsisfree/2009/oct/21/question-time-bbc-bnp-griffin, accessed 24 October 2013). For more information about the BNP, see Billig (1978, appendix 1), Richardson (2013a, 2013b), Solomos (2013).

33 Peter Hain, Secretary of State for Wales, made a final appeal to the BBC Trust to have the appearance blocked but this failed after an emergency meeting of the BBC Trust, held on 21 October 2009, which 'cleared' the way for Nick Griffin's participation. The *Guardian* cited former Home Secretary Alan Johnson, who also condemned the decision of the BBC to invite Nick Griffin (www.theguardian.com/politics/blog/2009/oct/16/alan-johnson-bnp-question-time, 16 October 2009), and Conservative leader David Cameron, who also stated that the BBC should not have invited him (*The Times*, http://login.thetimes.co.uk/?gotoUrl=http%3A%2F%2Fwww.thetimes.co.uk%2Ftto%2Fopinion%2Fcolumnists%2Fjaniceturner%2F, 21 October 2009).

34 www.theguardian.com/politics/2010/jan/22/nick-griffin-race-trial-details, accessed 12 March 2015. I am very grateful to John Richardson for providing me with this material and quote.

35 See http://hopenothate.org.uk/blog/nick/why-no-platform-means-something-different-today-2410, accessed 11 February 2014.

36 See www.socialistworker.co.uk/art.php?id=22373, accessed 11 February 2014.

37 A. Singh, 'BNP's Nick Griffin: "I was victim of Question Time's Lynch Mob"' (http://www.telegraph.co.uk/news/politics/6415588/BNPs-Nick-Griffin-I-was-victim-of-Question-Time-lynch-mob.html, accessed 11 February 2014).

38 'Nick Griffin on *Question Time*: BNP boss squirms as audience laugh' (*Mirror Online*; www.mirror.co.uk/news/uk-news/nick-griffin-on-question-time-bnp-426538); 'Griffin: Unfair that Question Time was filmed in "ethnically cleansed" London' *(Guardian*, 23 October 2009; www.theguardian.com/politics/2009/oct/23/bnp-nick-griffin-question-time, all accessed 11 February 2014).

6 PERFORMANCE AND THE MEDIA: THE POLITICS OF CHARISMA

'Talk scandals originate in speech acts, i.e. statements and discussions, and it is discursive norms and codes that are transgressed. At stake is the question of what people in a certain position are allowed to say and how they should behave in public discourses.'

Mats Ekström and Bengt Johansson (2008, 77)

The 'New Face' of Politics: 'Old Wine in New Bottles'?

One of the salient elements of right-wing politicians' success is their well-crafted strategic performance on frontstage, in traditional and new media, including social media, in election rallies, press conferences and speeches, always oriented towards the specific audience. As a cab driver emphasized in December 2014 while he was taking me to Manchester Airport, he felt that Nigel Farage, the leader of the British right-wing populist party UKIP, was talking *to* him, not *down* to him and not *about* him. Although the driver had actually voted for the Labour Party all his life, he now was, he explicitly stated, inclined to vote for UKIP at the general election in May 2015. Simultaneously, he repeated twice that he certainly did not endorse or support any racist views; however, he said that Nigel Farage understood his worries, also liked to go to the pub, and had the experience of real (manual) work and what this meant. When I pointed out that Nigel Farage came from a wealthy background, had gone to public school and had worked as a banker, the driver replied that he actually knew nothing about UKIP's leader but countered: 'That does not matter; he understands me; *he speaks my language*.' This brief anecdote (which, of course, cannot be generalized but does point to a quite common conviction amongst sectors of the British public) illustrates well that Farage, like other leaders of right-wing populist parties, is able to find the *right register* with which to convince many voters that he was on their side and that he took them seriously. In an atmosphere of huge distrust of politicians across the EU (more than 60 per cent do not believe that their governments are making the right decisions),[1] right-wing populist parties and their leaders convey empathy, address discontent and anger in simple and simplistic terms, use the phrase 'against those up there, against the elites', and position themselves as saviours of the people who feel 'left behind'. In other words, and in contrast to more accountable governmental positioning, right-wing populist politicians primarily construct themselves as '*being one of us*' ('Us' defined as the ordinary man/woman from the street), as *saving 'Us' from 'Them'* ('Them' being opponents, strangers and, more generally, all dangerous people or scenarios) and as knowing what 'We' want (as fulfilling the unspoken but shared common needs).

Of course, all politicians perform frontstage as part of their political everyday life. They are trained by spin doctors to satisfy the emotional and cognitive needs of their various audiences by being able to adapt to a range of contexts and predictable and unpredictable events (Wodak 2011a). As Tannen succinctly notes in her best-selling book *The Argument Culture*, 'fitting ideas into a particular camp requires you to oversimplify them. Again, disinformation and distortion can result. Less knowledge is gained, not more. And time spent attacking an opponent or defending against attacks is not spent doing something else' (1998, 289). It is therefore certainly legitimate to ask at this point what kind of specific performativity characterizes right-wing populist politicians differently from politicians per se. The *form of the performanc*e is only one – even if important – part of the specific right-wing populist habitus. *Form and content* are necessarily linked to construct the specific political agenda. In right-wing populist rhetoric, several elements are combined: *specific topics* which are addressed; *specific ideologies* which feed into and constitute utterances and performances; *strategies of calculated ambivalence and provocation* which are used to create and de-escalate intentionally provoked scandals; and a *continuous campaigning style*, an overall antagonistic habitus which does not comply with hitherto conventional rules of negotiation and compromise (Forchtner et al. 2013; Kienpointner 2009).

For example, on a poster by the German extreme right-wing party NPD (Image 6.1), a smiling white young man, Jens Gatter, dressed in a nice and clean, blue-white striped shirt, his gaze directed at 'Us', assures the viewers (and indirectly promises) that he will speak up for 'Us'; that he is brave and courageous enough to say explicitly what people ('We') only think and keep to 'Ourselves' as it might be seen as inappropriate (and politically incorrect) to voice such opinions.

Image 6.1   NPD campaign poster 2014

This strategy relates to the *double-positioning* as both *saviour of the people* and representing *the* people; and as being *one of the people*. Moreover, the *topos* of freedom of speech (e.g. Vignettes 11 and 12) is addressed which is based on the conditional 'If you vote for me, I am brave enough to voice everything which is important for you and "us" even if it might be politically incorrect or inopportune'. Closely related to this *topos* is the *topos* of critique – 'if you vote for me, I will utter important critique even if this is regarded as politically incorrect or inopportune'. Jens Gatter, who achieved the best result for the NPD in the 2014 regional elections in Saxony (Germany) and has been appointed regional chairman of North Saxony 2015 (see npd-sachsen.de/npd-kreisverband-nordsachsen-waehlte-jens-gatter-zum-neuen-kreisvor-sitzenden/), projects visually that he knows what people need and regards it as his duty and mission to address and fulfil these needs even, it is subtly implied, if others (the elites, the opposition) do not listen to the people and their specific requests, assessments or judgements.

Defining the Terms: Frontstage, Backstage and Habitus

Before listing some important dimensions and resources of right-wing populist performances and positioning, I shall briefly define the concepts of 'frontstage' and 'backstage' as well as 'habitus' and 'positioning' (see Wodak 2011a for an extensive discussion). When analysing politicians' behaviour, Goffman's seminal work on organizations offers a useful framework. Goffman's notion of *performance* is inherently related to the metaphor of 'being in the theatre and on stage'. He distinguishes between *frontstage* and *backstage*. *Frontstage* is where the *performance* takes place and where the performers and the audience are present (Goffman 1959, 17). *Backstage* is where performers are present but the audience is not, and the performers can step out of character without fear of disrupting the performance: 'the back region is the place where the impression fostered by the performance is knowingly contradicted as a matter of course' (ibid., 112). However, when performers are backstage, they are nonetheless engaged in another performance: that of a loyal team member, a member of the field of politics and of related communities of practice.

Habitus can be understood as a system of psychological, embodied and pre-reflexive dispositions that is constitutive of a field (Bourdieu and Wacquant 1992, 16). A *field* structures a habitus. It denotes a 'set of objective, historical relations between positions anchored in certain forms of power (or capital)' (ibid.). Thus, the political field is a particular social universe within the wider field of power: it has its own rules in which particular configurations of capital are seen as valuable and are subject to struggles in order to increase or defend their value (ibid., 115). An important part of frontstage performativity is the context-dependent construction of the politicians' identity, usually defined by the specific *participation framework* (Sclafani 2014). Indeed, Sclafani (ibid.) states that although antagonistic discourse has been studied extensively (e.g. Tannen 1998), how individual politicians actually manage a positive and affiliative presentation of self in ritually argumentative debates, especially in public mass-mediated events, has rarely been investigated on the micro-level. For example, in the primaries leading up to the 2012 US elections, all Republican candidates continually referred to similar values and frames (such as the family frame), while simultaneously attempting to position themselves in unique ways on other agenda (Lakoff 2008; Vignette 15). Hence, apart from the professional, political habitus, we are dealing with situational, genre-specific *positioning* which is frequently tied to the concept of *branding*: marketing/marking and indexing one's recognizable political stance and identity for all listeners and viewers alike. Habitus and positioning are, I claim, inherently related to the construction of *charisma* (see below).

Appeals to feelings are part and parcel of right-wing populist rhetoric. During a period of fieldwork in the US in February/March 2012, when I was able to observe the primaries running up to the presidential elections of 2012, a prominent journalist from *Newsweek* and a consultant and spin-doctor for the US Democrats emphasized in an interview:

Text 6.1

I(nterviewee)1: '[…] Glenn Beck has found the way to tap in to the feeling, he's saying it feels like we are spending too much, it feels like we are unsafe against terrorists, it feels like this president is leading us towards a darker day […] I think people got the taste for what that's like, what it tastes like; for you know the Pres is a Moslem you know we are gonna go, you know, we are gonna be attacked very soon, Osama Ladin is gonna repeat 9/11; you know all these things […] Obama wants to enslave our children which is very very insightful … Inciting language but you know I mean, but economically and financially enslaving, he wants to spend so much

RW: Ah so that they will always have to pay …

I 1: Right, so that we are enslaving, you know, the future of America to pay our debt to China or you know to …

RW: Yeah but it's really an interesting way because it's sort of, it's such a paradox reversal because he's black

I 1: Right, Yeah I mean the enslaving is just an insight to get media, attention, anger feelings …'

(Interview transcript, 27 February 2012, Washington DC)

When describing the typical style and content of news reports by Glenn Beck, a well-known conservative moderator from Fox News, the interviewee employs a mixture of metaphors, such as a 'path leading towards a darker day' and the 'enslaving of our children' as a paradoxical image of total oppression, and of talking about the possibility of new imminent attacks by terrorists such as Bin Laden. These are listed as examples of discursive triggers which create an all-encompassing atmosphere of uncertainty and fear for viewers and listeners. The metaphorical scenarios, the journalist argues, appeal solely to feelings as there are no facts which would substantiate such fears; indeed, the interviewee repeats the verb 'to feel' several times in order to emphasize the irrationality of such rhetoric. Accusing President Obama, the first African-American US President, who has repeatedly spoken about freedom from slavery, of attempting to 'enslave children' as is continually repeated by Glenn Beck, certainly needs to be interpreted as a strategy of victim–perpetrator reversal.

In the same vein, the second interviewee explains that somebody has to be blamed, most plausibly the government, by appealing to feelings, not to rationality, and painting dangerous scenarios such as major catastrophes, that is, the end of America, which 'will all fall apart':

Text 6.2

I2: 'But look I think it's very very difficult in current American culture where people are used to a certain standard of living and I think they feel entitled to a certain standard of living when they see the pathway to that more difficult than it has been in previous years at least over the past few years they have to have somebody to blame for that and the government is a very easy to blame, its large you don't really know exactly so it's got to be their fault […] I think in many ways it is an appeal to base emotion and that emotion in a lot of their core messaging is that fear as a primary factor; okay so they say you should be afraid of this situation; this is what America is gonna look like, it will all fall apart'

(Interview transcript, 2 March 2012, Washington DC)

Such vivid constructions of fear are used not only in the US; they are also employed by European right-wing populist politicians, such as HC Strache, the leader of the Austrian FPÖ, for instance in a speech delivered in a closed (party) meeting (i.e. backstage) to his followers on 2 January 2011 in Vienna, when addressing the so-called 'problems with integration of foreigners in everyday life'.[2] In such speeches HC Strache attempts uniting his followers and providing them with the main arguments to be used in debates on frontstage with more heterogeneous audiences:

Text 6.3

'But let us take a look inside the social housing projects of our cities, where there are no luxury flats, where there are no rooftop terraces, let us take a closer look what the problems are there and what things are like in these neighbourhoods, where people are faced with multiculturalism in a very different way than at a fancy Italian or Turkish restaurant or any other posh place. The situation is very different there, people have to face the fact that they are insulted, that there is noise annoyance, that there is Muslim Halal slaughter of animals in the cellars of various social housing projects, even in the community laundrettes, or barbequing in the inner yards, and when citizens call to order those citizens that do not follow the house rules, they are insulted, in the least of cases, if not threatened with violence or murder. Then let us talk about the fact that in these areas our children have already become a minority in the classrooms and that there are often only one, two, three Austrian children in a classroom and that therefore the educational area has fallen catastrophically.' [*applause, also several times during the speech*]

Apart from first constructing a Manichean division between those, on the one hand, who talk about '*Multikulti*', the derogative German term for multiculturalism, but don't know anything about real life as they are not confronted with the everyday life of people living in council housing, and those ordinary Austrian citizens, on the other hand, that Strache claims – in a sophisticated rhetorical way, using manifold repetitions, rhetorical questions, and appeals to finally 'talk about it' – are frequently verbally attacked by foreigners and otherwise molested by alleged Halal slaughter and barbequing, people not following the official rules and regulations, and even being threatened with violence and murder if they dare protest such changes. All these negative experiences which, as Strache maintains, are commonplace in everyday life, remain vague; no specific incident is mentioned; these are, he suggests emphatically, undisputable 'facts' that everybody is continuously confronted with and which have changed the Viennese (and Austrian) culture (e.g. Vignette 14).

Moreover, Strache continues, too many foreign children attend Austrian schools, thus necessarily causing education standards to decline. Strache succeeds to list all possible inconveniences and unsubstantiated threats in just one paragraph, all the while presupposing that 'they', the foreigners, and 'their culture' are not just different but actually offensive, threatening and disturbing to innocent Viennese and, by implicature, to all Austrian citizens. The *topoi of culture* (they are different and therefore don't want to integrate) and *of danger* (they disturb our culture and are frequently criminals) are evoked throughout his speech in general and this paragraph in particular, lending themselves to paint an overwhelming scenario of horror, of how the peaceful everyday Austrian world is endangered by foreigners from a different – Muslim – culture (see also Vignette 14).

Neuro-linguistic Programming, Propaganda and Repetition

Right-wing populist performances (both frontstage and backstage) link several dimensions, have specific characteristics and require a range of resources. In the 1990s, FPÖ protagonists were strategically trained by spin-doctors in persuasive and manipulative rhetoric for campaigning, via neuro-linguistic programming (NLP) in employing means of propaganda with maximal effect. NLP was actually developed as a kind of cognitive psychotherapy (Bandler and Grinder 1989; Ötsch 2000; Stettner and Januschek 2002) and offers a range of rhetorical techniques in order to gain assertiveness and win in arguments. FPÖ politicians quickly learnt to constantly interrupt other discussants, repeat their main points very loudly, change topics abruptly, and to viciously attack their opponents *ad hominem*, in televised debates, interviews or during election rallies. Such patterns became completely predictable; nevertheless, opponents and journalists were frequently caught in a dynamic where they were unable to position themselves adequately, that is, expose the fallacies and return to their own agenda (Reisigl and Wodak 2001).

Thus, 'repetition as a rhetorical device' became part and parcel of the FPÖ rhetorical brand, that is, repetition of slogans, arguments and lexical items as well as of ideological contents in varied forms. As Johnstone (1987, 208) elaborates, such repetition entails how assonance, alliteration and other devices 'make discourse sound elegant', help to create 'rhetorical presence', contribute to 'the linguistic foregrounding of an idea which can serve to make it persuasive even without logical support', and 'make[s] things believable by forcing them into the affective field of the hearer and keeping them there' (ibid., 208).[3] By repetition, it is presupposed that the utterance is more convincing; and that tireless repetition of an argument (possibly by different people) brings an end to the discussion because the opponent does not care to discuss the issue any more and hence retracts their standpoint. More fatigue means less resistance or even resignation, as could frequently be observed in television debates during the subsequent 'black and blue' period from 2000–2006. Moreover, repetition is frequently combined with an appeal to authority (*argumentum ad verecundiam*; *topos of authority*). In this way, a standpoint is presented as self-evident; there is no need to provide further proof.[4] As the German sociologist Leo Löwenthal argued in his seminal treatise (1982; translated as 'Prophets of Deceit') when describing the agitator in contrast to reformers or revolutionaries:

In the formulation of their fundamental accusation, reformers as well as the revolutionary replace emotional arguments with intellectual ones. In the domain of agitation, however, the relation between accusation and experience is rather indirect and unspoken. […] While the reformer as well as the revolutionary employ their own energies to elevate the thoughts and emotions of their audience to a higher level of consciousness, the agitator strives to exaggerate and intensify the irrational elements of the original accusation.

(1982, 22)

Löwenthal wrote these sentences under the impression of World War II and the impact of Nazi propaganda during his exile in the US. His analysis of the Führer-personality certainly remains valid to this day.

Performing Right-wing Populist Agenda: Authenticity and Charisma

In the political field, both frontstage and backstage, right-wing populist politicians have to be perceived as *authentic*, as 'one of us', that is, as understanding the problems and needs of everybody, and must avoid being (perceived as) distant to 'the people' (see Image 6.1). *Authenticity* implies and presupposes that such politicians represent, know and understand how 'normal' Austrian, British or Hungarian citizens feel and live. They are part of the in-group; not strangers, not elitist or intellectual, but firmly rooted in common-sense opinions and beliefs. They visit the same pubs as everybody else; they travel to similar places, drive similar cars, have similar problems in their family lives, and speak the same language, that is, the mother tongue (see Chapter 4). Simultaneously, they are also constructed as being the representatives of the common/ordinary people, having the necessary courage to say what the woman/man on the street only thinks; they dare oppose the powerful and be direct and explicit, not minding or even transcending the rules of political correctness and politeness. Below, I illustrate in detail how authenticity is enacted and performed in a case study of the leader of the Austrian Freedom Party, HC Strache (Vignette 13). So, for the moment, a few brief examples should suffice to illustrate the above.

During my fieldwork in Washington, DC, the journalist from *Newsweek* (Interviewee 1) explained to me why Sarah Palin was perceived as being authentic, whereas Barack Obama was not:

Text 6.4

I1: There is the divide, I think, between the parties in what you want in a leader, so Democrats are very much, Democrats tend to say, this is very simplified but for my reporting I noticed that the Democrats tend to say: You know what? I'm not an elite person, I'm not an eloquent person, I'm not a rich person, I can't be president personally, I want somebody who is better than me, who is smarter than me, who knows the nuance, who can understand, who can negotiate; and the Republicans, again very simplified, this is not everyone, but generally say: You know I'm a dad, I've got a lot of work to do, I have four kids, I have stuff on the weekends, I can't, don't have time to be president but I want someone who's just like me, who understands my struggle, who understand what's like to have job or have kids and so … yeah Democrats sound like they want someone better, Republicans sound like they want someone just like me. […] I think that's why you see the rise of Pres Obama who's you know who is, this Harvard educated elite, he's wealthy and then you see the popularity of somebody like Sarah Palin, who's just a mum from Wasilla, Alaska, she's just a hockey mum, right […]. You know – you cannot have a beer with him [Obama], chop some wood, go to his ranch you know […] So yeah, Republicans and Conservatives say, I want 'me' politics and anyone who doesn't look like us, anyone who doesn't get us, anyone who's elite, anyone who's wealthy or a snob, we don't want them in office because they are not gonna speak up for the Everyman.'

(Interview transcript, 27 February 2012, Washington DC)

Authenticity (for US voters) therefore seems to presuppose that manual labour, building one's own house, chopping wood in the forest, and apparently being part of the Wild West mythology are salient attributes for a (white) American man and successful politician; in any case, they have to sound and feel like everybody else – this is the heart of '*me*/everybody-politics', not elitist, not better and not different. Obviously, part of this cognitive frame implies that such men are necessarily white and certainly not Harvard-educated as the then incumbent candidate, Barack Obama. Latent racism is combined with *anti-intellectualism* and very traditional male roles.[5] Being like everybody else relates to another traditional gender-role: 'being the grizzly mom' was put forward by the former candidate for vice president 2008, Sarah Palin, asserting that 'moms just know when something's wrong'.[6] Here, it is presupposed that mothers intuitively know what their families and children need regardless of any education or training; indeed, it is possible to observe an explicit pride in *not* knowing specific facts because ordinary people also don't know and don't have to know. I have labelled this attitude the '*arrogance of ignorance*' (Wodak 2013a, 2013b; Chapter 7).

Moreover, being a 'grizzly mom' implies being prepared to protect your family and fight enemies. Such quasi-natural empathy and intuition, it is further presupposed, is inborn.[7] Of course, this female role was and is launched in opposition to Hillary Clinton, who constructs herself very differently, as a knowledgeable, educated and experienced politician (Tannen 2008). Considering the Tea Party candidates for the elections of both 2008 and 2012 in the US, it is obvious that such positionings as authentic and 'one of us' are virtual and artificial as none of the candidates could earnestly be considered as such: any US candidate for an election must be very wealthy or have very wealthy supporters, which certainly sets her/him apart from the man or woman on the street, particularly during the financial crisis of 2008. Ben Alpers, an expert in US contemporary history, summarizes the meaning of authenticity in the US (and, by implication, also beyond) as follows:

Authenticity as it's invoked in our political talk may be an empirically lousy concept, a buzzword borrowed from existentialism, shorn of any intellectual depth it might once have had. But authenticity talk actually makes a political difference, as all those who rightly complain about the way the media treated Gore and Bush in 2000 would acknowledge. In fact, I think authenticity talk has political significance beyond the crude levels of character assassination and political hagiography. Among its other functions:

- It's a way of discussing how much one can trust what a particular politician says.

- It's a way of describing the cultural fit (or, more sceptically, the imaginary cultural fit) between a politician and his or her potential (primary or general) electorate.

- It's a shorthand for a host of questions about character (another important concept whose concrete existence is hard to pin down).

The empirical dodginess of authenticity talk makes it an imperfect tool for all of these things. And one might more generally deplore the importance of some of them in our political culture. Why should it matter, for example, that a candidate is an appropriate cultural 'fit'? But what one can't do is pretend that these things don't matter simply on the basis of the fact that they shouldn't.

(Alpers, 2012)

Other examples of authenticity are easily found in European right-wing populist parties: Nigel Farage of UKIP, for example, likes being depicted in pubs and opposing the smoking ban as something illiberal and stupid;[8] Geert Wilders of the Dutch PVV joins the chanting of his followers and rages against Moroccans,[9] thus saying what his followers don't dare say; and so forth (see above). Of course, such chanting and slogans are intended as a strategy of provocation, causing typical 'talk scandals' (Ekström and Johansson 2008), and immediately make the headlines, also internationally. Jörg Haider used to change his outfits several times on one day during campaigning, always accommodating the immediate context and the audience, thus wearing casual trendy clothes when speaking to young urban audiences and folklore outfits in villages.

Furthermore, while performing, successful media-savvy politicians make use of their *charisma*. This concept has been developed by the sociologist Max Weber in his conceptualization of authority (Weber 1978, 217–46, 1111–57) as a 'quality of an individual personality' (ibid., 241) and a 'specific gift of body and mind' (ibid., 1112). However, perceiving charisma as 'gift or grace' ignores the socio-political aspects related to political leadership (Eatwell 2007). A Weberian perspective on Barack Obama's charisma and its impact on the US presidential election campaign would, for example, tend to reduce charisma to his personality. To the contrary, charisma in politics has to be linked to the audience's recognition of the 'right' set of social and cultural capital (habitus) within the 'right' context. Charisma is therefore socially constructed and has to be publicly recognized.

A purely psychological notion of charisma overlooks the actor's actual performance (Goffman 1971). It is necessary to de-naturalize charisma, stress its social-constructivist aspect, and explore how agents *become* charismatic (and possibly *lose* their charisma, as could be observed in many debates surrounding previously prominent politicians like Berlusconi or Sarkozy); by extension, it is equally necessary to look at how charisma becomes *routinized* (Weber 1978, 246–54, 1121ff.). Accordingly, Eatwell (2007, 6–11) conceptualizes charisma via four leadership traits, all of which have to be fulfilled by the politician in question:

1. Charismatic leaders have a mission, as saviour of the people.
2. Charismatic leaders portray themselves as ordinary men, as merely obeying the wishes of the people, and thus also as having a symbiotic relationship with the people they represent.

3. Enemies are targeted, indeed demonized.

4. Charismatic personalities have great personal presence, which is frequently described as 'magnetism'.

Apart from such personality traits, the unique bond with recipients, the interaction with and impact on the audience also has to be accounted for. Eatwell (2007) suggests that charismatic leaders have to be able to attract a hard core of supporters who are absolutely loyal and invest substantial energy by working for the leader and the party. This is called '*coterie-charisma*'. Also, such leaders are metonymically identified with their parties, which Eatwell labels as '*centripetal charisma*'. And, finally, Eatwell distinguishes the process of charismatization, that is, '*cultic charisma*', as the deliberate attempt to create something like a religious aura surrounding the leader (ibid., 16–17). Eatwell applies his model of charisma very plausibly to Mussolini and Hitler; it is quite obvious that these characteristics and dimensions fit charismatic politicians nowadays as well, reinforced and reproduced as they are via media outlets and their web performances, as will be illustrated for HC Strache, the current leader of the FPÖ, as a case in point below.

Media, Commodification and Branding

Grande (2000) argues convincingly that there are 'the two dimensions of politics, guided by different types of political logic': on the one hand, the functionally-oriented logic of political execution and implementation of power [*Verhandlungsdemokratie*]; on the other hand, the logic of gaining or sustaining power rooted in the socio-economic conditions of media-based representation of politics [*Mediendemokratie*] (ibid., 123–4). These two dimensions of politics are characterized by significantly different types of political behaviour and practices, which, in turn, also affect the relevance of certain political actors and their political imaginaries. Thus, *Verhandlungsdemokratie* is based on the constant search for political compromise and on the anonymization of individual contributions to the complex processes of negotiation-based consensus seeking (usually backstage). *Mediendemokratie*, however, is based on the recurrent foregrounding of political issues as well as on the 'personalization of successes and failures' (ibid., 29), which are then ascribed to selected media-savvy individual political actors (frontstage) (e.g. Chapter 1).

The development towards a (contradictory) celebrity culture goes hand in hand with other social changes in late modernity, such as 'a radical unsettling of the boundaries of social life', including, on a textual level, the unsettling of boundaries 'between different domains of social use of language', leading to a 'pervasive *discoursal hybridity*', that is, the mixing of discourses and genres (Chouliaraki and Fairclough 1999, 83). This hybridity is fuelled by – and further fuels – the *conversationalization* of public life (Fairclough 2010, 135ff.). Branding in respect to media personalities is characterized primarily by constructing the uniqueness of the political party and its leader; by developing a metonymic relationship between the people and its products; by developing *recognizability* via a standardized layout (of posters and slogans), focusing on specific agenda and frames, repeating slogans over and over; and finally by selling the brand through various everyday products (such as T-shirts, cups, caps and so forth) (Karmasin 2004, 473). Thus, politics and politicians become commodified.

While the FPÖ, for example, has always strived for a strong presence in the traditional media and communicated with its voters by means of more traditional political communication genres (in particular via rallies, speeches, etc., but also through official genres like party programmes), the recently 'revamped' FPÖ under HC Strache has turned increasingly to the new Web-based media as its main channels of political communication (Forchtner et al. 2013; Krzyżanowski 2013a). Currently, the FPÖ maintains its Web presence via the main party Web page (www.fpoe.at) and a party-related think-tank (www.fpoe-bildungsinstitut.at). Members of the FPÖ also operate a blog called 'Uncensored' (www.unzensuriert.at)[10] and an official YouTube channel (www.youtube.com/Oesterreichzuerst) called 'Austria First', a name employed in many campaigns and major referenda undertaken by the party in both the 1990s and 2000s (see Reisigl and Wodak 2000). The YouTube channel employs a variety of genres, ranging from recordings of HC Strache's speeches and interviews to his rap songs (see below; Image 6.11) and different election-campaign spots and short films. Moreover, beyond its official presence, the party also manages the Web presence of its leader – via his Web page (www.hc-strache.at) – as well as channels on Facebook (www.facebook.com/HCStrache?ref=mf) and Flickr (www.flickr.com/search/?q=strache&w=all) – yet with much content from HC Strache's official pages, also available at other FPÖ domains (see Pick, 2013). In this way, one can indeed buy caps and T-shirts with the HC Strache brand (see Image 6.2). To illustrate the ongoing branding, Strache uses word play and renames himself as HC Stra-Che, thus merging the name of the famous Cuban revolutionary leader Che Guevara with his own name and, subsequently, his positioning.

Image 6.2   HC Strache merchandise

Recent research on political discourse has emphasized the importance of Web 2.0 and social media, since such easily accessible, quasi-private and at the same time quasi-public communication platforms as Facebook and Twitter allow new forms of *participation in political discourse and deliberation* (Angouri and Wodak 2014; Morley and Robins 2002) as well as positioning and branding of one's unique political identity, one's unique selling point (USP) and one's stance. Thus, Jenkins argues that

> the new political culture – just like the new popular culture – reflects the pull and tug of these two media systems: one broadcast and commercial, the other narrowcast and grassroots. […] Broadcasting provides the common culture, and the Web offers more localized channels for responding to that culture.

(2008, 222)

The fact that political elites often demonstrate a stark lack of competence at using these new forms, whereas right-wing populist politicians seem to be very competent at it, poses further questions regarding participation and legitimization (Päivärinta and Sæbø 2006). The World Wide Web is seen as a hypertextually organized distribution medium that integrates all other digitally transmitted forms of communication and media of first and second order (Schlobinski 2005, 9) or, as argued by Castells (2007), establishes a 'network society'. Alongside websites and blogs, social networks provide a notable space for self-presentation and 'impression management' for politics; Facebook in particular has become an online-media 'machine' for performative-semiotic constructions of the self (Barton and Lee 2013; see Vignette 1). As illustrated by Reichert (2008, 62), the global market of narration is based on conceptualizations of a mediatized 'economy of attention', which conflates story-telling about oneself with entrepreneurial strategies of communication and commodification. Blasch (2012) takes this insight as her point of departure and develops the analytical categories of Kress (2003), van Leeuwen (1996) and Dyer (1998) into a framework for analysing the media constructions of (hyperreal) politicians' identities and positionings on the World Wide Web. Below, I draw on her framework of categories and *levels of multimodal identity construction* (Blasch 2012, 160–63) when analysing some incidents of HC Strache and the FPÖ's performance. I focus primarily on:

- *appearance* – gaze, dress;
- *staging, performativity* – actions and interactions, interpersonal relationships as represented on the various genres (posters, Facebook, homepage, and so forth);
- *objective context/setting* – background, room;
- *speech of character and of others* – in bubbles (e.g. comics);
- *gestures*;
- *visual style and composition* – colours, social media icons, layout, eye-catchers;
- *content* – slogans, *topoi*, intertextual references, interdiscursivity, ideologemes.

VIGNETTE 13
PERFORMING RIGHT-WING POPULIST POLITICS: HC STRACHE
Multiple Identities: A 'Man for All Seasons'

Pels characterizes media-savvy right-wing populist politicians as:

> political leaders [who] shed their elitist aura and try to become 'one of us'. On the other hand, distance is reasserted by the remoteness of the star who, while dwelling constantly in the public eye, is still seen as untouchable and as 'living in a different world'. In this sense, politicians increasingly share in the 'extraordinary ordinariness' which characterises the modern democratic celebrity'.

(2003, 59)

Indeed, such politicians oscillate between the abstract and concrete, between fiction and reality, between ordinariness and stardom, between governmental and campaign styles, hence representing many identities adapted to a range of audiences whose vote they strive to gain. HC Strache establishes his Facebook page as a 'war room' which – in contrast to his mainstream opponents – conceptualizes the metaphor of *war* via a boxing match and the battleground of his election campaign in Vienna 2010 as a boxing ring (Image 6.3).

Image 6.3   HC Strache Facebook page 2010

This screenshot illustrates many of the elements discussed above. First, HC Strache, standing in the middle of a podium, dressed in a suit with a tie, seems misplaced on this stage designed to remind the viewer of a boxing match. He blends politics and sports, addressing a nation (Austria) of sports enthusiasts, and reframing politics as winner-takes-all competition between individuals and nations. Simultaneously, Strache appears as a statesman; his gaze is directed at the viewer, surrounded by his small group of hard core male supporters who carry his bag and other important materials. Outside the fence, another group of supporters, young women, hold posters which manifest the typical 'HC brand': all posters are constructed with the same layout, red and white on the top (the colours of the Austrian flag) with blue at the bottom (the colour of the FPÖ, indexing freedom). The slogans vary at the top of the image, realizing the campaign agenda, while the bottom slogan remains the same throughout. Slogans read 'We are concerned with our fellow Viennese' and 'Clear the ring', that is, setting the stage for HC Strache and his speech. The core followers and other supporters are dressed casually, all wearing some accessories branded with 'Strache' (caps, T-shirts and sweaters); four men surround Strache, possibly bodyguards as their gaze is directed at the audience. The name of the 'star', HC Strache, functions as logo and brand throughout the stage (and war room) on all posters, on the podium, and on all other materials. Intertextual references are made to many other posters (via their recognizable layout) and via the colours which are used on all posters and establish indexicality to the Austrian flag. Moreover, the reoccurring metonymic relationship between the pronoun 'We' (i.e. Strache and the FPÖ)

(Continued)

137

(Continued)

and 'us Viennese' is realized in the slogan on the podium, thus constructing Strache as part of the Viennese in-group and as the main representative (and fighter for the Viennese) all at once. Strache positions himself as serious politician, sportsman, celebrity, saviour and star in the midst of his followers, surrounded by quasi-cheerleaders. In this way, he establishes the symbiotic bond between audience and himself, despite the contradictory elements present.

Indeed, for those in the know, the positioning as fighter insinuates Strache's youth in extreme right-wing groups, an identity Strache would like to sweep under the carpet and which does not fit well with the 'soft' image strategically conveyed by his current performance: leaked pictures show him in soldier-like uniform, practising with paintball guns together with a very well-known neo-Nazi, Gottfried Küssel, who has been convicted several times for neo-Nazi activities.[11] After having unsuccessfully denied such activities, HC Strache currently defines these as 'youth adventures' and thus attempts relativizing his former activities. However, this well-known past and some strategically placed coded messages time and again continue to appeal to the extreme right-wing core supporters of the FPÖ and leave no doubt whatsoever which ideologies underlie this party's programme,[12] that is, extreme right, frequently revisionist and neo-Nazi ideologemes.[13] Several examples of Strache's and the FPÖ's exclusionary ideologies and the related nationalistic and nativist body politics are documented and analysed throughout this book (e.g. Vignettes 1, 3, 5, 10, 11, 14; and below).

In positioning himself as a youthful, serious and approachable handsome politician (while distancing himself from 'sins of the past'), HC Strache smiles in various photographs of his election campaign in Styria (a region south of Vienna) that are accessible online (Image 6.4) and his gaze is always directed at the viewers.

Image 6.4   HC Strache campaigning in Gleisdorf 2014

The motif is similar to his Facebook page and thus, again, lends itself to intertextual references. Here, HC Strache is dressed casually, with a sweater on his shoulders, a neat striped shirt, and – in contrast to his main opponent, the mayor of Vienna (see Image 4.8) – appears above all youthful, confident, healthy, blue-eyed, tanned and with gleaming white teeth (incidentally, his vocation before a career in politics was as a dental assistant and technician).

In various downloadable comic books created for the election campaign in Vienna 2010 (see Forchtner and Wodak forthcoming; Wodak and Forchtner 2014), we encounter HC Strache mainly in his role as saviour, another feature of charisma as mentioned above. In two available comic books, HC Strache appears as Prince Eugene (referring to *Prince Eugen of Savoy* who saved Vienna from the Ottoman Empire in 1683), or as HC

Man (name and dress, complete with cape, clearly playing on the Superman character), or as HC Stra-Che (again, referring intertextually to Che Guevara, the revolutionary Cuban hero, fighting for liberty and freedom against various oppressors and enemies, i.e. capitalists, Americans and so forth). Thus, both comic identities construct HC Strache as a charismatic figure, the saviour from oppression. These comic book identities strategically target, of course, young audiences (see Image 6.5).

Image 6.5   HC Strache posing as Prince Eugene and HC Stra-Che 2010

Strache wears the blue Superman suit, with a small Austrian flag on his sleeve and the logo 'HC' on his chest. He is fit, healthy and full of energy, thus conveying the strength to save Vienna.

Image 6.6   HC Strache in a disco 2008

(Continued)

(Continued)

In Image 6.6 (a snapshot posted online in *Der Standard* 26 December 2008; http://derstandard.at/1229975033141/Generation-Zukunft-Out-of-touch---die-leben-alle-in-der-steinzeit), Strache is wearing his HC Stra-Che T-shirt and is positioning himself as a young, seductive and sexy male, one of 'Us', dancing in the disco like everybody else. He is signing a woman's breast, similar to pop stars like Keith Richards. He thus foregrounds his traditional male role merged with the image of a typical attractive male celebrity. Indeed, part of his campaigning habitus consists of specifically addressing and attracting the young generation. During his 2010 election campaign he promised that he would visit every disco and club in Vienna. Results illustrate that Strache was successful in addressing the young generation, in particular young men;[14] in 2010, 27 per cent of young men (under 25) voted for the FPÖ in Vienna (see Chapter 7 on the gender gap in voting for right-wing parties):

> [T]he youthful image of the FPÖ is tied to its leading candidate Heinz-Christian Strache and his inner circle, which projects a casual and youthful image. The FPÖ, so Heinzlmaier [an expert on youth culture], is an unpolitical party, but is authentic. At the same time, it is caught in a certain milieu and finds it difficult to reach beyond its core voters. 'This is also the party's fate', continues Heinzlmaier.
>
> (Die Presse n.d.)

In Image 6.7, HC Strache appears as saviour, carrying a cross during a campaign opposing plans to build a mosque in Vienna. In this image (launched by the FPÖ), Strache positions himself as a warrior dressed in black, pictured in strong contrast and shadows, utterly serious, with a threatening gaze, intertextually related to the frame of a crusade, fighting for the Occident, thus constructing a religious aura, another important dimension of charisma, as mentioned above.

Image 6.7 HC Strache with cross 2009

It is interesting to observe that the FPÖ strongly opposes migration and, at the same time, pursues a campaign strategy of targeting a specific immigrant electorate or, more precisely, Austrian citizens with Serbian roots. Why 'Serbs' in particular are being targeted can be explained, on the one hand, by their status as third largest immigrant group in Austria and, on the other hand, by their largely Christian denomination, which in the eyes of the FPÖ makes them culturally similar and thus 'capable of integration', but also, perhaps more importantly, viable for being integrated into his campaigning. The play on Christianity also seeks to exploit traditional animosity harboured by nationalist Serbs against other immigrants from former Yugoslavia such as 'Bosnians' and 'Albanians' identified with Islam. Indeed, it was as an institutional bridge to the Serbian minority in Austria that a 'Christian Freedom Platform' was founded in 2009. Beyond this exceptional case, the Austrian right is united in its opposition to immigration, stating reasons ranging from the social-demagogical (in the case of the FPÖ) to the ethno-pluralistic (in the case of the *'Bloc identitaire'*, a right-wing group established in 2013 and oriented towards a 'real' Austrian identity) and the openly racist (in neo-Nazi circles). As the common bracket for all these we can recognize the motive of defending the 'cultural identity' of Austria, allegedly threatened by immigration, that the various factions have diverging definitions of (i.e. as German in the traditional far-right, as Austrian in the more modern far-right).

The many positionings of HC Strache, some of which I have been able to illustrate above, construct a multi-faceted politicians' identity, oriented towards some and excluding others: as saviour of the Occident; as casual, smiling but also serious statesman; as fighter; as attractive young man; as extreme right-wing fraternity member with paramilitary experience; and as hero, revolutionary and superman, surrounded by loyal supporters, cheerleaders, bodyguards, and smiling young men and women. In this way, one could reiterate that Strache – like his predecessor Haider before him – is a 'man for all seasons' (Gingrich 2002), adaptable to the needs and desires of ordinary people, bonding with them as well as representing them. The party, through all of this, is metonymically identified with him and his agenda, consisting mainly of anti-immigration policies, anti-EU agenda and nativist nationalism as well as more-or-less explicit insinuations of Nazi ideology and a revisionist conception of Austria's (and Germany's) history.

To return to Strache's over two-hour-long speech, directed solely at his party members and core followers on 22 January 2011, thus quasi on 'frontstage in the backstage' (Text 6.3.): he sought to boost his personal biography by choosing the former, famous and widely admired social-democratic Austrian-Jewish Prime Minister Bruno Kreisky (Austrian chancellor in the 1970s) as his model.[15] This attempt forms part of the concluding remarks – which depict a new political imaginary for Austria with Strache as prospective chancellor – after having discussed the agenda for the party, having challenged opposing political voices as well as the policies of the EU, repeatedly speaking out firmly against immigration and foreigners and so forth. At the end of the speech, Strache reminds the audience that this day, 22 January 2011, is the 100th birthday of former Chancellor Bruno Kreisky and suggests that it is worth remembering the charismatic politician Kreisky. He lists some negative experiences and failures as well as many positive achievements and juxtaposes Kreisky's and his own vision to the current government, which he represents exclusively in a negative light.

Strache constructs his identity by appropriating Kreisky's positive characteristics, such as the ability to mobilize and fascinate people, to convince them of important political goals, to reinforce a strong, independent and neutral Austria, to befriend both Arab leaders and Israeli politicians, to inspire hope for the future and so forth. Kreisky, Strache emphasizes, was courageous, he worked for the people (implying that he was a generic populist), and he was an intellectual, with much humour and wit: 'he was a great Austrian' – a phrase he repeats several times. Most importantly, Strache argues, Kreisky was somebody who formed a coalition with the Freedom Party in the 1970s and did not isolate the FPÖ. Many positive flagwords are included in this short extract. Strache thus commemorates an ideal-type charismatic statesman who knew what was good 'for the people' and, simultaneously, was 'one of the people' – which is precisely the image that Strache wants to project.

By claiming that he is similar to Kreisky and could thus actually be perceived as his successor, Kreisky's highly praised attributes would then also automatically be transferred to him, that is, become part of his personality and his appeal. Moreover, Strache implicitly seeks to dismantle any accusations of being racist or antisemitic by identifying with Kreisky, a left-wing social-democratic intellectual and secular Austrian Jew who was in exile in Sweden during World War II and also incarcerated by the Austrian-fascist government in Vienna after the civil war of 1934. Finally, by appropriating Kreisky's social-democratic agenda, Strache is able to present himself as a caring and socially oriented, middle-of-the-road, responsible politician; *he* should therefore be perceived as Kreisky's successor, more capable and innovative than the current social-democratic chancellor Werner Faymann, whom he ridicules during large parts of his speech. *He*, Strache, would continue Kreisky's legacy and would be able to shape the country similar to his model, as a 'safe and just society'. Such positioning receives much applause; the identification with the most charismatic post-war Austrian politician (who, of course, was positioned on precisely the other extreme of the political spectrum, as socialist, internationally oriented, cosmopolitan, left-wing secular Jew) is obviously accepted and believed (or at least wished for):

Text 6.5

'Dear friends, today the 22 January 2011 is also a special day that we cannot completely ignore, the 100th birthday of Bruno Kreisky is today and I will tell you one thing, Bruno Kreisky was a great Austrian. [...] And Bruno Kreisky was a great Austrian, a great politician in foreign policy who reinvigorated the neutrality of our country like no other in the Second Republic. [...] And certainly there are many things that Kreisky did that we cannot condone in retrospect. [...] He was able to fill people with enthusiasm then, he was able to inspire hope, he brought our small country Austria with its neutral positioning on the international level, which I want to revive as well, into a very good position for the Arab as well as the Jewish side. Kreisky regarded the people as the aim of his work. [...] And one thing Kreisky had for certain, he had the will to shape. That distinguished him. He was someone with great intellect, with wit, with courage, but also someone who ultimately also always tried to reach consensus in our society. And he was the one socialist-democratic chairman who did not exclude the FPÖ, because he knew how important and valuable we are for our homeland, dear friends. (applause) Dear friends, with this will to shape things, which Bruno Kreisky exhibited, Bruno Kreisky can indeed for us, in this aspect be a model for me. We want to shape, we want to accept responsibility, we want to implement our right and valid concerns, to the advantage of the people, yes, and we want to become the strongest and decisive power [...] because at the end our homeland has a future again and the young people have a future development in a safe society and in a socially just society where we can hold our own. (applause)'

The argumentation scheme underlying the entire speech implies that Strache would be the right chancellor for Austria as *he* knows what everybody wants, as he would act responsibly and would protect Austrian interests (and the 'homeland'), as he is aware of imminent dangers and threats, and finally that he would succeed as he is similar to the eminent politician Bruno Kreisky; thus the *topoi of saviour, threat, urgency and responsibility* are used throughout (Figure 6.1).

The *topos* of saviour

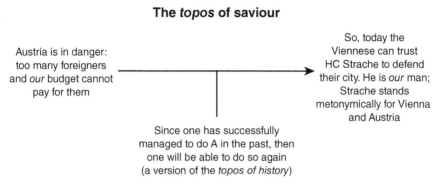

Figure 6.1 *Topos of saviour* combined with the *topos of history*

Performing the FPÖ's Agenda: Exclusionary Rhetoric

Identity always implies similarity and difference. Each of Strache's identities is thus inclusive (of young people, attractive women, Serbs and Christians etc.) and simultaneously exclusionary (of all non-Christians, specifically Muslim immigrants). Krzyżanowski characterizes the transformation of the FPÖ since the so-called Haider years in the following way:

> In contrast to the Haider era when FPÖ discourse was dominated by anti-immigrant, nationalistic, revisionist and anti-establishment rhetoric, recent years have been dominated by the party's overt turn to Islamophobia as its central discursive and policy frame.
>
> (2013a, 141)

Drawing on his analysis of a range of Islamophobic posters, slogans and policy documents, Krzyżanowski constructs the semantic field depicted in Figure 6.2 to represent the main concepts of the FPÖ's propaganda related to anti-Muslim campaigning (ibid., 143).

Different aspects of Islam are elaborated throughout the various genres. Topics range from minarets as symbols of Muslim violence and the rising number of Muslims living in Austria, to a specific understanding of gender politics and Muslims' and women's rights (see Vignette 14). All the dimensions of Islam are represented in a clearly negative light implying that, for example, Muslim education is 'radical' or that religious freedoms are 'abused' by Muslims. Islam is thus represented as an omnipresent threat to Austria and Europe as a whole. Accordingly, the arguments are constructed via the *topoi of danger and threat* as well as *urgency*.

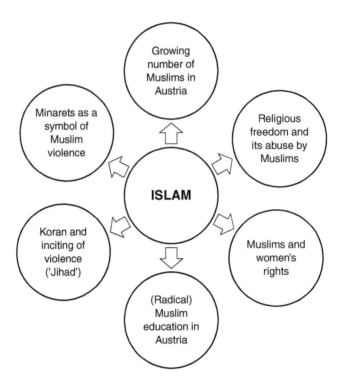

Figure 6.2 Semantic field of 'Islam' as used by the Austrian Freedom Party (FPÖ) (adapted from Krzyzanowski 2013a, 143)

In the traditionally anti-clerical FPÖ, a predominantly instrumental approach is apparent, drawing on religion as a carrier medium and means of justification for its xenophobic agenda. The anti-clerical legacy of the party also permeates the references to 'cultural Christianity' and the necessity to defend the 'Christian roots' of Europe as a repertoire of cultural traditions. This conception of Christianity as cultural rather than immediately religious also represents a major difference to the political programme and rhetoric of the US right-wing parties, which very explicitly strives to weaken the separation of Church and State (Weidinger 2014). Not only do we more frequently find Christian references in the immigration discourse of right-wing politicians in the US, they are also championed for heterogeneous motivations: both the immigration-friendly and the immigration-opposing right argues its respective position by way of Christianity, among other things. We find, for example, a balancing of immigration against abortion with the aim of prohibiting both (see Vignette 15).

In part, very similar motives and *topoi* can be identified in Austria, where the FPÖ built its campaign for the parliamentary elections of 2013 around the flagword '*Nächstenliebe*', a German term that carries the meanings of Christian love of one's neighbour, but explicitly used it to refer to 'our Austrians'. Christian resonances can be found in the FPÖ's use of symbols like the cross and St. Stephen's Cathedral (see Image 6.7). The dominant line of argument, once again, is to position Christianity as the cultural heritage and value system on which Austria or Europe are based and which must be defended against the so-called '*Überfremdung*', a German Nazi term that carries the meanings of 'foreign domination' and the feeling of 'being overwhelmed by immigrants' (see the slogan '*Abendland in Christen-hand*', i.e. 'Occident in Christian hands' from the FPÖ's campaign for the EU election in 2009; Wodak and Köhler 2010).

As illustrated in Chapters 1, 3 and 5, however, the FPÖ's ideology is characterized not only by Islamophobic statements and beliefs; antisemitic sentiments are also continuously addressed, ranging from caricatures depicting traditional stereotypes of the greedy 'capitalist Jew' (Vignette 1) to Holocaust denial as manifested in statements by the former FPÖ candidate for president, Barbara Rosenkranz (see Vignette 11). Indeed, HC Strache reversed the roles and suddenly labelled the FPÖ the 'new Jews' when an extreme right-wing fraternity ball was attacked by demonstrators (Image 6.8) because it was held on Holocaust commemoration day (27 January 2012),[16] thus appropriating Jewish suffering and victimhood for the FPÖ and himself, thereby trivializing and de-historicizing the Holocaust and Nazi war crimes. In Image 6.9, Strache and his fraternity colleague are wearing black ties and their fraternity caps, thus merging the usual dress code for balls with the fraternity uniform. Here, we encounter a further positioning of HC Strache as a member of the extreme right-wing duelling fraternity *Olympia*. Attacks by a few demonstrators during the ball were fallaciously compared and equated with the November pogrom of 9 November 1938, when violent Nazis terrorized the Jewish population in Vienna, destroyed almost all Viennese synagogues and murdered over 200 Viennese Jews. Thus, Strache obviously applies a trivializing discursive strategy combined with a *topos of history*.

Image 6.8   Screenshot of HC Strache TV evening news, 27 January 2012

Image 6.9   HC Strache wearing his duelling-fraternity cap, *Akademikerball*, 27 January 2012

In the 2010 local elections in Vienna,[17] the focus on an alleged 'non-Austrian threat' was reinforced in a poster (Image 6.10) appealing for *'More courage for our "Viennese Blood"* [in pure, saturated red]. *Too much otherness is not good for anybody* [maximally dark, taking the form of a stamp]'. The poster calls for 'courage', which is apparently manifested by the FPÖ, implying that those in power lack the necessary courage. The poster explicitly links the opposition of *us* against *them* to nativism, that is, to blood and thus to biologically constructed groups, facilitating an obviously racist categorization. The representation of HC Strache is similar to the positioning as serious politician (see Images 6.3 and 6.4. above): youthful, casual and healthy, a spotless white shirt, unbuttoned at the top, no jacket or tie, brilliant blue eyes and white teeth, a tanned complexion, dense brown hair with only a touch of grey at the temples; he smiles self-confidently from the poster's surface.

Image 6.10   FPÖ poster, Vienna election campaign 2010

At the top, on the poster's right, we find the party logo consisting of two elements: the party acronym FPÖ and the predication *'Die soziale Heimatpartei'*, meaning 'The Social Homeland-Party'. The logo thus emphasizes the self-presentation of the party as liberal, social and homeland-oriented, thus combining recurring flag-words of the FPÖ (e.g. Text 6.4). These three predications also fulfil the important principle of addressing multiple audiences as the party acronym satisfies both traditional FPÖ voters and the whole party. The attribute 'social' is a positive signal to socialist voters dissatisfied with current policies of the governing Social Democratic Party. The compound *'Heimatpartei'* with its specifying predication *'Heimat'* obviously targets conservatives and nationalists, and is intended to evoke patriotic feelings of belonging to the local community, oriented towards traditional rural values.

Beneath the logo, on the right, there is a rhyme in red letters: 'More COURAGE for our "Viennese blood"', in German *'Mehr MUT für unser "Wiener Blut"'*; slightly beneath the rhyme, in black, is the line 'Too much of the foreign is not good for anybody' (*'Zu viel Fremdes tut niemandem gut.'*). Rhyming slogans are integral to the Strache brand: most posters manifest rhymes (see Wodak and Köhler 2010). The rhyming speech act is an elliptical appeal and request in slogan-like nominal style, constructing a 'we-group' which is characterized by its *blood*. The blood is thus specified as having the quality of being 'Viennese'. Its use follows the strategy of *calculated ambivalence*, which allows for manifold convenient readings. 'Blood' represents biological descent, kinship and ancestry. The opposition of 'our Viennese blood' and the depersonalizing metonymy 'too much of the foreign' contributes to the naturalizing construction of a Viennese we-group which seems endangered by 'too' many foreign immigrants. The producers of the poster, however, took precautions against such a literal racist reading of 'Viennese blood' – which implies that they were indeed conscious of the phrase's biologizing meaning; that it was, in fact, intended. By framing the phrase in quotation marks, the authors distance themselves from the literal meaning (perspectivization strategy).

Beyond the biological, 'Viennese blood' also implies Viennese culture, since *Wiener Blut* is the title of the well-known waltz and operetta by Johann Strauss (junior). Strauss and his music are clear identity markers for a specific Austrian and particularly Viennese culture. The request for 'more courage for our Viennese blood' presupposes that, nowadays, political opponents are not brave enough to engage in protection of the 'Viennese essence'. Hence, the appeal suggests that the FPÖ, in contrast to the other political parties, is ready to protect this 'Viennese essence' against 'too much of the foreign'; and this 'fact' further implies that the party deserves to be elected. The ellipsis at the bottom of the poster concludes with the claim: 'Therefore, Yes for HC Strache.' ('*Deshalb Ja zu HC Strache.*'). The claim is visually supplemented by a circle marked with a quasi-hand-drawn red cross. In sum, the poster condenses the following argumentation scheme: 'You should vote for Strache and the FPÖ, because he and his party are more courageous than their political opponents and will protect our "Viennese blood" against "too much of the foreign"'.

At this point, one question remains: What do Strache and the FPÖ consider 'too much of the foreign'? The answer is not explicitly given in the poster, but it can be found in other election campaign material related intertextually to the poster, with anti-foreigner and particularly anti-Muslim statements and sentiments. The fear-mongering of the FPÖ had its intended effect: in the Viennese election 2010, the FPÖ received 25.8 per cent of the votes – 11 per cent more than in 2005. In a public opinion poll after the election, 68 per cent of the respondents who voted for the FPÖ stated that they did so because the FPÖ is active against migration (see Köhler and Wodak 2011, 73).

During the scandal, the FPÖ rejected all criticism and responded by producing a new advertisement, this one on the topic 'What do we mean by "Too much of the foreign is not good for anybody"?'.[18] On the surface, this creates the appearance of a rational discourse; the contents of its arguments, however, are recognizable as a mixture of insinuations and indirect statements, formulated as conditional clauses, which makes it almost impossible to reject them directly. The arguments brought forth in this poster do, however, clarify what is meant by 'the foreign'. On the one hand, they attack the FPÖ's main political opponent, the SPÖ, for its alleged political position regarding immigration and integration. On the other hand, they focus specifically on religion – on Islam.

The campaign this poster was part of was also characterized by the production of an intertextually related rap song entitled *Viennese Blood* and the publication of what has become widely known as the 'Mustafa Comic' (see above, Image 6.5, FPÖ 2010; Wodak and Forchtner 2014). These media, while addressing additional audiences – in particularly a disengaged youth – thematized the very same topics, such as immigration and 'Viennese blood'. Both new media caused massive public attention and scandals; for example, the rap song has been watched almost 200,000 times on YouTube (Image 6.11), while the comic had a circulation of 550,000 (and is still available for download on HC Strache's homepage).[19]

Significantly, the song itself was not simply made available via the party's YouTube channel, but was first presented in one of Vienna's best-known discotheques and featured prominently in an explicit effort to target the youth vote.[20] In Image 6.11, Strache constructs himself as a

Image 6.11   Web page promoting HC Strache's rap song 2010

pop singer, with dark sun glasses, and in the various snapshots on the right side as a performer, singing with the microphone and addressing the cheering audience. He is obviously having fun. The text of the song is centred and is represented like an old scroll or manuscript.[21]

Paradoxically, if not surprisingly, several contradictions arise within the anti-immigrant rhetoric and related practices of the FPÖ: American as well as European right-wing populists also oppose immigration of people with Christian background, yet they hardly object to well-off immigrants of other religious denominations; overall, they seem little concerned with the actual denomination of those whose presence they find irritating, and employ the attribute 'Christian' as a very dynamic, at times even arbitrary predication. Possibly, one could speculate, religion is not the (only) actual motive of anti-immigrant marginalization, but a pretext to conceal other reasons for opposing them. These would include, above all, social-political motives (fears of competition and decline caused by the socio-economic status of immigrants) and an interdependent racism that instrumentalizes religion in the service of white or autochthonous safeguarding of power and resources as a tool for Othering-processes; but also very traditional and perpetually reinvigorated collective fears and prejudices in the sense of *Iudeus ex machina*, that is, socio-psychologically internalized strategies of scapegoating.

Endnotes

1   See http://image.guardian.co.uk/sys-files/Guardian/documents/2011/03/13/Guardian_ Euro_Poll_day1.pdf?guni=Graphic:in body link&guni=Graphic:in body link, accessed 21 December 2014.

2   I am very grateful to journalists who attended this backstage meeting and gave me the recordings. Markus Rheindorf translated these text extracts into English; of course, I analysed the German original.

3   In argumentation, repetition of an argument is sometimes even fallaciously treated as legitimate evidence or proof (fallacy of repeated assertion, proof by assertion, argument by

repetition, proof by exhaustion (of the listener), *argumentum ad nauseam* or *argumentum ad infinitum*; see Hansson 2014).

4   It is certainly not by coincidence that Joseph Goebbels, Minister of Propaganda in Nazi Germany from 1933 to 1945, wrote that 'propaganda must […] always be essentially simple and repetitive. In the long run, basic results in influencing public opinion will be achieved only by the man (sic!) who is able to reduce problems to the simplest terms and who has the courage to keep forever repeating them in this simplified form, despite the objections of the intellectuals' (Manvell and Fraenkel 1960, 211; see Hansson 2014).

5   It proved difficult to construct authenticity for the Republican candidate Mitt Romney leading up to the election of 2012 as Romney does not appear to be an authentic American male either (see http://crookedtimber.org/2012/02/13/mitt-romney-and-the-fallacy-of-political-authenticity/, accessed 29 March 2014).

6   www.momlogic.com/2010/07/sarah_palin_compares_moms_to_mama_grizzlies.php, accessed 29 March 2014.

7   See also Carmen Gartelgruber, member of the Austrian Freedom Party and one of the few female members of FPÖ in the Austrian Parliament: www.zeit.de/2013/37/fpoe-frauenquote-petra-steger/seite-2, accessed 29 March 2014. She also believes that the only place a young mother should be is at home, taking care of the children.

8   See www.huffingtonpost.co.uk/2013/04/30/nigel-farage-smoking-ban-germany-_n_3182909.html, accessed 29 March 2014.

9   www.theguardian.com/world/2014/mar/20/dutch-politician-geert-wilders-moroccans-outrage-pvv-party-anti-islam, accessed 29 March 2014.

10 The blog – there is now also a print edition – was initiated by Martin Graf, a member of a far-right fraternity and former third president of the Austrian parliament. According to the Austrian chamber of commerce (www.wkoecg.at/Web/Ecg.aspx?FirmaID=0f68efff-25b9–46cd-9edd-b18a79a9b92d, accessed 22 October 2012), it is now managed by Walter Asperl, who was also Graf's office manager during his time in parliament as third president of the chamber.

11 www.youtube.com/watch?v=1pj2koTPqv8, accessed 31 March 2014.

12 A well-known example of this is a photograph of HC Strache using the known neo-Nazi greeting (three extended fingers), supposedly to order beer: www.oe24.at/oesterreich/Erstes-Foto-von-FPOe-Chef-Strache-mit-Neo-Nazi-Gruss/76669, accessed 31 March 2014; here, too, Strache sought to relativize the known neo-Nazi sign as a simple order for three pints of beer.

13 There is a vast amount of research dealing with the FPÖ, its former leader Jörg Haider and the current leader HC Strache from many perspectives. Here, I list only some publications which have analysed the rhetoric, i.e., the racist, Islamophobic and antisemitic utterances, for further information as it would be beside the point to summarize all analyses in this vignette, focusing on Strache's positionings and performance (e.g. Czernin 2000; Forchtner et al. 2013; Krzyżanowski 2013a; Krzyżanowski and Wodak 2009; Pelinka and Wodak 2002; Reisigl 2007, 2013; Richardson and Wodak 2009b; Wodak 2007a, 2013a, 2013b, 2013c; Wodak and Köhler 2010; Wodak and Pelinka 2002; Wodak and Reisigl 2002).

14 See http://derstandard.at/1285042394492/Wiener-Jungwaehler-Junge-finden-Blau-cool-waehlen-aber-Rot, accessed 25 August 2014.

15 Bruno Kreisky no doubt also inspired Jörg Haider in the early 1970s and the latter consciously sought Kreisky's proximity at times. Kreisky himself first took a liking to the young, eloquent politician-to-be of the FPÖ, supposedly judging him to be a young 'liberal'. At least since the so-called Frischenschlager-Reder-affair, Kreisky's opinion of Haider worsened dramatically (Wodak et al. 1990). Thus, on 17 October 1988, he stated in an interview with the magazine *Profil*: 'There are real Nazis, who are life-threatening, and always will be again. Today, I would count among them Jörg Haider' (Sickinger 2008, 189).

16 See http://derstandard.at/1326504047903/STANDARD-Bericht-Strache-auf-WKR-Ball-Wir-sind-die-neuen-Juden, accessed 30 March 2014.

17 See Köhler and Wodak (2011, 12–17), Wodak and Reisigl (2015), Wodak (2013a, 2013b) and Forchtner et al. (2013) for extensive analyses of this election campaign and the poster; here, I focus only on the most important features and refer interested readers to the above-mentioned publications.

18 See www.hcstrache.at/bilder/mediaordner/g10,14110782715,0830.jpg, accessed 12 March 2015.

19 This massive effort followed similar attempts to reach young voters in the 2006 and 2008 general elections as well as the European elections in 2009 (songs) and the publication of a graphic novel, *The Blue Planet*, during the 2009 elections to the European Parliament (Forchtner and Wodak 2015).

20 Photos of these visits are available at: www.hcstrache.at/home/?id=62&p=99 and www.hcstrache.at/home/?id=62&p=104, accessed 14 September 2012.

21 Analysis of the rap song reveals a scenario in which *Us* and *Them* are demarcated throughout the text: It posits 'the people' and 'our Viennese Blood' versus 'Islamists', 'the reds', 'other habits' (those practised in Istanbul) and (Mayor) 'Häupl'. References to blood are not applied in a strictly traditionally racist sense but with 'a wink of the eye', connecting it to *Us*, the majority of the people, while coding the 'Other', from Social-Democrats to Muslims, as belonging to the uncivil, barbaric – even undemocratic – side of the binary code, the 'Other' (see Wodak and Reisigl 2015 for more detail).

7 GENDER AND THE BODY POLITIC: THE POLITICS OF PATRIARCHY

> 'I maintain that the *people* of radical right populism may be envisioned as a family construction that contours a heteronormative worldview, which orders the society according to a paternalist logic that contains women in an inferior and dependent position, even when temporarily and conditionally allowing them in politics.'
>
> Ovidiu Cristian Norocel (2013, 51)

Contradictory Phenomena, Tendencies and Some Findings

To date, gendered discourses in the rhetoric of right-wing populist parties have been largely neglected and remain under-researched. Although there is much talk about right-wing 'families' and 'party families' as conceptual metaphors for the structure of such parties and their exclusionary ideology, there is little or no awareness of the relevance of gender politics and no acknowledgement that the 'archetypical family' focuses on the power hierarchies at work between men and women: white middle-class Christian women in the privileged position of power as *mater familias*, white middle-class heterosexual Christian men as 'normal', and all other individuals (i.e. those who differ in terms of gender, ethnicity/'race', religion, social class and sexual orientation) conceptualized as 'outside' of the family (i.e. as not belonging to the family at all). This conception persists, although it is obvious that the much quoted and invoked 'people' consist of men and women, of individuals of many sexual orientations, from a range of professions, different age groups and social classes; in fact, the frequently appealed-to homogeneity is rarely challenged with respect to gender dimensions.

Because of the explicit articulation of a patriarchal frame as well as the paradoxical power that some women have held and continue to hold in such parties, it is important to investigate both *why* the ideologemes of right-wing populism attract specific voters and *which* norms and values concerning gender politics are currently promoted. At this point, several levels need to be distinguished carefully: first, the composition of the electorate (which has been researched in depth); second, the values and norms that characterize right-wing populist propaganda and refer to gender politics (and, related to this, ethno-nationalism, antisemitism and exclusionary body politics); and third, the specific image(s) that male and female leaders of right-wing populist parties strive to propagate of themselves.

The few instances in which the gender gap has been briefly mentioned occur in discussions about 'modernization and globalization-losers' (see Chapter 4): as men are frequently the victims of modernization, 'having faced not only declining wages but also a loss of authority in their families at home vis-à-vis wives who are also wage earners' (Kitschelt 2007, 1200), they tend to vote for right-wing populist parties that claim to protect and help them against the so-called privileged elites and against immigrants who are alleged to threaten them and take away their jobs. Hence, the argument goes, one needs 'a firm hand that will control things such as rampant immigration, meddling by EU bureaucrats and so forth; in brief, a return to order' (Gingrich and Banks 2006, 16). Or, as Campbell argues,

> 'Woman' as commodity, as carer, as producer and reproducer […] is positioned anew as Other; the sovereignty of ideologies of masculinity is simultaneously rattled and reinstated. Gender, uniquely, exposes the limits of this articulation, its contradictions and – most important – its unsustainability. The old sexual contract is recognised as unsustainable but retained in modernised form. Neoliberal neo-patriarchy is the new articulation of male domination.[1]

> (2014, 4)

Strong, charismatic male leadership is frequently highlighted as a salient characteristic of right-wing populist parties (see Chapter 6). However, as Norocel (2013, 51) rightly points out, there are or were, in fact, a number of female politicians in positions of power in right-wing populist parties, such as Marine Le Pen (Front National), Pia Kjærsgaard (Danish Peoples Party, 1996–2011), Krisztina Morvai (as MEP for Jobbik, who does not hold a leadership function but exerts considerable influence), Barbara Rosenkranz of the Austrian FPÖ (who stood for election for Austrian President in 2010, as illustrated in Chapter 5) and Heide Schmidt (a former deputy in Jörg Haider's FPÖ before she left the party in 1993 and stood for election for Austrian President in 1992). Of course, we should not forget Sarah Palin or Michelle Bachmann, who are both very prominent Republican female politicians affiliated with the US Tea Party and, at first glance, seem to contradict the 'strict father' frame proposed by Lakoff (2008) which emphasizes male leadership. I will come back to this apparent paradox below. Suffice it to say at this point that these women all remain an important element in a patriarchal social order.

Two examples shall serve to illustrate the manifold contradictions of gendered body politics: the focus on veiled Muslim women as the ultimate 'Other' (Vignette 14) and the US Tea Party's debates about abortion (Vignette 15). In the following, I shall by necessity restrict myself to some important theoretical approaches as it would be impossible to discuss all dimensions in the necessary detail.

Plastic Woman and Cardboard Man

Conservative family values, homophobia and anti-abortion campaigns have become part and parcel of the ideologies of, at least, some of the right-wing populist movements in Central Europe and the former Eastern-Bloc countries as well of the US Tea Party.

The latter conservative tendency seems to be a reaction to what US journalist Hanna Rosin labels the '*end of men*' (2013) in a book with this title. She identifies a noticeable change in US middle class gender politics associated with, as she suggests, the emergence of *plastic women* and *cardboard men*:

> Plastic Woman has during the last century performed superhuman feats of flexibility. She has gone from barely working at all to working only until she got married to working while married and then working with children, even babies. If a space opens up for her to make more money than her husband, she grabs it. If she is no longer required by ladylike standards to restrain her temper, she starts a brawl at the bar […]. They earn more than single women and just as much as the men […]. Cardboard Man, meanwhile, hardly changes at all. A century can go by and his lifestyle and ambitions remain largely the same. A 'coalminer' or 'rigger' used to be a complete identity, connecting a man to a long lineage of men. […] They [men] lost the old architecture of manliness but they have not replaced it with any obvious new one […]. As a result men are stuck […].
>
> (2013, 7–9)

Gender relations are changing in a significant way, patriarchy is threatened, the world as 'We' know it no longer exists – with respect to the politics of race, gender and ethnicity. Thus, it is not surprising, I believe, that much fear constructed and launched by the extreme right-wing is projected onto fantasies and imaginaries of both empowered and independent white women as well as women symbolizing the 'Other', namely the veiled Muslim woman as metonym for the 'post-modern stranger' (see Chapter 4).

Creating scapegoats is certainly part and parcel of right-wing populist rhetoric. Fear of minorities existing 'inside' nation states is continuously emphasized, for example of Jews (perceived as a powerful group which allegedly dominates certain professions through a so-called worldwide conspiracy) as well as Roma (depicted as a symbol of the nomadic, uncivilized Other in Western and Eastern Europe). Both groups are marked as the 'modern strangers' that were already noted by Simmel (1950). Strangers within and outside are perceived as threatening (Christian) civilization, accompanied by a gendered discourse which, on the one hand, appeals to the liberation of women according to Human Rights Conventions and is directed against Muslim women and, on the other hand, restricts women's rights via traditional Christian religious values directed against the freedom to choose abortion and to live independent lives (see below).

This gendered discourse clearly attempts to govern and regulate women's bodies and minds, thereby objectifying and disciplining women. The 'national family' as imagined by such right-wing populist ideologies should preserve the traditional patriarchal order of the sexes and keep the nation's body white and pure. Of course, this ideology resembles, and also draws on, conservative and fascist imaginaries which have been extensively investigated by Musolff (2010) in his research on the concept of the '*Volk*' and the '*Volkskörper*' across German nationalistic writing since the 18th century which led, amongst other ideologies such as antisemitism and racism, to the national-socialist ideology of the superiority of the white Aryan race.

Such body politics is inherently nativist and exclusionary; it excludes the strangers within and outside, also via conceptual metaphors: Jews and Roma are cast as 'parasites' that 'destroy' the host body from inside; migration is cast as a 'disease' or 'illness' which befalls the national body from outside (e.g. Reisigl and Wodak 2001; Chapters 2 and 4).

Strangers are also gendered, of course; currently, the post-modern 'Other' in much of the political debate across Western Europe, as stated above, is represented as the veiled Muslim woman.

Intersectionality and the 'Authoritarian Personality'

These complex interrelations were studied in detail, long before the work of Rosin and Norocel, by the group of researchers around Theodor W. Adorno and Max Horkheimer in the 1940s in the US. Their studies on the authoritarian character (published as *Studien zum autoritären Charakter*) confirm the assumption that various ideological set pieces such as ethnocentrism, antisemitism, sexism or nationalism belong to a *single* – the anti-democratic – *mindset*, what they termed '*Einstellungssyndrom*'. Within this ideological system they are not simply interrelated but connected dialectically and can reinforce each other. In case antisemitism and open racism are regarded as taboo, as happened in Germany and Austria after the collapse of the national-socialist regime, a functionally equivalent ideology – such as a chauvinistic nationalism or Islamophobia – can move into the foreground, behind which, however, the dynamics of the other ideologies continue to operate (e.g. Stögner 2014; Stögner and Wodak 2014).

The corresponding conceptions of masculinity and femininity have been defined in *Authoritarian Personality* as *pseudo-masculinity* and *pseudo-femininity*, and correspond in several respects to *Plastic Woman* and *Cardboard Man*, but in reverse order: *Cardboard Men* tend to be passive, whereas *Plastic Women* are defined as rather active by Rosin. Gender roles have been adapted to new developments in social reality; the imagined traditional constructions of masculinity have been shattered, or seem at least to be under massive threat.

It is striking that the authors recognize a bundle of attributes as pseudo-masculinity and -femininity that corresponds exactly to the social norms regarding dichotomous gender relations and gender roles (e.g. Stögner 2014, 42). In particular male informants in the study showed a statistically significant connection between authoritarian character traits and encrusted traditional ideals of masculinity:

> In fact, there seems to be, in the high-scoring men, more of what may be called *pseudo-masculinity* – as defined by boastfulness about such traits as determination, energy, industry, independence, decisiveness, and will power – and less admission of passivity. An ego-accepted admission of passivity, softness, and weakness, on the other hand, is found predominantly in low-scoring men. [...] An analogous trend – although statistically not significant – toward what may be called *pseudo-femininity* is found in evaluating self-estimates given by high-scoring women. These women tend to think of themselves as feminine and soft; no masculine trends are being admitted [...].

> (Adorno et al. 1967, 428)

To attest pseudo-masculinity and femininity, of course, it is not sufficient to identify the traits described above; what is, in fact, decisive is the rigidity and strictness with which the social conventions regarding gender relations and gender roles are adhered to, reproduced and propagated, as will be described below with respect to the religiously dominated abortion debates in the US. This may deprive individuals of any possibility to resist and fight the repressive tendencies in society and its oppressive structures. At the same time there is fear of a looming loss of security, which the oppressive conditions do seem to offer – at least for some women.

Behind the ostentatious over-emphasis of masculinity, however, we can clearly recognize a fear of passivity, dependence and loss of control – aspects which in bourgeois, Christian-Occidental modernity are unequivocally assigned to femininity (e.g. Stögner 2014, 43ff.). This refers to exactly those fears and desires that are rediscovered in the *Cardboard Men* more than 60 years after the initial publication of Adorno et al.'s (1967) *The Authoritarian Personality*. Then, these were mostly fears; today, they are many men's real experience of an actual loss of power and longings for a positively imagined past.

The studies of Adorno and his fellow authors are far from being outdated; quite to the contrary, they can offer one explanation (of several) for the often conservative, even reactionary gender politics of right-wing populism in the 21st century. Similarly, complex interrelations with other ideologies of exclusion as already described in the 1940s are still to be observed. The following discussion focuses on exactly such (an) *intersectionality*, that is, on the connections between new and old gender roles and regulations, the conservation of old social, patriarchal and authoritarian orders by calls for the ideals of tough men and leader figures as well as – in some instances such as the Tea Party in the US – by a ban on abortion and homophobia, but also by the defence against threatening gender politics from the Orient. This engenders apparent and virulent contradictions that need to be revealed and studied.

The Gender Gap in the Right-wing Populist Electorate

Most right-wing populist movements have more male than female followers and voters. Accordingly, in the elections to the European Parliament in May 2014, more men participated than women overall (see Figure 7.1[2]), except for Estonia, Ireland, Malta, Finland and Sweden. Historically, women's votes have risen from 16 per cent in 1979 to 37 per cent in 2014 in the EU-wide elections to the European Parliament.

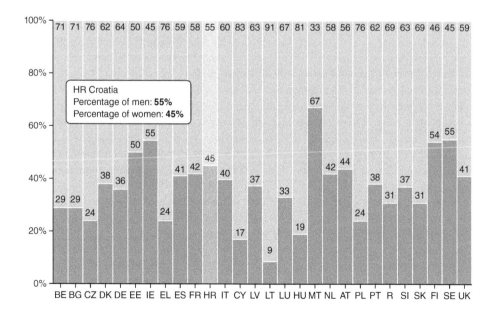

Figure 7.1   Gender distribution, European Parliament elections 2014

The distribution of voters according to the categories of age, profession, education and sex clearly shows that the highest percentage of voters for the Austrian Freedom Party, for example, are male workers between 16 and 29 years of age. Comparing left-liberal voters with the FPÖ voters in the age group below 29 years of age, it is noteworthy that 54 per cent of women cast their votes for the Social Democrats and Green Parties, whereas 51 per cent of male voters opted for right-wing and extreme right-wing parties (ÖVP and FPÖ).[3] This tendency can be observed throughout Western Europe.

There have, of course, been various attempts to explain the gender gap and the differences between East and West, once such differences were finally acknowledged. Historically, women used to vote like their male partners (Inglehart and Norris 2000); moreover, they usually tended to vote for conservative family values, thus for the conservative right-wing. This changed slowly from 1968 on, picking up pace particularly in the 1980s, due to women's growing independence, professionalism and new legislation related to women's equality and gender mainstreaming.

In Eastern Europe, the trend is quite the opposite: here, women tend to vote for conservative parties. Explanations of the differences between East and West have suggested that Western emancipatory movements were not attractive after 1989 in the former Eastern Bloc countries and that high unemployment rates usually affected women (see Meinhart and Zöchling 2014). Moreover, left-wing parties, especially in Scandinavia, integrate more female politicians, who also attract female voters. However, right-wing populist parties draw male voters, even if they have female figureheads and leaders like the Front National. The aggressive campaigning habitus seems to be more attractive for male voters than female voters in spite of Marine Le Pen's female leadership (at the 2012 national elections, 21 per cent and 15 per cent of the male and female electorate, respectively, voted for Marine Le Pen); the same is true for the Danish populist right-wing party, whose politicians are largely female. One factor, in particular, seems to attract female voters to elect Front National – the vehement anti-Muslim positioning. The self-styled role as protector of female liberties effectively counteracts the aggressive campaign habitus which many women do not seem to endorse.

Therefore at least three factors should be regarded as important when attempting to explain the manifest gender gap: the change of gender roles and the implementation of more liberal gender legislation after 1968; religious beliefs and related family values; and xenophobia (including, but not limited to, anti-Muslim beliefs). Notably, the biggest gap between female and male voters exists amongst young voters, which might seem counter-intuitive as younger generations are usually described as more open-minded and cosmopolitan. Even in countries with massive youth unemployment, women tend to vote for the centre-left. The male core voters of populist right-wing parties come from the working class and – as Meinhart and Zöchling (2014) argue – lose themselves in nostalgic memories of a mystified past, the 'good old days', fearing globalization and unemployment, and are therefore attracted to the typical scapegoat rhetoric of the right wing (see Chapters 1, 3 and 6).

In the US, the respective voting behaviour of women and men seems to follow a different tendency related to strong value struggles. Although more women voted for Clinton, Gore and Obama for president than for their Republican counterparts, there are nevertheless large groups of women who position themselves to the right and campaign against abortion and for traditional family values (Vignette 15). In such movements, religious value conflicts seem to override other, more traditional left/right cleavages. This is why debates about abortion (Pro-Life versus Pro-Choice) dominate the US public and have acquired the status of a litmus-tests: Pro-Choice indicates Democratic alignment, Pro-Life Republican alignment.

An inherently female agenda amongst other highly sensitive value judgements, such as pro or against gun control and pro or against national health legislation, thus serves to distinguish party preferences (Rosin 2013). These value conflicts have become more manifest with the rise of the Tea Party and the (frequently also racist) anti-Obama campaigns, usually identified with the former candidate for Vice President 2008, Sarah Palin (see Chapter 6). Indeed, the two polarized positions are symbolized by two famous women: Hillary Clinton on the one hand and Sarah Palin on the other. In this dichotomy, Palin symbolizes the attractive white woman who protects her family and draws almost exclusively on her intuition and common sense to achieve this. Hillary Clinton, in contrast, symbolizes experience with politics, with foreign affairs and intellectual engagement. Despite Palin's (efforts to) appeal to women, the core electorate of the Republican Party remains male. In fact, men tend to vote based on political ideology, while women remain a critical voting constituency that has to be attracted during each election cycle (Abramowitz 2011, 2014).

VIGNETTE 14
HEADSCARVES AND BURQAS – BODY POLITICS

Reviewing Islamophobic rhetoric in the 1990s and the first decade of the 21st century reveals that specific iconic images of the 'female' have become the ultimate 'Other'. Countless political debates have surrounded and continue to surround the so-called 'headscarf' (the *hijab*, which covers hair and sometimes shoulders, and the *burqa*, which covers hair, face and the entire body) as symbols of uncivilized, barbaric Islam and of the oppressed woman who should be liberated by the rules of Western culture. In this enterprise, interestingly, right-wing populist movements have aligned with some left-wing intellectuals and parties as well as feminists, assuming and presupposing that all veiled Muslim women are being forced to wear headscarves or the burqa and that the West faces a two-fold challenge and responsibility: to protect its women from oppression by Islam, and to empower and liberate oppressed Muslim women. This discourse has constructed a dichotomous and homogenous out-group which is perceived as extremely dangerous for Western societies; as mentioned in Chapter 6, this Islamophobic discourse is also instrumentalized to cover up other socio-political and, most importantly, socio-economic agenda: indeed, appeals to liberate women from 'textual-sexual oppression' (Amin 2014) unite more voters around the right-wing populist agenda than anti-modernization and anti-globalization agendas. Marsdal (2013) convincingly deconstructs the traditional left/right cleavage with respect to a change in voting behaviour related to social class in detail. He emphasizes that votes for (moral) values have substituted votes for parties and amply illustrates (e.g. for developments in Norway in 2010) that

> [c]lass issues are shoved into the background and value issues come to the fore. Tensions over economic distribution and fairness are demobilized. This takes place, however, at the top level of party politics, and not in society. In society, economic and social inequalities and tensions have been rising over the last decades, not only in Denmark, but also all over Europe. The political demobilizing of class conflicts does not take place because most voters have come to emphasize value issues more than

(Continued)

(Continued)

> class issues, which they have not, but rather because, under the neo-liberal élite consensus on class issues, confrontation on moral and cultural issues ('values') has become the only available means of party-political and ideological demarcation [...]. Economic policy debates are dull and grey. Then, someone says something about the Muslim veil and media hell breaks loose.
>
> (ibid., 51–2)

The Swiss Debate about Minarets

Let us look at an infamous example of such construction, one that has been discussed in the context of anti-Muslim and Islamophobic campaigning, but not in relationship to gender dimensions (see also Betz 2013, 73–4; Kallis 2013, 64). In November 2009, a majority of Switzerland's voters supported a proposal to ban the construction of minarets (*Minarettverbot*) throughout the country. This outcome signified a huge political victory for the SVP, the Swiss populist right.[4] Challenging the building of minarets fitted well into the Swiss populist right's identitarian strategy, which is supposed to reinforce Swiss traditional identity while suppressing all others. The poster used by the SVP (Image 7.1) shows a Swiss flag pierced by black caricatured minarets resembling missiles and the silhouette of an equally caricatured Muslim woman in a burqa who is represented as leading this onslaught of missiles, standing on top of the Swiss flag, casting long shadows over it (thus metaphorically threatening and conquering the national body of Switzerland).

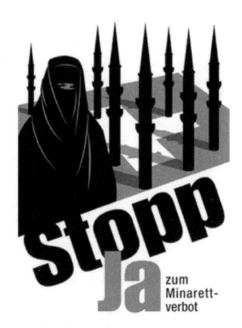

Image 7.1 SVP poster 2009 calling for a ban on minarets

One woman stands metonymically for all Muslim women, for Islam per se and for the danger posed by Islam as she is not simply armed by missiles but has deployed them on

Swiss territory. The image also expresses a conceptual metaphor of war. Islam is thus alleged to be at war with Switzerland; Islam is presented as in the process of attacking Switzerland. An implicit and condensed argumentation scheme can also be deconstructed: continuing to allow minarets to be built would imply to stand by and idly watch Islam overrun Switzerland, a clear *topos of danger*. Presupposed as evidence (datum) is the – not proven – proposition that Islam is dangerous and will change Western (Christian) civilization through something unknown (and by implication dangerous); as unknown as the covered woman whose face remains invisible. At the same time, however, the covered woman symbolizes female (sexual) oppression, as she is seen as being forced to wear a burqa and abstain from Western clothing and, by implication, liberty. Of course, this begs the question as to why the poster does not depict bearded men or a combination of Muslim women and men. Arguably, religious Muslim women are most discernible in public space; they are marked and visible, gazed at by by-passers and frequently harassed.[5] According to Betz (2013, 73), Oskar Freysinger, a SVP Member of Parliament, characterized minarets as a 'symbol of a political and aggressive Islam' and a 'symbol of Islamic law', alleging that the 'minute you have minarets in Europe it means Islam will have taken over' (ibid.). Freysinger also justified the campaign with the argument that the Islamic doctrine was fundamentally incompatible with Switzerland's order, based on secular law.[6] Most importantly, the construction of minarets was perceived as a first step towards the alleged 'creeping Islamization of Switzerland' (ibid.): banning minarets would make Islam invisible, prevent public calls to prayer and block the alleged attempt of introducing Sharia law in the country. Thus, the 2009 referendum achieved its purported goal: protecting and preserving Switzerland's Christian and Western liberal values and traditions.

It is not by coincidence that the headscarf and burqa have become the symbols of the danger allegedly posed by Islam: the discourse about defending women's rights against Islam has become ubiquitous and has been appropriated both by right-wing populist parties and by some feminists and left-wing parties. Surprisingly and suddenly, many men have become very concerned with women's liberties and women's rights. As Ho (2005), Sauer (2005) and Stögner (2014) argue, sexism is closely tied to nationalism and chauvinism, and thus also to body politics (see above):[7]

> Both Muslim and non-Muslim women are the subject of this paternalistic, anti-Muslim nationalism. The 'oppression' of Muslim women by their menfolk is used to portray Islam as inherently misogynistic and oppressive, while instances of Muslim men harassing and sexually assaulting non-Muslim women have triggered a nationalistic response founded on the protection of our women.
>
> (Ho 2005, 4)

(Muslim) women are thus caught in a double-bind, a typical no-win situation. Islam is depicted as inherently dangerous, to Muslim and non-Muslim women alike (Elver 2012, 7). Of course, many Muslim women are oppressed in their families and by their male siblings. However, this kind of discourse makes it virtually impossible to discuss the Islam-internal situation as every example would invariably reinforce the overall negative generalizations about Islam (Hamzeh 2011). Controversies about headscarves have thus become an arena of passionate debates and conflict about culture and civilization, about national identities and European identity. The struggle over identity is linked to sexual difference and sexual identities; in this case, a modern gender-egalitarian 'Us' against

(Continued)

(Continued)

a pre-modern, patriarchal and sexist 'Them'. Similarly, Sauer (2005, 1) emphasizes that the headscarf or burqa should not be understood merely as a piece of cloth; rather, 'the body of the women is used as a signifier for cultural, religious and ethnic difference' (ibid.): the body of the generic Muslim women is used to illustrate and depict the threat posed by religious fundamentalism as well as the failure of ideologies and policies of multiculturalism. In short, we are dealing with value conflicts related to body politics. In the discourse, as evidenced by the poster analysed above, conflicts about values and religion, about what ultimately amounts to national identities, are carried out as power struggles over female bodies.

Media representations of Muslim women add to propaganda such as the SVP's by focusing primarily either on Muslim men or on the female 'Other' (Navarro 2010), but rarely, for example, on the large number of successful Muslim female university professors, lawyers and so forth. In this way, we are confronted with a new kind of orientalism which has substituted the former sensual image of Muslim women from the 19th and early 20th centuries (ibid., 98). By avoiding other salient issues such as women's rights, public freedoms or access to education, the discussion has been reduced primarily to the visual characteristics of the burqa and headscarf. Such media coverage also legitimizes the scarce reporting on women's rights in the Western world by presupposing a clear contrast between the East and West, between Islam and the Occident, which is equated with Christianity: unveiled women are assumed to be liberated and modern, while veiled women are seen as backward, traditional and intellectually retarded (ibid., 101). A fallacious argument is constructed by two hasty generalizations: first, by assuming two homogenous groups, Muslim women and non-Muslim women; and second, by backgrounding all other class, educational, professional and other markers of female identities. Following Ramirez (2006), this kind of imagination and construction of the 'Muslim woman' may be labelled as *'neo-colonial sexism'*,[8] thus identifying a tendency striving to maintain the superiority of the West.

British Debates about the Burqa

A second example, taken from the British context, serves to confirm and illustrate the above analysis and interpretation. Here, I rely on joint research with John E. Richardson (Richardson and Wodak 2009a).[9]

On 1 May 2008, local government elections took place in England and Wales, along with elections for the Greater London Authority and London Mayor. The BNP stood over 600 candidates across 74 wards in England and Wales.[10] A BNP leaflet, headed *The Londoner*, was a prominent feature of the party's London campaign. On their first 'National Weekend of Action' alone, the party apparently delivered over 100,000 leaflets across the capital (ibid.). Laid out in the style of a newspaper – complete with a clear sans-serif masthead – the remainder of the front page is arranged under the headline 'The Changing Face of London' (see Image 7.2).

The expression 'Changing Face' is used both metaphorically, to refer to the ways in which the character or disposition of London has (allegedly) changed, as well as literally, referring to actual individual faces of London's inhabitants, who metonymically represent the city in a generic way. The upper of two images show white families, the vast majority of whom are women and children, out socializing on a terraced street; food and drink are clearly included

Image 7.2   The BNP 'Londoner' campaign leaflet 2008

on stalls in the foreground of the image and flag bunting between the houses. From this and the clothes worn by the women and children, one can conclude that the photo was taken on the day of a social event during the late 1940s or early 1950s. Men are absent in this photo – and we can only speculate why this is so: a traditional social event where men are absent, working while women have free time? Or, as Richardson and Wodak (2009a) also propose, the poster may represent post-war London: men might still be in the army, as part of the Allied forces in continental Europe. Whatever the reason, a contrast between London then and now is constructed by juxtaposing white modern British women/families enjoying themselves and smiling, with traditional Muslim women whose faces are covered and thus cannot be seen. The combination of fun, friendliness and the place of the nation (metonymically represented by the flag, an instance of banal nationalism like the Swiss flag in Image 7.1) in everyday life constructs an idealized past for working-class Londoners (this is a terraced street, not one filled with Georgian mansion houses, which are modern despite the fact that they are in the 1950s, thus combining the notions of 'modernity' and the 'good old days').

The women in the lower image are less friendly. They are Muslim and wear the burqa. The viewer's attention is again directed by the use of the arrow on the left, this time pointing to a woman putting up two fingers – a gesture directed at the photographer and hence also at the viewer. This is an interesting and, ironically, rather English gesture, usually taken as a sign of defiance or abuse – in effect meaning 'fuck off'. The lower image is much darker than the upper, an effect mostly achieved by the black clothes worn by the three women. In contrast to the image above, this image is dominated by the three women – we are in closer proximity to them. The flier thus represents smiling white women with children in contrast with three huge women without children in black who, by implication, appear threatening and dangerous.

The selection of the image of the white women enjoying leisure time with their children at the very least represents a 'modern traditional' patriarchal view, in which women may well be 'allowed' to work but 'remain primarily responsible for the family and the home' (Mudde 2007, 93). Through various cuts (prams and children were digitally removed from the photograph) which we were able to trace (Richardson and Wodak 2009a, 66), the Muslim women are reduced to being instances of only *a Muslim woman*, not a mother, sister, aunt and so forth. As a result of the editing, cutting and enlarging of the original picture, the shape of the women has also been distorted – they look more squat and dumpy than they are in the original.[11] They are presented not only as dangerous but also as unfeminine and ugly, in contrast to the pretty white women above.

Thus, this flier supports the BNP's ideal picture of London positioned at the top of the composition whilst their idea of the city's terrible reality at present is situated underneath. The repeated use of 'this' is a particularly effective rhetorical device on the front page, and the principal element that allows a rhetorical integration of visual and verbal components of the argument. The first use ('consider this') forms part of a directive to cue up the argument presented on the front page: 'they' functions as a cataphoric pronoun, referring to the argument that the BNP wishes the viewer to consider. The second 'this' is a far more complex pronoun, simultaneously referring to the image above: the white street scene, as well as presupposing the qualities that London obviously used to possess. The pronoun is linked to the upper photograph through the semantic consonance between 'the way London used to be', 'From this …', as a starting point contrasting with a change of state used on the intrusive arrow, and the global topic of 'change', introduced in the headline. The photo and the description of the represented London-past should be viewed and understood together: the street scene, depicting a universally white and predominantly female group, should be taken to denote a city which is seemingly 'at ease with itself, friendly, happy and secure'.

This indexical slippage between image and description allows the BNP to insinuate that the 'community values' of the past are something to be desired and that the BNP aims to reintroduce them. However, the use of the second image, in opposition to the street party, enables the BNP to project issues of race, gender and religion as the cause of this alleged loss of 'community values'. The choice to depict Muslim women in the burqa, the selection of this particular point in time (of someone making an abusive gesture) and the production decision to frame them in close-up, thereby denying them a sense of place and context, makes it difficult to construct any interpretation of the image other than one emphasizing their Muslimness. In turn, this foregrounding of the women's Muslimness acts to emphasize the white, non-Muslimness of the women and children in the upper image. Hence, from this contrast, viewers can construe that London has changed drastically, and it is this change that has apparently brought with it the loss of a variety of positive social characteristics, such as 'From this [friendly] to this [abusive]' or 'From this [happy] to this [unexpressive]'.

The final use of 'this' in the central verbal component of the front page – 'If you would like London to be like *this* again …' – retains the complex way that this pronoun is used.

Here, 'this' refers anaphorically to the list of positive social and civic qualities listed imme-diately beforehand, as well as to the image from London's past. Hence, the leaflet implicitly proposes a return to the positive social values listed – a list that triggers certain contemporary liberal values that most people would endorse. By foregrounding women, this flier obviously presents a gendered argument for the racial purification of the British capital. From this, it is possible to reconstruct a specific political stance and its underlying arguments:

1. London used to be white.

2. When it was white, London was at ease with itself, friendly, happy and secure.

3. The BNP wants London to be at ease with itself, friendly, happy and secure.

4. Islam is dangerous, that is, dark and black.

5. When Muslims live in London, London turns black.

6. Being at ease, friendly, happy and secure means being white.

7. Therefore, the BNP will make London white again.

8. Hence, Muslims should leave London (or be made to leave).

Muslim women stand metonymically for all 'Others' living in London (or Great Britain) as the agenda of the BNP is, as is well-known, significantly wider than this (see also Chapter 5; Richardson 2013a, 2013b). As in the Swiss example, a gendered argumentation is employed for exclusionary nativist body politics: Muslim women stand metonymically for Britain's non-white and non-Christian, that is, minority ethnic communities in general. It seems, however, that this kind of exclusionary and racist rhetoric did not lead to the aspired victory at the elections. The results of the BNP were significantly below what had been widely pre-dicted. Across the country, the party gained 10 local councillors, significantly fewer than the 40 they were reported as aiming for.

Austrian Debates about the 'Headscarf'

The final example for the gendered discourse of right-wing populist parties illustrates the appeal to liberate Muslim women from being coerced into wearing a headscarf – referenced in a slogan from the Austrian FPÖ during the Vienna 2010 election (Köhler and Wodak 2011) (see Image 7.3).

The translation of the message on this poster implies that 'We', written in capital letters and pointing to the image of HC Strache on the right who symbolizes the FPÖ and the

Image 7.3 FPÖ poster, Vienna election campaign 2010

'proper' Viennese, are the party that protects free women. This is juxtaposed with: 'The SPÖ [the Social Democratic Party, until then holding an absolute majority in the local government] [protects] the compulsory wearing of head-scarfs' (*Kopftuchzwang*, in German, is a composite noun). The verb is missing in this elliptic sentence, but is easily inserted via implicature from the first sentence. A contrast is established between the FPÖ as protector of women's liberties and the SPÖ, which allegedly supports their oppression symbolized here, for the purposes of the FPÖ campaign, by the headscarf. At the most obvious level, there is a particularly insidious reversal of positions: the FPÖ is, in fact, arguing for a ban or prohibition of headscarves (to be precise, only against the religiously motivated wearing of headscarves, and only in the case of Islam), seeking to remove, much like the BNP in our previous example, what is seen as disturbing from the face of the city, that is, public space. The campaign is about enforcing – by social pressure if not by legislation – conformity to an idea of 'modern' femininity. The second proposition is moreover fallacious in so far as the SPÖ does not endorse the oppression of any women; nor does it endorse a compulsory wearing of the headscarf. What the SPÖ does support, however, is multiculturalism and the freedom of wearing whatever garments people choose as long as such conventions do not impinge on the Austrian constitution, the freedom of opinion and religious freedom (e.g. Sauer 2005). In this way, a straw man fallacy is used for positive self-presentation of the FPÖ, reversing the associations of 'enforcing' and 'liberating'.

'Free women' in English stands for '*freie Frauen*' in German, establishing alliteration with the name of the FPÖ in German, namely *Freiheitliche Partei Österreichs*, favouring a reading of *freiheitlich* as describing a party which stands for freedom. What kind of freedom, we might therefore ask, does the FPÖ envisage for women? In Chapter 5, media and FPÖ slogans of and about a prototypical ideal FPÖ woman, Barbara Rosenkranz, when standing for election for Austrian President were already briefly summarized: she is first and foremost a good mother, indeed a mother of 10 children; being a good mother implies that she cares for her family. By implication, and drawing on a particularly old-fashioned idea of the nation (and the national body), she is also credited with the ability to care for her political family and in consequence for Austria, should she be elected as President. In her book *MenschInnen. Gender Mainstreaming – Auf dem Weg zum geschlechtslosen Menschen* (2008) she warns Austrians that feminism, if left unopposed, would destroy the 'right', that is, 'proper' or 'true', order of the sexes. She declares that:

> It is clear that the position of woman in our society must be entirely equal, there can be no exceptions to this. But it is equally a fact that successful femininity and motherliness must not be separated, if we as a whole want to have a future.
>
> (ibid.)[12]

Femininity and motherliness (though not the more biological 'motherhood') are thus the salient characteristics of any good woman, not just by preference or social convention, but as responsibility and existential duty to an obscure community of 'us as a whole', presumably Austrian society or even humanity – this relates well to definitions of the 'Grizzly Moms' by the US Tea Party (see Chapter 6 and Text 7.3. below). *Freie Frauen* in the campaign poster shown above could also imply a number of other meanings, being a collocation open to many readings: women who are free (free from what?); women who are free of any obligations, thus not committed and not married (free for whom?), with a subtext implying a woman who is (too) sexually liberated or even a woman who could be used for sex (thus, actually a prostitute).

Below, the usual FPÖ slogan (reproduced on all posters in this election) is repeated as a brand: 'WE [capitalised and thus emphasizing contrast] are here for the Viennese' in a rather idiomatic German phrasing. This slogan relates to the capitalised 'We' in the first sentence and clarifies the in-group: the 'real Viennese', consisting of free women, thus non-Muslims. Muslims are excluded from the Viennese and signified by women wearing the headscarf. Apart from excluding Muslims, the political opponents – in the case of the local Vienna elections, most prominently the Social Democratic Party – are also excluded from the real Viennese (as are the Jews, Roma, and other ethnic minorities; see Image 1.1). The metonymy of the headscarf serves political goals: the Social Democratic Party and its multicultural policies are implicitly defined as too lenient and self-sacrificing vis-à-vis foreign cultures, most notably Islam, accepting their traditionalist and anti-modern ways, thus becoming at least complicit in constraining (women's) freedom and rights. This claim is fallacious on many levels as the FPÖ endorses traditional and conservative family values, whereas the Social Democrats support women's rights and – since the 1970s – have implemented much legislation protecting and enforcing women's equality, women's chances to combine family and career options, and women's free choice for abortion. 'Free' in the context of the FPÖ thus suggests precisely the opposite meanings of the common and conventional usage of the term in current political rhetoric and thus constitutes an attempt at redefining and reformulating meanings (and subsequently, values). Such Manichean rhetoric necessarily prohibits any differentiated and rational discussion about the existing oppression of some Muslim women. The use of such strategies of exaggeration and the *straw man* fallacy leaves no space for other opinions or views.

US Debates about Abortion: Campaigning against *Pro Choice Roe* vs. *Wade* and its consequences

On 27 February 2012, I was able to interview a journalist working for Aljazeera America, in Washington DC. Talking about the Republican primaries and their conservative values, the journalist told me that 'abortion as topic serves as a joker. Whenever candidates have nothing else to say about any other topic, abortion as hot topic appears in the debate or interview'. I had noticed, of course, that in the US abortion has remained one of the most salient issues – in contrast to Western European countries, where this issue has been marginalized since the 1970s and certainly could not serve any candidate in any party as a possibly successful electoral agenda – usually debated, legislated and regulated by male politicians and many fundamentalist religious groups led by women. Nevertheless, I was surprised that this topic would be seriously discussed for almost 20 minutes in the Republican Primary Presidential debate in Arizona on 22 February 2012, televised live on CNN, this being one of the main debates between the four Republican candidates standing for election in the primaries for presidential candidate against Obama. Moreover, I must admit that I was shocked that some female Tea Party candidates, amongst them Michelle Bachmann and Sarah Palin, actually argued that women should be forbidden to undergo an abortion even if conception occurred as a result of rape. In contrast to the European right-wing populist and conservative body politics, it is thus not the headscarf or the burqa which dominates the gendered political discourse on the right in the US – it was and continues to be control over abortion (and contraception) as symbolized in the controversy between 'Pro Life' and 'Pro Choice', in addition to other salient issues such as gun control, national healthcare and so-called illegal immigration from South America (e.g. Abramowitz 2011; Greenhouse and Siegel 2012; Staggenborg 1991).

On 22 January 1973, the Supreme Court of the United States decided on the now famous *Roe* vs. *Wade* case (410 US 113 (1973)), which is widely regarded as one of the landmark decisions by the US Supreme Court on the issue of abortion. As Staggenborg (1991, 37) elaborates, *Roe* vs. *Wade* was decided simultaneously with a second case, *Doe* vs. *Bolton*. The Supreme Court ruled 7 to 2 that a right to privacy under the due process clause of the 14th Amendment extended to a woman's decision to have an abortion, but that this right must be balanced against the state's two legitimate interests in regulating abortions: protecting prenatal life and protecting women's health (ibid., 192). Greenhouse and Siegel (2012, 253) present much documentation regarding the case where the Court tied state regulation of abortion to the third trimester of pregnancy. This decision marked the end of a long struggle between the women's movement and medical associations, on the one hand, and – as main protagonist of the anti-abortion movement at that point in the time – the Catholic Church. *Roe* vs. *Wade* essentially reshaped national politics, dividing much of the US into Pro-Choice and Pro-Life camps, while engendering many grassroots movements on both sides.

However, this decision did not mark the end of the debate but actually prompted an enormous public reaction which persists even today, revolving around issues including whether and to what extent abortion should be legal, who should decide the legality of abortion, what methods the Supreme Court should use in constitutional adjudication, and what the role of religious and moral views should be in the political sphere. The more recent polarization on abortion has many reasons: the opposition to President Obama per se (see Chapter 6) and to the Patient Protection and Affordable Care Act (PPACA; usually labelled derogatively as 'Obamacare' and vehemently opposed by the US Republican Party and the Tea Party as well as fundamentalist Christian religious groups)[13] has to be considered as a salient factor as well. The (PP)ACA actually presents the first, more or less successful, legislation for national healthcare designed to be available to almost all Americans, including contraception and abortion costs.[14]

The 'Arrogance of Ignorance' – Grizzly Moms

The US Tea Party was founded in its current form by Republican Congressman Ron Paul on 16 December 2007, the 234th anniversary of the famous Boston Tea Party. This launch served libertarian agenda and created a divide in the Republican Party. The main target of the Tea Party was and continues to be Barack Obama (see Glossary for more details). Sarah Palin, a prominent member of the Tea Party, was nominated as candidate for Vice President by the Republican Party in 2008 and quickly became a symbol for the agenda of the Tea Party, which consists mainly of elderly white middle-class men with extremely conservative views (Abramowitz 2011). Indeed, having conducted multiple opinion polls and surveys, and having compared these results with other members of the Republican

Party, Abramowitz states that Tea Party members oppose *inter alia* the healthcare reform, the economic stimulus programme, federal funding of stem cell research, federal funding of clean energy research, financial reform and raising taxes on upper income households, gun control, foreign aid programmes and – abortion (ibid., 13). Importantly, however, and apart from such ideological conservatism, both racial resentment and dislike for Barack Obama had significant effects on support for the Tea Party (ibid.). In short, anti-government stance, neo-liberal policies, Christian religious fundamentalism, racism and the disciplining of female bodies are part and parcel of the US Tea Party movement and hence of the Republican Party.

Sarah Palin's Grizzly Moms were strategically introduced to the campaign to attract more female voters as the gender gap is most apparent amongst Republican voters. By endorsing all of the above-mentioned neo-liberal ideologies, conservative values and gendered disciplining policies, this successful female politician (and media celebrity), who continuously stated that she was able to combine her family obligations with her commitment to being Alaska's governor, contributed substantially to reproducing the patriarchal order of the sexes (e.g. Rodino-Colocino 2012; Schowalter 2012). She was able, as McLaren aptly describes, to instrumentalize her charm and attractive looks, 'to inject herself as the new face (literally and figuratively) of the Republican Party, employing abecedarian attempts at crafting her "knowing wink" for the titillated cameras that seem transfixed by her beauty queen looks' (2009, 805). In this way, Palin strategically polarized the country between 'rural Americans and the Eastern elites, between people of color (including immigrants) and hard-working White males' (ibid.). Finally, she also played the race card as many voters could not imagine a black man in the White House (see Chapter 6).

Broxmeyer provides an acute analysis of Sarah Palin's persona, her self-presentation as well as the reasons for choosing her as candidate in the 2008 presidential election:

> By choosing Palin as a running mate, the septuagenarian McCain strove to find a symbolical midwife to birth conservatism anew after the disastrous effects of the Bush administration on the electoral prospects of the Republican Party. After all, she was the mother of five children and yet a self-proclaimed political virgin, barely into her first term as governor of Alaska and virtually unknown on the national scene. Channelling the forces of sentimental populism, Palin fused the supposed inherent goodness and patriotism of market fundamentalism and heteronormative culture together with the possibility of a national-capitalist future. During the election, Sarah Palin brought infantile citizenship to the forefront of American politics as never before and demonstrated its potency as a national fantasy, as well as its internal contradictions. Despite, or more likely because of, her electoral defeat, Palin has become a 'singular national industry,' amassing a twelve-million-dollar postelection bonanza from her book deal [and] her Fox News show, *Real American Stories*.

(2010, 144)

The 'Mama Grizzly' coalition emphasizes 'kitchen table economics', that is, the position that the state budget should be run like the family budget. As women are daily involved in caring for their families and living costs, they should know – by common sense and experience – how to run the state. The conservative group Concerned Women for America (CWA) actually provides members with a brochure entitled 'How to Lobby From Your Kitchen Table'. This anti-intellectualism is vehemently directed against the elites, and more specifically against Obama, who studied at Harvard and personifies intellectualism.

In a speech given in Washington, DC in May 2010, Palin campaigned for a Pro-Life agenda as well as fiscal policy while employing motherhood and 'frontier feminism' (a term insinuating the courageous female pioneers in the Wild West) as supposedly valid evidence. In her 2010 book *America by Heart: Reflections of Family, Faith, and Flag*, she makes this connection explicit:

> Moms just kind of know when something's wrong. It's that mother's intuition thing, I think. We can tell when things are off-base, off-course, and not right. And we're not afraid to roll up our sleeves and get to work and get the job done and set things straight. Moms can be counted on to fight for their children's future.

(cited in Schowalter 2012, 44–5)

Such a common-sensical, anti-intellectual and anti-elitist stance resonates well with the political figure of Barbara Rosenkranz, the BNP's and FPÖ's gender ideology, and the nativist-nationalistic body politics as presented by Norocel (2013). Comaroff highlights the specific right-wing populist agenda of Palin in the run-up to the 2008 US election and argues that 'if Palin's populism was of the right-wing, "call it like I see it" kind', then many defined Barack Obama 'a left-wing populist (the phrase is often used interchangeably with socialism among US conservatives)' (2011, 100). Grizzly Moms are, the Tea Party members claim, the core of the traditional white Christian family and, by consequence, the core of the American nation, as imagined by the founding fathers, the Constitution, and the pioneers who conquered the Wild West. By implicature, only white, middle-class, heteronormative Christian mothers are appealed to and also attracted as voters and activists; the Tea Party has almost no non-white members (Abramowitz 2011, 2014). Men do not feel threatened by the Grizzly Moms as the patriarchal male position of power is not challenged by what they represent – the traditional family and conservative values remain sacrosanct. Media studies and opinion polls after the 2008 election provide evidence that Palin neither harmed nor helped McCain; indeed, her candidacy may have contributed to a loss of support amongst swing voters (Kenski 2010; Knuckey 2011; Wasburn and Wasburn 2011).

VIGNETTE 15
MEN DEBATING ABOUT WOMEN'S RIGHTS: THE CASE OF ABORTION

On 22 February 2012, four male candidates participated in the Republican presidential primary debate in Arizona, televised live on CNN: Rep. Ron Paul, Texas; former Speaker of the House Newt Gingrich; former Senator Rick Santorum, Pennsylvania; and former Governor of Massachusetts Mitt Romney. John King, CNN anchor and chief national correspondent, moderated the debate. Questions were asked from the public, some spontaneous, some prepared beforehand, and read out by the moderator.

This was the final of a course of 20 debates during which some candidates had already stepped down or had been voted out.[15] The first question concerns the national debt, posed by a member of the audience. After about 20 minutes of heated discussion, CNN takes the first break. King then poses the second question himself:

Text 7.1

'Since birth control is the latest hot topic, which candidate believes in birth control, and if not, why? As you can see – it's a – it's a very popular question in the audience, as we can see. Look, we're not going to spend a ton of time on this but it is – please.'

The formulation of the question implies that the audience insists on this topic, that it is important, but also that not too much time will be spent on it – in this way, the moderator relativizes the relevance of this issue and emphasizes that it is on the agenda due to popular request (but possibly in spite of CNN or himself). Newt Gingrich is the first to respond. In his turn he first defines birth control, that is, abortion, as a religious issue in which the state should have no say; second, he attacks his fellow participants for not having opposed Obama when voting for 'legalizing infanticide'. He then immediately turns against Obama himself, whom he accuses of 'protecting doctors who killed babies who survived abortion':

Text 7.2

Gingrich: No, I think – look, I think there's – I want to make two – I want to make two quick points, John.

The first is there is a legitimate question about the power of the government to impose on religion activities which any religion opposes. That's legitimate.

[*applause*]

King: Sure is.

Gingrich: But I just want to point out, you did not once in the 2008 campaign, not once did anybody in the elite media ask why Barack Obama voted in favor of legalizing infanticide. OK? So let's be clear here.

[*applause*]

If we're going to have a debate about who the extremist is on these issues, it is President Obama who, as a state senator, voted to protect doctors who killed babies who survived the abortion. It is not the Republicans.

This segment illustrates that abortion is a highly politicized issue, instrumentalized here as a means to an end against both opponents in the same party, the Republicans, and against the incumbent presidential candidate of the Democratic Party, Barack Obama. The discussants have to address each other, the live audience and the many million viewers on CNN, nationally and globally. The Gingrich example exemplifies how this multi-addressing is achieved by mentioning and drawing on many instances of the past (voting behaviour in the House and Senate), usually realized as *topoi of history and authority*, as well as by providing different narratives of the candidates' own campaigning against abortion (and thus justifying their previous decisions) over the years. In the context of the debate, each candidate has to distinguish himself from the other three and 'tell his own story'.

By labelling abortion as 'infanticide', Gingrich implies that what is at stake here is the life of an already fully grown infant and not an embryo. Listeners and viewers would thus associate the killing of a baby or even a young child with this term. Second, he accuses

(Continued)

(Continued)

Obama of protecting murderers – doctors who killed babies (in his wording, not embryos), without giving any evidence for this claim. Third, he attacks his fellow Republicans for not having opposed such murder. The first turn thus sets the scene for viewing abortion fallaciously as the killing of full-grown babies, that is, as murder, and thus as a terrible crime. Notably, mothers and women are absent in this first turn and, as will be illustrated in the following, throughout the entire debate about abortion.

Immediate reactions amongst the three other candidates are necessarily oriented towards the accusation of not having opposed Obama and other state bills sufficiently as well as providing their own stance. Mitt Romney, second to speak, focuses on the religious dimension by continuously repeating the adjective 'religious' (e.g., religious conscience, religious freedom, religious tolerance), the first point on Gingrich's list, and agrees that the state should not intervene in religious issues:

Text 7.3

Romney: [...] Well, we found out when Barack Obama continued his attack on religious conscience. I don't think we've seen in the history of this country the kind of attack on religious conscience, religious freedom, religious tolerance that we've seen under Barack Obama. Most recently, of course –

[applause]

– most recently requiring the Catholic Church to provide for its

employees and its various enterprises health care insurance that would include birth control, sterilization and the morning-after pill. Unbelievable.

And he retried to retreat from that but he retreated in a way that was not appropriate, because these insurance companies now have to provide these same things and obviously the Catholic Church will end up paying for them.

But don't forget the decision just before this, where he said the government – not a church, but the government – should have the right to determine who a church's ministers are for the purposes of determining whether they are exempt from EEOC or from workforce laws or labor laws.

He said the government should make that choice. That went all the way to the Supreme Court. There are a few liberals on the Supreme Court. They voted 9–0 against President Obama. His position –

[applause]

– his position – his position on religious tolerance, on religious

conscience is clear, and it's one of the reasons the people in this country are saying we want to have a president who will stand up and fight for the rights under our Constitution, our first right, which is for freedom of religion.

Romney uses his turn to generalize the attack on Obama, claiming that the President never considers religious conscience and even dominates the Catholic Church, a typical straw man fallacy, generalizing and exaggerating specific opinions which, however, remain unsubstantiated. Thus, he argues, even the Catholic Church will be forced in one way or the other to allow for birth control without mentioning any evidence for this claim. His disgust with the situation he has just described is performed and intensified by the exclamation 'Unbelievable'. He then continues to list some other state interventions into religion which were, however, rejected by the Supreme Court. This fact now allows him to represent Obama as unrealistic, non-strategic, non-religious, or even as unintelligent – when all Supreme Court judges vote against a bill, the bill (by implication) has to be truly wrong. Moreover, Romney draws on the Constitution as legitimation – a *topos of authority* as everything written in the Constitution is accepted as right per se, even after centuries have passed and interpretation of laws has necessarily changed. The constitution is thus regarded as a sacred text, including the obligation to interpret it literally.

At this point King interrupts and steers the discussion back to the original topic and addresses Rick Santorum directly, by quoting the former Senator's publicized opinion that contraception is dangerous. In his reply, Santorum ventures even further from the original topic of birth control and starts elaborating on overall heteronormative and conservative family and social values. He first quotes – again a *topos of authority* – from the *New York Times* that many children are born out of wedlock (i.e. if the NYT reports a survey it must be right) and continues by emphasizing the plight of such children – indeed, in this short turn, the word 'children' is repeated seven times in order to highlight and foreground his focus:

Text 7.4

Santorum: What we're seeing is a problem in our culture with respect to children being raised by children, children being raised out of wedlock, and the impact on society economically, the impact on society with respect to drug use and all – a host of other things when children have children.

And so, yes, I was talking about these very serious issues. And, in fact, as I mentioned before, two days ago on the front page of *The New York Times*, they're talking about the same thing. The bottom line is we have a problem in this country, and the family is fracturing.

Over 40 percent of children born in America are born out of wedlock. How can a country survive if children are being raised in homes where it's so much harder to succeed economically? It's five times the rate of poverty in single-parent households than it is in two-parent homes. We can have limited government, lower tax – we hear this all the time, cut spending, limit the government, everything will be fine. No, everything's not going to be fine.

There are bigger problems at stake in America. And someone has got to go out there – I will – and talk about the things.

And you know what? Here's the difference.

The left gets all upset. 'Oh, look at him talking about these things.' You know, here's the difference between me and the left, and they don't get this. Just because I'm talking about it doesn't mean I want a government program to fix it.

That's what they do. That's not what we do.

(Continued)

(Continued)

Santorum sets out by identifying an existing problem: poor teenagers having children. The solution he suggests to this problem is to protect and save traditional families, without resorting to any intervention by the government, as he alleges the political left would do. He does not propose any practical solutions such as programmes for schools or even allowing teenagers to access contraception or undergo abortion should no other help be available. His fallacious argument is founded on the premise that the core heteronormative family is dissolving ('is fractured') and that, as a consequence, poverty is rising and children are not protected. No evidence is provided, however, that 'healthy' families would be able to avoid falling into poverty. In this turn focused on children, mothers (and fathers) are not mentioned. Children are the victims of a destruction of family values. These values are essentialized and not challenged: marriage between a man and a woman is taken as a given – no mention is made during the entire debate of mothers or women, the two terms or even synonyms are not uttered once. In terms of the Republican candidates' positioning, relevant social global changes such as new family patterns are not accepted, but are perceived as deviant, as the causal consequence of fractured families and the primary cause for poverty, drug abuse and the suffering of children. Santorum typically positions himself as courageous and brave enough to speak out for the poor and for the children; he constructs a clear distinction between 'me and the left' as well as between 'we' and 'they', i.e. 'the government', and criticise the status quo should he be elected; thus he would be able to propose changes but nevertheless, the government should not intervene (*topos* of saviour combined with *topos* of critique).

As the final candidate to respond, Ron Paul takes the floor and emphasizes his general and well-known libertarian values with respect to abortion:

Text 7.5

Paul: As an OB [obstetrician] doctor, I've dealt with birth control pills and contraception for a long time. This is a consequences [*sic*] of the fact the government has control of medical care and medical insurance, and then we fight over how we dictate how this should be distributed, sort of like in schools. Once the government takes over the schools, especially at the federal level, then there's no right position, and you have to argue which prayer, are you allowed to pray, and you get into all the details.

The problem is the government is getting involved in things they shouldn't be involved in, especially at the federal level.

[*applause*]

But sort of along the line of the pills creating immorality, I don't see it that way. I think the immorality creates the problem of wanting to use the pills. So you don't blame the pills.

I think it's sort of like the argument – conservatives use the argument all the time about guns. Guns don't kill, criminals kill.

[*applause*]

So, in a way, it's the morality of society that we have to deal with. The pill is there and, you know, it contributes, maybe, but the pills can't be blamed for the immorality of our society.

[*applause*]

Ron Paul introduces his statement by drawing on his expertise as obstetrician. He equates the state's intervention on birth control (via nationalized healthcare) with other interventions on religious practices. Due to his libertarian values, the state per se should have no say, not on health or abortion or schools or religion. In this way, Paul frames the abortion issue as an example of the more general policy as enacted by the Obama government (i.e. the Democratic Party), which is allegedly supporting strong state intervention. Independence of the state and individual responsibility are core elements of such a libertarian, neo-liberal stance.

Moreover, he introduces concrete actors to the discussion – people taking contraception (pills) or people using guns. Referring to a popular argument on gun control, he iterates that it is not the pills or guns that deserve blame but the immoral people who use them to perform criminal acts. By putting pills and guns on the same level, he also fallaciously equates them and their users in a completely decontextualized way: people taking contraception pills kill (babies), just as much as people using guns do if they are criminal and immoral. It is thus immoral society that is to blame, since (it is presupposed) it supports immoral people (i.e. women) who then take pills and kill (per implicature) babies/embryos (a *post hoc propter hoc* fallacy). The primary presupposition in this brief statement, however, is that the state (i.e. Obama and his healthcare act) are to blame – for providing access to contraception, the morning-after pill and birth control via abortion.

In their first turns, all four participants effectively discuss values, not concrete policies, and put the blame on immoral society and state intervention into birth control (as well as either explicitly or implicitly the healthcare bill and the Obama administration, who allow for access to abortion and contraception paid by the Affordable Care Act). Moreover, a specific scenario is created via the *topos of danger* and the straw man fallacy according to which the traditional core family is being destroyed, society has become immoral, and social, moral and religious values are being challenged because of recent political developments. The victims are infants, babies and children born 'out of wedlock'. Nevertheless, the four candidates position themselves differently and also perform differently in this debate: Gingrich is direct and immediately sets the frame by labelling abortion as 'infanticide'; Romney presents himself as the overall protector of religion and religious conscience; Santorum puts social issues, society and family, and especially poverty on the agenda, and he presents himself as the courageous would-be saviour of the traditional family and American values; and Paul puts forth the obviously fallacious argument of equating pills with guns, thus referring to Gingrich's 'abortion-equals-murder-frame' albeit on a quasi-expert level. Not surprisingly, the debate then turns to a discussion of core Republican and Tea Party values while re-enforcing the attack on the Obama administration and Obama personally, for example, when Romney postulates that 'this isn't an argument about contraceptives, this is a discussion about, are we going to have a nation which preserves the foundation of the nation, which is the family, or are we not?' and thus endorses the agenda highlighted by Santorum.

The (traditional) family is metonymically equated with the nation – a strikingly obvious example of gendered body politics. A few minutes later, Gingrich agrees with Paul in arguing that '[w]hen you have a government as the central provider of services, you inevitably move towards tyranny, because the government has the power to force ... and this is true whether it's Romneycare or Obamacare or any other government centralized system'. In this way, Gingrich reframes the current democratic election as a choice between tyranny (allegedly the current government) and freedom (the Republican positioning).

Afterthoughts

Clearly, as Vignettes 14 and 15 amply illustrate, gendered ideologies have to be considered when analysing right-wing populism. Values related to traditional patriarchy are part and parcel of the exclusionary and nativist, nationalistic belief systems which most right-wing populist parties endorse. However, they manifest themselves in different images, symbols and domains.

In Europe, specifically in Western Europe and in Scandinavia, the burqa-wearing woman stands for danger and threat to European civilization: indeed, the veiled women has become the generic 'Other', symbolizing the alleged dangers posed by Islam, by different cultures and religions, different rituals and customs, and a different way of life. Dichotomies are erected between quasi-homogenous 'civilized' Europeans and 'anachronistic, even barbaric' Others from the Orient. A *neo-colonial sexism* has emerged in which the Muslim female body is seen as incorporating all evil, everything the West (and Western females) should beware of. Of course, such disciplining and regulating of the female body implies that women should be subject to patriarchal domination which can, as has been illustrated above, be implemented both by men and women. This ideological positioning has become salient and overrides the former left/right cleavage. It has become a *conflict about values, not about social class, age or education* and so forth.

In the US, on the other hand, we encounter a different bio-politic: the debates in the US are concerned with protecting the white heteronormative American family, thus emphasizing family values. These family values are related to women's duties – they are the primary care-takers as mothers and wives; they also possess the necessary common-sense intuition which is deemed – as proposed by frontier feminism – salient to be able to govern the country. Thus, women as care-takers and as mothers are foregrounded, firmly repositioned in their traditional gender roles. The primary value conflict is centred on this female role: abortion and contraception are viewed as endangering the values of the white heteronormative family and the 'pure' American population. In this way, the Tea Party and parts of the Republican Party retain a conservative ideology which has been transcended in Western Europe and is not part of the usual right-wing populist agenda there. Indeed, these values contradict the attempt to 'liberate women' (see above, Vignette 14); whereas in the US, this value conflict retains the status of a litmus test, distinguishing between Democrats and Republicans. This difference can also be explained by the important role of Christian religion in the US and the prominence of secularism in Western Europe. The investigation of gendered body politics, both in Europe and the US, substantiates the assumption that the conceptual metaphor of the 'family' has taken on a nativist dimension, related to the 'authoritarian syndrome' as well as to post-modern bio-politics and the threat, experienced by many in our globalizing societies, of changing gender roles.

Endnotes

1 See www.opendemocracy.net/5050/beatrix-campbell/neo-liberal-neopatriarchy-case-for-gender-revolution, accessed 21 May 2014.

2 Figure 7.1 lists the countries in alphabetical order with their conventional acronyms: BE – Belgium; BG – Bulgaria; CZ – Czech Republic; DK – Denmark; DE – Germany; EE – Estonia; IE – Ireland; EL – Greece; ES – Spain; FR – France; HR – Croatia;

IT – Italy; CY – Cyprus; LV – Latvia; LT – Lithuania; LU – Luxembourg; HU – Hungary; MT – Malta; NL – Netherlands; AT – Austria; PL – Poland; PT – Portugal; RO – Romania; SI – Slovenia; SK – Slovakia; FI – Finland; SE – Sweden; UK – UK (see www.results-elections2014.eu/en/gender-balance.html, accessed 23 July 2014).

3 www.profil.at/articles/1422/576/375649/europawahl-2014-warum-frauen-maenner?google_editors_picks=true, accessed 23 July 2014.

4 As Betz (2013, 74) notes, the leader of the SVP, Christoph Blocher, was opposed to this campaign; it seems that the SVP was far from unanimous in supporting the initiative.

5 See Ho (2005), Sauer (2005), Navarro (2010), Flam and Beauzamy (2011), Read-Ghazal and Bartkowski (2000) and Wodak (2008) for more details on the impact of 'the gaze' as experienced by male and female migrants and, specifically, by veiled Muslim women.

6 Interview with Oscar Freysinger, 16 December 2009, quoted after Betz (2013); www.swissinfo.ch/eng/Specials/Minaret_Debate/Result_and_reactions/Minaret_vote_was_a_lesson_in_civic_spirit.html?cid=7916178, accessed 16/9/11; also www.reitschule.ch/reitschule/mediengruppe/Medienspiegel/09–04–28-MS.html, accessed 16 September 2011.

7 See also Rosenberger and Sauer (2013) for more details.

8 As Navarro (2010, 112) emphasizes, such racist discourse does not only occur in the West: 'In Muslim countries, the representation of Western women highlights prostitution, pornography and lack of respect for women.'

9 Here, I only discuss the gendered dimension extensively and refer readers to the original article for a comprehensive analysis of the racism propagated by the BNP compared to posters of the Austrian right-wing populist parties (Richardson and Wodak 2009a, 61–9). I am very grateful to John Richardson for allowing me to use the poster and parts of our analysis in this chapter.

10 The BNP also entered 10 candidates for the GLA London-wide candidate list, one constituency candidate (for the London constituency of City and East) as well as Richard Barnbrook as their Mayoral Candidate. The London Assembly is made up of 25 members and is a unique case in British politics, being decided by a partial system of proportional representation: 14 members of the Authority are elected via a 'first past the post' system to represent constituencies; these are supplemented by 11 London-wide members elected through PR. Political parties need 5 per cent of the vote to get one of these 11 seats, 8 per cent for two and 11 per cent for three (see Richardson and Wodak 2009a for more details).

11 The original image, entitled 'Many British Asians don't feel British', taken by a Press Association photographer, is available to view at http://prints.paphotos.com/pictures_679845/Many-British-Asians-dont-feel-British.html, accessed 19 May 2008.

12 The German original reads 'Es ist klar, dass der Rang der Frau in unserer Gesellschaft ein gänzlich gleichberechtigter sein muss, da kann es keine Abstriche geben. Ebenso aber ist es eine Tatsache, dass erfolgreiche Weiblichkeit und Mütterlichkeit nicht auseinanderfallen dürfen, wenn wir im Gesamten eine Zukunft haben wollen' (Rosenkranz 2008).

13 http://obamacarefacts.com/obamacare-facts.php, accessed 13/8/14. Indeed, in an interview on CNN, 3 June 2014, Dr Ben Carson from John Hopkins University stated that, 'Obamacare was the worst thing what happened to the United States since slavery' (www.youtube.com/watch?v=_toMKpsGW2o, accessed 13 August 2014).

14 One example of the enormous struggle is indicated by the filibuster by Texas senator Wendy Davis on 25 June 2013. She held an 11-hour long filibuster to block State Bill 5, which featured restrictive abortion regulations and would have led to the closure of all but five clinics in the state. The bill would have required abortion clinics to have hospital privileges and be

classified as ambulatory surgical centres, which supporters say would ensure better care for women but others say are simply intended to make it more difficult for women to access health services. The conservative majority in the Senate was convinced the bill was certain to pass if it came to a vote, so Davis launched a filibuster, a procedure in which a speaker attempts to talk and therefore hold the floor until the session ends, making a vote impossible. Davis filibustered for 11 of the 13 hours necessary, talking and standing for the entire time. This event caused an enormous tweet storm (see Dewey, 2013). The pink sneakers she wore during the 11 hours quickly became a metonymy for the 'Pro-Choice Movement' (www.google.hr/search?q=wendy+davis+pink+sneakers&tbm=isch&imgil=oN0oivsxgYrz7M%253A%253Btlk5Jor2ToFI2M%253Bhttp%25253A%25252F%25252Fblog.chron.com%25252Fshopgirl%25252F2013%25252F06%25252Fwendy-davis-pink-sneakers-kick-up-funny-reviews%25252F&source=iu&usg=__Xy-52HpKPEHxnlQQRKk-iAKdPlk%3D&sa=X&ei=bzrrU4j-KKnmyQOehICQBQ&sqi=2&ved=0CBwQ9QEwAA&biw=1188&bih=585, accessed 13 August 2014).

15 See http://en.wikipedia.org/wiki/Republican_Party_presidential_debates,_2012 (accessed 13 August 2014) for the entire list of debates and candidates. In the following detailed analysis of the sequence focused on abortion, I use the official transcript provided by CNN (http://transcripts.cnn.com/TRANSCRIPTS/1202/22/se.05.html). As the focus of my analysis of the debate is not its typical interactional aspects, I neglect many hesitation phenomena, intonation and a multimodal analysis. Instead I focus primarily on the specific arguments employed by each candidate to support his respective Pro-Life stance, having also to simultaneously distinguish himself from the other discussants (although they all seem to agree in general and maintain a Pro-Life stance).

8 MAINSTREAMING: THE NORMALIZATION OF EXCLUSION

The *Haiderization* of Europe

The Austrian 'Faustian' Coalition: Breaching Post-war Taboos

On 3 October 1999, Austria drew international attention: the Freedom Party FPÖ won 27.2 per cent of the votes, after running an election campaign centred on blatant and explicit racist slogans against foreigners. During the campaign, the Social Democratic Party SPÖ as well as the People's Party ÖVP (both forming a grand coalition government up to October 1999) seemed paralysed. The headline of the tabloid *Neue Kronenzeitung* (Austria's most popular newspaper and, in terms of readership in relation to population, the most widely read newspaper in the world) already celebrated Haider's 'March into the Chancellery' four days ahead of the actual election. At first, this was still perceived as a purely 'Austrian phenomenon', similar to other scandals in Austria which eventually made the headlines across the globe, such as the infamous 'Waldheim Affair' in 1986 (Wodak 2011c; Wodak et al. 1990). Both the Waldheim Affair and Haider's success were regarded as manifestations of Austria's Nazi past which had not been overcome in any adequate way: indeed, Austria continued to live comfortably (*gemütlich*) with its *Lebenslüge* (a lie that is told so as to live with a clear conscience), reassured by the self-told and continuously reasserted tale that it had been the first victim of Nazi aggression on 12 March 1938, and that Hitler and his SS were to blame for all Nazi atrocities.

Few scholars at that point in time already understood that the so-called *Haider phenomenon* would need to be evaluated as a new social movement carried by a charismatic and clever demagogue (Haider was an academic and had also worked as assistant professor in law at the University of Vienna for several years; Krzyżanowski and Wodak 2009).

On 4 February 2000, the Haider Party joined the Austrian government and formed a coalition with the ÖVP after some months of negotiations between the SPÖ which had, in fact, won the elections of 1 October 1999, and the ÖVP, which had come third (the FPÖ coming second). The then 14 other EU member states were deeply concerned as a *salient taboo of post-war Europe was breached for the first time*, that is, not to invite an extreme right-wing party into government, a party that did not distance itself clearly and was ambivalent towards the values (and the rhetoric) of Nazi times. They consequently approved of sanctions against the Austrian 'black and blue' government, named after the party colours of the coalition, which were quickly recontextualized as being directed against all Austrians and against Austria (Wodak and Pelinka 2002): a chauvinistic backlash was instigated in Austria, carried by almost all Austrian media and throughout the political system.

As a result of this and subsequent developments since 2000, a *normalization* of formerly tabooed racist, xenophobic and antisemitic rhetoric, as well as of exclusionary legislation implemented, can be observed in Austria – and is paralleled by similar developments throughout Europe, manifested in a range of explicit and coded expressions in public. *Haider is a case in point: his ascension marks the threshold when right-wing populist parties started to become acceptable for being integrated into a national government in an EU member state.* This is why I recapitulate some of the Austrian developments since 1989 and 2000, as other European right-wing populist parties and national governments seem to follow the 'Austrian model' and trajectory. Of course, analogies are never full analogues; nevertheless, the Austrian experience allows us to understand and explain some of the developments we have been confronted with ever since.

The Haider Phenomenon

The FPÖ in 2000 had many characteristics of what would soon be labelled as the *Haiderization of Europe*: a right-wing populist party espousing an ideology composed of a revisionist history (see Chapters 2 and 3), a nativist chauvinistic construction of a German cultural nation (see Chapter 4), vehement anti-immigration, Islamophobic and antisemitic rhetoric (see Chapters 1, 3, 5 and 7), and a staging of politics that soon blurred the boundaries between entertainment and serious politics, between a fictionalization of politics and the politicization of fiction (see Chapter 6).

Haider's right-wing populist rhetoric, aptly continued by HC Strache after Haider's sudden and unexpected death in 2008 (he died in car accident at night, drunk and driving at 88 miles per hour in his VW Phaeton, in a small Carinthian village with a speed limit of 30 miles per hour), was directed against 'those up there', that is, anti-elitist and anti-intellectual campaigning against 'Brussels' and the EU, and against corruption and privileges of the elites, endorsing conservative family policies and traditional gender roles as well as presenting himself as the 'saviour' of the 'man and woman of the street' or, as it suited him, of the imagined homogenous 'real Austrian people' (Wodak 2013a, 2013b). Under his leadership, the FPÖ constructed itself as a national-social movement, clearly insinuating the national-socialist slogans of the Nazi past. Hence, all the dimensions characterizing right-wing populist ideologies listed in Chapter 1 were already apparent – for those looking closely enough – in the 1990s.

Scapegoating, blaming the victim, victim–perpetrator reversal, trivialization and denial were, as we could observe on many occasions, among the most common discursive strategies used to convince voters or listeners/viewers of 'necessary' political measures, such as restricting immigration and legitimizing such restrictions, which often enough contradicted the democratic traditions and values of many nation states. Of course, depending on the genre and field of political discourse, the linguistic realizations would differ as elaborated in Chapter 3: the more anonymous the genre, the more explicit exclusionary rhetoric tends to be. The more official the setting, the more such prejudices and stereotypes are embedded into positive self-presentation and realized in implicit or latent linguistic units or clauses (presuppositions, implicatures, inferences, allusions etc.) introduced by disclaimers. Thus, as frequently emphasized throughout this book, the *context of each utterance* must be taken into account when analysing its exclusionary force. Moreover, tracking these developments revealed once and for all that *form and content of utterances (written, oral and visual) have to be analysed simultaneously* as meanings are always constructed via form and content. Utterances gain their meanings in use, in specific socio-political, historical and local contexts.

After the sanctions by the 14 other EU member states had been imposed against the Austrian government, it was quickly alleged that Austria was being victimized by the EU, a conspiracy supposedly organized by the left-wing parties inside Austria and the social-democratic parties throughout Europe was apparently directed against Austria. Concomitantly, a justificatory discourse similar to the one employed during the Waldheim Affair in 1986 united 'all Austrians' against the EU. Of course, there were many oppositional voices and the largest demonstration since 1945 (totalling over 300,000 protesters) marched through Vienna on 17 February 2000, protesting against the 'black and blue' government. Nevertheless, the sanctions were lifted after much consultation, and an investigatory commission, the so-called 'Three Wise Men', concluded that Austria was still abiding by all EU treaties and had remained a democratic country.

The 'Three Wise Men' were the former Finnish president Martti Ahtisaari, the then Spanish chancellor Marcelino Oreja, and a prominent German political scientist, Jochen Frowein. These three men visited Austria twice, spoke to many delegates, officials and NGOs, and published an extensive report on 8 September 2000. The report also judged the rhetoric of the FPÖ:

c) The continual use of ambiguous formulations by leading members of the FPÖ.

§88. It seems indeed to have become a typical feature of Austrian politics, that representatives of the FPÖ use extremely misleading formulations. Senior party members of the FPÖ have, over a long period of time, adopted attitudes that could be understood as xenophobic or even as racist. Many observers have recognised, in the formulations used, nationalistic undertones, and sometimes even undertones that come close to typical national-socialist expressions, or they sense in them a trivialisation of the history of that period.

(Ahtisaari et al. 2000, 26)

The report then became more specific:

§89. Clearly the FPÖ has taken no measures against members who have publicly projected xenophobic attitudes; it has neither condemned nor curtailed these attitudes and has made no clear apology for them. Whenever the perpetrators are confronted with these utterances, they deny any national-socialist intention or any corresponding character of the utterance. (ibid.)[1]

These two paragraphs (which are followed by several more in a similar vein and assess the programme and actions of FPÖ functionaries very critically) document the fact that a prominent commission of two elder statesmen and a highly respected political scientist does, in fact, attribute a salient role to political communication, to the language of politics and the language in politics, and to the prejudiced discourse of the FPÖ. Indeed, the report clearly pointed to the 'coded' exclusionary rhetoric of the FPÖ, to the many instances of 'double-speak' and calculated ambivalence.

The reactions to this report were manifold: the government quickly stated that everything was now alright, that the EU had judged Austria to be democratic and acting according to European values. The paragraphs quoted above, in contrast, were hardly mentioned or spoken of at all. If and when some government officials reacted to the assessment of the FPÖ, they tried to reformulate it and, for example, changed the negative connotation of 'radical' to a positive one, emphasizing the Latin etymology of 'radical' as 'going back to the roots'. On the surface, the conflict had thus been managed well or even solved, and the EU sanctions disappeared from the media agenda, which they had dominated for months (Wodak and Pelinka 2002).

In this way, the single explicit attempt of the EU and their organizations to date to set clear boundaries to arguably extreme-right ideologies and related movements had failed; indeed, it had resulted in the opposite, uniting Austrians behind their government and triggering even more support for the government. In the subsequent breaches of the Human Rights Charter, which is part of the EU Treaty – for example by Berlusconi in Italy or Orban in Hungary (by constraining the freedom of the press) – such sanctions could not be attempted any more as the range of possible interventions by the EU has been significantly altered.[2] The *Treaty of the European Union* Article 7 does suggest a legal strategy of intervention in case of a 'clear risk of a serious breach by an EU member state of EU values' and has been employed several times to date; however, the possibilities and forms of implementation are currently quite restricted:

> The intention to use the Article 7 TEU mechanism has come about on several occasions. The French Roma expulsions, the Romanian political struggle between President Băsescu and Prime Minister Ponta and its consequences are amongst the most relevant examples. Furthermore, the European Parliament has recently highlighted its willingness to activate this democracy protection mechanism if the Hungarian government does not take action to restore the rule of law in Hungary. Nevertheless, the political unwillingness to use Article 7 leaves several questions unanswered: what are the precise EU values protected by this mechanism? What is the threshold for a measure or a non-measure to classify as serious breach? etc.
>
> (Andreagimis 2013)[3]

In Austria, cases of hate incitement such as the Facebook Incident (Vignette 1) were taken to court, but usually resulted in a dismissal of the charge: the calculated ambivalence and double-speak of specific utterances could frequently be denied successfully by the respective politicians – except in cases of Holocaust denial (see Chapter 5) or explicitly revisionist Nazi rhetoric (see Wodak 2007a).[4] With respect to the Facebook incident (Image 1.1), for example, the court's assessment of the caricature stated that

> the caricature had not 'enticed sedition against the entire Jewish population' but wanted to voice criticism against the Austrian government and the Euro rescue fund.[5]
>
> (http://derstandard.at/1363707385450/Strache-Karikatur-Karl-verteidigt-weiter-Einstellung-der-Ermittlung)

What was meant by the peculiar phrase 'the entire Jewish population' was never clarified. We would be justified in asking, for instance, which Jewish population? The Austrian Jewish population? Jewish Israelis? A 'Jewish race', thus alluding to racist beliefs? Or – possibly insinuating a traditional stereotype – a 'Jewish world conspiracy'? The judgment thus implied that the traditional antisemitic stereotype of 'the Jewish banker who exploits the workers and the government' and – in the context of the Eurozone crisis and the measures proposed by the European Bank and the EU Commission against this – insinuated that the Jewish bankers did, indeed, have the power to manipulate governments and the EU and that it was therefore not antisemitic as the caricature 'only' targeted bankers and not 'all Jews'.

In view of the vast amount of literature and research about such stereotypes and the alleged 'power of Jewish bankers', this decision can only be regarded with scepticism. The consequence of such court rulings, of course, supports ever more messages employing calculated ambivalence and rhetoric based on a politics of denial. Breaching taboos, playing with hate incitement, and posting discriminatory slogans and images have thus become part and parcel of right-wing populist strategies – apparently tolerated by jurisprudence.

As already mentioned in Chapters 1 and 6, the media support such scandals at least indirectly as these hold the headlines for days and weeks, thus forcing all other political agenda into the background. The media also seem caught in a double-bind: if they do not report such incidents, they seem to accept these. If they do report them in detail, they give ever more attention to such incidents and reinforce the scandalization – a dynamic I have labelled as the *Right-wing populist perpetuum mobile* (see Chapter 1 and below). In this way, the FPÖ (and similar parties across Europe and beyond) set the frames in everyday politics; traditional antisemitic and racist stereotypes have become acceptable again.

Mainstreaming and Normalization

Although I was convinced in 2000 that right-wing populism would prove not to be a short-lived phenomenon, probably very few scholars could have imagined that in 2014, such parties would be able to win the elections for European Parliament in France or the UK, countries which had always formed a *cordon sanitaire* against the participation of right-wing populist parties in government since the end of World War II. Nowadays, right-wing populism in all its varieties has become a mainstream political force in many European countries and beyond. It is an almost trivial consequence that the respective policies and strategies, the ideologies and imaginaries must therefore be taken seriously, analysed, interpreted and explained. The many genres in which such policies are disseminated have to be examined carefully in order to understand the electoral success of such parties, why they are deemed attractive by so many young and old, male and female voters in some national contexts but not in others. This is why close and systematic critical analysis of the communicative dynamics, the rhetorical patterns and argumentative schemata used is pertinent. After having analysed the rhetoric of exclusion, body and border politics, the politics of the past and the history of right-wing populist movements in Europe and beyond in much detail, it is important to come back to some of the questions posed in Chapter 1: *Why are these parties so successful? Are there general patterns to be detected or is each so specific as to be incomparable? And why is it now, in 2014, that some parties are climbing to the very top of the electoral ladder?*

In 1992, huge protests against Jörg Haider's anti-immigration proposals led to one of the largest post-war demonstrations, referred to as a 'sea of light' ('*Lichtermeer*'), against such exclusionary and racist politics (Reisigl and Wodak 2000). By 2014, however, many of the proposals of the *Austria First* petition had already been implemented and legalized, had in fact become integral to everyday policies and experience. The many walls in stone or barbed wire, erected since 2010 against the alleged threat of migrants and refugees (in Greece, Bulgaria and Spain), manifest the politics of exclusion in re-semiotized ways: the 'postmodern strangers' are to be kept outside; exclusion has now been set in stone. The 'strangers within' carry the borders with them, they have embodied them; they have to pass language tests, citizenship tests, acquire working permits, adapt to many rules and regulations, that is, assimilate, and experience a range of everyday exclusionary practices both explicit and latent. In this way, borders have become reinstated, allowing only specific individuals to pass them while others are kept waiting outside or are denied entry:

> Variously invoked as a geographic term for delineating territories, a political expression of national sovereignty, a juridical marker of citizenship status, and an ideological trope for defining terms of inclusion and exclusion, the border circulates as a robust spatial metaphor in the public vernacular.

> (DeChaine 2012, 1)

As evidenced by the 15 vignettes throughout this book, many factors have to come together to facilitate success for right-wing populist parties. These factors are influenced by both local and global developments: by national traditions and histories, by the global financial crisis and the related neo-liberal austerity politics leading to rising unemployment figures in many European countries and beyond, by the urge to protect the welfare state ('welfare chauvinism'), by enormous poverty in the 'developing countries' and subsequent migration, by the developments of the 'Arab Spring' and by emerging new fundamentalist religious movements, by launching ever more security measures after 9/11 and so forth. And, of course, by the disenchantment of many citizens by dysfunctional traditional politics – politics which are perceived as no longer able to confront new risks and dangers in our societies in adequate ways. New media-savvy leaders instrumentalize such disenchantment in text, image and talk, via many discursive and material practices.

The fundamental European values were stated explicitly in the Copenhagen Declaration, 14 September 1973:[6]

> The Nine European States might have been pushed towards disunity by their history and by selfishly defending misjudged interests. But they have overcome their past enmities and have decided that unity is a basic European necessity to ensure the survival of the civilization which they have in common. The Nine wish to ensure that the cherished values of their legal, political and moral order are respected, and to preserve the rich variety of their national cultures. [...] they are determined to defend the principles of representative democracy, of the rule of law, of social justice – which is the ultimate goal of economic progress – and of respect for human rights. All of these are fundamental elements of the European Identity.

> (Copenhagen Declaration on European Identity)

As Zielonka (2012, 58) argues, these values have unfortunately been backgrounded, possibly even forgotten, during the many crises in recent years and decades: accordingly, EU member states have been harshly criticized 'for failing to offer their citizens sufficient means of participation, representation, and accountability' (ibid.). Although participation in such complex decision-making processes far away from home is necessarily difficult, the use of power has to be legitimated. However, there is a lack of channels for pan-European deliberation and bargaining even though the European Parliament has recently gained more rights and power. Moreover, due to the financial crisis since 2008, Zielonka maintains that 'the electorates in both creditor and debtor states are profoundly disenchanted with demands coming from Europe […] In the EU, technocrats dominate policy making while populists dominate politics' (ibid.). Frustration and EU-scepticism strengthen both left-wing and right-wing populist movements which are otherwise ideologically far apart: both the left-wing populist Greek Syriza and the right-wing populist Austrian FPÖ, the British UKIP and Dutch Freedom Party are campaigning to take power away from Brussels and bring it 'back home'.

Hence, *renationalizing tendencies* can generally be observed, manifest in new frontiers and borders, new walls which are being erected across Europe to protect the traditional nation state – a Fortress Europe – in times in which globalized media and new communication modes simultaneously allow for an unprecedented speed of sharing news and spreading change. Slogans that propose a return to a homogenous nation state, the mother tongue and conservative family values, which highlight 'pure' Christian white people as the 'real' Austrians, Finns, Hungarians or Danes, are voiced ubiquitously, as answers to the many – constructed and real – fears and anxieties. The answers given by populist right-wing parties are oriented backward, towards a nostalgic imaginary, clinging to parochial, chauvinistic and traditional values, trying to turn back the wheel of history and social developments.

Comaroff (2011, 103) emphasizes three points she regards as relevant in respect of right-wing populist agenda:

> I seek to make three points: first, that populism in some form is a necessary condition of *all* anti-establishment movements, past and present, progressive or conservative; second, that it is in itself never enough to fuel sustained, politically constructive mobilizations; and third, that in all these respects, populism would seem to take on particular, and particularly disquieting, features in late modern times.
>
> (ibid.)

Following Comaroff's view, we can pose the question of what will happen now that right-wing populist movements actually are becoming part of the establishment. To date, there are only a few examples of government coalitions (in Austria, Italy, Switzerland, Norway and the Netherlands) or of support of governments (in Denmark). This does not yet allow – as I have indicated in previous chapters – clearly predictable and generalizable patterns to be identified. Indeed, the coalition government between ÖVP and FPÖ in Austria lost its majority in the 2006 national elections, and the FPÖ lost many voters partly due to its performance in government; however, the FPÖ under HC Strache quickly won new support and, in 2014, stood at 29 per cent in the opinion polls.

The continuous oppositional habitus was not successful when confronted with the difficult 'job' of governing; right-wing populist parties seem to be more successful when in opposition. In Denmark, however, the Danish People's Party held on to power for 10 years; the programme to protect the welfare benefits for the 'Danish people' seems to have resonated well even during government participation. The same is true for Switzerland, where the Swiss People's Party continues to hold strong support and anti-immigration policies put forward in various referenda find agreement in large population segments. And even in countries where right-wing populist parties have to date been excluded from government, as in France or the UK, centre-right and centre-left parties seem to pre-emptively implement right-wing populist policies in the attempt to retain their voters (see Chapter 4). Evidence indicates that this strategy, previously initiated in many countries (including Austria), is doomed to fail as voters tend to elect the party that traditionally stands for specific policies instead of parties which opportunistically and superficially jump onto the respective bandwagon. However, the consequence of the *normalization of right-wing populist policies* implies that almost the entire political spectrum moves to the right, that exclusionary policies are effectively promoted and implemented, and that societies which have a strong oppositional party become polarized (e.g. Greece). Agonistic struggle as suggested by Ernesto Laclau (see Chapter 2), in which the success of right-wing populist parties might trigger new alternatives amongst the mainstream and force such parties to abandon their comfort zone, has not had any observable positive effect to date.

Nativist Body Politics – East and West

A nativist nationalistic agenda has become hegemonic in the rhetoric and manifestos of right-wing populist parties, articulating a desire to establish a homogenous white, Christian population in the borders of the traditional nation state, all speaking the same language – the mother tongue. In some of these parties, a fascist 'blood and soil' rhetoric and related metaphors of 'strangers' visualized as 'parasites, disease and illness' have come to the fore, frequently drawing on fascist and national-socialist traditions and pasts, on rewritten foundational myths of lost power and territory (see Chapters 2, 4 and 5). Such nostalgic imaginaries are combined with and reinforced through anger and fear: anger about the alleged loss of power and fear of alleged new threats. These in turn lead to opposition against any transnational and globalized policies, against the EU specifically – which is perceived as initiating undesirable changes, and against cosmopolitanism more generally. Conspiracies are subsequently detected and imagined in the background, claimed to be the cause of such loss of power, usually related to traditional antisemitic tropes; Jews or other allegedly powerful groups which, the right-wing populist ideology assumes, are to be blamed for all the common woes and problems. Complexity is reduced to simplistic dichotomies; scapegoats are created and instrumentalized as reasons for any current problems or troubles. The traditional left/right cleavages seem obsolete: we are confronted with struggles about (*inter alia* religious and social, family and feminist) values which cut across the former social divides. Calls for strong leaders able to solve all problems are becoming louder and clearer once more.

Related to such body and border politics, some important differences between right-wing political parties in East and Western Europe should be emphasized. Due to the Communist past of Eastern European countries, current politics are faced with very different legacies than those of Western European countries. Hungary, Poland, the Czech Republic, Slovakia, Bulgaria, Ukraine, Russia and the Baltic States do not only have to cope with the trauma of World War II, that is, with having been occupied by Nazi Germany (such as Czechoslovakia, Poland and Bulgaria) or by having had fascist regimes (Hungary and Romania) or collaborated with Nazi Germany in many respects (Ukraine), but also by having been part of the Eastern Bloc, the Warsaw Pact, until 1989. Thus, at least two histories have to be integrated into collective memories: on the one hand, World War II, and on the other hand, the Communist era and various forms of resistance.

The upheavals of 1989 meant that nation states and national identities, which had been long thought lost or which had never truly existed, had to be reinvented. As Judt (2007, 821) reminds us, 'Auschwitz was the most important thing to know about World War II' – but only for the West. For the East, however, 'the *fin de siècle* Western preoccupation with the Holocaust of the Jews carries disruptive implications'. (ibid.) In schoolbooks and memorials, the horrors and victims of World War II certainly appeared and were documented, but, as Judt argues, 'Jews were not part of the story' (ibid., 822). Indeed, as he continues, it is obvious that huge dilemmas exist in Eastern European memory culture – should one thus commemorate the Hungarian Revolution 1956, the Prague Spring 1968, or the fall of the Berlin Wall? Which victims are, so to speak, more worthy of being mentioned, when, where and why? This huge paradox is well summarized by Judt:

> Before 1989 every anti-Communist had been tarred with the 'Fascist' brush. But if 'anti-Fascism' had been just another Communist lie, it was very tempting now to look with retrospective sympathy and even favour upon *all* hitherto discredited anti-Communists, Fascists included. […] Execrated until very recently as nationalists, Fascists and Nazi collaborators, they would now have statues raised in honour of their wartime heroism.

> (ibid., 824)

Apart from memory and identity politics, the transformation/transition to a capitalist economy produced new categories of winners and losers. Many wanted to become part of 'the West' as quickly as possible, others wanted to remain neutral, and other groups nostalgically longed for 'the better past' (Kovács and Wodak 2003). The very different memories and experiences in Western Europe and Eastern Europe serve as one at least partial explanation for different political developments and different kinds of right-wing populist movements and their programmes, for different electorates and gender politics, and for the different scapegoats: Muslims and migrants in Western Europe, Jews and Roma in Eastern Europe. It must be noted that Roma are discriminated against everywhere, in the East and in the West, in France, Ireland and Italy, as well as in Hungary, Slovakia, Romania, Bulgaria and the Czech Republic. They certainly were and remain the most vulnerable group in Europe.

As elaborated in Chapter 2, we have to abandon the idea of a *one-size-fits-all explanation for the rise and success of right-wing populist movements*. Histories, collective memories and experiences as well as different narratives form a range of complex ideologies. These ideologies draw on many traditional discourses interwoven with the new 'Western' agenda and practices constructing new identity politics and an explicitly xenophobic, antisemitic and racist politics of exclusion in Eastern Europe. Thus, they differ from a 'softer', coded and frequently accepted discrimination in Western Europe that is legitimized due to security measures, neo-liberal austerity politics and welfare chauvinism.

The Politics of Fear

Leaders of right-wing populist parties have also changed their looks and performance – from radical right-wing 'thugs' to well-educated and well-dressed demagogues, typifying overtly 'soft', caring and responsible politicians (Chapter 6). A *politics of denial* dominates – all proponents of such parties would necessarily deny that they condone racist or antisemitic beliefs as illustrated in Vignette 1. Such parties present themselves as primarily patriotic, as protecting the needs of the 'real' Danish/Finnish/Hungarian/Greek and so forth people, as saving the 'people' from globalization and other (frequently alleged) threats, and as opposing the obvious fact: Europe and the EU have become countries of immigration, diverse, multilingual and multicultural. They would also deny that this fact has to be confronted with new policies in politics, education, legislation and everyday life. A general politics of fear is mobilized against all new developments, a *negative mobilization* as suggested by Comaroff (2011). This mobilization does not serve constructive programmes but a backwards-oriented politics, an anachronistic agenda attempting to preserve some illusionary past, infused with much nostalgia and anti-intellectualism. This '*arrogance of ignorance*', as I have termed it, permeates many domains of our societies.

As illustrated in Chapter 7, gendered discourses seem to serve such politics well and co-construct an ideology that combines nativist body politics, exclusionary border politics, racism, xenophobia and antisemitism, sexism as well as homophobia – constituting the authoritarian syndrome as described by Adorno et al. (1967). The claim put forward by the so-called 'frontier feminism' of Tea Party followers, that is, that 'kitchen table economics' would be able to solve complex state economic issues and the global financial crisis, illustrates such naivety and ignorance. The tendency to return to traditional gender roles, to strong and strict fathers on the one hand, and to caring mothers on the other hand, instantiates the wish to control and discipline, once more, the female body in order to revive strong masculinities. This is also why right-wing populist parties and their leaders (e.g. Marine Le Pen or HC Strache) seem to admire strong political male leaders such as Vladimir Putin, who manifest and implement (frequently against any international human rights conventions) authoritarian, even dictatorial policies (Chapter 7). Comaroff emphasizes the need for the strong leader as follows:

> In their fatal dependency on dualism, populist movements often resurrect the patriarch in place of the vanquished 'elite': hence the troubling return to language of the paterfamilias and male dominance […]. For this kind of populace, the leader serves as fetish, a *deus ex machina* who short-circuits the more sustained structures of debate, democratic governance, and the pursuit of justice.

(2011, 205)

'Cardboard men' and 'plastic women' embody, manifest and perform new gender roles, leaving many (in particular working-class) men at a loss, as modernization losers, unemployed and with no perspective for the future, especially amongst the young generation. Thus, in many EU member states, high unemployment amongst the young triggers both an understandable fear of the future and desires for change, frequently projected onto strong leaders. Fear is easily converted into scapegoating and politically instrumentalized: 'Others' who take away 'our jobs', usually migrants, are perceived as the root cause instead of inequality, austerity politics and neo-liberal economics. We witness some rich countries with low unemployment, such as *inter alia* Austria, Germany, Denmark, Sweden, Norway and Switzerland, who strive to protect their welfare economy resulting in welfare chauvinism and strong body politics; and some poor countries with high unemployment, such as *inter alia* Spain, Portugal, Italy, Greece, France, Hungary and the UK, where the economic situation leads to rising xenophobia. In both cases, successful populist right-wing movements are the result. Due to historical legacies, however, this does not happen everywhere in the same way; not by means of the same *topoi* and discursive strategies, and not with the same force and success.

Nohrstedt (2013, 311–12) illustrates via careful analysis of various incidents – such as the so-called 'Mohammed Cartoon crisis' in 2006 – that the complex interdependence between media, scandalization and a politics of fear (and threat) is a necessary and constitutive element for the rise of right-wing populist parties, apart from the dynamic of the *right-wing populist perpetuum mobile* already mentioned above. He provides evidence that 'threats and dangers dominate in the political rhetoric. Political changes are driven by worst-case scenarios' (ibid); moreover, distrust amongst fellow citizens abounds as individuals seem to feel more and more vulnerable and, indeed, feel completely and utterly at the mercy of unpredictable and unknown powers or developments which nobody could possibly influence – including abstract phenomena like globalization, climate change or the financial crisis. Instead of positive imaginaries being concretized in alternative party programmes and manifestos, such as 'solidarity' (Dean 1996), a politics of 'well-being' (Nussbaum 2013), 'encounter cultures' (Amin 2012) or, indeed, acceptance and living with difference (Benhabib 1987), we witness an increase of divisiveness and the normalization of discriminatory policies, resulting in the kinds of border and body politics elaborated throughout this book.

(Not) Falling into the Trap?

Fear dominates the political agenda at the present historical juncture; and, of course, some of these anxieties and fears or, more to the point, some of the dangers and threats associated with them should be taken seriously, such as climate change, poverty, fundamentalism, the widening gap between rich and poor, between the so-called 'First World' and the 'developing countries' and so forth. Mainstream parties would be well advised to address the many problems which have emerged due to recent global and local developments – they should not be swept under the carpet but confronted with alternative policies:

> The roots of public anxiety that make it easy to scapegoat the stranger need to be tackled head on, through reforms aiming at job generation, fair pay, equal access, universal well-being, […] and shared common life. Only then will the temptation to name the migrant and subaltern as the threat to the prosperity, well-being and cohesion of the many, seem anomalous.
>
> (Amin 2012, 125)

Instead of a politics of denial, a *politics of 'well-being'*, an *inclusive politics* should be the goal, articulating a more integrative and inclusive 'We' instead of ever more strict Manichean divisions between 'Us' and 'Them'. Nussbaum (2013, 118) maintains that societies should not only be concerned about GDP per capita as the only indicator of quality of life. Instead, she proposes that societies should aim at 'human development', 'meaning the opportunities of people to lead rich and rewarding lives' (ibid.). Along a similar vein, *solidarity* is promoted by few scholars and politicians (Judt 2010), a notion which has lost its original positive meaning and impact, and is now endorsed by some and ridiculed by others. There is no doubt that the rising inequality across the globe is the primary cause of current social problems. As Judt rightly argues, '[I]nequality is corrosive. It rots societies from within' (2011, 6). He continues:

> How should we begin to make amends for raising a generation obsessed with the pursuit of material wealth and indifferent to so much else? Perhaps we might start by

reminding ourselves and our children that it wasn't always thus. Thinking 'economistically,' as we have done now for thirty years, is not intrinsic to humans. There was a time when we ordered our lives differently.

(ibid., 6)

Proponents of solidarity are frequently labelled as do-gooders, naive and over-zealous (the German term *Gutmenschen* encapsulates this derogatory notion); solidarity is viewed as an anachronistic concept not suitable for an individualistic, neo-liberal and globalized world. However, even quite conservative European intellectuals such as Biedenkopf et al. (2004, 8–10) call for more solidarity in their reflections on Europe; more pessimistically, however, they state that '[m]arkets cannot produce a politically resilient solidarity [...]. European solidarity is not something that can be imposed from above. [...] When individual solidarity is not there, institutionally based solidarity is not enough to bring a polity into being.'

Cutting through the Gordian knot – Setting Alternative Frames

In his widely acknowledged book *Don't Think of an Elephant: Know Your Values and Frame the Debate* (2004), which points to some electoral failures of Democratic candidate John Kerry against G.W. Bush in the US presidential election 2004, George Lakoff suggested that alternative frames should be promoted. Simply reacting to the frames of the US Republican Party implied a foregone conclusion in the sense of losing the agenda-setting force. The struggle for values, initiatives and alternatives should not be neglected; quite to the contrary – instead of opposing the Republican agenda, the Democratic Party should strive to set their own themes and retain their egalitarian position. He claims that the Democratic Party has not been able to prevent the Republican Party in reframing and recontextualizing their own, traditionally Democratic agenda – and was thus, Lakoff argues, actually left without any significant programme. Taking Lakoff's views on board, I believe – also in a quite similar vein – that not falling into the demagogic and political trap of right-wing populism entails setting *alternative frames and agenda*, endorsing and also disseminating alternative concepts, such as equality, diversity and solidarity. Nussbaum also mentions 'human dignity' and respect as concepts with such potential (2013, 120).

Alternative policies and programmes, into which form and content necessarily have to be integrated, must be launched. If change reaches no deeper than the rhetoric, including argumentation schemes, metaphors and so forth, right-wing ideologies will merely become softer on the surface, more implicit and possibly even more difficult to deconstruct.

Not falling into the trap entails developing and maintaining alternative patterns of media reporting – less oriented towards reinforcing scandalous incidents and appearances of right-wing populist politicians, but towards deconstructing them. Instead of highlighting ever more outrageous utterances, it would be much more sensible to point out the underlying dynamics and the related intentions, that is, getting on the front page at whatever cost. For example, it would make a substantial difference to point to recurring patterns, to ever new allegations of conspiracies and to deconstruct these explicitly on a meta-level. The frame of 'anything goes' could thus be firewalled and limited by exposing blatant lies and by contextualizing and embedding incidents in their appropriate context and history. Instead of highlighting fear, solidarity and inclusiveness lend themselves as positive imaginaries. Not falling into the trap would thus entail a *politics of solidarity* instead of a *politics of fear or envy*.

Moreover, it would be important to stop generalizing and attributing specific characteristics to seemingly homogenous groups, that is, '*All* Americans, Muslims, Israelis, British, Austrians, Roma or Jews do or are X'. Groups are never homogenous; such rhetoric only serves reinforcing and perpetuating dangerous stereotypes. Complexity should therefore not give way to simplistic dichotomies which are frequently used to fallaciously 'explain' difficult phenomena.

Finally, it is imperative no longer to react, imitate or adapt to the right-wing populist agenda via *the right-wing populist perpetuum mobile*, to resist the temptation to jump on the right-wing populist bandwagon out of fear of losing voters. Instead, parties should formulate alternative positions or maintain or even reinvigorate their traditional position: to (re)formulate values such as equality, justice, democracy, education, multilingualism, diversity and solidarity – all of which are fundamental European values as stated in the Copenhagen Declaration of 1973 mentioned above – in ways attuned to the necessities of the 21st century.

Epilogue

Although I had strictly planned to stop revising this book to comment on ever new and interesting as well as surprising political events after submitting my manuscript, new developments in Germany starting in late autumn 2014 have to be at least briefly mentioned.

A new social movement, PEGIDA ('Patriotic Europeans against the Islamisation of the West'), is dominating the headlines in German media and beyond.[7] By recontextualizing the salient slogan of the sweeping demonstrations of 1989 in the former GDR, namely '*Wir sind das Volk*' (i.e. 'We are the people'), which was directed against the Communist dictatorship in East Germany and accompanied the fall of the Berlin Wall, PEGIDA is now attacking asylum seekers and migrants, primarily if not exclusively those of Muslim faith. Analogous to other right-wing populist movements I have described, PEGIDA is also combining supposedly liberal agenda – the defence of democratic and liberal values – with reactionary and anti-feminist demands.

The new right-wing populist party in Germany established in spring 2014, *Alternative für Deutschland* or AFD,[8] has already aligned itself with PEGIDA, which succeeded in mobilizing approximately 20,000 demonstrators in Dresden every Monday; PEGIDA has been described as a gathering of so-called *Wutbürger*, that is, angry citizens. While the demographics of these demonstrators are diverse, they include many citizens who feel left behind and ignored by the political establishment, who fear for their jobs and, most importantly, fear a loss of 'real' German identity. This phenomenon is new for post-war Germany, where to date only small extreme-right parties or neo-Nazis such as the NPD (see Chapter 6) had been occasionally visible; of course, such extreme and exclusionary positions were expressed in recent years in various editorials or in Thilo Sarrazin's best-selling book *Deutschland schafft sich ab* (2010), but this had remained primarily an intellectual debate and had not yet become the programmatic agenda of a party or movement.

Most German mainstream politicians, media and religious communities have reacted very strongly against this new movement, emphasizing Germany's openness for all refugees. Counter-demonstrations organized by anti-racism NGOs, by all mainstream parties, by students, by the churches and so forth have also taken place.[9] Indeed, on 10 January

2015, a much larger demonstration of 35,000 people marched in Dresden, protesting against PEGIDA and proclaiming Germany's openness for refugees and ethnic as well as religious minorities. Although PEGIDA has not achieved the status of a political party as yet, and although AFD remains under 10 per cent, the entire political establishment is embarrassed, worried and indeed appalled. Subsequently, German chancellor Angela Merkel requested all Germans to reject PEGIDA's programme, in her annual New Year speech, as top priority for 2015.[10] These developments remind me of the *Lichtermeer* in Vienna in 1993 and the strong opposition to the FPÖ and Jörg Haider in the 1990s. While many other historical scenarios suggest themselves as parallels, it is certainly much too early to draw any analogies or valid comparisons to the 1930s and the Weimar Republic. The contexts differ significantly.

We cannot predict at this stage how these new developments will impact Germany's politics. PEGIDA may soon disappear again; it may change or evolve into something larger yet; German politics may accommodate to the right-wing populist agenda as has happened in many other EU member states. Or maybe not? Let us hope that people have learnt from the past. And that at least some do not fall in the many traps outlined above.

Endnotes

1 See www.ag-friedensforschung.de/regionen/Austria/bericht.html, accessed 6 September 2014, for more details.

2 See www.europarl.europa.eu/comparl/libe/elsj/charter/default_en.htm, accessed 12 March 2015, for more information.

3 See http://epthinktank.eu/2013/10/07/article-7-teu-a-mechanism-to-protect-eu-values/, accessed 6 September 2014.

4 See www.news.at/a/strache-karikatur-karl-verteidigt-staatsanwaltschaft, accessed 7 September 2014.

5 See Vignette 1 (Facebook Incident, Chapter 1): The antisemitic caricature posted by Strache on his Facebook site was judged not to be antisemitic as the caricature allegedly did not relate to 'all Jews'. Vignette 1 traces this incident and the subsequent scandalization in much detail.

6 The Copenhagen Declaration was signed by nine EU member states (France, Germany, Belgium, the Netherlands, Luxembourg, Italy, Denmark, Ireland and the UK) (www. cvce.eu/obj/declaration_sur_l_identite_europeenne_copenhague_14_decembre_1973-fr-02798dc9-9c69-4b7d-b2c9-f03a8db7da32.html, accessed 4 September 2014).

7 See e.g. www.faz.net/aktuell/politik/inland/pegida-in-dresden-polizisten-muessen-demonstranten-aufhalten-13355174.html, accessed 6 January 2015.

8 See www.alternativefuer.de/for more information.

9 See www.sueddeutsche.de/politik/erfolg-deutschlandweiter-gegendemos-pegida-floppt-ausserhalb-dresdens-1.2291802, accessed 5 January 2015.

10 See www.youtube.com/watch?v=-televisionNyMXFLeg, accessed 5 January 2015.

GLOSSARY OF RIGHT-WING POPULIST PARTIES[1]

Q AUSTRIA
Freiheitliche Partei Österreichs (FPÖ)
Freedom Party of Austria

FOUNDED	EUROPEAN AFFILIATION
April 1956	EAF (European Alliance for Freedom)

IDEOLOGY
Nationalism; Anti-immigration; Anti-Islam; Antisemitism;
Euroscepticism

ELECTION RESULTS

Year	Type of Election	Votes	Percentage	Mandates
2009	European Parliament	364,207	12.7	2/17
2008	National Parliament	857,028	17.5	34/183
2013	National Parliament	958,285	20.5	40/183
2014	European Parliament	556,835	19.72	4/18

The FPÖ was founded in 1956, 30 years before Haider became the party's leader; it was a successor to the Federation of Independents, which gathered former NSDAP members after the end of World War II. The party saw an electoral comeback under the leadership and populist, xenophobic, revisionist and antisemitic rhetoric of Jörg Haider (Wodak and Pelinka 2002). In the 1999 national election, the FPÖ won 26.9 per cent of the vote and became the second strongest party in Austria. This electoral success led to a coalition government between the Austrian People's Party (ÖVP) and the FPÖ, accompanied by the introduction of sanctions from the EU claiming that participation of the FPÖ in a coalition government 'legitimized the extreme Right in Europe' (Krzyżanowski and Wodak 2009; Meret 2010). Under Haider's leadership, the party transformed into a far-right populist party claiming that its intention was to protect 'Austrian culture and national identity' and to safeguard Austrian people's rights and prosperity. The issue that continues to dominate the political agenda of the party is immigration. In 1993 the party launched a petition to collect signatures in favour of a popular referendum on the control of immigration in Austria. While this caused a political crisis within the party (Meret 2010), it did not put a halt to the anti-immigration discourse of the party's leadership. Its plans for restrictive amendments to the country's migration policy were accomplished during its participation in coalition government (2000–2006). The FPÖ adopted a more radical, anti-immigrant and especially anti-Muslim agenda under HC Strache. The party now presents itself as guarantor of Austrian identity, social welfare, and social and financial stability through the prism of its *Heimat* (homeland) profile and has developed a Eurosceptic rhetoric (McLaughlin 2013). During the 2013 national election campaign, HC Strache used strong anti-immigration or racist discourse that increased the party's popular support; the FPÖ is now openly described as far-right and xenophobic (McLaughlin 2013).

Q BELGIUM

Vlaams Belang (VB)
Flemish Interest

FOUNDED	EUROPEAN AFFILIATION
November 2004	EAF (European Alliance for Freedom)

IDEOLOGY
Flemish nationalism; Separatism; Anti-Islam; Euroscepticism

ELECTION RESULTS

	Type of Election	Votes	Percentage	Mandates
2009	European Parliament	647,170	9.9	2/22
2010	Chamber of Representatives	506,697	7.8	12/150
2010	Senate	491,519	7.6	3/40
2014	European Parliament	284,891	4.26	1/21

Vlaams Belang (VB), which originates from Vlaams Block – which was forced to disband in 2004 due to its xenophobic, antisemitic and discriminatory discourse (Mudde 2003; Osborn 2001) – is a Flemish nationalist party that advocates independence for Flanders and the establishment of a Flemish Republic. Immigration and security issues still dominate VB's political agenda. The party opposes multiculturalism, claims that strict limits on immigration are necessary and that immigrants should be obliged to adopt the Flemish culture and language (Coffé 2005). Although the new party's members have attempted to moderate the 'radical' character of VB's political programme, the leader of the new party and former chairman of Vlaams Block, Frank Vanhecke, soon maintained that 'the party changed its name but not its tactics or programme' (Coffé 2005; Erik 2005). Hence, the leadership of the party adopted anti-Muslim rhetoric on the basis of Islamist terrorism and emphasized the threat of 'immigrants' criminality' in general (Coffé 2005). In 2009 VB participated for the first time in the European Parliament election and began an alliance with other Eurosceptic nationalist parties. All other Flemish parties in Belgium have agreed not to participate in a coalition with Vlaams Belang, forming a cordon sanitaire (Coffé 2005).

Q BULGARIA

Ataka
Attack

FOUNDED	EUROPEAN AFFILIATION
April 2005	NF (National Front) France

IDEOLOGY
Ultranationalism; Antisemitism; Anti-Roma; Euroscepticism

ELECTION RESULTS

Year	Type of Election	Votes	Percentage	Mandates
2009	National Election	395,707	9.4	21/240
2009	European Parliament	308,052	12.0	2/17
2013	National Election	258,481	7.3	23/240
2014	European Parliament	66,210	2.96	0/17

ATAKA is an example of political-media links, in so far as a popular television talk-show presented by the journalist Volen Siderov evolved into a political party in 2005. ATAKA can be defined as an ultra-nationalist party that views Bulgaria as a one-nation state and claims that 'differences of origin or faith have no priority over nationality' (ATAKA 2014). The country's Muslim minority was presented as 'evil' by the party's leadership (Pencheva 2009). Moreover, the party emphasizes Bulgarian culture, language and the Orthodox religion, and opposes Bulgaria's participation in the

EU and NATO, attacking those who signed Bulgaria's membership of the EU as 'national traitors'. Furthermore, the party presents itself as fighting for the spiritual, social, educational and financial prosperity of the Bulgarian nation via the party's main slogan: 'Let's regain Bulgaria for the Bulgarians' (ATAKA 2014). The party blames the Roma for an increase in criminality in Bulgaria, and Jews and the EU for the financial and humanitarian crisis in the country (Rensmann 2011). The party also opposes the accession of Turkey to the EU as a 'Turkish threat' that intends to recolonize the Balkan region. ATAKA became the fourth largest party in Bulgaria by blaming both the colonial West-EU and Muslim Turkey (Tsolova 2013). ATAKA saw a sharp fall in its electoral percentages in the 2014 European Parliament elections.

⚲ CYPRUS

Εθνικό Λαϊκό Μέτωπο, Ethniko Laiko Metopo
National Popular Front (ELAM)

FOUNDED	EUROPEAN AFFILIATION
May 2011 (as political party)	ENF (European National Front)

IDEOLOGY
Far-right; Greek nationalism; Anti-immigration

ELECTION RESULTS

Year	Type of Election	Votes	Percentage	Mandates
2011	Parliamentary	4,354	1.08	0
2013	Presidential	3,899	0.88	
2014	European Parliament	6,957	2.69	0/6

The National Popular Front (ELAM) was approved by the Greek Cypriot Authorities as a legal political party in May 2011. Prior to its official formation into a political party, ELAM was a nationalist movement that was established in the late 2000s and led by Christos Christou, who was an active member of the Golden Dawn far-right party in Greece and still remains ELAM's leader (Katsourides 2013). He had already organized the political satellite of Golden Dawn in Cyprus under the name 'Golden Dawn-Cypriot Kernel', whose registration was rejected by the authorities, and then adopted the name ELAM (Kosmas 2013). The links between Golden Dawn and ELAM go beyond the party's name or leader in the form of support for their 'brother' or 'sister' movement (Katsourides 2013). ELAM identifies itself as an antisystemic, nationalist movement that supports the interests of the Greek Cypriots and fights illegal immigration. The party has been accused by the Cypriot media of promoting racism and being involved in acts of violence against immigrants, Turkish Cypriots and students.

⚲ DENMARK

Dansk Folkeparti (DF)
Danish People's Party (DPP)

FOUNDED	EUROPEAN AFFILIATIONS
October 1995	MELD (Movement for a Europe of Liberties and Democracy) EFD (Europe of Freedom and Democracy)

IDEOLOGY
Ultranationalism; Anti-immigration; Euroscepticism

ELECTION RESULTS

Year	Type of Election	Votes	Percentage	Mandates
2009	European Parliament	357,942	15.3	2/13
2011	National Election	436,726	12.3	22/179
2014	European Parliament	605,889	26.6	4/13

The Danish People's Party (DPP) was founded in 1995 after the split of the Danish Progress Party. It is a nationalist party that seeks to protect the monarch, the Church of Denmark and the rights and cultural heritage of the Danish people. The party's leadership opposes the transformation of Denmark into a multi-ethnic, multicultural society and adopts an anti-immigration, especially anti-Muslim, stance (Rydgren 2004). According to the former leader of the party, Pia Kjærsgaard, 'a multiethnic Denmark would be a national disaster' (DPP statements 1997). In 2001, after its electoral success, the party participated in the conservative-liberal coalition government (2001–2011) and implemented stricter policies on immigration. The DPP is responsible for establishing Europe's strictest law on immigration in 2002 (see BBC News 2005). In response to criticism from the Swedish government regarding its strict immigration rules, Pia Kjærsgaard maintained that '[i]f they want to turn Stockholm, or Malmö, into a Scandinavian Beirut, with clan wars, honour killings and gang rapes, let them do it. We can always put a barrier on the Øresund Bridge' (BBC News 2005). In 2010, the party proposed a complete halt to all immigration from non-Western countries and justified this on the basis of the party's moral responsibility to 'keep Denmark Danish' (DPP 2002).

FINLAND

Perussuomalaiset
Finns Party or True Finns

FOUNDED
May 1995

EUROPEAN AFFILIATIONS
MELD (Movement for a Europe of Liberties and Democracy)
EFD (Europe of Freedom and Democracy)

IDEOLOGY
Finish nationalism; Anti-immigration; Euroscepticism

ELECTION RESULTS

Year	Type of Election	Votes	Percentage	Mandates
2009	European Parliament	162,930	9.79	1/13
2011	National Parliament	560,075	19.05	39/200
2012	Presidential	287,571	9.40	4th
2014	European Parliament	222,457	12.9	2/13

The Finns Party was founded in 1995 after the dissolution of the Finnish Rural Party. Supporting the ideological and political pillars of its predecessor, the Finns Party is described as a populist, nationalist party that currently forms the main opposition in the Finnish Parliament, after its electoral success in 2011 (Mars 2011). The party developed its rhetoric on the basis of Finnish nationalism, authoritarianism and Euroscepticism. It opposes Finland's membership of the EU and NATO, criticizes globalism, attempts to minimize the Swedish influence in Finnish society by removing the obligatory character of Swedish as national second language in all levels of education, and promotes 'Finnish identity' (Arter 2010). The Finns Party supports limitations on and strict rules for immigration. It also demands that immigrants to Finland accept and adopt Finnish culture, emphasizing the threat of 'immigrants' criminality' (Arter 2010; Mars 2011). The Finns Party is typical of Scandinavian populist, far-right parties that often justify their anti-immigration views on the basis of 'welfare chauvinism' rather than racism; their nationalism is milder and connections with extreme groups weaker than the right-wing populists of central Europe (Kitschelt and McGann 1995).

🔍 FRANCE

Front National (FN)
National Front

FOUNDED	EUROPEAN AFFILIATION
October 1972	EAF (European Alliance for Freedom)

IDEOLOGY
Nationalism; Anti-immigration; Antisemitism; Euroscepticism

ELECTION RESULTS

Year	Type of Election	Votes	Percentage	Mandates
2007	National Assembly	1,116,136	4.3	0/577
2009	European Parliament	1,091,691	6.3	3/72
2012	National Assembly	3,528,373	13.6	2/577
2014	European Parliament	4,711,339	24.85	24/74

The National Front was founded in 1972 in an effort to unify the different French nationalist movements of that period (Shields 2007). Until his resignation in 2010, Jean-Marie Le Pen was the leader of the party. Its first electoral success was in the 1984 European election, where the party won 11 per cent of the vote and 10 MEPs were elected (Hainsworth 2000). In the presidential election of 2002, Le Pen won against the socialist candidate Lionel Jospin in the first round and became the first far-right leader to participate in the final round of a presidential election, although he was beaten by the right-wing candidate, Jacques Chirac. In January 2011, Le Pen's daughter, Marine, was elected as the new leader of the FN. Under her leadership the party attempted to downplay its fascist, antisemitic and far-right pillars, moderate its discourse and construct itself as a mainstream right-wing party (Shields 2007). This new image of the FN increased its popularity and led to the party's victory in the 2014 European elections, but principles of nationalism and populism still dominate the party and are accompanied by anti-immigration, especially anti-Muslim, and Eurosceptic ideas (Shields 2007). The party claims that it will fight 'illegal immigration' and suggests the deportation of 'illegal immigrants', a reduction in legal immigration to France, and 'zero tolerance' of criminality (FN Programme, 2012). The FN also considers multiculturalism a threat to French national identity and opposes the Schengen Agreement. The party opposes France's membership of the EU and the Eurozone and argues that the EU is a supranational organization that acts against the best interests of European peoples. Instead, it suggests the formation of a 'Europe of nations', which would respect the national characteristics and principles of every country, and would include Russia and Switzerland, but not Turkey (FN Programme 2012). In November 2013, Marine Le Pen and Geert Wilders announced their intention to cooperate in the 2014 European election during a press conference in The Hague. As Wilders noted, their aim is to 'fight this monster called Europe' which, according to Le Pen, 'has enslaved our various peoples' (see *Economist* 2013). The FN won the first place in France in the European Parliament elections of 2014.

⚲ GERMANY

Nationaldemokratische Partei Deutschlands (NPD)
National Democratic Party of Germany

FOUNDED	EUROPEAN AFFILIATION
November 1964	ENF (European National Front)

IDEOLOGY
Neo-Nazism (revisionist, racist, antisemitic, anti-democratic, *völkisch*); Anti-immigration

ELECTION RESULTS

Year	Type of Election	Votes	Percentage	Mandates
2009	Federal Parliament	768,442	1.8	0/631
2009	European Parliament	–	less than 1	0/99
2013	Federal Parliament	634,842	1.5	0/631
2014	European Parliament	300,815	1.03	1/96

The National Democratic Party of Germany was founded in 1964 as a successor to the German Reich Party and is a far-right party usually described as a neo-Nazi organization (Backer 2000). Members and supporters of the party are considered to participate not only in anti-immigrant protests, but also in hate crimes and attacks against immigrants, while the party's leadership is noted for its use of xenophobic, antisemitic and homophobic rhetoric (Deutsche Welle 2013b). The federal government has attempted to ban the NPD several times, in 2003, 2011 and 2012, claiming it is an 'anti-constitutional' party (Deutsche Welle 2013a; Rising 2012), but has not been successful. In March 2013, the government announced that it would not try again to ban the NPD (Eddy 2013). The NPD has never been elected to the national parliament (Bundestag), though its members have sat in regional parliaments. In 2004, the party won seats in the regional parliament of Saxony, and won six seats in the 2006 parliamentary election for Mecklenburg-Western Pomerania. In the 2009 municipal elections, the party saw electoral success in eastern parts of Germany (see *Local* 2009; BBC 2006a). In the 2014 European Parliament elections, the NPD was elected for the first time with one member to the European parliament.

⚲ GREECE

**Λαϊκός Ορθόδοξος Συναγερμός,
Laikós Orthódoxos Synagermós
(LAOS)**
Popular Orthodox Rally

FOUNDED	EUROPEAN AFFILIATIONS
September 2000	MELD (Movement for a Europe of Liberties and Democracy) EFD (Europe of Freedom and Democracy)

IDEOLOGY
Ultranationalism; Antisemitism; Anti-immigration; Euroscepticism

ELECTION RESULTS

Year	Type of Election	Votes	Percentage	Mandates
2009	National Election	386,205	5.63	15/300
2009	European Parliament	366,615	7.15	2/22
May 2012	National Election	183,467	2.90	0/300
June 2012	National Election	97,099	1.58	0/300
2014	European Parliament	154,027	2.69	0/21

The Popular Orthodox Rally was founded in 2000 by Georgios Karatzaferis, a few months after he was expelled from the conservative New Democracy party. Like many far-right parties, LAOS emphasizes its 'patriotic' profile. The ambiguities and discrepancies between the party's official programme and LAOS representatives' daily statements and speeches illustrate, however, the leading group's attempt to mask the extreme-right features of the party (Psarras, 2010). LAOS' programme reveals the populist ideology of the party, based on the idea of Greekness's superiority (LAOS 2007). At the same time, the party demands the expulsion of all 'undocumented' immigrants from Greece and focuses alleged migrants' criminality, especially in addressing their voters (Psarras 2010; Tsiras 2012). In this way, the party demonstrates its nationalist and racist characteristics along with its anti-communist, antisemitic and pre-dictatorship (supporters of the Greek military junta 1967–1974) pillars. Moreover, LAOS presented itself (in the 2009 national election) as an anti-systemic party fighting against political and financial powers and supporting the Greek people's interests. The party lost its populist, anti-system credentials by supporting the bailout agreement between the Greek government and the so-called 'troika' (European Central Bank, European Commission and International Monetary Fund) in 2010, and later (November 2011) by participating in a coalition government with two mainstream parties, centre-left PASOK and centre-right New Democracy (Tsiras 2012). Although the party left the coalition after a few months, its participation was a strategic miscalculation that marginalized the party's role (see national election results in May and June 2012 as well as the European Parliament elections 2014).

⚲ GREECE
Χρυσή Αυγή, Chrysí Avgí
Golden Dawn

FOUNDED	EUROPEAN AFFILIATIONS
February 1983	ENF (European National Front)

IDEOLOGY
Ultranationalism; Neo-Nazism; Antisemitism; Anti-immigration

ELECTION RESULTS

Year	Type of Election	Votes	Percentage	Mandates
2009	National Election	19,636	0.29	0/300
2009	European Parliament	23,566	0.5	0/22
May 2012	National Election	440,966	6.97	21/300
June 2012	National Election	426,025	6.92	18/300
2014	European Parliament	536,910	9.39	3/21

Golden Dawn was founded in 1983 by Nikolaos Michaloliakos, a supporter of both Greek military dictatorships (1936–1941, 1967–1974), who had been arrested several times (in 1974, 1976 and 1978) for his terrorist activities as a member of far-right extremist groups (Psarras 2012). The statutes of the party imply that it is a popular movement, 'with faith in the ideology of Nationalism' (Golden Dawn 2012, 2). However, Golden Dawn's neo-Nazi profile is clearly visible in the party's symbolism, with its flag resembling a swastika, Nazi salutes and chant of 'Blood and Honour' encapsulating its xenophobic and racist ideology. The party relies on a strict military hierarchy and includes hit squads committed to perpetrating hate crimes against migrants, leftists and homosexuals (Psarras 2012). Golden Dawn reappeared on the political landscape in 1993, in the midst of nationalist fervour due to a dispute between Greece and the Republic of Macedonia over use of the name Macedonia (Ellinas 2013; Psarras 2012). Golden Dawn members present themselves as nationalists who fight the so-called 'enemies' of the Greek nation, though explicit references to the ideology of National Socialism are avoided. As Michaloliakos notes: 'Back in the 1980s we flirted with all sorts of ideas of the interwar years including National Socialism and fascism. But by the 1990s, we settled the ideological issues and positioned ourselves in favour of popular nationalism' (Ellinas 2013). Golden Dawn's hit squads continued to carry out hate crimes and acts of violence against immigrants and political opponents, especially after their electoral success and the entry of the party into the Greek Parliament. At the same time Golden Dawn challenged the democratic reflexes of the Greek authorities by building ties to the Greek police; these were revealed when almost 50 per cent of Greek policemen voted for Golden Dawn in the 2012 national elections (Dalakoglou 2013). The first attempt by the Greek authorities to react against the Neo-Nazi threat and stop the far-right militias came in September 2013, when an antifascist hip-hop artist, Pavlos Fyssas or Killah P, was stabbed to death by a Golden Dawn member. This time it was a Greek who was killed by the neo-Nazis, not an anonymous immigrant, and the authorities proceeded to arrest party members and MPs, including Nikolaos Michaloliakos. Golden Dawn increased its percentage of votes in the European Parliament elections in 2014 despite the jailing of its party leaders.

⌕ HUNGARY

Jobbik
Movement for a Better Hungary

FOUNDED	EUROPEAN AFFILIATION
October 2003	AENM (Alliance of European National Movements) 2009

IDEOLOGY
Ultranationalism; Antisemitism; Antiziganism; Euroscepticism

ELECTION RESULTS

Year	Type of Election	Votes	Percentage	Mandates
2009	European Parliament	427,773	14.77	3/22
2010	National Election (1st round)	855,436	16.67	
2010	National Election (2nd round)	141,323	12.26	47/386
2014	European Parliament	340,287	14.67	3/21

Jobbik was founded as a right-wing youth association in 2002 and transformed into a political party in 2003. After its electoral success in 2010, it became the main opposition party in the Hungarian Parliament. The party is described by scholars and journalists as a far-right, ethno-nationalist, populist political group (Huggan and Law 2009; Schori Liang 2007), features that the leadership of Jobbik rejects, in so far as it presents itself as a conservative, radical-patriotic, Christian party (Jobbik 2014a). The party's main European Parliament election slogan in 2009, 'Hungary belongs to the Hungarians', criticized by the European Electoral Commission, illustrates the ideological position of the party. Jobbik dedicates itself to supporting Hungarian minorities in Romania, spreading solidarity among Hungarians and fighting so-called 'foreign financial interests' in the country (Jobbik 2014b). The leadership of the party openly expresses antisemitic beliefs through the prism of a 'Jewish threat' allegedly wanting to dominate the country. The party organized a protest against the World Jewish Congress in Budapest in May 2013, and many members of the party have made explicit antisemitic statements (see BBC news, 4 May, 2013b). Although Jobbik denies allegations of racism and violence, its members and supporters have been accused of racist incidents against Roma and homosexuals (ibid.). Moreover, the party refers to alleged 'gypsy crime' and declares its intention to face up to it (Jobbik 2014b). In 2007, Jobbik's leader, Gábor Vona, founded the 'Hungarian Guard', which soon transformed into the party's paramilitary wing that harasses and intimidates members of the Roma community and homosexuals. Jobbik's Euroscepticism, antisemitism and racism are also expressed in the European Parliament, where they have found partners such as BNP's Nick Griffin, who supported Jobbik and cooperated with the party in the 2009 European Parliament election (LeBor 2009; Waterfield 2009).

⚲ ITALY

Forza Nuova (FN)
New Force

FOUNDED	EUROPEAN AFFILIATION
September 1997	ENF (European National Front)

IDEOLOGY
Ultranationalism; Neo-Fascism; Anti-Immigration

ELECTION RESULTS

Year	Type of Election	Votes	Percentage	Mandates
2008	Chamber of Deputies	108,837	0.3	0
2008	Senate of the Republic	85,630	0.26	0
2013	Chamber of Deputies	89,811	0.26	0
2013	Senate of the Republic	81,521	0.26	0
2009	European Parliament	146,619	0.47	0

The Italian neo-fascist party Forza Nuova was founded in 1997 by Roberto Fiore and Massimo Morsello. In 1985 the founders were sentenced for being members of Armed Revolutionary Nuclei – a fascist terror group that was implicated in the Bologna bombing of 1980, which killed 85 people. They both escaped to London where they stayed for more than 10 years as political refugees. In Britain, Fiore, who identifies himself as a fascist (Pallister 1999), became a close friend of Nick Griffin (BNP); and in 1986, thanks to his friendship with the leader of the BNP, he founded, with Massimo Morsello, 'Easy London', a society offering help to young people living and working in London; together they set up the International Third Position, a neo-fascist organization (Ryan 2004). Although Forza Nuova was founded in 1997, its founders, Fiore and Marsello, only returned to Italy in 1999; and after Marsello's death in 2001, Fiore, who had maintained his ties with the British far-right organizations through educational and charity activities (Cobain 2008; Pallister 1999), became the sole leader of the party. He also became a member of the European Parliament when he replaced Alessandra Mussolini in 2007. Forza Nuova has been criticized for its political campaigns and acts of violence against immigrants and homosexuals. The party seeks repeal of the abortion law and openly expresses its opposition to immigrants (FN Programme 2012). Indeed, in March 2011, Fiore led Forza Nuova protests on the island of Lampedusa against immigration to Italy. Forza Nuova didn't participate in the European Parliament elections of 2014 in so far as the party's supporters failed to collect and submit the necessary 300,000 signatures.

⚲ ITALY

Lega Nord (LN)
North League

FOUNDED	EUROPEAN AFFILIATION
February 1991	EFD (Europe of Freedom and Democracy)

IDEOLOGY
Ultranationalism; Federalism; Islamophobia; Euroscepticism

ELECTION RESULTS

Year	Type of Election	Votes	Percentage	Mandates
2008	Chamber of Deputies	3,024,758	8.3	60/630
2008	Senate of the Republic	2,644,248	7.9	26/315
2013	Chamber of Deputies	1,390,156	4.1	20/630
2013	Senate of the Republic	1,328,555	4.3	18/315
2009	European Parliament	3,126,915	10.2	9/72
2014	European Parliament	1,686,556	6.16	5/73

Lega Nord was officially founded as a federal political party in February 1991. The party's electoral breakthrough came in 1992, transforming Lega Nord into a leading political actor (Gallagher 1992b, 2000). In 1994, the party proceeded to form an alliance with Berlusconi's Forza Italia and doubled its parliamentary representation in that year's national election. In 1995, Lega Nord joined the National Alliance (Alleanza Nazionale), a coalition of conservative and neo-fascist parties including the Italian Social Movement (MSI) led by Gianfranco Fini, who later became the leader of the Alliance (Gallagher 2000). The National Alliance participated in the coalition government under Berlusconi and the Lega Nord was represented in five ministries in Berlusconi's government in May 1994. That government collapsed in December 1994 (McCarthy 1995). In the 1996 national election, Lega Nord had an important electoral success (59 deputies and 27 senators), although it stayed outside party coalitions. Thereafter, the leaders of the party developed their rhetoric regarding the secession of northern Italy under the name *Padania*. The party's federalist, populist ideology dominated its discourse, and federalism became a major strand of the party's political agenda. Indeed, the official programme of the party cited 'federalist libertarianism' as its ideological basis. While Euroscepticism is another ideological characteristic of the Lega Nord, the party openly supports the direct election of the President of the European Commission and requests more powers for the European Parliament and European Central Bank (Lega Nord Programme 2012). The same contradictory tactics and discourses appear in the party's strategy on migration. Although the official party rejects charges of xenophobia and Islamophobia, illustrating the leadership's attempt to present a more moderate character to justify participation in right-wing coalitions, such as Berlusconi's House of Freedom (2000–2007) and People of Freedom (2007–2013), many members of Lega Nord make racist and xenophobic statements when they speak to audiences that consist of party members and sympathizers (Parenzo and Romano 2009). In December 2013, Matteo Salvini was elected as the new federal secretary of the party. He took a critical view of the EU, especially of the Eurozone, and before the 2014 European Parliament elections started to cooperate with Marine Le Pen (NF) and Geert Wilders (PoVV).

⚲ LATVIA

Nacionālā Apvienība
National Alliance
(Coalition of 'For fatherland and freedom/LNNK' and 'All for Latvia')

FOUNDED	EUROPEAN AFFILIATIONS
July 2011 (as party) 2010 (as alliance)	AECR (Alliance of European Conservatives and Reformists) AEN (Alliance for Europe of the Nations)

IDEOLOGY
Nationalism; Anti-immigration; Anti-Russian

ELECTION RESULTS

Year	Type of Election	Votes	Percentage	Mandates
2010	National Election	74,028	7.7	8/100
2011	National Election	127,208	13.9	14/100
2014	European Parliament	58,991	7.45	1/8

The National Alliance is a coalition of conservative, liberal and nationalist parties. It first appeared as an electoral alliance for the 2010 national election and unified the conservative party For Fatherland and Freedom with the nationalist, far-right party All for Latvia, which is considered racist and neo-Nazi (Muižnieks 2005; Nathan 2011). The alliance won eight seats in that election. In 2011 it became a party and increased its seats to 14 in the national election. It is now the fourth largest party in the Latvian Parliament and participates in the centre-right government of Latvia. The National Alliance emphasizes the importance of Latvian culture and language, opposing multiculturalism and immigration. The party, and especially its ally All for Latvia, regards Russians and Russian imperialism as a threat to the Latvian nation and calls for cooperation between Latvia and the EU (FN Programme 2012). One of the partners of the alliance, the conservative For Fatherland and Freedom, participated in the 2014 European Parliament elections and succeeded in having one MEP elected.

⚲ NORWAY

Fremskrittspartiet
Progress Party

FOUNDED	**EUROPEAN AFFILIATION**
April 1973	None

IDEOLOGY
Liberalism; Anti-immigration

ELECTION RESULTS

Year	Type of Election	Votes	Percentage	Mandates
2009	National Election	614,724	22.9	41/169
2013	National Election	463,560	16.3	29/169

The Progress Party was originally founded in 1973 as Party for a Strong Reduction in Taxes, Duties and Public Intervention by the right-wing political activist Anders Lange. Lange sought to establish an anti-tax, anti-bureaucracy protest movement, which transformed into the Progress Party in 1977 (Andersen and Bjorklund 2000). According to the party's leadership, 'the Progress Party is a classical liberal party that shall work for a major reduction in taxes, duties and government intervention, and for the safeguarding of the rights of the people and their freedom, as the Constitution presupposes' (Progress Party 2013) and its ideology is described as 'classical liberalism' (ibid.). However, media and academics describe it as a far-right party with xenophobic agenda (Andersen and Bjorklund 2000; Mudde 2000; Nilsen 2013). Although the Progress Party purports to be based on 'Christian and humanistic values', to oppose discrimination and support the integration of migrants into Norwegian society, its members usually resort to anti-immigration rhetoric (Paterson 2013). In the 1997 national election the Progress Party became the main opposition party in the country, a position that it also held following the national elections in 2005 and 2009. In 2013, the Progress Party in coalition with the Conservative Party won the national election and currently participates in a coalition government. This coalition has been criticized in the international media, especially because of the alleged links between the Progress Party and the terrorist Anders Behring Breivik, who was a member of the Progress Party in his youth and only left the party in 2006 (McDonald-Gibson 2013; Paterson 2013).

⚲ POLAND

Prawo i Sprawiedliwość (PiS)
Law and Justice

FOUNDED	**EUROPEAN AFFILIATION**
June 2001	AECR (Alliance of European Conservatives and Reformists)

IDEOLOGY
Nationalism; Euroscepticism; Antisemitism; Homophobia

ELECTION RESULTS

Year	Type of Election	Votes	Percentage	Mandates
2009	European Parliament	2,017,607	27.4	15/50
2007	National Election	5,183,477	32.1	166/460
2011	National Election	4,295,016	29.89	157/460
2014	European Parliament	2,246,870	31.78	19/51

The Law and Justice Party (PiS) presents itself as a conservative party, although there are close links between the party and the far right (Ciobanu 2013). Some of its tactics and aims, however, reveal its extreme-right ideological basis. PiS was founded in 2001 by the Kaczyński twins, Lech and Jarosław. The party won the 2005 election and Jarosław became Poland's Prime Minister, while Lech won the presidency. Since 2007, PiS has been the second largest party in the Polish Parliament. The main aims of the party are a struggle against alleged corruption and the ardent 'de-communication' of the country. On foreign policy, the party opposes the EU as a supranational organization; but supports economic and military integration with the EU on terms beneficial for Poland (Jungerstam-Mulders 2006). In contrast, the party supports Poland's strong alliance with the US. In other words, PiS can be characterized as a Eurosceptic and Atlanticist party. The discriminatory nature of the party first became apparent in 2002, when Lech Kaczynski, then mayor of Warsaw, refused permission for a Gay Pride parade, stating that it would be obscene and offensive to other people's religious beliefs. Thereafter, homophobia and opposition to homosexual rights were presented as ideological pillars of the party, together with distrust of minorities, antisemitism and nationalism (Day 2009; Traynor 2009).

ꞯ PORTUGAL

Partido Nacional Renovador (PNR)
National Renewal Party

FOUNDED	EUROPEAN AFFILIATION
February 2000	ENF (European National Front)

IDEOLOGY
Nationalism; Anti-immigration; Euroscepticism

ELECTION RESULTS

Year	Type of Election	Votes	Percentage	Mandates
2009	National Election	11,503	0.2	0/230
2009	European Parliament	17,548	0.31	0/22
2011	National Election	13,214	0.37	0/230
2014	European Parliament		less than 0.5	0/21

Since the 'carnation revolution' Portugal has not witnessed resurgence in electoral success for extreme-right parties; quite to the contrary, the post-revolution has been characterized by the electoral failure of far-right parties that brought back memories of the old authoritarian regime. Hence, there was a 'marginalization of the far right' (Gallagher 1992a) in Portugal that still characterizes the country's political landscape (Zuquete 2007). The results of the recent national and European Parliament elections illustrate the marginalized role of the National Renewal Party, though the party's ideological core and discourse cannot be ignored by analysts of far-right rhetoric. At the time of its foundation, the party appeared to be neo-fascist and pro-Salazar's ideas. However, since then the party has transformed into a counterpart of the Western European organizations, especially after the election of Pinto Coelho to the party's leadership in 2005 (Zuquete 2007). One of the party's main slogans is 'Portugal for the Portuguese', and nationalism is proposed as the only way of solving the country's problems (Mudde 2000). At the same time, immigration is presented as an invasion that threatens Portuguese national identity and security as well as the survival of the Portuguese people (Zuquete 2007). The party's discourse targets immigrants and internal and external forces, such as the EU, that are considered to be responsible for the 'decadence' in and destruction of Portugal. The Eurosceptic ideology of the party combined with anti-systemic and populist elements, dominates the party's rhetoric and ensures its participation in the European National Front.

⚲ RUSSIA

Политическая партия ЛДПР
Liberal Democratic Party (LDPR)

FOUNDED	EUROPEAN AFFILIATION
1991	none

IDEOLOGY
Ultranationalism; Anti-communism; Anti-West; Antisemitism; Homophobia

ELECTION RESULTS

Year	Type of Election	Votes	Percentage	Mandates
2011	Duma Election	7,664,570	11.67	56/450
2012	Presidential Election	4,458,103	6.2	-

The LDPR was founded in 1991 and is led by the 'charismatic' figure of Vladimir Zhirinovsky, well-known to Russian and international audiences for his populist, nationalist and racist rhetoric (see BBC News 2012). The party is described as far-right, anti-communist and ultranationalist and is centred on Zhirinovsky's controversial personality (Cox and Shearman 2000). He encourages violent action and war in the name of a 'Greater Russia', supports the restoration of Russia with Belarus, Ukraine and other former Soviet republics and criticizes the discrimination by Baltic countries' leadership against Russian minorities (Dunlop 2011). The party is also opposed to both communism and capitalism, presents the West as the main threat to the Russian nation and favours a mixed economy and liberalism (Cox and Shearman 2000). The LPDR noted its first electoral success in the 1993 Duma election, receiving a sizeable minority of the vote (almost 23 per cent). In the 2011 Duma elections the party's percentage was 11.4 per cent, making it the fourth strongest party in Russia.

⚲ SLOVAKIA

Slovenská národná strana (SNS)
Slovak National Party

FOUNDED	EUROPEAN AFFILIATIONS
December 1989	EFD (Europe of Freedom and Democracy) MELD (Movement for a Europe of Liberties and Democracy)

IDEOLOGY
Ultranationalism; Euroscepticism; Anti-Hungarian; Anti-Roma

ELECTION RESULTS

Year	Type of Election	Votes	Percentage	Mandates
2009	European Parliament	45,960	5.55	1/13
2010	National Election	218,490	5.08	9/150
2012	National Election	116,420	4.55	0/150
2014	European Parliament	20,244	3.61	0/13

The Slovak National Party (SNS) was founded in December 1989, its ideological base being the historical Slovak National Party of Czechoslovakia (1871–1938). The SNS presents itself as a nationalist party that emphasizes Christianity (Jeffries 2002). Its members' statements regarding Roma and the Hungarian minority in Slovakia illustrate the racist, ultranationalist character of the party (see BBC News 2006). Its former leader, Ján Slota, has received media attention because of his racist statements and violent attacks against Hungarians (Balogova 2008). Since 1990 SNS has won seats in every Slovak Parliament and participated in the coalition government from 2006 to 2010. In the 2012 national election SNS noted its first electoral collapse, failing to meet the 5 per cent electoral threshold, losing its deposit and any parliamentary representation.

The Politics of Fear

⚲ SPAIN

España 2000
Spain 2000

FOUNDED	EUROPEAN AFFILIATION
2002	NF (National Front) France

IDEOLOGY
Nationalism; Anti-immigration; Euroscepticism

ELECTION RESULTS

The party won five council seats in the municipal elections of 2011

Year	Type of Election	Votes	Percentage	Mandates
2011	National election	9,266	0.04	0

España 2000, considered to be a far-right party, was founded in 2002 in Spain. The extreme-right remains a marginal ideology linked to the Franco era and the Spanish Civil War, and this is demonstrated by the party's weak national electoral results. However, the financial and social crisis in Spain led to an increase in España 2000 sympathizers (see Mason 2012). The party's main slogan is 'Spaniards first' and its aims relate to protection of Spanish national identity and Spaniards' social rights. The party's leading members maintain that they fight 'illegal migration' and globalization and support Spain's position in a Europe of nation-states, but not in a supranational organization such as the EU (España 2000, 2000a). Hence, the party has similarities with the French Front National, which has supported España 2000 at its national congress (España 2000, 2000b). Indeed, the decision of the party's leading team to congratulate Marine Le Pen for her success in the 2014 European Parliament elections illustrates the links between the French Front National and España 2000. Although the party's electoral success is limited to the districts of Valencia and Madrid, its actions extend beyond the borders of these areas, given that it has organized demonstrations against immigration from Muslim countries in various Spanish cities.

⚲ SWEDEN

Sverigedemokraterna (SD)
Sweden Democrats

FOUNDED	EUROPEAN AFFILIATION
February 1988	EAF (European Alliance for Freedom)

IDEOLOGY
Swedish nationalism; Anti-immigration; Euroscepticism

ELECTION RESULTS

Year	Type of Election	Votes	Percentage	Mandates
2009	European Parliament	103,584	3.3	0/18
2010	National Election	339,610	5.7	20/349
2014	European Parliament		9.7	2/20

The Sweden Democrats' rhetoric is based on xenophobic, populist and nationalist arguments (Kitschelt and McGann 1995). There is, however, an important difference between the SD and other Scandinavian far-right parties that hinges on the ideological roots of the SD. It was founded in February 1988 as a successor to the xenophobic, racist Sweden Party and Progress Party that provided the SD with its fascist roots and connections (Rydgren 2006). During the 1990s, the SD's leadership rejected the party's fascist past and sought ideological identification with the French National Front, the Freedom Party of Austria and the Danish People's Party (Rydgren 2006). Since the 2000s, different leaders have continued the party's policy of moderation, which involves the expulsion of any extremist members

204

and the establishment of a nationalist Eurosceptic profile (Mudde 2007; Rydgren 2006). The SD promotes 'Swedish culture and national identity', opposes the special rights given to the Sami population of northern Sweden and criticizes the EU and the Eurozone. Moreover, the party's leadership claims that Swedish identity and Swedes are threatened by immigrants, and thus rejects their integration into Swedish society and multiculturalism, and seeks to restrict the number of immigrants on the basis of the Danish People's Party political agenda (Rydgren 2006). In the 2010 national election, the SD crossed the 4 per cent threshold and entered the Swedish Parliament for the first time, and since then has increased in popularity (see the 2014 European Parliament elections).

Q SWITZERLAND
Schweizerische Volkspartei (SVP)
Swiss People's Party

FOUNDED	EUROPEAN AFFILIATIONS
September 1971	None

IDEOLOGY
Liberalism; Anti-immigration; Euroscepticism; Anti-Islam

ELECTION RESULTS

Year	Type of Election	Votes	Percentage	Mandates
2011	Federal Election	641,106	26.6	54/200
2007	Federal Election	672,562	28.9	62/200

At the time of writing, the Swiss People's Party is the strongest party in the Swiss Parliament and presents itself as a centre-right party for the middle classes. The orientation of the party's electoral platform for 2011–2015 is expressed by the slogan 'SVP – the party for Switzerland'. The SVP was founded in 1971 via a merger of the Party of Farmers, Trades and Independents (BGB) and the Democratic Party, and had become the strongest party in Switzerland by the 2000s (Stockemer 2012). According to the SVP's programme (2011–2015), the party intends to protect the Christian culture, rights, freedom and prosperity of the Swiss people, and is committed to lower taxes and less state control and bureaucracy; it supports an 'immigration policy tailored to the needs of Switzerland, instead of unlimited mass immigration' and the deportation of foreign criminals. Although these aims are not directly linked to a far-right party, its xenophobic ideology is apparent in its references to immigrants; they are represented as a threat to the security of the Swiss people and Swiss national identity (Stockemer 2012). Moreover, the party alleges that 50 per cent of the crimes in Switzerland are committed by foreigners. The anti-immigrant and especially anti-Islamic character of the party is illustrated by its usage of racist posters during election campaigns (BBC News 2007; Day 2011; Mir 2011). Another threat to Swiss identity, prosperity and independence alleged by the SVP is the possibility of Switzerland's entry into the EU, which the party vehemently opposes (Stockemer 2012; SVP Programme 2011–2015). The Eurosceptic, anti-immigration character of the party was also revealed by its role in the referendum concerning the anti-immigration law in 2014 and its leading position in the 'Yes' vote (Baghdjian and Schmieder 2014; Traynor 2014).

⚲ THE NETHERLANDS

Partij voor de Vrijheid (PVV)
Party for Freedom

FOUNDED February 2006	EUROPEAN AFFILIATION EAF (European Alliance for Freedom)
	IDEOLOGY Anti-immigration; Anti-Islam; Euroscepticism

ELECTION RESULTS

Year	Type of Election	Votes	Percentage	Mandates
2009	European Parliament	769,125	17.0	5/25
2010	House of Representatives	1,435,349	15.5	24/150
2012	House of Representatives	950,263	10.1	15/150
2014	European Parliament	630,139	13.3	4/26

The Party for Freedom (PVV) is based on the 'charismatic' figure of its founder and leader, Geert Wilders. In the 2010 national election it became the third strongest party in the Netherlands; Wilders gave the governmental coalition his support, though without having ministers in the cabinet. In 2012, the PVV withdrew its support from the government due to its opposition to austerity measures, a decision that led to a political crisis. During the difficult political situation following the 2010 national election and PVV's support for the minority government, the party pushed for anti-immigration measures, such as the 'burqa ban' that was never implemented (CNN 2012). In this way, the PVV revealed its anti-immigration basis that has been further developed in the party's programme. The PVV calls for a halt to immigration from Muslim countries and intends to forbid Islamic schools, headscarves and the Quran. Moreover, the party seeks the deportation of criminals with foreign citizenship and restrictions on immigrant labour. Simultaneously, Wilder's party aims to protect 'Judeo-Christian culture' and punish any violent acts against Jews or homosexuals. It has a Eurosceptic profile, demanding withdrawal from the EU and the Eurozone, and a return to the old Dutch currency (see PVV Political Agenda 2010–2015). The anti-Muslim ideas dominate the rhetoric of Wilder, who usually emphasizes the alleged 'Islamic threat' to European Judeo-Christian civilization (Traynor 2008; Wodak and Boukala 2014). This anti-immigration and especially anti-Muslim ideological basis of the party have led to the PVV's characterization as a far-right party (Art 2011). The international media usually refer to the PVV as extreme-right and anti-Muslim, although Wilders maintained he was not anti-Muslim: 'I have a problem with Islamic tradition, culture and ideology, not with Muslim people [...] I don't hate Muslims, I hate Islam' (Traynor 2008).

⚲ UKRAINE

Vseukrayinske obyednannia 'Svoboda'
All-Ukrainian Union 'Svoboda'

FOUNDED October 1991	EUROPEAN AFFILIATION AENM (Alliance of European National Movements)
	IDEOLOGY Ultranationalism; Fascism; Antisemitism

ELECTION RESULTS

Year	Type of Election	Votes	Percentage	Mandates
2007	National Parliament	178,660	0.76	0/450
2012	National Parliament	2,129,246	10.45	36/450

Svoboda was originally founded in Lviv in 1991 as the Social-National party of Ukraine and was based on the collaboration of a number of ultra-nationalist movements that define themselves as enemies of communist ideology (Olszanski 2011; Rudling 2013). The name of the party was an intentional reference to the Nazi Party in Germany. Membership was restricted to ethnic Ukrainians, although the party also recruited skinheads and football hooligans (Rudling 2013). The Social-National party of Ukraine, Svoboda, was renamed the All-Ukrainian Union Svoboda, in February 2004 with the rise of Oleh Tyahnybok to party leader. Tyahnybok made significant efforts to moderate the party's extremist character and use of Nazi symbols. The new leader, however, did not deny the nationalist, antisemitic and anti-communist tradition of the party; quite the contrary as, in 2004, Tyahnybok was expelled from the parliament for a speech calling for Ukrainians to fight against a 'Muscovite-Jewish mafia' and praised the Organization of Ukrainian Nationalists for having fought 'Muscovites, Germans, Jews and other scum who wanted to take away our Ukrainian state' (Rudling 2013). Svoboda's ideological base is (ultra-) nationalism. The party opposes ethnic minorities and languages, and its members openly express opposition to Russians, Jews, immigrants and homosexuals. In the 2012 Ukrainian parliamentary election, Svoboda won its first seats in the Ukrainian Parliament. In October 2012, Svoboda joined a formal coalition with the centre-right Batkivshchyna and UDAR parties to form the Parliament's collective opposition. Svoboda actively participated in the pro-EU protest campaign, February–March 2014, aiming to influence regime change and integration with the EU. Five members of Svoboda held positions in Ukraine's government following the clashes in February 2014 (Salem 2014).

⚲ UNITED KINGDOM

UK Independence Party (UKIP)

FOUNDED	EUROPEAN AFFILIATION
September 1993	EFD (Europe of Freedom and Democracy)

IDEOLOGY
Anti-immigration; Euroscepticism; Anti-Islam

ELECTION RESULTS

Year	Type of Election	Votes	Percentage	Mandates
2009	European Parliament	2,498,226	16.6	13/72
2010	House of Commons	919,546	3.1	0/650
2014	European Parliament	4,376,635	26.6	24/73

UKIP was founded in 1993 and is described by the UK media and academics as a Eurosceptic, populist party (Abedi and Lundberg 2009), although UKIP identifies itself as a 'democratic, libertarian party' (UKIP 2013a). In the local election of 2013 the party saw some electoral success and won several council seats nationwide; in the national election 2015, UKIP won one seat in the House of Commons. The party is characterized as a one-issue party (Euroscepticism) and by the populist rhetoric and performance of its leader, Nigel Farage (see Abedi and Lundberg 2009; BBC News 2006b), who has been a UKIP MEP since 1999. UKIP was founded on the basis of Euroscepticism and still emphasizes the UK's withdrawal from the EU. It adopted a British anti-European stance and came second in the 2009 European Parliament election, behind the Conservatives, with 13 elected representatives (Underwood 2010). In the 2014 European elections, UKIP came first in the UK and had 24 MEPs elected. UKIP states that the UK should leave the EU and all other European organizations and institutions, such as the European Convention on Human Rights and the European Convention on Refugees and the Protection of Refugees. The party claims that as long as Britain remains under the EU's umbrella, the immigration issue that dominates the party's political agenda cannot be solved and the British authorities cannot 'deport foreign criminal and terrorist suspects where desirable' (UKIP 2013b). Moreover, the introduction to UKIP's policy on immigration mentions that the party aims to reduce 'uncontrolled immigration', introduce a 'freeze' on immigration for permanent settlement and deal with 'illegal immigrants' and their deportation (UKIP 2013b).

ᑫ UNITED KINGDOM

British National Party (BNP)

FOUNDED 1982	**EUROPEAN AFFILIATION** AENM (Alliance of European National Movements)
	IDEOLOGY Nationalism; Anti-immigration; Antisemitism; Fascism; Euroscepticism

ELECTION RESULTS

Year	Type of Election	Votes	Percentage	Mandates
2009	European Parliament	943,598	6.3	2/72
2010	House of Commons	563,743	1.9	0/650
2014	European Parliament	179,694	1.09	0/73

The British National Party (BNP) was founded in 1982 by John Tyndall, previously leader of the far-right National Front, a party with neo-Nazi ideology and links (Hill and Bell 1988). The BNP's ideological platform is considered fascist and nationalist (Copsey 2007; Renton 2005; Richardson 2013a, 2013b). The party has never won a seat in Parliament, though it did see electoral success in the 2009 European Parliament election, when two of its leading members, Nick Griffin and Andrew Brons, were elected MEPs. From the very beginning, the BNP's leadership has sought to distance itself from fascist and neo-Nazi groups, although the ideological pillars of the BNP are nationalism and fascism (Copsey 2007). In 1999, Nick Griffin was elected as the new leader of the party. Griffin's main aim was to modernize the party's image and moderate its ideological basis. An anti-immigration stance, however, remained the number one issue on the BNP's agenda, transforming quickly into Islamophobia, especially after 9/11 in New York and the 7/7 London bombings in July 2005 (Copsey 2007). The party's manifesto refers to freedom, security and democracy as important values of the British nation at risk. In particular, the party claims that 'democracy is under threat from the EU and mass immigration, both of which threaten to extinguish all of our traditions and culture' (BNP 2010). The BNP demands the deportation of all 'illegal immigrants' and those foreigners who are convicted of crimes in Britain (ibid.). It also demands Britain's immediate withdrawal from the EU, which is allegedly destroying Britain's national identity and nationhood. Moreover, the party describes immigration from Muslim countries to Britain as 'the Islamic colonization of Britain' and demands that 'Islamic immigration be halted and reversed as it presents one of the most deadly threats yet to the survival of our nation' (ibid.). Furthermore, the party opposes multiculturalism, and although it attempts to downplay its nationalist, fascist and antisemitic characteristics, it refers directly to 'British superiority': 'British people may take pride from knowing that the blood of an immense column of nation-building, civilization-creating heroes and heroines runs through their veins [...]. Being British is more than merely possessing a modern document known as a passport. It runs far deeper than that; it is to belong to a special chain of unique people who have the natural law right to remain a majority in their ancestral homeland' (BNP 2010). According to the UK media, several BNP members have attempted to 'protect' their British rights through violent activities (see BBC News 2013a). John Tyndall himself has convictions for assault and organizing neo-Nazi activities (Human Rights Watch 1997) and Nick Griffin was convicted of hate speech (Botsford 2013). The BNP cooperates with far-right or neo-Nazi parties, such as the Greek Golden Dawn, the Italian Forza Nuova and the Hungarian Jobbik, and plays a leading role in the Alliance of European National Movements (AENM).

1.1. United States of America[2]

The US Tea Party Movement

Many academics, political scientists and journalists describe the Tea Party as an example of cor-porate-funded astroturfing associated with the Republican Party (Formisano 2012). Skocpol and Williamson define the Tea Party as 'neither solely a mass movement nor an astroturf creation, arguing for something in between: a grassroots movement amplified by the right-wing media and supported by elite donors' (2012, 50–51). The name 'Tea Party' refers to the 'Boston Tea Party', a protest by colonists who objected to a British tax on tea in 1773 without having the right to representation, and dumped British tea taken from docked ships into the harbour (Leopore 2010). The origins of the current Tea Party movement were, on the one hand, grassroots in nature, developing outside the existing power centres in Washington, DC, and in the more remote regions where conservative politics meet a more libertarian, right-wing opposition. On the other hand, roots derived directly from elements within the Republican Party apparatus and began as proxies for the party itself (Burghart and Zeskind 2010, 15). Among the earliest moments that led to the establishment of the Tea Party movement were the events of the 234th anniversary of the Boston Tea Party, primarily directed at the libertarian part of the Republican Party and focused on the Republican Congressman Ron Paul as the intellectual 'godfather' of the party. His supporters held a 'tea party moneybomb' to raise cam-paign funds for his campaign in the 2008 Republican presidential primaries (ibid.). After the election of President Barak Obama (2008) and the signature of the American Recovery and Reinvestment Act (February 2009), which led to many protests nationwide, the first official 'tea parties', such as the 'Freedom Works', appeared and continued to emerge throughout the summer. According to Burghart and Zeskind (2010), the turning point for the Tea Parties was the Freedom Works rally on 12 Septem-ber 2009 in Washington, DC, when a massive event gave Tea Party groups an opportunity to work together. Hundreds of thousands of Tea Parties met in the streets and shared their stories and their anger with the Obama government. Tea Parties had turned from periodic protests into a full-fledged social movement (ibid., 17).

Most politicians who support the Tea Party have participated in various electoral campaigns as Republicans (since 2008); however, as Abramowitz (2014) notes, Republican primaries have been the site of competitions between the more conservative Tea Party wing of the party and the more moderate establishment wing. The Tea Party is not a typical political party as it does not have a formal structure and hierarchy, and does not promote one single political agenda. However, most of the Tea Party groups focus on budget deficits, taxes and the power of the federal government. Moreover, Tea Party groups request tighter border security, and oppose amnesty for illegal immigrants, abortion and gun control. They also emphasize issues of (nativist) nationalism: many voiced concerns regard-ing Barack Obama's birth certificate and promoted the idea that the President of the US was not a 'real American' (Formisano 2012; Skocpol and Williamson 2012). Burghart and Zeskind (2010) studied the six main national organizational networks at the core of the Tea Party movement. They provide much evidence that the leading figures of the 1776 Tea Party (the faction more commonly known as TeaParty.org) were imported directly from the anti-immigrant vigilante organization called the Minuteman Project. Tea Party Nation seems to gather so-called birthers and has attracted Christian nationalists and nativists. Tea Party Express frequently outraged the public with the racist pronounce-ments of its leaders. Finally, both ResistNet and Tea Party Patriots, the two largest networks, have provided a home to well-known anti-immigrant nativists and racists (ibid., 57–65).

Opinion poll data reveal that the majority of the Tea Party supporters are white, middle-class, conservative men who used to vote Republican. However, they are more conservative and much more politically active than other Republicans (see opinion data in Abramowitz 2011; Burghart and Zeskind 2010). The close link between the Tea Parties, anti-immigrant politics and media support can be observed, for example, in Congresswoman Michele Bachmann's Tea Party Caucus in the House of Representatives. Founded in July 2010, the Tea Party Caucus quickly grew to include 51 representa-tives, all of them Republicans.

Endnotes

1   I am very grateful to Salomi Boukala for helping me with the literature search and review for the glossary. Obviously all the listed parties are right-wing populist parties; however, some of them can certainly be described as Neo-Nazi or fascist parties. I have added such characteristics whenever appropriate.

2   Because the Tea Party movement is embedded into the Republican Party, I cannot provide similar information on election results and so forth. As I have in respect to all the other parties in the Glossary.

REFERENCES

Abedi, A. and Lundberg, T. C. (2009) 'Doomed to failure? UKIP and the organisational challenges facing right-wing populist anti-political establishment parties', *Parliamentary Affairs*, 62/1: 72–87.

Abramowitz, A. (2014) 'The Republican Establishment versus The Tea Party', Charlottesville, VA: University of Virginia Center for Politics.

Abramowitz, A. I. (2011) 'Partisan polarization and the rise of the Tea Party Movement', paper presented at American Political Science Association, Seattle Washington, 1–2 September.

Adelung, J. C. (1782) *Deutsche Sprachlehre.* Vienna: Johann Thomas Edler von Trattner.

Adorno, T. W. (1963) 'Was bedeutet Aufarbeitung der Vergangenheit?', in Adorno, T. W. (ed.), *Eingriffe: Neun kritische Modelle*. Frankfurt: Suhrkamp.

Adorno, T. W. (1966) *Negative Dialektik*. Frankfurt: Suhrkamp.

Adorno, T. W., Frenkel-Brunswick, E., Levinson, D. and Sanford, R. N. (1967 [1950]) *The Authoritarian Personality*. New York: Harper.

Ahlzweig, C. (1990) 'Die Deutsche Nation und ihre Muttersprache', in Ehlich, K. (ed.), *Sprache im Faschismus*. Frankfurt: Suhrkamp, 35–57.

Ahtisaari, M., Orejo, M. and Frowein, J. (2000) *Der Bericht*. Paris. Available at http://images.derstandard.at/upload/images/bericht.pdf, accessed 22/4/2015.

Albertazzi, D. (2007) 'Addressing "the People" – A comparative study of the Lega Nord's and Lega dei Ticinesi's political rhetoric and style of propaganda', *Modern Italy*, 12/3: 327–47.

Alexander, J. C. (2006) *The Civil Sphere*. Oxford: Oxford University Press.

Alfahír (2008a) *Két emberkép között folyik a harc*, 27 August. Available at http://alfahir.hu/node/17448, accessed 16/3/15.

Alfahír (2008b) *A Magukfajták ideje lejárt: Morvai Krisztina reagál az Élet és Irodalom cikkére in Barikad*, 12 November. Available at http://alfahir.hu/node/20313, accessed 16/3/15.

Alleanza Nazionale – Fratelli d'Italia (2015). Political Programme available at http://www.fratelli-italia.it/

Allport, G. (1979 [1954]) *The Nature of Prejudice*. New York: Perseus.

Alpers, B. (2012) 'What use are the politics of authenticity?' *US Intellectual History Blog*, 14 February. Available at http://s-usih.org/2012/02/what-use-are-politics-of-authenticity.html, accessed 1/3/14.

Altheide, D. L. (2002) *Creating Fear: News and the Construction of Crisis*. New York: Transaction.

Altweg, J. (2007) 'Welch ein Artgenosse ist der Eidgenosse', *Frankfurter Allgemeine Zeitung – Feuilleton* 20 Oktober. Available at http://www.faz.net/aktuell/feuilleton/wahl-in-der-schweiz-welch-ein-art genosse-ist-der-eidgenosse-1490524.html, accessed 7/1/15.

Amin, A. (2012) *Land of Strangers*. Cambridge: Polity.

Amin, T. (2015) 'The Discursive Construction of Women in the Quran and Tafsir.' Unpubl. PhD Thesis, Lancaster University (forthcoming).

Andersen, J. and Bjorklund, T. (2000) 'Radical right-wing populism in Scandinavia: From tax revolt to neoliberalism and xenophobia', in Hainsworth, P. (ed.), *The Politics of the Extreme Right: From the Margins to the Mainstream*. London: Pinter, 193–223.

Anderson, B. (1991 [1983]) *Imagined Communities: Reflections on the Origin and Spread of Nationalism*. London: Verso.

Angouri, J. and Wodak, R. (2014) '"They became big in the shadow of the crisis": The Greek success story and the rise of the far right', *Discourse & Society*, 25/4: 540–65.

Aristotle (2004) *Rhetoric*. Thessaloniki: Zitros.

Arneil, B. (2009) 'Disability, self-image, and modern political theory', *Political Theory*, 37/2: 218–42.

Arsenal for Democracy (2012) '2014-european-election-results-table', 1 June. Available at http:// arsenalfordemocracy.com/2014/06/01/eu-elections-the-rising-populists-and-why-europe-is-worried/2014-european-election-results-table/#.U-8IT7I__mR, accessed 16/8/14.

Art, D. (2011) *Inside the Radical Right*. Cambridge: Cambridge University Press.

Arter, D. (2010) 'The breakthrough of another West European populist radical right party? The case of the True Finns', *Government and Opposition*, 45/4: 484–504.

ATAKA (2014) *ATAKA's 20 Principles*. Sofia: ATAKA. Available at www.ataka.bg/en/index.php? option=com_content&task=view&id=14&Itemid=27, accessed 11/3/15.

Backer, S. (2000) 'Right-wing extremism in unified Germany', in Hainsworth, P. (ed.), *The Politics of the Extreme Right: From the Margins to the Mainstream*. London: Pinter, 87–120.

Baghdjian, A. and Schmieder, A. (2014) 'Swiss vote to set limits on immigration from EU', Reuters, 9 February. Available at http://uk.reuters.com/article/2014/02/09/uk-swiss-vote-immigration-idUKBREA180MI20140209, accessed 11/3/15.

Baker, P., Gabrielatos, C., KhosraviNik, M., Krzyżanowski, M., McEnery, T. and Wodak, R. (2008) 'A useful methodological synergy? Combining critical discourse analysis and corpus linguistics to examine discourses of refugees and asylum seekers in the UK press', *Discourse & Society*, 19/3: 273–305.

Balogova, B. (2008) 'Editorial: The journalist's dilemma: How to report Ján Slota', *Slovak Spectator*, October. Available at http://spectator.sme.sk/articles/view/33193/11/the_journalists_dilemma_how_to_report_jan_slota.html, accessed 11/3/15.

Bandler, R. and Grinder, J. (1989) *The Structure of Magic: A Book about Language and Therapy*. Ann Arbor, MI: University of Michigan Press.

Barton, D. and Lee, C. (2013) *Language Online: Investigating Digital Texts and Practices*. London: Routledge.

Bauböck, R. and Goodman-Wallace, S. (2012) *EUDO Citizenship Policy Brief 2*. Florence: European University Institute.

Bauböck, R. and Joppke, C. (eds) (2010) 'How liberal are citizenship tests?', *EUI Working Papers* 41. San Domenico di Fiesole: European University Institute.

Bauman, Z. (1995) 'Making and unmaking of strangers', *Thesis Eleven*, 43/1: 1–16.

Bauman, Z. (2009) *Europe of Strangers*. Available at http://docs.google.com/viewer?url=www. transcomm.ox.ac.uk/working%20papers/bauman.pdf, accessed 11/3/15.

BBC News (2005) 'Denmark's immigration issue', 19 February. Available at http://news.bbc.co.uk/2/hi/europe/4276963.stm, accessed 11/3/15.

BBC News (2006a) 'Poll boost for German far right', 18 September. Available at http://news.bbc.co.uk/2/hi/europe/5349696.stm, accessed 11/3/15.

BBC News (2006b) 'Profile: Nigel Farage', 12 September. Available at http://news.bbc.co.uk/2/hi/uk_news/politics/5338364.stm, accessed 11/3/15.

BBC News (2007) 'Swiss row over black sheep poster', Foulkes, I., 6 September. Available at http:// news.bbc.co.uk/2/hi/europe/6980766.stm, accessed 7/7/12.

BBC News (2009) 'BBC defends BNP move amid protest', 22 October. Available at http://news.bbc.co.uk/1/hi/uk_politics/8319596.stm, accessed 31/1/14.

BBC News (2012) 'Profiles of Russia's 2012 presidential election candidates', 30 January. Available at http://bbc.co.uk/news/world-europe-16750990, accessed 11/3/15.

BBC News (2013a) 'BNP: Under the skin', 2 April. Available at www.news.bbc.co.uk/hi/english/static/in_depth/programmes/2001/bnp_special/membership/organisers/criminal.stm, accessed 11/3/15.

BBC News (2013b) 'Jobbik Ralley against World Jewish Congress in Budapest', 4 May. Available at www.bbc.co.uk/news/world-europe-22413301, accessed 11/3/15.

BBC News (2013c) 'Council "horrified" over scheme for immigrants to go', 23 July. Available at www.bbc.co.uk/news/uk-england-london-23419848, accessed 29/4/14.

BBC News (2013d) 'Downing Street says "go home" van ads are working', 29 July. Available at www. bbc.co.uk/news/uk-politics-23489925, accessed 29/4/14.

Beauzamy, B. (2013a) 'Explaining the rise of the Front National to electoral prominence: Multi-faceted or contradictory models?', in Wodak, R., KhosraviNik, M. and Mral, B. (eds), *Right-wing Populism in Europe: Politics and Discourse*. London: Bloomsbury, 177–90.

Beauzamy, B. (2013b) 'Continuities of fascist discourses, discontinuities of extreme-right political actors? Overt and covert antisemitism in the contemporary French radical right', in Wodak, R. and Richardson, J. E. (eds) *Analysing Fascist Discourse: European Fascism in Talk and Text*. London: Routledge, 163–80.

Beirich, H. (2013) 'Hate across the Waters: The Role of American Extremists in Fostering an International White Consciousness', in Wodak, R., KhosraviNik, M. and Mral, B. (eds), *Right-wing Populism in Europe: Politics and Discourse*. London: Bloomsbury, 89–103.

Benhabib, S. (1987) 'The generalized and the concrete Other', in Benhabib, S. and Cornell, D. (eds), *Feminism as Critique*. Minneapolis, MN: University of Minneapolis Press.

Benz, W. (1995) 'Realitätsverweigerung als antisemitisches Prinzip: Die Leugnung des Völkermords', in Benz, W. (ed.), *Antisemitismus in Deutschland: Zur Aktualität eines Vorurteils*. Stuttgart: DTV, 121–39.

Berger, P. L. and Luckmann, T. (1966) *The Social Construction of Reality*. Garden City, NY: Anchor.

Best, J. (2001) 'Social progress and social problems: Towards a sociology of gloom', *The Sociological Quarterly*, 42/1: 1–12.

Betz, H. G. (1993) 'The new politics of resentment: Radical right-wing populist parties in Western Europe', *Comparative Politics*, 25: 413–27.

Betz, H. G. (1994) *Radical Right-wing Populism in Western Europe*. New York: St. Martins' Press.

Betz, H. G. (1996) 'Review: The Radical Right in Western Europe', *Political Science Quarterly*, 111/4: 716.

Betz, H. G. (2013) 'Mosques, minarets, burqas and other essential threats: The populist right's campaign against Islam in Western Europe', in Wodak, R., KhosraviNik, M. and Mral, B. (eds), *Right-wing Populism in Europe: Politics and Discourse*. London: Bloomsbury, 71–88.

Betz, H. G. and Immerfall, S. (1998) *The New Politics of the Right: Neo-Populist Parties and Movements in Established Democracies*. New York: St. Martins' Press.

Biedenkopf, K., Geremek, B., Rocard, M. and Michalski, K. (2004) *The Spiritual and Cultural Dimension of Europe: Reflection Group – Concluding Remarks*. Brussels: The European Commission.

Billig, M. (1978) *Fascists: A Social Psychological View of the National Front*. London: Harcourt, Brace, Jovanovich.

Billig, M. (1995) *Banal Nationalism*. London: SAGE.

Billig, M. (2006) 'Discourse and discrimination', in Brown, K. (ed.), *Encyclopaedia for Language and Linguistics*. Oxford: Elsevier.

Blackledge, A. (2006) 'The racialisation of language in British political discourse' *Critical Discourse Studies*, 3/1: 61–79.

Blamires, C. (ed.) (2006) *World Fascism: A Historical Encyclopedia*. Santa Barbara, CA: ABC-CLIO.

Blasch, L. (2012) 'Die PolitikerIn als (hyper)mediales Identitätskonstrukt'. Unpublished MA Dissertation, Dept. of Linguistics, Vienna University.

BNP (2010) *Democracy, Freedom, Culture and Identity: British National Party General Elections Manifesto 2011*. Welshpool: BNP. Available at www.bnp.org.uk/sites/default/files/british_national_party_manifesto_2010.pdf, accessed 12/3/15.

Bos, L., van der Brug, W. and de Vreese, C. H. (2010) 'How the media shape perceptions of right-wing populist leaders', paper prepared for *Politicogenetmaal*, Leuven, 27–8 May.

Botsford, D. (2013) *The British State versus Freedom of Expression: The case of R. v. Griffin*. London: Libertarian Alliance. Available at www.libertarian.co.uk/lapubs/legan/legan029.pdf, accessed 13/3/15.

Boukala, S. (2013) 'The Greek media discourse and the construction of European Identity: Islam as radical otherness, collective identity and "Fortress Europe"'. Unpublished PhD Thesis, Lancaster University.

Bourdieu, P. (1999) *On Television*. New York: The New Press.

Bourdieu, P. (2005) 'The political field, the social science field, and the journalistic field', in Benson, R. and Neveu, E. (eds), *Bourdieu and the Journalistic Field*. Cambridge: Cambridge University Press, 29–47.

Bourdieu, P. and Wacquant, L. (1992) *An Invitation to Reflexive Sociology*. Chicago, IL: University of Chicago Press.

Broxmeyer, J. D. (2010) 'Of politicians, populism, and plates: marketing the body politic', *Women's Studies Quarterly*, 38/3–4: 138–52.

Bull, P. and Simon-Vendenbergen, A.-M. (2014) 'Equivocation and doublespeak in far right-wing discourse: an analysis of Nick Griffin's performance on BBC's *Question Time*', *Text & Talk*, 34/1: 1–22.

Bunzl, M. (2007) *Anti-Semitism and Islamophobia: Hatreds Old and New in Europe*. Chicago, IL: Prickly Paradigm Press.

Burghart, D. and Zeskind, L. (2010) *Tea Party Nationalism: A Critical Examination of the Tea Party Movement and the Size, Scope, and Focus of Its National Factions*. Kansas City, KS: Institute for Research and Education on Human Rights.

Butterwegge, C. (1996) *Rechtsextremismus, Rassismus und Gewalt*. Darmstadt: Primus.

Cameron, D. (2011) 'Prime minister's address to Conservative party members on the government's immigration policy', *Guardian*, 14 April. Available at www.theguardian.com/politics/2011/apr/14/david-cameron-immigration-speech-full-text, accessed 26/6/13.

Cameron, D. (2012) 'House of Commons Liaison Committee – Oral evidence from the Prime Minister – Minutes of Evidence', HC 484-i. Available at www.publications.parliament.uk/pa/cm201213/cmselect/cmliaisn/484/120703.htm, accessed 26/6/13.

Campbell, B. (2014) 'After neoliberalism: The need for a gender revolution', www.eurozine.com/articles/2014-05-14-campbell-en.html, accessed 12/8/14.

Canovan, M. (1981) *Populism*. London: Junction Books.

Canovan, M. (1999) 'Trust the people! Populism and the two faces of democracy', *Political Studies*, 47/1: 2–16.

Castells, M. (2007) 'Communication, power and counter-power in the network society', *International Journal of Communication*, 1: 238–66.

CeiberWeiber (2010) 'Das (freie) Frauenbild der FPÖ', 1 September. Available at www.ceiberweiber.at/index.php?p=news&area=1&newsid=541, accessed 12/8/14.

Charter, D. (2007) '"Black sheep" cartoon ignites bitter row on racism before Swiss election', *The Times*, 10 October. Available at http://www.thetimes.co.uk/tto/news/world/europe/article2596010.ece, accessed 22/4/2015.

Charteris-Black, J. (2013) *Analyzing Political Speeches*. Basingstoke: Palgrave.

CHdata123 (2007) 'Criminal Fascist Nazi SVP (Swiss Popular Party): criminality of foreigners - black sheep bad seed - a goat - Blocher kicked out'. Available at www.chdata123.com/eu/ch/kr/criminal-SVP-ENGL/07-crim-foreigners-black-sheep-goat-Zottel-Blocher-kicked-out-2007.html, accessed 16/7/13.

Checkel, J. and Katzenstein, P. (2009) *European Identity*. Cambridge: Cambridge University Press.

Chouliaraki, L. and Fairclough, N. (1999) *Discourse in Late Modernity: Rethinking Critical Discourse Analysis*. Edinburgh: Edinburgh University Press.

Chouliaraki, L. and Morsing, M. (eds) (2010) *Media, Organizations and Identity*. Basingstoke: Palgrave.

Cicero, M.T. (84BC) *De Inventione*. Available at http://www.classicpersuasion.org/pw/cicero/dnv2-1.htm, accessed 23/4/15.

Cinpoes, R. (2008) 'From national identity to European identity', *Journal of Identity and Migration Studies*, 2: 1–19.

Ciobanu, C. (2013) 'Conservative culture and the Far Right in Poland', *Open Democracy*. Available at www.opendemocracy.net/can-europe-make-it/claudia-ciobanu/conservative-culture-and-far-right-in-poland, accessed 11/11/13.

CNN (2012) 24 April. http://edition.cnn.com/2012/04/23/world/europe/netherlands-politics/.

Cobain, I. (2008) 'Language School run by Italian fascist leader', *Guardian*, 29 February. Available at www.theguardian.com/politics/2008/feb/29/thefarright.italy, accessed 12/3/15.

Coffé, H. (2005) 'The adaptation of the extreme right's discourse: The case of the "Vlaams Blok". Ethical perspectives', *Journal of the European Ethics Network*, 2: 205–30.

Comaroff, J. (2011) 'Populism and late liberalism: A special affinity?', *The ANNALS of the American Academy of Political and Social Science*, 637: 99–111.

Copsey, N. (2007) 'Changing course or changing clothes? Reflections on the ideological evolution of the British National Party 1999–2006', *Patterns of Prejudice*, 41/1: 61–82.

Corner, J. and Pels, D. (eds) (2003) *Media and the Restyling of Politics: Consumerism, Celebrity and Cynicism.* London: SAGE.

Council of the European Union (2003) 'Effective management of the external borders of the EU Member States – 10274/03'. Brussels: CEU.

Cox, M. and Shearman, P. (2000) 'After the fall: The extreme nationalism in the post-communist Russia', in Hainsworth, P. (ed.), *The Politics of the Extreme Right: From the Margins to the Mainstream.* London: Pinter.

Cutts, D. and Goodwin, M. J. (2013) 'Getting out the rightwing extremist vote: Extreme right party support and campaign effects at a recent British election', *European Political Science Review*: 1–22.

Czernin, H. (ed.) (2000) *'Wofür ich mich meinetwegen entschuldige' – Haider, beim Wort genommen.* Vienna: Czernin Publishers.

Dalakoglou, D. (2013) 'Neo-Nazism and neoliberalism: A few comments on violence in Athens at the time of crisis', *Working USA: The Journal of Labor and Society*, 16/22.

Day, M. (2009) 'European elections: Poland's controversial Law and Justice Party', *Telegraph*, 1 June. Available at www.telegraph.co.uk/news/worldnews/europe/eu/5418173/European-elections-Polands-controversial-Law-and-Justice-Party.html, accessed 12/3/15.

Day, M. (2011) 'Swiss far-right party on course for record-breaking election win', *Telegraph*, 20 October. Available at www.telegraph.co.uk/news/worldnews/europe/switzerland/8839006/Swiss-far-right-party-on-course-for-record-breaking-election-win.html, accessed 12/3/15.

De Cillia, R. and Dorostkar, N. (2013) 'Integration und/durch Sprache', in Dahlvik, J. Reinprecht, C. and Wiebke, S. (eds), *Migration und Integration – wissenschaftliche Perspektiven aus Österreich.* Vienna: Vienna University Press, 143–62.

De Cleen, B. (2012) 'The rhetoric of the Flemish populist radical right party Vlaams Blok/Belang in a context of discursive struggle: A discourse-theoretical analysis'. Unpublished PhD thesis, Vrije Universiteit, Brussels.

De Cleen, B. (2013) 'The stage as an arena of political struggle: The struggle between the Vlaams Blok/Belang and the Flemish City theatres', in Wodak, R., KhosraviNik, M. and Mral, B. (eds), *Right-wing Populism in Europe: Politics and Discourse.* London: Bloomsbury, 209–21.

De Lange, S. (2008) 'From pariah to power: The government participation of radical right-wing populist parties in West European democracies'. Unpublished PhD Thesis, University of Antwerp.

Dean, J. (1996) *Solidarity of Strangers: Feminism after Identity Politics.* Berkeley, CA: University of California Press.

DeChaine, R. D. (ed.) (2012) *Border Rhetorics: Citizenship and Identity on the US–Mexican Frontier.* Tuscaloosa, AL: University of Alabama Press.

Delanty, G. and Kumar, K. (2006) 'Introduction', in Delanty, G. and Kumar, K. (eds), *The SAGE Handbook of Nations and Nationalism.* London: SAGE, 1–4.

Delanty, G. and Kumar, K. (eds) (2006) *The SAGE Handbook of Nations and Nationalism.* London: SAGE.

Delanty, G., Wodak, R. and Jones, P. (eds) (2011) *Migration, Identity, and Belonging*, 2nd edn. Liverpool: Liverpool University Press.

DerStandard.at (2001) 'FPÖ für Verschärfung des Asylrechts', 27 September. Available at http://derstandard.at/725783/FPOe-fuer-Verschaerfung-des-Asylrechts, accessed 28/9/01.

DerStandard.at (2012) 'Streit um antisemitisches Bild auf Strache-Seite', 19 August. Available at http://derstandard.at/1345164507078/Streit-um-antisemitisches-Bild-auf-Strache-Seite, accessed 4/5/13.

DerStandard.at (2014) 'Mölzer vergleicht EU mit dem Dritten Reich', 24 March. Available at http://derstandard.at/1395362877057/Moelzer-soll-EU-mit-dem-Dritten-Reich-verglichen-haben, accessed 15/4/15.

Dettke, D. (2014) 'Hungary's Jobbik Party, the challenge of European ethno-nationalism and the future of the European project', *Reports and Analyses* 4. Warszawa: Centre for International Relations, Wilson Center.

Deutsche Welle (2013a) 'German states repeat effort to ban far-right NPD', 3 December. Available at www.dw.de/german-states-repeat-effort-to-ban-far-right-npd/a-17266103, accessed 12/3/15.

Deutsche Welle (2013b) 'Is Germany's far-right NPD set to self-destruct?', 30 December. Available at www.dw.de/is-germanys-far-right-npd-set-to-self-destruct/a-17329887, accessed 12/3/15.

Devlin, R. and Pothier, D. (2006) *Critical Disability Theory*. Vancouver: University of British Columbia Press.

Dewey, C. (2013) 'Wendy Davis "tweetstorm" was planned in advance', *Washington Post*, 26 June.

Die Grünen (2010) *Dossier Barbara Rosenkranz*. Vienna: Parliamentary Club, Green Party.

Die Presse (n.d.) *'Jungwähler: FPÖ und Grüne fast gleichauf'*. Available at http://diepresse.com/home/politik/wienwahl/601074/Jungwaehler_FPO-und-Grune-fast-gleichauf, accessed 25/8/14.

Dirven, R., Wolf, H. G. and Polzenhagen, F. (2007) 'Cognitive linguistics and cultural studies', in Geeraerts, D. and Cuyckens, H. (eds), *The Oxford Handbook of Cognitive Linguistics*. Oxford: University Press, 1203–21.

Discover Society (2014) '"Swamped" by anti-immigrant communications?', 6 May. Available at www.discoversociety.org/2014/05/06/swamped-by-anti-immigrant-communications/, accessed 18/8/14.

Doerr, N. (2013) 'Bonding or bridging: Right wing and cosmopolitan images of immigrants'. Unpublished paper, Harvard University.

DPP (1997) *Pia Kjærsgaards Tale om Udlændingepolitik*. Copenhagen: Dansk Folkeparti. Available at www.danskfolkeparti.dk/Pia_Kj%C3%A6rsgaards_tale_om_Udl%C3%A6ndingepolitik_%C3%85rsm%C3%B8det_1997, accessed 12/3/15.

DPP (2002) *Principprogram*. Copenhagen: Dansk Folkeparti. Available at www.danskfolkeparti.dk/Principprogram, accessed 12/3/15.

Dumneazu (2010) 'Election day in Hungary: Mudslinging with mud. Zsidesz. Fun!', 11 April. Available at http://horinca.blogspot.co.uk/2010/04/election-day-in-hungary-mudslinging.html, accessed 30/4/14.

Dunlop, J. (2011) *The Rise of Russia and the Fall of the Soviet Empire*. Princeton, NJ: Princeton University Press.

Dyer, R. (1998) *Stars* (with a Supplementary Chapter and Bibliography by Paul McDonald; new edition). London: BFI British Film Institute Publishing.

Eatwell, R. (2007) 'The concept and theory of charismatic leadership', in Pinto, A. C., Eatwell, R. and Stein, U.L. (eds), *Charisma and Fascism in Interwar Europe*. London: Routledge, 3–18.

Economist, The (2013) 'This monster called Europe', 16 November. Available at www.economist.com/news/europe/21589894-marine-le-pen-and-geert-wilders-form-eurosceptic-alliance-monster-called-europe, accessed 12/3/15.

Eddy, M. (2013) 'Berlin won't join effort to ban far-right party', *New York Times*, 20 March. Available at www.nytimes.com/2013/03/21/world/europe/merkels-government-wont-pursue-ban-of-german-far-right-party.html?_r=0, accessed 12/3/15.

Edelman, M. (1967) *The Symbolic Uses of Politics*. Chicago, IL: University of Illinois Press.

Ekström, M. and Johansson, B. (2008) 'Talk scandals', *Media, Culture & Society*, 30/1: 61–79.

Ellinas, A. (2009) 'Chaotic but popular? Extreme-right organisation and performance in the age of media communication', *Journal of Contemporary European Studies*, 17: 209–21.

Ellinas, A. (2013) 'The rise of Golden Dawn: The new face of the far right in Greece', *South European Society and Politics*, 18/4: 543–65.

Elver, H. (2012) *The Headscarf Controversy: Secularism and Freedom of Religion*. Oxford: Oxford University Press.

Engel, J. and Wodak, R. (2009) 'Kalkulierte Ambivalenz' "Störungen" und das "Gedankenjahr": Die Causen Siegfried Kampl und John Gudenus', in De Cillia, R. and Wodak, R. (eds), *Gedenken im "Gedankenjahr": zur diskursiven Konstruktion österreichischer Identitäten im Jubiläumsjahr 2005*. Innsbruck: Studienverlag, 79–100.

Engel, J. and Wodak, R. (2013) '"Calculated ambivalence" and Holocaust denial in Austria', in Wodak, R. and Richardson, J. E. (eds), *Analysing Fascist Discourse: European Fascism in Talk and Text*. London: Routledge, 73–96.

Erik, J. (2005) 'From Vlaams Blok to Vlaams Belang: The Belgian far-right renames itself', *West European Politics,* 28/3: 493–502.

Ersbøll, E., Kostakopoulou, D. and Van Oers, R. (eds) (2010) *A Redefinition of Belonging? Language and Integration Tests for Newcomers and Future Citizens*. Leiden: Martinus Nijhoff.

España 2000 (2000a) *Presentación*. Available at http://espana2000.org/?page_id=32, accessed 12/3/15.

España 2000 (2000b) *Programa político*. Available at http://espana2000.org/?page_id=39, accessed 12/3/15.

European Commission (2004) 'Action Paper in response to the terrorist attacks on Madrid', Memo 04/65, Brussels, 18 March.

Extramiana, C., Pulinnx, R. and Van Avermaet, P. (2014) *Linguistic Integration of Adult Migrants: Policy and Practice Draft Report on the 3rd Council of Europe Survey*. Strasbourg: Council of Europe.

Fairclough, N. (2010) 'Discourse, change and hegemony', in Fairclough, N. (ed.), *Critical Discourse Analysis: The Critical Study of Language*. Harlow: Longman, 126–45.

Feldman M. and Jackson, P. (eds) (2013) *Doublespeak: The Rhetoric of the Far-Rights Since 1945*. Frankfurt: Ibidem.

Fella, S. and Ruzza, C. (2013) 'Populism and the fall of the centre-right in Italy: The end of the Berlusconi model or a new beginning?', *Journal of Contemporary European Studies*, 21/1: 38–52.

Fieschi, C. (2004) *Fascism, Populism and the French Fifth Republic: In the Shadow of Democracy*. Manchester: Manchester University Press.

Fine, R. (2009) 'Fighting with phantoms: A contribution to the debate on antisemitism in Europe', *Patterns of Prejudice*, 43/5: 459–79.

Flam, H. and Beauzamy, B. (2011) 'Symbolic violence', in Delanty, G., Wodak, R. and Jones, P. (eds), *Identity, Belonging and Migration*. Liverpool: Liverpool University Press, 221–40.

FN Programme (2012) 'Le Projet du Front National'. Available at www.frontnational.com/le-projet-de-marine-le-pen/, accessed 4/4/15.

Forchtner, B. and Wodak, R. (forthcoming) 'Conveying regression through comics – the case of the Austrian Freedom Party: A critical discourse analysis', in Virchow, F. (ed.), *The Far Right and Visual Politics*. Wiesbaden: VS.

Forchtner, B., Krzyżanowski, M. and Wodak, R. (2013) 'Mediatisation, right-wing populism and political campaigning: The case of the Austrian Freedom Party (FPÖ)', in Ekström, M. and Tolson, A. (eds), *Media Talk and Political Elections in Europe and America*. Basingstoke: Palgrave, 205–28.

Ford, R. and Goodwin, M. (2014) *Revolt on the Right: Explaining Support for the Radical Right in Britain*. London: Routledge.

Formisano, R. (2012) *The Tea Party: A Brief History*. Baltimore, MD: The Johns Hopkins University Press.

Fortier, A-M. (2010) 'The body as evidence and the endurance of "race"', Plenary Lecture, Conference on Migrations: Interdisciplinary Perspectives, Vienna, 2 July 2010.

Fortier, A-M. (2012) 'Genetic indigenisation in "the people of the British Isles"', *Science as Culture*, 21/22: 153–75.

FPÖ (2010) *Comic-Sagen aus Wien*. Vienna: FPÖ. Available at https://www.youtube.com/watch?v=QSQ2qgKsrrU, accessed 23/4/2015.

Freeden, M. (1998) 'Is nationalism a distinct ideology?', *Political Studies*, 46/4: 748–65.

Freud, A. (1992) *The Ego and the Mechanisms of Defence*. London: Karnac Books.

Freud, S. (1982 [1930]) *Das Unbehagen in der Kultur*, Gesammelte Werke XIV. Frankfurt: Fischer, 419–506.

Fusi, N. (2014) 'Beppo Grillo'. Unpublished seminar paper, Georgetown University, Washington, DC.

Gallagher, T. (1992a) 'Portugal: The marginalization of the extreme right', in Hainsworth, P. and Anderson, M. (eds), *The Extreme Right in Western Europe and the USA*. London: Continuum International, 232–45.

Gallagher, T. (1992b) 'Rome at bay: The challenge of the Northern League to the Italian State', *Government and Opposition*, 27/4: 47–86.

Gallagher, T. (2000) 'Exit from the ghetto: The Italian far-right in the 1990s', in Hainsworth, P. (ed.), *The Politics of the Extreme Right: From the Margins to the Mainstream*. London: Continuum International, 64–86.

Gatter, J. (2014) 'Campaign poster', available at www.jens-gatter.de, accessed 14/4/14.

Gellner, E. (1983) *Nations and Nationalism*. Oxford: Blackwell.

Gingrich, A. (2002) 'A man for all seasons', in Wodak, R. and Pelinka, A. (eds), *The Haider Phenomenon in Austria*. New Brunswick, NJ: Transaction, 87–102.

Gingrich, A. and Banks, M. (eds) (2006) *Neo-Nationalism in Europe and Beyond: Perspectives from Social Anthropology*. New York: Berghahn.

Girnth, H. (1996) 'Texte im politischen Diskurs. Ein Vorschlag zur diskursorientierten Beschreibung von Textsorten', *Muttersprache*, 106/1: 66–80.

Goffman, E. (1959) *The Presentation of Self in Everyday Life.* New York: Anchor.

Goffman, E. (1971) *Relations in Public: Microstudies of the Public Order.* New York: Basic Books.

Golden Dawn (2012) *Καταστατικό του Πολιτικού Κόμματος με την Επωνυμία « Λαϊκός Σύνδεσμος – Χρυσή Αυγή »* [Statutes of the Political Party with the name 'Popular Association – Golden Dawn']. Athens: Golden Dawn.

Goodman-Wallace, S. (2010) 'Integration requirements for integration's sake?', *Journal of Ethnic and Migration Studies*, 36/5: 753–72.

Gramsci, A. (1975) *Selections from the Prison Notebooks.* London: Lawrence and Wishart.

Grande, E. (2000) 'Charisma und Komplexität: Verhandlungsdemokratie, Mediendemokratie und der Funktionswandel politischer Eliten', *Leviathan*, 28/1: 122–41.

Greenhouse, L. and Siegel, R. B. (2012) *Before Roe v. Wade: Voices that Shaped the Abortion Debate before the Supreme Court's Ruling.* New Haven, CT: Yale Law School.

Griffin, R. (1999) 'Afterword: Last rights?', in Ramet, S. (ed.), *The Radical Right in Central and Eastern Europe since 1989.* Philadelphia, PA: Penn State University Press, 297–321.

Guardian (2013) '"Go home" vans to be scrapped after experiment deemed a failure', 22 October. Available at www.theguardian.com/uk-news/2013/oct/22/go-home-vans-scrapped-failure, accessed 29/4/14.

Guardian (2014) 'Immigration minister resigns for employing illegal immigrant', 8 February. Available at www.theguardian.com/uk-news/2014/feb/08/immigration-minister-resigns-illegal-immigrant-mark-harper, accessed 30/4/14.

Hainsworth, P. (2000) 'The Front National', in Hainsworth, P. (ed.), *The Politics of the Extreme Right: From the Margins to the Mainstream.* London: Pinter.

Hamzeh, M. (2011) 'Deveiling body stories: Muslim girls negotiate visual, spatial, and ethical hijabs', *Race, Ethnicity and Education*, 14/4: 481–506.

Hansson, S. (2014) 'Calculated overcommunication: Strategic uses of prolixity, irrelevancy, and repetition in administrative language' (forthcoming).

Hansson, S. (2015) 'Discursive strategies of blame avoidance in government: A framework for analysis', *Discourse & Society*, 26/3: 297–323.

Harrison, S. and Bruter, M. (2011) *Mapping Extreme Right Ideology.* Basingstoke: Palgrave.

Hart, C. (2010) *Critical Discourse Analysis and Cognitive Science: New Perspectives on Immigration Discourse.* Basingstoke: Palgrave.

Hay, C. (2007) *Why We Hate Politics.* Cambridge: Polity.

HC Strache (2010) Campaign poster. Available at http://www.hcstrache.at/home/?id=48#, accessed 14/10/12.

Heer, H., Manoschek, W., Pollak, A. and Wodak, R. (eds) (2008) *The Discursive Construction of History: Remembering the Wehrmachts War of Annihilation.* (trans. S. Fligelstone). Basingstoke: Palgrave.

Heitmeyer, W. (ed.) (1996) *Was hält eine multi-ethnische Gesellschaft zusammen?* Frankfurt: Suhrkamp.

Higgins, M. (2008) *Media and Their Publics.* Maidenhead: McGraw-Hill.

Hill, R. and Bell, A. (1988) *The Other Face of Terror: Inside Europe's Neo-Nazi Network.* London: Grafton.

Ho, C. (2005) 'Muslim women's new defenders: Women's rights, nationalism and Islamophobia in contemporary Australia', Project Report: Sanctuary and Security in Contemporary Australia, ARC Project LP0562553. Sydney: Australian Research Council.

Home Office (2013) *Operation Vaken: Evaluation Report – October 2013.* London: Home Office. Available at www.gov.uk/government/uploads/system/uploads/attachment_data/file/254411/Operation_Vaken_Evaluation_Report.pdf, accessed 29/4/14.

Horaczek, N. and Reiterer, C. (2009) *HC Strache: Sein Aufstieg, seine Hintermänner, seine Feinde.* Vienna: Ueberreuter.

Huggan, G. and Law, I. (2009) *Racism Postcolonialism Europe.* Liverpool: Liverpool University Press.

Human Rights First (2014) *'We are Not Nazis, but …': The Rise of Hate Parties in Hungary and Greece and Why America Should Care.* New York: Human Rights First. Available at www.humanrightsfirst.org/sites/default/files/HRF-report-We-Are-Not-Nazis-But.pdf, accessed 5/8/14.

Human Rights Watch (1997) *Racist Violence in the United Kingdom*. New York: Human Rights Watch.

ICERD (1969) *International Convention on the Elimination of all Forms of Racial Discrimination*. United Nations, Office of the High Commissioner for Human Rights. Available at www.ohchr.org/EN/ProfessionalInterest/Pages/CERD.aspx, accessed 19/3/15.

Ignazi, P. (1992) 'The silent counter-revolution: Hypotheses on the emergence of extreme right-wing parties in Europe', *European Journal of Political Research*, 9: 75–99.

Igounet, V. (1998) 'Holocaust denial is part of a strategy', *Le Monde Diplomatique*, 8 May. Available from http://mondediplo.com/1998/05/08igou, accessed 2/3/14.

Inglehart, R. and Norris, P. (2000) 'The developmental theory of the gender gap: Women's and men's voting behaviour in global perspective', *International Political Science Review*, 21/4: 441–63.

Jeffries, I. (2002) *Eastern Europe at the Turn of the Twenty-first Century*. London: Routledge.

Jenkins, H. (2008) *Convergence Culture: Where Old and New Media Collide*. New York: New York University Press.

Jobbik (2014a) 'A short summary about Jobbik', available at www.jobbik.com/short_summary_about_jobbik, accessed 12/3/15.

Jobbik (2014b) 'Policies', available at www.jobbik.com/policies, accessed 12/3/15.

Johnstone, B. (1987) 'An introduction: Perspectives on repetition', *Text*, 7/3: 205–14.

Joppke, C. (2010) *Citizenship and Immigration*. Cambridge: Polity.

Judt, T. (2007) *Postwar: A History of Europe since 1945*. London: Penguin.

Judt, T. (2008) 'The problem of evil in postwar Europe', *New York Review of Books*, 14 February.

Judt, T. (2010) 'Ill fares the land', *New York Review of Books*, 29 April.

Judt, T. (2011) *Ill Fares the Land*. London: Penguin.

Jungerstam-Mulders, S. (2006) *Post-Communist EU Member States: Parties and Party Systems*. London: Ashgate.

Kahn, R. A. (2005) *Holocaust Denial and the Law: A Comparative Study*. Basingstoke: Palgrave.

Kallis, A. (2013) 'Breaking taboos and "mainstreaming the extreme": The debates on restricting Islamic symbols in contemporary Europe', in Wodak, R., KhosraviNik, M. and Mral, B. (eds), *Right-wing Populism in Europe: Politics and Discourse*. London: Bloomsbury, 55–70.

Kampf, Z. (2009) 'Public (non-)apologies: The discourse of minimizing responsibility', *Journal of Pragmatics*, 41: 2257–70.

Kaplan, J. and Weinberg, L. (1998) *The Emergence of a Euro-American Radical Right*. New Brunswick, NJ: Transaction.

Karmasin, H. (2004) *Produkte als Botschaften*, 3rd edn. Frankfurt: Redline Wirtschaft/Ueberreuter.

Karvonen, L. (2010) *The Personalisation of Politics: A Study of Parliamentary Democracies*. Colchester: ECPR.

Kasprowicz, D. (2012) 'Filling in the niche. The populist radical Right and the concept of solidarity', *Eurozine*, 14 February. Available at http://www.eurozine.com/articles/2014–02–14-kasprowicz-en.html, accessed 17/8/14.

Katsourides, Y. (2013) 'Determinants of extreme right reappearance in Cyprus: The National Popular Front (ELAM), Golden Dawn's sister party', *South European Society and Politics*, 18/4: 567–89.

Kenski, K. (2010) 'The Palin Effect and vote preference in the 2008 presidential election', *American Behavioral Scientist*, 54/3: 222–38.

KhosraviNik, M. (2010) 'The representation of refugees, asylum seekers and immigrants in British newspapers: A critical discourse analysis', *Journal of Language and Politics*, 9/1: 1–28.

Kienpointner, M. (1996) *Vernünftig argumentieren: Regeln und Techniken der Argumentation*. Hamburg: Rowohlt.

Kienpointner, M. (2009) 'Plausible and fallacious strategies to silence one's opponent', in Van Eemeren, F. H. (ed.), *Examining Argumentation in Context: Fifteen Studies on Strategic Manoeuvring*. Amsterdam: Benjamins, 61–75.

Kienpointner, M. (2011) 'Rhetoric', in Ostman, J. and Verschueren, J. (eds), *Pragmatics in Practice*. Amsterdam: Benjamins, 264–77.

Kitschelt, H. (1997) *The Radical Right in Western Europe: A Comparative Analysis*. London: Macmillan.

Kitschelt, H. (2007) 'Growth and persistence of the radical right in postindustrial democracies: Advances and challenges in comparative research', *West European Politics*, 30/5: 1176–206.

Kitschelt, H. and McGann, A. (1995) *The Radical Right in Western Europe: A Comparative Analysis.* Ann Arbor, MI: University of Michigan Press.

Klein, J. (1996) 'Insider-Lesarten. Einige Regeln zur latenten Fachkommunikation in Partei-programmen', in Klein, J. and Diekmannshenke, H. (eds) *Sprachstrategien und Dialogblockaden.* Berlin: Springer, 201–9.

Kluge, F. (1999) *Etymologisches Wörterbuch.* Berlin: De Gruyter Mouton.

Knuckey, J. (2010) 'The "Palin Effect" in the 2008 U.S. Presidential Election', *Political Research Quarterly*, 20/10: 1–15.

Köhler, K. and Wodak, R. (2011) 'Mitbürger, Fremde und "echte Wiener": Ein- und Ausgrenzungen über Sprache', *Deutschunterricht*, 6/11: 64–74.

Körte, M. and Stockhammer, R. (eds) (1995) *Ahasvers Spur. Dichtungen und Dokumente vom 'Ewigen Juden'.* Leipzig: Reclam.

Kosmas, P. (2013) 'Cyprus: ELAM, Like Golden Dawn (ΚΥΠΡΟΣ: ΕΛΑΜ ΟΠΩΣ ΧΡΥΣΗ ΑΥΓΗ)', *Iskra.gr.*, 5 January.

Kovács, A. (2010) *The Stranger 'At Hand'.* Antwerp: Brill.

Kovács, A. (2013) 'The post-communist extreme right: The Jobbik Party in Hungary', in Wodak, R., KhosraviNik, M. and Mral, B. (eds), *Rightwing Populism in Europe: Politics and Discourse.* London: Bloomsbury, 223–34.

Kovács, A. and Szilágyi, A. (2013) 'Variations on a theme: The Jewish "Other" in old and new antisemitic media discourses in Hungary in the 1940s and in 2011', in Wodak, R. and Richardson, J. E. (eds), *Analysing Fascist Discourse: European Fascism in Talk and Text.* London: Routledge, 203–27.

Kovács, A. and Wodak, R. (eds) (2003) *NATO or Neutrality? The Austrian and Hungarian Cases.* Vienna: Böhlau.

Kress, G. (2003) *Literacy in the New Media Age.* London: Routledge.

Krzyżanowski, M. (2010) *The Discursive Construction of European Identities: A Multi-level Approach to Discourse and Identity in the Transforming European Union.* Frankfurt: Lang.

Krzyżanowski, M. (2013a) 'From anti-immigration and nationalist revisionism to Islamophobia: Continuities and shifts in recent discourses and patterns of political communication of the Freedom Party of Austria (FPÖ)', in Wodak, R., KhosraviNik, M. and Mral, B. (eds), *Right-wing Populism in Europe: Politics and Discourse.* London: Bloomsbury, 135–48.

Krzyżanowski, M. (2013b) 'Right-wing populism, opportunism and political catholicism: On recent rhetorics and political communication of Polish PiS (Law and Justice Party)', in Sir Peter Ustinov Institut, Pelinka, A. and Haller, B. (eds), *Populismus. Herausforderung oder Gefahr für eine Demokratie?* Vienna: New Academic Press, 11–126.

Krzyżanowski, M. and Oberhuber, F. (2007) *(Un)Doing Europe: Discourses and Practices of Negotiating the EU Constitution.* Oxford: Peter Lang.

Krzyżanowski, M. and Wodak, R. (2009) *Politics of Exclusion: Debating Migration in Austria.* New Brunswick, NJ: Transaction.

Krzyżanowski, M. and Wodak, R. (2011) 'Political strategies and language policies: The "rise and fall" of the EU Lisbon strategy and its implications for the Union's multilingualism policy', *Language Policy*, 10/2: 115–36.

Laclau, E. (2005) *On Populist Reason.* London: Verso.

Lakoff, G. (1987) *Women, Fire, and Dangerous Things: What Categories Reveal about the Mind.* Chicago, IL: Chicago University Press.

Lakoff, G. (2004) *Don't Think of an Elephant: Know Your Values and Frame the Debate.* White River Junction, VT: Chelsea Green.

Lakoff, G. (2008) *The Political Mind: Why You Can't Understand 21st-century American Politics with an 18th-century Brain.* New York: Penguin.

Lakoff, G. and Turner, M. (1989) *More than Cool Reason: Field Guide to Poetic Metaphor.* Chicago, IL: University of Chicago Press.

Lakoff, R. T. (2001) 'Nine ways of looking at apologies: The necessity for interdisciplinary theory and methods in discourse analysis', in Schiffrin, D., Tannen, D. and Hamilton, H. E. (eds), *The Handbook of Discourse Analysis.* Oxford: Blackwell, 199–214.

Lamont, M. (2000) *The Dignity of the Working Man: Morality and the Boundaries of Race, Class and Immigration.* Cambridge, MA: Harvard University Press.

Lamont, M. and Molnar, V. (2002) 'The study of boundaries in the social sciences', *Annual Review of Sociology*, 28: 167–95.

LAOS (2007) '*Πλαίσιο Θέσεων*' [Framework of Positions]. Athens: LAOS.

LeBor, A. (2009) 'Jobbik: Meet the BNP's fascist friends in Hungary', *The Times*, 9 June. Available at www.thetimes.co.uk/tto/news/politics/article2028568.ece, accessed 12/3/15.

Lebsanft, F. (2000) 'Die eigene und die fremden Sprachen', in Dahmen, W., Holtus, G., Kramer, J., Metzeltin, M., Schweickard, W. and Winckelmann, O. (eds), *Schreiben in einer anderen Sprache.* Tübingen: Narr, 3–20.

Lega Nord Programme (2012) Available at www.leganord.org/index.php/il-movimento/lo-statuto-della-lega-nord, accessed 12/3/15.

Leopore, J. (2010) *The Whites of Their Eyes: The Tea Party's Revolution and the Battle over American History.* Princeton, NJ: Princeton University Press.

Lipstadt, D. (1993) *Denying the Holocaust: The Growing Assault on Truth and Memory.* New York: Free Press.

Local, The (2009) 'Neo-Nazis make headway into town councils', 9 June. Available at www.thelocal.de/20090609/19800, accessed 12/3/15.

Löwenthal, L. (1982 [1949]) *Falsche Propheten. Studien zum Autoritarismus.* Frankfurt: Suhrkamp.

Loitfellner, S. (2003) '"Furchtbar war der Blutzoll, den Österreich entrichten musste …". Die Wehrmacht und ihre Soldaten in österreichischen Schulbüchern', in Heer, H., Manoschek, W., Pollak, A. and Wodak, R. (eds), *Wie Geschichte gemacht wird.* Vienna: Czernin, 171–91.

Loitfellner, S. (2008) '"The appalling toll in Austrian lives". The Wehrmacht and its soldiers in Austrian schoolbooks', in Heer, H., Manoschek, W., Pollak, A. and Wodak, R. (eds), *The Discursive Construction of History: Remembering the Wehrmachts War of Annihilation* (trans. S. Fligelstone). Basingstoke: Palgrave, 155–74.

Lowndes, J. and Warren, D. (2011) 'Occupy Wall Street: A twenty-first century populist movement?', *Dissent*, 21 October.

Lucardie, P. (2000) 'Prophets, purifiers, and prolocutors: Towards a theory on the emergence of new parties', *Party Politics*, 6/2: 175–86.

Lynch, D., Whitaker, R. and Loomes, G. (2012) 'The UK Independence Party: Understanding a niche party's strategy, candidates and supporters', *Parliamentary Affairs*, 65: 733–57.

Maas, U. (1985) '*Als der Geist der Gemeinschaft eine Sprache fand*'. *Sprache im Nationalsozialismus.* Opladen: Westdeutscher Verlag.

Mădroane, D. (2013) 'New times, old ideologies? Recontextualizations of radical right thought in postcommunist Romania', in Wodak, R. and Richardson, J. E. (eds) *Analysing Fascist Discourse: European Fascism in Talk and Text.* London: Routledge, 256–76.

Mammone, A. (2009) 'The eternal return? Faux populism and contemporarization of neo-fascism across Britain, France and Italy', *Journal of Contemporary European Studies*, 17/2: 171–94.

Mancini, P. (2011) *Between Commodification and Lifestyle Politics: Does Silvio Berlusconi Provide a New Model of Politics for the 21st Century?* Oxford: Reuters Institute for the Study of Journalism.

Manvell, R. and Fraenkel, H. (1960) *Dr Goebbels: His Life and Death.* New York: Simon and Schuster.

Mars, C. (2011) '"The rise of right-wing populism in Finland": The True Finns', *Transform*, 8.

Marsdal, M. E. (2013) 'Loud values, muffled interests: Third way social democracy and right-wing populism', in Wodak, R., KhosraviNik, M. and Mral, B. (eds), *Right-wing Populism in Europe: Politics and Discourse.* London: Bloomsbury, 39–54.

Mason, P. (2012) 'Amid scars of past conflicts Spanish far right grows', *BBC News*, 18 December. Available at www.bbc.co.uk/news/world-20773516, accessed 12/3/15.

Matouschek, B., Wodak, R. and Januschek, F. (1995) *Notwendige Maßnahmen gegen Fremde?* Vienna: Passagen.

McCarthy, P. (1995) *The Crisis of the Italian State: From the Origins of the Cold War to the Fall of Berlusconi.* London: Macmillan.

McDonald-Gibson, C. (2013) 'Norway's Far Right May Come to Power Despite Memory of Anders Breivik's Killing Spree', *Time*, 19 August. Available at http://world.time.com/2013/08/19/

norways-far-right-may-come-to-power-despite-memory-of-anders-breiviks-killing-spree/, accessed 12/3/15.

McGlashan, M. (2013) 'The branding of European nationalism: Perpetuation and novelty in racist symbolism', in Wodak, R. and Richardson, J. E. (eds) *Analysing Fascist Discourse: European Fascism in Talk and Text.* London: Routledge, 297–314.

McLaren, P. (2009) 'Rehearsing disaster's rehearsal: The election and its aftermath in Obamerica', *Cultural Studies – Critical Methodologies*, 9/6: 803–15.

McLaughlin, L. (2013) 'Are the Austrian FPÖ party really neo-Nazis?', *New Statesman*, 9 October. Available at www.newstatesman.com/politics/2013/10/are-austrian-fpo-party-really-nazis, accessed 12/3/15.

Meinhart, E. and Zöchling, C. (2014) 'Europa Wahl 2014: Warum Frauen und Männer unterschiedlich wählen', *Profil*, 31 May. Available at www.profil.at/articles/1422/980/375649/europawahl-2014-warum-frauen-maenner, accessed 20/7/14.

Mény, Y. and Surel, Y. (2000) *Par le people, pour le people: le populisme et les démocraties.* Paris: Fayard.

Mény, Y. and Surel, Y. (eds) (2002) *Democracies and the Populist Challenge.* Basingstoke: Palgrave.

Meret, S. (2010) 'The Danish People's Party, the Italian Northern League and the Austrian Freedom Party in a comparative perspective: Party ideology and electoral support'. Unpublished PhD thesis, Series 25, University of Aalborg.

Michalowski, I. (2011) 'Required to assimilate? The content of citizenship tests in five countries', *Citizenship Studies*, 15/6–7: 749–68.

Mileti, F. P. and Plomb, F. (2007) 'Addressing the link between socio-economic change and right-wing populism and extremism: A critical review of European literature', in Flecker, J. (ed.), *Changing Working Life and the Appeal of the Extreme Right.* Aldershot: Ashgate, 9–34.

Minkenberg, M. (2002) 'The radical right in post socialist central and eastern Europe: Comparative observations and interpretations', *East European Politics and Societies*, 16/2: 337–9.

Minkenberg, M. and Perrineau, P. (2007) 'The radical right in the European elections 2004', *International Political Science Review*, 28/1: 29–55.

Mir, M. (2011) 'How a far-right party came to dominate Swiss politics', *The Local*, 7 October. Available at www.thelocal.ch/20111007/1422, accessed 12/3/15.

Molé, N. J. (2013) 'Trusted puppets, tarnished politicians: Humor and cynicism in Berlusconi's Italy', *American Ethnologist*, 40: 288–99.

Morley, D. and Robins, K. (2002) *Spaces of Identity: Global Media, Electronic Landscapes and Cultural Boundaries.* New York: Routledge.

Mouffe, C. (2000) *The Democratic Paradox.* London: Verso.

Mouffe, C. (2005) *On the Political.* London: Routledge.

Mudde, C. (2000) *The Ideology of the Extreme Right.* Manchester: Manchester University Press.

Mudde, C. (2003) *The Ideology of the Extreme Right*, 2nd edn. Manchester: Manchester University Press.

Mudde, C. (2004) 'The populist zeitgeist', *Government and Opposition*, 39/4: 542–63.

Mudde, C. (2005) 'Racist Extremism in Central and Eastern Europe', *East European Politics & Societies*, 19/2: 161–84.

Mudde, C. (2007) *The Populist Radical Right Parties in Europe.* Cambridge: Cambridge University Press.

Mudde, C. and Kaltwasser, C. R. (2012) *Populism in Europe and the Americas: Threat or Corrective for Democracy?* Cambridge: Cambridge University Press.

Muižnieks, N. (2005) 'Latvia', in C. Mudde (ed.), *Racist Extremism in Central and Eastern Europe.* London: Routledge, 101–28.

Musolff, A. (2006) 'Metaphor scenarios in public discourse', *Metaphor and Symbol*, 21/1: 23–38.

Musolff, A. (2010) *Metaphor, Nation, and the Holocaust.* London: Routledge.

Nathan, J. (2011) 'A hatred that refuses to die', *Independent*, 22 March.

Navarro, L. (2010) 'Islamophobia and sexism: Muslim women in the western mass media', *Human Architecture*, 8/2: 94–113.

Nilsen, A. G. (2013) 'Norway's disturbing lurch to the right', *Guardian*, 10 September. Available at www.theguardian.com/commentisfree/2013/sep/10/norway-lurch-to-right, accessed 12/3/15.

Nohrstedt, S-A. (2013) 'Mediatization as an echo-chamber for xenophobic discourses in the threat society: The Muhammad cartoons in Denmark and Sweden', in Wodak, R., KhosraviNik, M. and Mral, B. (eds), *Right-wing Populism in Europe: Politics and Discourse*. London: Bloomsbury, 309–20.

Norocel, O. C. (2013) *Our People – A Tight-knit Family under the Same Protective Roof.* Helsinki: Unigrafia.

Norris, P. (2004) *Electoral Engineering: Voting Rules and Political Behavior.* New York: Cambridge University Press.

Norris, P. (2005) *Radical Right: Voters and Parties in the Electoral Market.* Cambridge: Cambridge University Press.

Nussbaum, M. C. (2013) *Emotional Politics: Why Love Matters for Justice.* Cambridge, MA: Belknap.

Oesch, D. (2008) 'Explaining workers' support for right-wing parties in Western Europe: Evidence from Austria, Belgium, France, Norway, and Switzerland', *International Political Science Review*, 29/3: 349–73.

Oje, S. and Mral, B. (2013) 'The Sweden Democrats came in from the cold: How the debate about allowing the SD into media arenas shifted between 2002 and 2010', in Wodak, R., KhosraviNik, M. and Mral, B. (eds), *Right-wing Populism in Europe: Politics and Discourse.* London: Bloomsbury, 277–92.

Olszanski, T. A. (2011) 'Svoboda Party – the new phenomenon on the Ukrainian right-wing scene', *Centre for Eastern Studies*, OSW Commentary, 56: 6.

Orgad, L. (2010) 'Illiberal liberalism: Cultural restrictions on migration and access to citizenship in Europe', *American Journal of Comparative Law*, 58: 53–105.

Orwell, G. (2006 [1946]) *Politics and the English Language.* Peterborough: Broadview Press.

Osborn, A. (2001) 'Belgian's far right party in Holocaust controversy', *Guardian*, 9 March. Available at www.theguardian.com/world/2001/mar/09/worlddispatch.thefarright, accessed 12/3/15.

Ötsch, W. (2000) *Haider Light.* Vienna: Czernin.

Päivärinta, T. and Sæbø, Ø. (2006) 'Models of e-democracy', *Communications of the Association for Information Systems*, 17: 818–40.

Palin, S. (2010) *America by Heart: Reflections of Family, Faith, and Flag.* New York: HarperCollins.

Pallister, D. (1999) 'Neo-fascist clear to resume charity role', *Guardian*, 6 August. Available at www.theguardian.com/uk/1999/aug/06/davidpallister, accessed 12/3/15.

Parenzo, D. and Romano, D. (2009) *Romanzo padano. Da Bossi a Bossi. Storia della Lega.* Milan: Sperling and Kupfer.

Paterson, T. (2013) 'Norway election results: Anti-immigrant party with links to mass murderer Anders Behring Breivik set to enter government under Conservative leader Erna Solberg', *Independent*, 10 September. Available at www.independent.co.uk/news/world/europe/norway-election-results-antiimmigrant-party-with-links-to-mass-murderer-anders-behring-breivik-set-to-enter-government-under-conservative-leader-erna-solberg-8805649.html, accessed 12/3/15.

Pelinka, A. (2013) 'Right-wing populism: Concept and typology', in Wodak, R., KhosraviNik, M. and Mral, B. (eds), *Right-wing Populism in Europe: Politics and Discourse.* London: Bloomsbury, 3–22.

Pelinka, A. and Wodak, R. (eds) (2002) *'Dreck am Stecken' – Politik der Ausgrenzung.* Vienna: Czernin.

Pels, D. (2003) 'Aesthetic representation and political style: Re-balancing identity and difference in media-democracy', in Corner, J. and Pels, D. (eds), *Media and the Restyling of Politics: Consumerism, Celebrity and Cynicism.* London: SAGE, 41–66.

Pels, D. (2012) 'The New National Individualism – Populism is here to stay', in Meijers, E. (ed.), *Populism in Europe.* Linz: Planet, 25–46.

Pencheva, M. (2009) 'The electoral strategies of the populist parties in Bulgaria', University of Kent Working Papers.

Pick, Y. (2013) *'Blaue Wahrnehmungsblase: Die FPÖ beherrscht es, ihre Botschaften ungefiltert ans Publikum zu bringen'*, *ZeitOnline Politik*, 19 September. Available at www.zeit.de/2013/39/kolumne-digitaler-wahlkampf-yussi-pick-oesterreich, accessed 30/3/14.

Pinero-Pinero, G. and Moore, J. (in press) 'Metaphorical conceptualization of migration control laws: Narratives of oppression', *Journal of Language and Politics*.

Pipes, D. (1997) *Conspiracy: How the Paranoid Style Flourishes and Where It Comes From.* New York: Free Press.

Pohl, W. and Wodak, R. (2012) 'The discursive construction of "migrants" and "migration"', in Messer, M., Schroeder, R. and Wodak, R. (eds), *Migrations: Interdisciplinary Perspectives.* Berlin: Springer, 205–13.

Posch, C., Stopfner, M. and Kienpointner, M. (2013) 'German postwar discourse of the extreme and populist right', in Wodak, R. and Richardson, J. E. (eds), *Analysing Fascist Discourse: European Fascism in Talk and Text.* London: Routledge, 97–121.

Prince, M. (2009) *Absent Citizens: Disability Politics and Policy in Canada.* Toronto: University of Toronto Press

Psarras, D. (2010) *Το Κρυφό Χέρι του Καρατζαφέρη* [The hidden hand of Karatzaferis] Athens: Alexandria.

Psarras, D. (2012) *Η Μαύρη Βίβλος της Χρυσής Αυγής* [The Black Bible of Golden Dawn]. Athens: Polis.

Purple-er (2010) 'Switzerland bans Minarets', 19 January. Available at https://purpler.wordpress.com/tag/ban/, accessed 10/8/14.

PVV Political Agenda (2012–15) Available at: http://pvv.nl/images/stories/verkiezingen2012/VerkiezingsProgramma-PVV-2012-final-web.pdf, accessed 12/3/15.

Ramirez, A. (2006) 'Sexismo neocolonial', *El País*, 8/10.

Read-Ghazal, J. N. and Bartkowski, J. P. (2000) 'To veil or not to veil?', *Gender and Society*, 14/3: 395–417.

Reichert, R. (2008) *Amateure im Netz. Selbstmanagement und Wissenstechnik im Web 2.0.* Bielefeld: Transcript.

Reisigl, M. (2007) 'Discrimination in discourses', in Kotthoff, H. and Spencer-Oatey, H. (eds), *Handbook of Intercultural Communication (Handbooks of Applied Linguistics*, Vol. 7). Berlin: Mouton de Gruyter, 365–94.

Reisigl, M. (2013) 'Zur kommunikativen Dimension des Rechtpopulismus', Sir Peter Ustinov Institut, Pelinka, A. and Haller, B. (eds), *Populismus. Herausforderung oder Gefahr für eine Demokratie?* Vienna: New Academic Press, 141–62.

Reisigl, M. (2014) 'Argumentation analysis and the discourse-historical approach: A methodological framework', in Hart, C. and Cap, P. (eds), *Contemporary Critical Discourse Studies*, London: Bloomsbury, 67–96.

Reisigl, M. and Wodak, R. (2000) '"Austria First": A discourse-historical analysis of the Austrian "anti-foreigner-petition" in 1992 and 1993', in Reisigl, M. and Wodak, R. (eds), *Semiotics of Racism: Approaches in Critical Discourse Analysis.* Vienna: Passagen, 269–304.

Reisigl, M. and Wodak, R. (2001) *Discourse and Discrimination: Rhetorics of Racism and Antisemitism.* London: Routledge.

Reisigl, M. and Wodak, R. (2009) 'The discourse-historical approach (DHA)', in Wodak, R. and Meyer, M. (eds), *Methods of Critical Discourse Analysis.* 2nd edn. London: SAGE, 87–121.

Rensmann, L. (2011) '"Against globalism": Counter-cosmopolitan discontent and antisemitism in mobilizations of European extreme right parties', in Rensmann, L. and Schoeps J. (eds), *Politics and Resentment: Antisemitism and Counter-Cosmopolitanism in the European Union.* Boston, MA: Brill, 117–46.

Renton, D. (2005) '"A day to make history"? The 2004 elections and the British National Party', *Patterns of Prejudice*, 13/9, 25–45.

Rheindorf, M. and Wodak, R. (2014) 'Der Wandel des österreichischen Deutsch: Eine textsortenbezogene Pilotstudie (1970–2010)', *Zeitschrift für Deutsche Sprache,* 42/2: 139–67.

Richardson, J. E. (2013a) 'Ploughing the same furrow? Continuity and change on Britain's extreme right fringe', in Wodak, R., KhosraviNik, M. and Mral, B. (eds), *Rightwing Populism in Europe: Politics and Discourse.* London: Bloomsbury, 105–20.

Richardson, J. E. (2013b) 'Racial populism in British fascist discourse: The case of COMBAT and the British National Party (1960–1967)', in Wodak, R. and Richardson, J. E. (eds), *Analysing Fascist Discourse: European Fascism in Talk and Text.* London: Routledge, 181–202.

Richardson, J. E. and Colombo, M. (2014) 'Race and immigration in far- and extreme-right European political leaflets', in Hart, C. and Cap, P. (eds), *Contemporary Critical Discourse Studies*. London: Bloomsbury, 521–43.

Richardson, J. E. and Wodak, R. (2009a) 'The impact of visual racism: Visual arguments in political leaflets of Austrian and British far-right parties', *Controversies*, 6 (2): 45–77.

Richardson, J. E. and Wodak, R. (2009b) 'Recontextualising fascist ideologies of the past: Rightwing discourses on employment and nativism in Austria and the United Kingdom', *Critical Discourse Studies*, 4: 251–67.

Ricoeur, P. (1992) *Oneself as Another*. Chicago, IL: University of Chicago Press.

Rising, D. (2012) 'Germany seeks to ban far-right party', *3 News*, 6 December. Available at www.3news.co.nz/Germany-seeks-to-ban-far-right-party/tabid/417/articleID/279402/Default.aspx, accessed 12/3/15.

Roberts, K. M. (2012) 'Populism and democracy in Venezuela under Hugo Chavez', in Mudde, C. and Kaltwasser, C.R. (eds), *Populism in Europe and the Americas*. Cambridge: Cambridge University Press, 136–59.

Rodino-Colocino, M. (2012) 'Men up, women down: Mama grizzlies and anti-feminist feminism during the year of (conservative) women and beyond', *Women and Language*, 35/1: 79–95.

Rosenberger, S. and Sauer, B. (eds) (2013) *Politics, Religion and Gender: Framing and Regulating the Veil*. London: Routledge.

Rosenkranz, B. (2008) *MenschInnen. Gender Mainstreaming – Auf dem Weg zum geschlechtslosen Menschen*. Graz: Ares.

Rosin, H. (2013) *The End of Men and the Rise of Women*, 2nd edn. London: Penguin.

RT News (2012) 'Neo-Nazi march in Lvov in honour of the Waffen-SS'. Available at http://rt.com/news/155364-ukraine-nazi-division-march/, accessed 30/4/14.

Rubinelli, S. (2009) *Ars Topica: The Classical Technique of Constructing Arguments from Aristotle to Cicero*. Berlin: Springer.

Rudling, P. A. (2013) 'The return of the Ukrainian far right: The case of VO Svoboda', in Wodak, R. and Richardson, J. E. (eds), *Analysing Fascist Discourse: European Fascism in Talk and Text*. London: Routledge, 228–55.

Rupert, M. (1997) 'The patriot movement and the roots of fascism', in Nan, S. A., Shapiro, I. et al. (eds), *Windows to Conflict Analysis and Resolution: Framing our Field*. Fairfax, VA: Institute for Conflict Analysis and Resolution, 81–101.

Ruzza, C. and Balbo, L. (2013) 'Italian populism and the trajectories of two leaders: Silvio Berlusconi and Umberto Bossi', in Wodak, R., KhosraviNik, M. and Mral, B. (eds), *Right-wing Populism in Europe: Politics and Discourse*. London: Bloomsbury, 163–76.

Ryan, N. (2004) *Into a World of Hate: A Journey among the Extreme Right*. London: Taylor and Francis.

Rydgren, J. (2004) 'Explaining the emergence of radical right-wing populist parties: The case of Denmark', *West European Politics*, 27/3: 474–502.

Rydgren, J. (ed.) (2005) *Movements of Exclusion*. New York: Nova.

Rydgren, J. (2006) *From Tax Populism to Ethnic Nationalism: Radical Right-wing Populism in Sweden*. Oxford: Berghahn.

Rydgren, J. (2007) 'The sociology of the radical right', *Annual Review of Sociology*, 33: 241–62.

Salem, H. (2014) 'Who exactly is governing Ukraine?', *Guardian*, 4 March. Available at www.theguardian.com/world/2014/mar/04/who-governing-ukraine-olexander-turchynov, accessed 12/3/15.

Sarrazin, T. (2010) *Deutschland schafft sich ab: Wie wir unser Land aufs Spiel setzen*. Berlin: DVA.

Sauer, B. (2005) 'Conflicts over values: The issue of Muslim headscarves in Europe'. Paper presented at Conference 'Culture meets Culture', Vienna, 5 May 2005.

Sayer, A. (2015) *Why We Can't Afford the Rich*. University of Bristol: Policy Press.

Scharsach, H.-H. (2012) *Strache im braunen Sumpf*. Vienna: Kremayr & Scheriau.

Schinkel, W. (2010) 'Populism: Comments on a democratic desire', *Open*, 20: 114–20.

Schlobinski, P. (2005) 'Sprache und internetbasierte Kommunikation. Voraussetzungen und Perspektiven', in Siever, T., Schlobinski, P. and Runkehl, J. (eds), *Websprache.net*. Berlin: De Gruyter Mouton, 1–14.

Schmidt, R. (2002) 'Racialisation and language policy: The case of the USA', *Multilingua*, 21: 141–62.

Schmitt, C. (2007) *The Concept of the Political: Expanded Edition*. Chicago, IL: University of Chicago Press.

Schori Liang, C. (2007) *Europe for the Europeans: The Foreign and Security Policy of the Populist Radical Right*. London: Ashgate.

Schowalter, D. (2012) 'Financialisation of the family: Motherhood, biopolitics, and paths of power', *Language and Gender*, 35/1: 39–57.

Schweitzer, E. C. (2012) *Tea Party. Die weiße Wut*. Munich: DTV.

Sciolino, E. (2007) 'Immigration, Black Sheep and Swiss Rage', *New York Times*, 8 October. Available at www.nytimes.com/2007/10/08/world/europe/08swiss.html, accessed 22/4/15.

Sclafani, J. (2014) 'Family as a framing resource in political identity construction: Introduction sequences in presidential primary debates', *Language in Society* (in press).

Semino, E. and Koller, V. (2009) 'Metaphor, politics and gender: A case study from Italy', in Ahrens, K. (ed.), *Politics, Gender and Conceptual Metaphors*. Basingstoke: Palgrave, 36–61.

Shermer, M. and Grobman, A. (2000) *Denying History: Who Says the Holocaust Never Happened and Why Do They Say It?* Berkeley, CA: University of California Press.

Shields, J. (2007) *The Extreme Right in France: From Pétain to Le Pen*. London: Routledge.

Sickinger, H. (2008) 'Jörg Haider', in Pelinka, A., Sickinger, H. and Stögner, K. (eds), *Kreisky-Haider. Bruchlinien österreichischer Identitäten*. Vienna: Braumüller, 111–220.

Sicurella, F. (2015) 'Speaking for the nation: A critical discourse study of intellectuals and nationalism in the post-Yugoslav context'. Unpubl. PhD thesis, Lancaster University (forthcoming).

Simmel, G. (1950) *The Sociology of Georg Simmel*. New York: Free Press.

Sir Peter Ustinov Institut, Pelinka, A. and Haller, B. (eds) (2013) *Populismus. Herausforderung oder Gefahr für eine Demokratie?* Vienna: New Academic Press.

Skenderovic, D. (2009a) *The Radical Right in Switzerland: Continuity and Change 1945–2000*. New York: Berghahn.

Skenderovic, D. (2009b) 'Immigration and the radical right in Switzerland: Ideology, discourse and opportunities', *Patterns of Prejudice*, 41/2: 155–76.

Skocpol, T. and Williamson, V. (2012) *The Tea Party and the Remaking of Republican Conservatism*. Oxford: Oxford University Press.

Smith, A. D. (1995) *Nations and Nationalism in a Global Era*. Cambridge: Polity.

Smith, H. (2013) 'Greek Golden Dawn member arrested over murder of leftwing hip-hop artist', *The Guardian*, 18 September. Available at http://www.theguardian.com/world/2013/sep/18/greece-murder-golden-dawn, accessed 10/10/13.

Solomos, J. (2013) 'Contemporary forms of racist movements and mobilization in Britain', in Wodak, R., KhosraviNik, M. and Mral, B. (eds), *Right-wing Populism in Europe: Politics and Discourse*. London: Bloomsbury, 121–34.

Staggenborg, S. (1991) *The Pro-Choice Movement: Organization and Activism in the Abortion Conflict*. Oxford: Oxford University Press.

Stettner, K. and Januschek, F. (2002) 'Entlarven – Ein Handlungsmuster des politischen Diskurses (am Beispiel der Haider-Talkshow von und mit Erich Böhme)', *Conflict and Communication Online*, 1/1. Available at www.cco.regener-online.de/2002_1/pdf_2002_1/stett_jan.pdf, accessed 12/3/15.

Stocchetti, M. (2007) 'The politics of fear', in Hodge, A. and Nilep, C. (eds), *Discourse, War and Terrorism*. Amsterdam: Benjamins, 223–41.

Stockemer, D. (2012) 'The Swiss radical right: Who are the new voters of the Swiss People's Party?', *Representation*, 48/2: 197–208.

Stögner, K. (2014) *Antisemitismus und Geschlecht. Historisch-gesellschaftliche Konstellationen*. Baden-Baden: Nomos.

Stögner, K. and Wodak, R. (2014) '"Nationale Einheit" und die Konstruktion des "fremden Juden": die politische Instrumentalisierung rechtspopulistischer Ausgrenzung in der *Daily Mail*', *OBST* 42 (special issue edited by F. Januschek and M. Reisigl): 130–61.

Stögner, K. and Wodak, R. (forthcoming) '"The man who hated Britain" – Old beliefs with new faces. The discursive construction of national unity against "the Jewish alien"', *Critical Discourse Studies*.

Stone, D. (2002) *The Policy Paradox: The Art of Political Decision Making*, 2nd edn. New York: Norton.

Stråth, B. and Wodak, R. (2009) 'Europe – Discourse – Politics – Media – History: Constructing crises?', in Triandafyllidou, A., Wodak, R. and Krzyżanowski, M. (eds), *European Media and the European Public Sphere*. Basingstoke: Palgrave, 15–33.

Street, J. (2004) 'Celebrity politicians: Popular culture and political representation', *British Journal of Politics & International Relations*, 6: 435–52.

Street, J. (2010) *Mass Media, Politics and Democracy*. Basingstoke: Palgrave.

Strömbäck, J. (2008) 'Four phases of mediatisation: An analysis of the mediatisation of politics', *International Journal of Press/Politics*, 13/3: 228–46.

SVP Programme (2015–19) Available at: www.svp.ch/positionen/parteiprogramm/, accessed 12/3/15.

Taggart, P. (2000) *Populism*. Buckingham: Open University Press.

Taguieff, P-A. (1984) 'La rhétorique du national-populisme', *Mots*, 9/9: 113–39.

Tannen, D. (1994) *Taking from 9 to 5*. New York: William Morrow.

Tannen, D. (1998) *The Argument Culture – Moving from Debate to Dialogue*. New York: Random House.

Tannen, D. (2008) 'The double-bind: The damned-if-you do, damned-if-you-don't paradox facing women leaders', in Morrison, S. (ed.), *Thirty Ways of looking at Hillary: Reflections of Women Writers*. New York: HarperCollins, 126–39.

Toulmin, S. (2003 [1958]) *The Uses of Argument*. Cambridge: Cambridge University Press.

Townson, M. (1992) *Mother-tongue and Fatherland: Language and Politics in German*. Manchester: Manchester University Press.

Traynor, I. (2008) 'I don't hate Muslims, I hate Islam', *Guardian*, 17 February. Available at www.theguardian.com/world/2008/feb/17/netherlands.islam, accessed 12/3/15.

Traynor, I. (2009) 'Anti-gay, climate change deniers – meet David Cameron's new friends', *Guardian*, 3 June. Available at www.theguardian.com/politics/2009/jun/02/david-cameron-alliance-polish-nationalists, accessed 12/3/15.

Traynor, I. (2014) 'Switzerland backs immigration quotas by small margin', *Guardian*, 10 February. Available at www.theguardian.com/world/2014/feb/09/swiss-referendum-immigration-quotas, accessed 12/3/15.

Triandafyllidou, A., Wodak, R. and Krzyżanowski, M. (eds) (2009) *The European Public Sphere and the Media: Europe in Crisis*. London: Palgrave Macmillan.

Tsiras, S. (2012) Έθνος και ΛΑ.Ο.Σ.: Νέα Άκρα Δεξιά και Λαϊκισμός [Nation and LAOS: New Far Right and Populism]. Thessaloniki: Epikentro.

Tsolova, T. (2013) 'Bulgarian anger over living standards lifts nationalist party', *Reuters*, 19 March. Available at www.reuters.com/article/2013/03/19/us-bulgaria-government-nationalists-idUSBRE92I0RV20130319, accessed 12/3/15.

UKIP (2013a) *Constitution*. Available at www.ukip.org/the_constitution, accessed 23/4/15.

UKIP (2013b) *Immigration Policy*. Available at www.ukip.org/issues/policy-pages/immigration, accessed 30/4/14; see also Z Stanworth UKIP, September 2013 zstanworthukip.wordpress.com/2013/09/, accessed 30/4/14.

Underwood, S. (2010) 'UKIP's political strategy: Opportunistic idealism in a fragmented political arena'. University Association for Contemporary European Studies Annual Conference, 6 September, Bruges, Belgium. Available at www.uaces.org/documents/papers/1001/usherwood.pdf.

United Nations (1948) *Universal Declaration of Human Rights*. Geneva: United Nations. Available at www.un.org/en/documents/udhr, accessed 5/1/14.

Unzensuriert (2013) 'Hofburg-Premiere für Wiener Akademikerball', 27 January. Available at www.unzensuriert.at/content/0011545-Hofburg-Premiere-f-r-Wiener-Akademikerball/, accessed 28/1/13.

Van Dijk, T. A. (1991) *News as Discourse*. New York: Erlbaum.

Van Dijk, T. A. (1992) 'Discourse and the denial of racism', *Discourse and Society*, 3/1: 87–118.

Van Eemeren, F. (2010) *Strategic Maneuvering*. Amsterdam: Benjamins.

Van Leeuwen, T. (1996) 'The representation of social actors', in Caldas-Coulthard, C. R. and Coulthard, M. (eds), *Texts and Practices: Readings in Critical Discourse Analysis*. London: Routledge, 32–70.

Van Leeuwen, T. and Wodak, R. (1999) 'Legitimizing immigration control: A discourse-historical analysis', *Discourse Studies*, 1/1: 83–118.

Veugelers, J. (2005) 'Ex-colonials, voluntary associations, and electoral support for the contemporary far right', *Comparative European Politics*, 3: 408–31.

Von Krusche, M. (2014) *'Reportage: Hans Christian Strache in Gleisdorf'*. Available at www.unplugged.at/krusche/feat01/txt02/txt81.htm, accessed 30/3/14.

Walton, D. (1996) *Argumentation Schemes for Presumptive Reasoning*. Hillsdale, NJ: Erlbaum.

Wasburn, P. C. and Wasburn, M. H. (2011) 'Media coverage of women in politics: The curious case of Sarah Palin', *Media, Culture & Society*, 33/7: 1027–41.

Waterfield, M. (2009) 'BNP could be at the heart of far-right EU Group', *Telegraph*, 15 May. Available at www.telegraph.co.uk/news/worldnews/europe/eu/5329638/BNP-could-be-at-heart-of-far-right-EU-group.html, accessed 12/3/15.

Weber, M. (1978) *Economy and Society: An Outline of Interpretive Sociology*. Berkeley, CA: University of California Press.

Weidinger, B. (2014) 'The sacral framing of exclusion. Christian references in far-right immigration discourses and right-wing interaction between Europe and the USA after 9/11'. Unpublished manuscript, University of Vienna.

Weiss, G. (2002) Searching for Europe: The problem of legitimisation and representation in recent political speeches on Europe. *Journal of Language and Politics*, 1/1: 59–83.

Wengeler, M. (2003a) *Topos und Diskurs. Begründung einer argumentationsanalytischen Methode und ihrer Anwendung auf den Migrationsdiskurs (1960–1985)*. Tübingen: Niemeyer.

Wengeler, M. (2003b) 'Argumentationstopos als sprachwissenschaftlicher Gegenstand. Für eine Erweiterung linguistischer Methoden bei der Analyse öffentlicher Diskurse', in Geideck, S. and Liebert, W-A. (eds), *Sinnformeln. Linguistische und soziologische Analysen von Leitbildern, Metaphern und anderen kollektiven Orientierungsmustern*. Berlin: De Gruyter Mouton, 59–82.

Williams, M. (2003) 'Words, images, enemies: Securitization and international politics', *International Studies Quarterly*, 47: 511–31.

Wilson, R. and Hainsworth, P. (2012) *Far-right Parties and Discourse in Europe: A Challenge for Our Times*. Brussels: European Network against Racism (ENAR).

Winnett, R. and Kirkup, J. (2012) 'Theresa May: We'll stop migrants if euro collapses', *Telegraph*, 25 May. Available at www.telegraph.co.uk/news/uknews/immigration/9291493/Theresa-May-well-stop-migrants-if-euro-collapses.html, accessed 12/3/15.

Wodak, R. (1989) '"Iudeus ex Machina"', *Grazer Linguistische Studien*: 153–80.

Wodak, R. (1990) 'The Waldheim Affair and Antisemitic Prejudice in Austrian Public Discourse', *Patterns of Prejudice*, 24/2–4: 18–33.

Wodak, R. (2006) 'Blaming and denying: Pragmatics', in K. Brown (ed.), *Encyclopedia of Language and Linguistics*, 2nd edn. Oxford: Elsevier, 59–64.

Wodak, R. (2007a) 'Pragmatics and critical discourse analysis', *Pragmatics and Cognition*, 15/1: 203–25.

Wodak, R. (2007b) 'Discourses in European Union organizations: Aspects of access, participation, and exclusion', in Briggs, C. (ed.), 'Four decades of epistemological revolution: Work inspired by Aaron V. Cicourel', Special Issue: *Text and Talk*, 27/5–6: 655–80.

Wodak, R. (2008) 'Controversial issues in feminist critical discourse analysis', in Harrington, K., Litosseliti, L., Sauntson, H. and Sunderland, J. (eds), *Gender and Language: Research Methodologies*. Basingstoke: Palgrave, 193–210.

Wodak, R. (2010) 'The glocalization of politics in television: Fiction or reality?', *European Journal of Cultural Studies*, 13/1: 1–20.

Wodak, R. (2011a) *The Discourse of Politics in Action: Politics as Usual*, 2nd edn. Basingstoke: Palgrave.

Wodak, R. (2011b) '"Us" and "them": Inclusion/exclusion – discrimination via discourse', in Delanty, G., Wodak, R. and Jones, P. (eds), *Migration, Identity and Belonging*. Liverpool: Liverpool University Press, 54–77.

Wodak, R. (2011c) 'Suppression of the Nazi past, coded languages, and discourses of silence: Applying the discourse-historical approach to post-war antisemitism in Austria', in Steinmetz, W. (ed.), *Political Languages in the Age of Extremes*. Oxford: Oxford University Press, 351–79.

Wodak, R. (2012) 'Language, power and identity', *Language Teaching*, 44/3: 215–33.

Wodak, R. (2013a) '"Anything goes!" The Haiderization of Europe', in Wodak, R., KhosraviNik, M. and Mral, B. (eds), *Right-wing Populism in Europe: Politics and Discourse*. London: Bloomsbury, 23–38.

Wodak, R. (2013b) 'The strategy of discursive provocation – a discourse-historical analysis of the FPÖ's discriminatory rhetoric', in Feldman, M. and Jackson, P. (eds), *Doublespeak: The Rhetoric of the Far-rights since 1945*. Frankfurt: Ibidem, 101–22.

Wodak, R. (2013c) 'Dis-citizenship and migration: A critical discourse-analytical perspective', *Journal of Language, Identity, and Education*, 12: 173–8.

Wodak, R. (2014a) 'Argumentation, political', in Mazzoleni, G. (ed.), *The International Encyclopedia of Political Communication*. New York: Wiley (in press).

Wodak, R. (2014b) 'It would be dangerous to regard European populism as a triumph of style over substance', *LSE Comment*. Available at http://blogs.lse.ac.uk/europpblog/2014/07/23/ it-would-be-dangerous-to-regard-modern-european-populism-as-devoid-of-serious-content-or-as-a-triumph-of-style-over-substance/, accessed 12/3/15.

Wodak, R. (2014c) 'Political discourse analysis – Distinguishing frontstage and backstage contexts. A discourse-historical approach', in Flowerdew, J. (ed.), *Discourse in Context*. London: Bloomsbury, 522–49.

Wodak, R. (2015) 'Saying the unsayable: Denying the Holocaust in media debates in Austria and the UK', *Journal of Language Aggression and Conflict*, (in press).

Wodak, R. and Auer-Boreo, G. (eds) (2009) *Justice and Memory – Confronting Traumatic Pasts: An International Comparison*. Vienna: Passagen.

Wodak, R. and Boukala, S. (2014) 'Talking about solidarity and security in the age of crisis: The revival of nationalism and protectionism in the European Union – a discourse-historical approach', in Carta, C. and Morin, J. F. (eds), *EU Foreign Policy through the Lens of Discourse Analysis: Making Sense of Diversity*. Farnham: Ashgate, 171–90.

Wodak, R. and Boukala, S. (2015) 'European identities and the revival of nationalism in the European Union – a discourse-historical approach', *Journal of Language and Politics* 14/1: 87–109.

Wodak, R. and de Cillia, R. (2007) 'Commemorating the past: The discursive construction of official narratives about the "Rebirth of the Second Austrian Republic"', *Discourse & Communication*, 1/3: 337–63.

Wodak, R. and Fairclough, N. (2010) 'Recontextualizing European higher education policies: The cases of Austria and Romania', *Critical Discourse Studies*, 7/1: 19–40.

Wodak, R. and Forchtner, B. (2014) 'Embattled Vienna 1683/2010: Right-wing populism, collective memory and the fictionalization of politics', *Visual Communication*, 13/2: 231–55.

Wodak, R. and Kirsch, P. (eds) (1995) *Totalitäre Sprachen*. Vienna: Passagen.

Wodak, R. and Köhler, K. (2010) 'Wer oder was ist "fremd"? Diskurshistorische Analyse fremdenfeindlicher Rhetorik in Österreich', *Sozialwissenschaftliche Studien*, 1: 33–55.

Wodak, R. and Pelinka, A. (eds) (2002) *The Haider Phenomenon*. New Brunswick, NJ: Transaction.

Wodak, R. and Reisigl, M. (2002) '"Wenn einer Ariel heißt …": Ein linguistisches Gutachten zur politischen Funktionalisierung antisemitischer Ressentiments in Österreich', in Pelinka, A. and Wodak, R. (eds), *'Dreck am Stecken'. Politik der Ausgrenzung*. Vienna: Czernin, 134–72.

Wodak, R. and Reisigl, M. (2015) 'Discourse and racism', in Tannen, D., Hamilton, H. and Schiffrin, D. (eds), *Handbook of Discourse Analysis*, 2nd edn. Chichester, UK: John Wiley & Sons, Ltd, 576–96.

Wodak, R. and Richardson, J. E. (eds) (2013) *Analysing Fascist Discourse: European Fascism in Talk and Text*. London: Routledge.

Wodak, R. and Weiss, G. (2004) 'Visions, Ideologies and Utopias in the Discursive Construction of European Identities: Organizing, Representing and Legitimizing Europe', in Pütz, M., Van Neff, A., Aerstselaer, G. and Van Dijk, J. (eds), *Communicating Ideologies: Language, Discourse and Social Practice*. Frankfurt: Peter Lang, 225–52.

Wodak, R. and Wright, S. (2006) 'The European Union in cyberspace: Multilingual democratic participation in a virtual public sphere?', *Journal of Language and Politics*, 5/2: 251–75.

Wodak, R. and Wright, S. (2007) 'The European Union in cyberspace: Democratic participation via online multilingual discussion boards', in Danet, B. and Herring S. (eds), *The Multilingual Internet: Language, Culture and Communication Online*. Oxford: Oxford University Press, 385–407.

Wodak, R., De Cillia, R., Reisigl, M. and Liebhart, K. (2009 [1999]) *The Discursive Construction of National Identities*. Edinburgh: Edinburgh University Press.

Wodak, R., Johnstone, B. and Kerswill, P. (eds) (2010) 'Introduction', *The SAGE Handbook of Sociolinguistics*. London: SAGE, 1–8.

Wodak, R., KhosraviNik, M. and Mral, B. (eds) (2013) *Right-wing Populism in Europe: Politics and Discourse*. London: Bloomsbury.

Wodak, R., Menz, F., Mitten, R. and Stern, F. (1994) *Sprachen der Vergangenheiten*. Frankfurt: Suhrkamp.

Wodak, R., Nowak, P., Pelikan, J., Gruber, H., de Cillia, R. and Mitten, R. (1990) *'Wir sind alle unschuldige Täter!' Diskurshistorische Studien zum Nachkriegsantisemitismus*. Frankfurt: Suhrkamp.

Woodley, D. (2013) 'Radical right discourse contra state-based authoritarian populism: Neoliberalism, identity and exclusion after the crisis', in Wodak, R. and Richardson, J. E. (eds), *Analysing Fascist Discourse: European Fascism in Talk and Text*. London: Routledge, 17–41.

Worth, J. (2011) 'The True Finns followed a well-known recipe for success', *Guardian*, 21 April. Available at www.theguardian.com/commentisfree/2011/apr/21/true-finns-nationalist-populists-european-parties, accessed 30/4/13.

Zielonka, J. (2012) 'Elusive solidarity', *Journal of Democracy*, 23/4: 54–61.

Zuquete, J. (2007) 'Portugal: A new look at the extreme-right', *Representation*, 43/3: 179–98.

INDEX